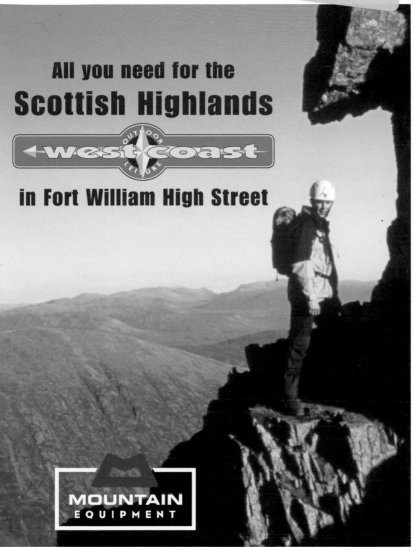

THE SCOTTISH
MOUNTAINEERING
CLUB JOURNAL

| Vol. XXXVIII | 2003 | No. 194 |

AN INWARD ADVENTURE

By Dave MacLeod

I HAD been climbing at Dumbarton Rock since the start, nine years ago now. I had come a long way in that time and learned a lot. The general theme was to focus on one thing at a time, beavering away for days or weeks on a problem just above my current level, learning what my body could do and how to get the most out of the rock to help me find a way through. Between repeated bouts of probing around a few feet off the ground only to be deposited coldly at my starting place, I would often glance up at my ultimate aim on the main face above, the great crack of *Requiem*. From my first visit to the rock, the extreme nature of this climb was the direction I wanted to take, and all the learning taking place on the boulders below was stored up in preparation for one day climbing at this level.

I fought and won my battle with *Requiem* in 2000, and thus arrived at an uncomfortable position in my progression as a climber. Having climbed the hardest thing around, where could I go now? I needed another battle to fight. The next challenge was not hard to find. All the routes on the face so far took crack or groove lines, essentially lines of weakness, despite their grandeur. The obvious step forward was to leave behind the safety of one of these cracklines and take on one of the great sheets of smooth wall in between. The Iron Road of *Chemin de Fer* provides access to the most attractive of these orange and brown streaked walls, leading from the kink in the crack all the way to the top. It was a long section of wall and it wasn't hard to see, even from 120ft below, that it was going to take a lot of work on the friendly end of a rope to unlock its secrets. With an open mind and excitement at venturing into new territory, I made the first of many trips to the top of the rock to set up a top rope.

The first big session was one of the best. It was free from reality. The line of the route was nothing more than a nice idea that existed firmly in my imagination. To bring reality in at this stage would have been the immediate end of it. I barely made a whole move in three hours. I shuttled up and down countless times on the rope, back and forth on a particular 10ft section. Work on each move was done in stages. Firstly, I spent 15 minutes feeling around, fascinated, like a baby discovering a new texture for the very first

Dave MacLeod on Requiem, E8 6b, Dumbarton. Photo: Nick Tarmey, (Dave MacLeod collection).

Dave MacLeod on Silver's Route Sit Start, Font 7a. Photo: Richard McGhee, (Dave MacLeod collection).

time. Then 15 minutes of pulling hard, introducing brawn where brain failed to turn a smooth undulation into a handhold. Finally, I spent the rest of the time just sitting in my harness, 120ft up on the headwall, staring at the rock in front of me, computing all the information I had just soaked up and trying to take it from the imaginary towards a sequence of movements which might one day be a route.

With appointments beckoning back in Glasgow and legs on the point of paralysis from hours suspending myself in a stringy sport climbing harness, I abseiled down into the shadows to catch the '10 to'. I was left with some homework which would fill my mind until my return. How to work my left foot up onto a handrail without the luxury of taking my weight off it and, higher up, a problem with a sidepull which was only a sidepull if I could get to the other side of it.

The hard thinking was done on the walk in to university over the coming weeks. This was the perfect place to learn the moves. For this route, optimism was needed to even believe those little holds could become a route. After eight hours dreaming in bed, the morning walk through Partick often felt strangely more enjoyable than it should. My mind had just been having climbing adventures all night and was in just the right mood for believing I could work out a way forward.

I decided that the left foot problem necessitated going back to square one with the lower crux, unless another hold could be found. The sidepull problem had three or four possible solutions. Unfortunately, I had tried all of them already and would just have to try harder or give up. These conclusions were rather unimpressive considering they had taken up a whole week of daydreaming!

After another couple of lonely sessions on the wall, I solved these obstacles and the line progressed from an imaginary hypothesis to an unlikely possibility. A big step forward. The left foot problem was overcome by the discovery of the poorest of sidepulls which, when cold enough for my ring fingertip to stick to, allowed me to scrape my left foot up the wall, reaching the next foothold just in time to slow and stop my body falling away from the wall. The sidepull problem was overcome by the same sequence I had initially worked on, but with the addition of some subtle shuffling of my trunk. There seemed to be a window in space that I had to move my body through for the move to work. I crossed under from a tiny pinch and placed my finger tips on the sidepull. Then I had to twist round in three stages, separate and crucial. I bent my whole body leftward into a C-shape, twisted it round and rotated my shoulder down, letting my head lean back. Once this was executed, the little flat sidepull became a real hold and a half-moon shaped sloper came within slapping distance, providing an escape leftward to improving holds.

With renewed optimism, I moved on to trying the whole route in one push. Doing all the crux section was great, even if it was right at my limit, but the big problem was that the first hard moves were 120ft of E5 crack climbing above the ground. I was quickly stopped in my tracks once again. After working on the route I tried finishing off by climbing up and down *Chemin De Fer* repeatedly to build up endurance and fine tune every move. Although this seemed to be working and I felt fitter than ever, I still couldn't even reach the top crux. With the summer heat fast approaching and waning interest in a route which appeared to be above me, I decided to come back in the autumn cool. In my mind, I doubted I would try it again.

That lingering doubt persisted whenever I thought about the line. However, late on a windy evening in early September, after a couple more sessions alone on the shunt, I climbed from the ground and slapped my way to the top of the crag, shocked at the sudden success after so much failure. Just as with *Requiem* the previous year, I realised instantly that I had to grab the chance of success and get on the lead before I developed a mental block about the route. I told my friends and girlfriend that I was going to lead the route within the week. There was no going back, I had invested too much effort to back off now.

A feeling of utter dread filled me slowly over the days that followed. I was all too aware of what I was asking of myself. I knew just how focused I would have to be and how flawless my climbing would have to be. A voice from inside was telling me that I was stretching my abilities and my luck much too far. I arranged with friends to make an evening visit to the rock and spread the word that I was going to have a go at the lead. I hoped that telling as many people as I could would help galvanise my inner motivation to draw a line under this long process of preparation.

On the day of the attempt, the weather was perfect. A funny sort of perfect. A strong cold wind was blowing light spots of rain from a threatening sky. Thus, a firm decision to go for it could not be made until the last minute. With a wet weather excuse looking like the likely outcome of the evening, I could happily bypass getting nervous, yet the attempt was still possible if the rain did not get any worse. I warmed up by climbing *Chemin de Fer* to the point where my project left the crack. I placed the highest gear, stared up at the blank wall above and all around me, taking it all in. Climbing back to the ground, I felt an uplifting feeling of excitement at doing something new, climbing the route 'for real' instead of the repetitive, almost robotic process of working the moves on a top rope.

An hour later, the sky darkened as dusk approached and the spits of rain, although constantly present, were not heavy enough to justify backing out. With a large audience gathered and a buzz in the air, I tied back into the rope ends and announced that I was 'having a look'. I told myself I would just climb the crack again and then come down. Pretending to be going for it might be good mental practice for controlling my emotions on the final day.

Halfway up the crack, it all went so very wrong. I felt a huge and horrible temptation to commit myself. In the cold wind, the holds felt sticky and I floated upwards on a cloud of adrenalin. I tried to remind myself of just how hard the wall actually was. But the crack was feeling like V. Diff rather than E5. In no time I was leaning out from the flat jug where the crack kinked leftward. Decision time. "This is stupid," I said out loud. But I could see the final jug just 40ft above. I could end this right now, climb E9, and never have to get nervous about this piece of rock again. Temptation, temptation.

I was still deciding when moments later I pulled through an overlap and slapped aggressively away from the last gear. A voice in my mind screamed at me as I approached the left foot drag move.

"Jump off NOW before it's too late. It's not a game Dave, you are going to be in hospital for weeks."

As I looked down at the crucial left foothold, I could see the two ropes dangling below me and just how far above the gear I was. It was already too late. All that was left was the moves or the fall.

My whole body trembled with the effort of resisting gravity as my left foot desperately scuffed and stabbed at the crucial edge. This effort and the elimination of my options concentrated my mind and I pushed on with aggressive resolve. Through the wind I could hear my breath squeak and hold as I locked down on each tiny finger edge, only to come back in sharp gasps as I moved my feet and repositioned.

I felt lonely and vulnerable as I continued up, through the desperate twist move until finally my fingers snatched and held the half-moon shaped hold which signalled the beginning of the end of the 6c moves. Matching this hold was the highest move I had failed at on the top rope. I bridged wide, chest against the rock, and slowly brought my right hand over my head towards the hold. Feeling strong on the move, I savoured the moment.

"Here it is. I'm about to climb my first E9. This feels great. And to think I could have just climbed down and gone home."

Just as my fingers curled over the crimp, my right elbow nudged the rock and the outward force caused my left hand to explode off the rock. I screamed as I arched away from the face and dropped through the air. I looked down and grabbed the rope with both hands. When I looked back up, everything was blurred. Suddenly, the picture became focused again and the rope whipped tight, cutting my hands. My trajectory was horizontal now and as I braced my feet, I smashed against the smooth face.

The voices from below which moments ago had been shouting encouragement were awkwardly silent. Hanging limp in my harness, I didn't know what to say, so I broke the silence with a laugh and an explanation for my failure. As I was lowered down, my shock and buzzing excitement turned to pain. I wished I hadn't come so close. Not only did it mean I couldn't give in, but the expectations from within and from those watching were an immense burden. The line had become a real prospect, rather than just an imaginary possibility. It was there for the taking, but what would I have to go through to take it? I hoped that only one more effort would be enough given how close I had come, but in the back of my mind, I knew that I could have failed on any of the hard moves. So the experience became one of constant failure once more. Over the next three weeks I visited the rock 10 times. I would either visit at 9am for the cool morning air if I could persuade my girlfriend, Claire, to hold the ropes, or at dusk if the evening was cool and windy enough. On each visit I underwent the familiar, but relentlessly demanding, process of mental and physical preparation – only to take the fall every time. The whole experience hijacked my thoughts and my life. I realised that the only escape was to succeed on the route. But despite the fact I had been so close before, I also had to accept that failure was inevitable every time I made the tiniest of mistakes and this pattern could go on indefinitely. With my ankles and wrists in a worrying state following each swing and slam off the headwall, I asked myself how much more of this could I and the people around me take?

At the time I wondered how I managed to find the will to go back and throw myself off the crux time after time and deal with the upset in my life, in the remote hope that I might just sneak through and finish it. After all, I could have just walked away and trained for two years before returning to complete a much more certain outcome. Only in hindsight, and without the cloud of an uncertain outcome, do the enjoyable and fulfilling aspects shine through. For each of those 11 times I took the fall, I have a photographic image of looking down as I dropped away from the wall of the exposure, the ropes whipping around at weird angles and the world rushing past. Each time I took the pleasure of focusing with my whole mind on each move and moment, the next instant was my whole world. Such a feeling is the deepest relaxation I can imagine. Your name and status and every worry you ever had is let go and forgotten in order to align every thought to perfect execution of the next move. These were special moments and experiencing them more than once was good fortune rather than purgatory. I realised later that such experiences in climbing are by necessity very rare due to the enormous effort which is required to reach the true limits of your ability. But when the chance comes around, it must be grabbed with both hands.

Finally, just as my long university summer break ran out and my ankles reached the point of medical emergency, my sheer persistence paid off. I stood at the bottom of the route, stamped out my anxieties once again and half shook, half floated my way through the final crux moves on a wave of cerebral opiates. As I reached the final move for the first time since the very first lead attempt, I detached myself from the growing anticipation of success for a vital few moments more and scuffled through to the finishing bucket. It was over, and I felt happiness, relief, but also emptiness. The route had provided me with direction, excitement and reward for over a year. What could fill the gap now that it was complete?

A DREAM TIME IN AULD REEKIE

By Dennis Gray

THEY say if you can remember the Sixties you were not there. But I was and for a period during the middle of that decade I resided in Manor Place in Edinburgh. Across the road from me lived Graham Brown of Brenva fame and, sharing his abode, was Robin Campbell an enthusiastic climbing pioneer in Scotland and a future SMC Journal Editor and President.

Auld Reekie was a ferment of climbing activity at the time, with Heriots and the Edinburgh University Clubs imbued with the recently departed spirit of Robin Smith. The JMCS and the Jacobites were inspired by Munro bashing and the driving stamina of Tranter, later and sadly to meet his demise at the wheel. Those old stalwarts of the SMC, the Marshalls (Jimmy and Ron), Eli Moriarty and Graham 'Typhoo' Tiso were ageing but still very capable, and finally there were the Squirrels. It was into the bosom of the latter that I was gathered when I arrived and first impressions did not disappoint, varying little from the forecast made by an old acquaintance Tom Patey, regarding the hedonistic possibilities of climbing with such an organisation. It mirrored my previous experience of such loosely knit climbing groups, firstly the one I had grown up with, the Bradford Lads, and then matured alongside, the Rock and Ice.

Besides climbers, Edinburgh was full of arty-crafty folk in that era and there were crossovers. You might go into a pub and find that the guy playing the piano was a chap you had met on Cairngorm the previous weekend. Or the poet reading his own work in the George had also give a drunken rendition of *The Cremation of Sam McGee* the previous Saturday night in Jimmie Ross's in Carrbridge. But I was astonished when, a couple of nights after my arrival I wandered randomly into a bar to find three living guitar legends jamming together in an impromptu session, John Redbourne, Bert Jansch and Davy Graham.

The Squirrels used to meet mid-week in the Castle Rock and the Wee Windaes and occasionally after closing time – not very late in these days – we would repair to the SMC club rooms in the High Street. I recall one memorable occasion when we bought a barrel of beer and rolled it up over the cobbles scattering courting couples and drunks as we progressed. Sometimes from the pub we would go forth and climb in the forbidden grounds of Salisbury Crags. On my first such foray it was icy and covered in snow and I was totally unprepared for the outing. Fortunately, in order to cross the icy pavements of the capital to reach the Castle Rock, I had put on my 'Desmaisons' (climbing boots of the day) but I was wearing a smart work suit and over this a sheepskin jacket against the cold. With Ian McEachran and Brian Robertson (BR) in the vanguard we stole into Holyrood Park on a 'moonlicht nicht' and arrived at the foot of a route that was graded V. Diff in summer. Climbing on 'Heavy' is as bad as driving on same and I must admit that the alcohol had blunted my reason. I followed the leader, solo, climbing close behind BR who chuckled like a wild thing as we ascended.

After about 40ft we arrived on a ledge below a small roof that nonetheless looked fearsome in the gloom, for we carried not a headtorch between us. However, Brian had been there before and assured me it was full of big holds and, to prove this, he climbed up to the obstacle and, after a slight hesitation at the prow, over he went almost hand over hand. His example demanded that I follow and so, casting off my sheepskin jacket and throwing it down onto the snowy ground below, I set out. When I reached the roof it was icy but BR had cleared the rock of powder snow as he ascended and the large holds were there as promised, but as I pulled over onto the easier ground above I heard a rip as my expensive work suit gave way in the seat of the pants. Everyone wore them extra tight in that era! All of our party eventually ascended the route in good order, despite our state of inebriation. It has to be said, that with one or two glaring exceptions, Edinburgh's Tartan Tigers could hold their liquor.

While walking out of Holyrood I became aware of a young fellow at my elbow who was still high on the adventure and bubbling with talk of epics on future nordwands. This despite a plea for silence from his elders in case any of the Park Rangers were out patrolling looking for trespassers in the Royal Park (at 11o'clock at night this might have impressed even the SNP). This tyro was Alistair 'Bugs' McKeith and soon he and I were to become climbing partners and we subsequently remained friends until his death on Mount Assiniboine in 1978.

I worked for a printing and publishing firm in the Anderston district of Glasgow and, among other contracts, we printed the Cairngorm Chairlift vouchers, produced the bus tickets for Aberdeen, leaflets for biscuit firms in Inverness and, of course, material for some of the distilleries. I had a roving commission the length and breadth of Scotland with a company car and free petrol to boot! Everywhere I went my climbing gear went with me. On a Wednesday night I occasionally stayed over in Glasgow and went to the Langside climbing wall. This was in the college of that name and it must have been among the first such facilities built in this country. Regular users included the likes of Johnny Cunningham, Jimmy McDowell and Willy Rowney. Afterwards the Creag Dhu met in a pub in West Nile Street that had sawdust on the floor and spittoons in the corners of the room.

Outside Glasgow in Balmore, on the edge of the Campsies, lived Mary Stewart an American climber who was a veterinary researcher at Glasgow University and her house was the scene of several memorable parties. On one occasion, her countrymen John Harlin, Layton Kor and Gary Hemming were present along with such regulars as Tom Patey, Rusty Baillie and Eric Beard. The entertainment was of a high order and professional folk musicians such as Alex Campbell, Hamish Imlach and The Incredible String Band kept the troops amused in between cameo performances by Patey and Beardie.

Edinburgh has, within short distance, several outcrops and in the summer months during the light evenings after work we might repair down the A1 to Traprain Law or across the Forth Bridge to the Aberdour sea cliffs in Fife. Sometimes such man-made facilities as the Currie Walls received a visit and, for those without transport, there was always BR's tree. This was a high arboreal near to his home which he had pegged, and to climb it using only these for holds and without etriers was both adventurous and strenuous. If we could get away from work early enough we might even go as far north as Dunkeld for an evening's climbing where the cliffs of Craig-y-Barns boasted some modern test pieces like The Rat Race pioneered by Robertson.

The Squirrels were good rock climbers but even stronger winter mountaineers. On their fringe was Dougal Haston, someone I had known for many years before I moved to Auld Reekie and, like him, Dave Bathgate, Jock Knight, Fred Harper, Bugs, Ian McEachran, BR and others were all snow and ice gymnasts. I think the strongest rope on this type of terrain was Bathgate and Knight and on one of our winter weekend meets on Ben Nevis they pioneered The Curtain, a route which was to become an instant classic. Bugs and I were more enamoured of Creag Meaghaidh farther north than Nevis and we enjoyed both the mountain's unspoilt and undeveloped nature as well as the outstanding social scene to be found at its base in the Loch Laggan Inn. Mine Hosts were John and Margaret Small and although they looked the part of Highlanders and wore the tartan John was, dare I say it, a 'Der Englander'. He had started climbing at more than 50 years of age in the company of Patey and if you were a regular in his hotel you helped yourself from a five pint bottle of Glenmorangie from off the bar and settled up at the end of the evening! Behind the wooden structure that was the main hotel, John had set up a free rudimentary bothy where we used to stay.

Tom Patey was also often at Laggan with Aberdonian colleagues from the Etchachan Club also occasionally in residence. Many climber/musicians such as George McLeod, Clive Freshwater and Eric Beard, all based in Aviemore, would often appear out of a winter's night and a ceilidh would soon be under way.

Unfortunately, the hotel caught fire and John, who was in the bath at the time, could only watch from outside, naked except for a towel, as it burned to the ground while he waited for the fire engine to arrive from Kingussie. After this sad event we based ourselves in the Cairngorms most weekends but not before Bugs and I had made the first winter ascents of The Scene and Apolyon Ledge on Meaghaidh.

On one occasion during my journeys around Scotland I was in Inverness on business and Patey phoned. "Why not drive out towards Ullapool and meet up for a dram," he suggested. It was mid-winter and the roads were like a rink but I dare not suggest to Tom that it might be an unwise journey to make in such conditions. Subsequently, following the winding snow-covered road north-west, it took many hours to reach the hostelry which was our rendezvous. Once I arrived, Patey decided, after a single malt, that we might as well head on back to his house in Ullapool in order to get his accordion. I had my tenor banjo with me and so a good evening developed in Tom's bothy behind his house singing along with some of the Ullapool locals. The next morning I had an important business meeting in Inverness and so I reluctantly quit this gathering and headed back to the capital of the Highlands.

The roads were even worse on the return journey and it was to be the early hours of the morning before I arrived back at my hotel in Inverness to find it locked and in complete darkness.

"Sod this," I thought, I'm not paying good money to spend a freezing night out on the pavement and so I hammered on the front door and after a while the manager appeared dressed like Wee Willie Winkie in a long nichtshirt and let me in. After profuse apologies I crept up to my room, undressed and piled into bed. However, after some little time I felt the need to visit the bathroom next door. This I did, only to find on my return that the bedroom door had slammed shut leaving me stood in a draughty corridor in nothing but a pair of skimpy blasters. I crept downstairs and had to ring the bell at reception several times before the manager once again appeared in his night attire. To say he was not pleased is a half-truth and the next morning after breakfast, when I went to settle my account, the girl at reception handed me a personal letter from himself requesting me never to visit the hotel again.

I often travelled to Dundee where we had several contracts and I climbed in Glen Clova. One interesting meeting there was with Ron Butchart the founder and original editor of *Climber* magazine. He confessed he had not known originally whether to launch a mountaineering or a fishing magazine. It had been a toss-up and climbing had won simply because there was already a fishing magazine available on the bookstands in Dundee. I used to stay outside the city in Broughty Ferry where the local folk club was led by singer/songwriter Ewan MacColl and American banjo maestro Peggy Seeger. It was undoubtedly the best such gathering I have ever been to. I always believed Ewan to be 100% native Scot but, like many of us in these islands, it turned out he was a bit of a mixture. I was intrigued to learn years later that his real name was Jimmy Millar and that he was from Salford in Lancashire. He had taken part in the 1932 Kinder Scout trespass for which he had penned the famous hillwalking song *The Manchester Rambler*.

The winter scene in the Cairngorms in the Sixties was dynamic. The skiing developments had rendered the mountains very accessible and a series of keen winters, especially in the early part of that decade, yielded some outstanding conditions. My own hardest lead of that period was an early ascent of Savage Slit in the Northern Corries. I guided an officer from the Royal Marines up this and Eric Beard tagged along as our third man. After the climb, Beardie and I descended riding two up by way of a huge shovel down the White Lady on Cairngorm. This was at the end of the day after the lift had stopped working and we attained a speed that would have done credit to an Olympic luge competition but, as can be imagined, it did not endear us to the skiing fraternity. In the evenings we would assemble at Karl Fuchs's Struan House Inn or at Jimmie Ross's Rowanlea in Carrbridge. Beardie also held his singsong twice weekly in the Cairngorm Hotel which was attended by literally hundreds of climbers and skiers on occasion. Jimmie Ross was one of the finest fiddlers in the Highlands and he loved having Tom Patey accompany him as he played jigs and reels that it was impossible to keep one's feet from tapping to.

The Squirrels owned a hut, The Drey in Glencoe, high up above the road in the pass. It was an amazing place for it had been built at the same time as that group were all keenly engaged in exploratory climbing. I was staying there once with Bugs and Margery Thomson and, after pioneering a new route in the Lost Valley, we returned to find that my vehicle was stuck firmly in the mud. Fred Harper was also there and offered to help us free it and to do this he began placing stones under my front wheels. Unfortunately, I misunderstood the instructions given by him from underneath the vehicle and, revving the engine, I bolted out of the mire but unfortunately, ran Fred over. For a second I thought: "Oh my God I've killed him." But on climbing out of the car I was met with the sight of him standing up out of the mud, covered in goo but saved from serious injury by its cushioning effect. He limped around for many weeks afterwards but, typical of Fred, he never complained or swore at me when this happened.

Many of the Squirrels subsequently enjoyed fine mountaineering careers. Bugs pioneered several new routes in Scotland and, perhaps more significantly, in his adopted country Canada. His most famous first ascent was perhaps The Polar Circus. Dave Bathgate became a keen expedition climber making journeys to Peru and the Himalaya. Brian Robertson climbed in Peru on Huandoy with Dave, Ian MacEacheran and Don Whillans. He also pioneered King Kong on Carn Dearg before moving to live in Colorado. Finally, Fred Harper became president of the British Mountain Guides and was an outstanding figure in the instructional field. He was for many years Director of Glenmore Lodge in the Cairngorms. The last time I climbed with him was only a couple of years ago shortly before he succumbed to cancer. He was visiting the Cow and Calf Rocks at Ilkley and we met up there by chance. He confessed he had always wanted to climb the classic route, Waleska, and so he led it and I seconded him never guessing that he was so ill. It was obvious when we later said our goodbyes, he to head off back north and me on the short ride home to Leeds, that our climb together that day had meant a lot to him although this was conveyed more by gesture than word. I think this was typical of the Squirrels and indeed of the Edinburgh climbers in general.

I hope I am not falling into the trap of 'selective memory syndrome' by recalling only the good times? But in retrospect it was, for me, a special time in the company of some outstanding personalities and, for the friendship they showed to me, I will always be grateful. And so, to all the Edinburgh climbers still surviving from those days, I wish: "Lang may yer lum reek!"

EASTER, LOCH CLUANIE   John Mitchell

DEATH ON THE MOUNTAIN

By Gair Swanson

'As the warmth of sleep overtook him on the third night of storm
He never once thought that he should have stayed home
To wash the car or mow the lawn'

IT WAS poetry, he had read it somewhere, sometime. It was floating in his head now, or maybe it really was hanging on a sign above the entrance to the snow hole. He was cold, so, so, cold. Maybe that was a good sign. Strange word that, 'good.' All relative really. Mary was dead, yesterday or was it the day before? Warmth of sleep, warmth? Good? Why warmth? It's just before you die see, he had seen it before in a close in the Grassmarket, remember, cold winter, thought she had been raped, ripped all her clothes off. Mind tricks, you see, just before it gets you, think your too hot. Clothes all over the place, blood, stumbling, banging, falling. Just because she didn't have anywhere to stay.

Alistair had seen the neighbours as he left on Saturday, same routine every weekend, Welly boots, B&Q pressure hose and a tin of polish. The big decision was whether to do the grass before the car or maybe do the car first. It looked like rain and the forecast wasn't that good. Be good for the sprouts though, the sprouts could do with a bit of rain. Far too cynical Mary had told him as they started the drive north. Live and let live she had said. He didn't want to die like the pruners and polishers. They had died long ago. It wouldn't be like that for him, it wasn't his choice, but at least he had lived.

He needed her clothes, duvet jacket, trousers. Arms rigid, unbendable, a mixture of death and bone-numbing cold. Crunching bone, breaking as he bent it hard against the side of his unfeeling boot, would only have to do one. Tailor's dummy, not her, spirit gone. Feeling hot tears on his cheeks, dropping, melting into the icy floor of her tomb.

"Hers, it's her tomb not mine," he screamed as he wrenched the bright orange jacket from her marble cold body. Feathers, floating feathers, down, floating down, duck down, laughter muffled under snow as he remembered Geoff's sleeping bag, the 'Prince of Wales' model the boys had christened it – only three feathers. He slumped to the ground exhausted and felt a bit of comfort as he pulled the jacket over his head. Blocking out death, blocking out fear. Black, dark and warm. Yes, real warmth, sleeping warmth. He shot upright. No, no,

"Cold, cold,
bold, bold,
hold, hold,
cold, cold,
bold, bold,
hold, hold."

He repeated the mantra as his wooden fingers tried to unlace her boots.
"Cold, cold,
bold, cold,
hold, bold,
cold."

"Shit, shit, shit," fingers gone, he needed her overtrousers. Slumping to his knees he rolled back onto the ground. Get them off he thought, just get them off.

Mary's mother began to worry as darkness fell on the Sunday. She had said she would phone, she had her mobile. Her father was more matter of fact, preferring to think it was a bad area for phone signals. He was right, the Cairngorm plateau is indeed a bad area for signals but Mary didn't know that. She died blaming herself, thinking the mobile she had left in the car would have been their salvation.

Every three minutes it was, his body convulsed with shivers, he had read somewhere that this was the body's way of keeping the vital organs warm. But had he not also read that women survive better than men in extreme cold.

"Mary was dead,
Mary was blue,
Mary was gone,
Mary and you."

No, not you, not you, not just to complete a crap rhyme. He was screaming again, the snow muffling his anguish.

"Mary was dead,
Mary was blue,
Mary was gone.
Only Mary, only her."

Blank verse, only her not me, not me.

"Mary marry me
How did it go,
Mary marry me,"

he bawled at the moon except there was no moon, only the grey white interior of his survival chamber and the howling gale driven blizzard outside. Jim Reeves or was it Buddy Holly? The Holly and the Ivy, Christmas Time Mistletoe and Wine. Mary won't be full grown now, no but I will and my children and my children's children. Not with Mary no, not with Mary.

"Mary Mary quite contrary
how does your garden grow."

"Cold, cold,
bold, bold,
hold, bold,
cold, hold,
bold, cold,
hold, hold."

So tired now, so tired, closing, hold, eyes closing, bold, cold mustn't, mustn't sleep, mustn't sleep.

Alistair Colin Morgan, born 11.7.53, at Edinburgh, Church of Scotland, freelance journalist, married, three children, Died 17.01.03, Cairngorm plateau, Scotland. Cause of death, Hypothermia.

"Well Alistair here you are, you made it. Surprised?"
This from some sort of security guard type in a uniform that made him look like a cross between a bus driver and a South American dictator.
"Made it, made it where?"
"The afterlife of course,' says he, as if it was an everyday occurrence. Maybe it was, there had been a queue right enough."
"Come on mate, stop taking the piss, where am I? I know I was drunk last night and the last thing I remember was getting off with that blonde bird, Mary I think her name was. We went back to her place and well, you don't want to hear about all that, or do you, you little rascal you. Come on stop mucking about. Is this where she stays, she was a bit posh – you the doorman or what?"
"No Alistair, my position here is simply that of – receptionist I suppose is the closest analogy to what you'll have been used to, yes receptionist, that's about right."
It was all a bit surreal but he decided to go along with it.
"You're a climber I believe," said the bus driver/dictator/receptionist as he started to fill in a form on the desk where he sat.
"Yes, yes I am," said Alistair wondering where this was leading.
"Winter or Summer?"
"Sorry?"
"Winter Mountaineering or rockclimbing, your preference?"
"Oh I see. I eh, both, I do both."
"I'm afraid I'll have to press you on this Alistair, we are a big organisation but there are limits and we do have to keep to budget. Winter or Summer?"
"Winter then, ice climbing, technical ice climbing is what I enjoy most."
"Shoe size?"

"Nine."

"That's 42 American isn't it?"

"Yes, I'm not in America am I?"

"No Mr. Morgan," he laughed. "You're not in America, but I've heard our organisation and America described in similar terms but no, not America."

The form filling took some time and covered everything from inside leg measurement to next of kin. He found the next of kin a bit strange. Here was this guy trying to tell him he was in the afterlife and at the same time asking him for his next of kin. Surely, it was a bit late for that.

"Take this form with you, we'll keep a copy here in case of problems. Take the lift to the basement and ask for Michael Scott, he'll get you kitted out with everything you need."

'Pinochet' got up from the desk and, without further ado, handed the form to Alistair wishing him good luck as he left the room. Nice guy.

There were two elevators, he was even thinking American now, lifts, two lifts, one for up and one down. Maybe he had been in some sort of clearing room but that couldn't be right could it. He was going down certainly, but he was going climbing and that had to be good.

"Michael Scott at your service, your form sir."

Now here *was* a dude. He was like a throwback from the Sixties, Timothy Leary type very peace and love, tie dyed shirt, long hair, you know the thing. As he handed over his form Alistair was looking around for the Volkswagen surfing van he felt sure must be parked nearby.

"Ah ah! a climber. We had one of you cats here before, same name as you, spelt it Alisteir though not Alistair, Crawley or Crowley something like that, didn't take to him much, a bit pushy tried to take over the place, you know the type. Come this way Mr Morgan and we'll get you fixed up."

Alistair found himself standing in the middle of a climber's retail paradise, it was like all the climbing shops you'd care to name rolled into one and then some, and the most exciting thing was, it looked like he wasn't going to have to pay.

"Help yourself," the Scott guy said with an expansive if not expensive sweep of his arm. "Anything you need, help yourself it's all the best of gear."

He was like the proverbial wee laddie in a sweetie shop. In all the years he had been climbing Alistair had never been what you would term a 'gear freak'. He had always been three or four years behind the new technology but now, well! Titanium curved shaft ice-axes and Footfang crampons, light as a feather, Gore-Tex and down from head to foot and boots as comfy as slippers. More than £1500 worth of kit in under half-an-hour.

"If this is the afterlife bring it on!"

He went to sleep that night in a room in the basement not far from the 'shop' and was awakened by the sun shining in on his face. From his wooden bunk bed he looked out onto a pristine snow slope leading up to the base of a 500ft icefall approaching the vertical. He got up and after inspecting the interior of the well-appointed mountain hut he found himself in, he put a pot of coffee on the stove and took great delight in dressing in his new gear and boots.

Later that morning he revelled in the wonderful views over a beautiful valley as he kicked his way up the firm snow and into the bottom of the icefall and, hefting his axes, he was delighted to find that they struck home first time into the perfect ice of the fall. Not only did he have the climb to himself, he had the mountain to himself and although at first he was a bit worried about soloing, conditions were so good that his axe placements were 'bombproof' and half-an-hour later he had topped out on a superb Grade IV/V route which he named *Heaven's Gate.*

He slept comfortably that night after cooking himself an excellent curry from the well-provisioned store, and the next morning ventured out again in the same perfect weather with the intention of exploring a wonderful-looking buttress he had seen farther to the west. But strangely enough within half-an-hour he found himself once more at the foot of *Heaven's Gate* and although the ice was again in perfect condition, he knew the climb and didn't get the same kick out of it.

He slept comfortably that night after cooking himself an excellent curry from the well provisioned store and the next morning ventured out again in the same perfect weather with the intention of exploring a wonderful looking buttress he had seen farther to the west. But strangely enough within half-an-hour he found himself once more at the foot of *Heaven's Gate* and although the ice was again in perfect condition. He knew the climb and didn't get the same kick out of it.

He slept comfortably. "Whoa hold on a minute, what kind of loop is this I'm in," he thought "same today, yesterday, day before. Rest day, I'll have a rest day."

He tried to stay in bed but couldn't and after a mug of the same delicious coffee he found himself climbing the flawless ice of *Heaven's Gate* yet again.

On returning to the hut he was about to start cooking once more, what used to be his favourite dish, when his eye was drawn to Scott sitting quietly in the corner.

"Nice to see you're settling in Mr Morgan, is the accommodation to your liking?" he asked smiling broadly.

"Yes, very comfortable, but I would like to know what's happening here. You've put me in this climber's heaven, the conditions are superb and I have this fantastic ice climb minutes from the cabin, but I can't seem to explore anywhere else. And what about a rest day?"

Evening light on Loch Roe, Loch Dubh and Suilven. Photo: Niall Ritchie.

Scott started laughing.

"No rest days here I'm afraid Mr Morgan. This is the reaction we get from all our clients in the early days, from whatever background. The fishermen are the same. Cottage by the loch, lovely weather and a four-pound trout every hour on the hour, eight hours a day, seven days a week. Heavenly." He laughed again.

"This, Mr Morgan, is the other place and we try our best to suit the surroundings to our client's preferences. Welcome to Hell he laughed again, a long, crackling laugh and was gone.

"No dogs, no dogs, whose dog is this? Scott, Scott is this your dog? Get off, off."

"Cairngorm Leader to Glenmore," the radio crackled with static, "Search and Rescue Dogs have located targets. Snow hole. Coire Etchachan 242653 repeat 242653.

"Female dead, male severely hypothermic, poor pulse. Chopper immediate 242653 on red smoke flare. Cairngorm Leader over."

"Glenmore we read, Glenmore we read, contacting air crew will advise, Glenmore over."

Three toes on his right foot, three fingers and half his nose was the price. Who was Mary? Well the tabloids tried to make something of their relationship in their *Death on Killer Mountain* pieces, you know the kind of thing. Personally, I don't think there was much in it. Alistair was always a bit scathing of those who took their partners climbing. 'Fit and Fast' was his credo for mountain safety and I think this was nothing more than the case of a middle-aged guy being flattered by the attentions of a young girl and letting that flattery rule his head. Had he been on his own, I feel sure he would have forced his way down on the first day.

He was out of it for about a fortnight what with the drugs and all. He didn't make the funeral and as far as I know her parents never visited him. He's never really talked much about it and he's not been climbing since the accident. Spends most of his time reading. He's got a thing about this Alisteir Crowley guy the self-styled 'Great Beast', lived up Loch Ness way back in the 1920s. Into black magic, orgies and the like but, funnily enough, he was also a member of the Scottish Mountaineering Club. We were out for a curry the other night and I asked him where he found out about this guy Crowley, apparently some friend of his, Michael Scott introduced them.

There is one other strange side effect of his accident. When I say *we* were out for a curry, that's not strictly true he had a steak, he used to love his Rogan Josh but since the accident he seems to have gone right off them.

DOW SPOUT

By Stephen Reid

VIEWED from the far bank of the Cooran Lane on the edge of the Silver Flowe, Craignaw was a fantastic sight. The East Face of this huge whaleback of a mountain is nearly 1000ft high and one-and-a-half-miles long, and it was in full winter garb, plastered in snow and rime and bathed in the rosy glow of a low, early January sun. Under the summit, three short gullies could just be discerned. The right hand of these we knew was merely a grassy scramble, but the central was *Drainpipe Gully,* a summer V. Diff. discovered by that veteran Galloway enthusiast and explorer, Andrew Fraser, 20 years earlier.

Now Andrew had returned for the first winter ascent, partnered by another Ayr climber Ian Magill, and myself. As an off-comer and Sassenach from south of the Border, I felt privileged to have been invited, though I rather suspected that it might have less to do with my climbing skills and more with the fact that I had managed (quite legitimately) to acquire a vehicle permit for the forest track leading into the climb.

Over the last decade Andrew and I had been involved in some fairly intensive development on the Galloway crags, though strangely enough, never on the same crag at the same time. As a result we had exchanged many a phone call, e-mail and letter, but we had only met once and had never climbed together before. Naturally, each of us was convinced that his own routes and crags were best! I was thus fully prepared to spend the day fending off endless leg-pulls and good-natured chaffing and to give as good as I got.

To the left of *Drainpipe* was *Silver Flow,* a gully that had only had one winter ascent and which was definitely due a repeat, but far to the left again was the main reason for our visit, *Dow Spout,* a swathe of frozen silver water that tumbled the full length of the mountain-side in a series of icy steps, pink and glistening in the dawn. From our view point, it looked magnificent and forbiddingly steep, but the foreshortening effect of distance was deceptive. *Dow Spout* in good conditions is one of the best Grade II routes of its type in the British Isles. That its first recorded ascent did not take place until 1997 becomes less of a puzzle when it is realised that the only way to reduce the approach time to a reasonable 1hr 30mins is to use a mountain bike on the forestry track for the first leg, and hardly a puzzle at all when one knows how few climbers there are actually operating in the Galloway Hills. Though that is perhaps a puzzle in itself.

The Spout owes its existence to the Dow Loch, a lochan situated just south of the summit of Craignaw. A small stream carries the outflow to the top of the East Face whence it exits through a notch and cascades, splashes and tumbles over a series of granite slabs and heather ledges until it finally disappears into the floating bog of the Silver Flowe far below. In times of drought it dries up and for good winter conditions heavy rain, followed by at least seven days of hard frost, seem to be required.

The idea of climbing *Dow Spout* as a winter route was that of Jim Lawrence, a doctor from Dumfries, who had noticed the fall featured in that seminal work on the area *The Merrick and the Neighbouring Hills,* published in 1929. According to the author, J. McBain: "Ordinarily, there is but a mere trickle of water down the rocks, but when the *Dow Spout* pours its flood waters over the brink it is by far the most picturesque thing of its kind in the uplands, and as a spectacle it is probably not surpassed in Scotland. It then comes down the mountainside in the guise of a beautiful white ribbon clinging to the declivity from top to bottom. I have seen the *Dow Spout* in a thunder storm transformed from a state of quiescence into a white mass of descending water within the space of 10 minutes: and it is only when its small watershed is saturated with water, and during the continuance of heavy rain or rapidly melting snow, that it can be seen in all its picturesqueness."

On reading this, Jim had duly set off to view this marvel but found a 'mere trickle'. Perseverance paid off, however, when one December a cloud of spray being blown in the wind betrayed the Spout in all its glory, moreover he noted ice forming around its edges. A week later the temperatures were still low and the ice thicker, and a further week on, on New Year's Day 1997, he and Simon Mortlock were finally rewarded with as fine a first ascent as any Scottish winter climber could wish for.

With so few ascents to date, less than 10 as I write, it is hard to be certain as to what exactly is required for good conditions, but certainly the Spout is a fickle beast and, however deep and long-lasting the cold spell, is not likely to form if there has not been sufficient rain. For example, Stuart Lampard and Jim Thompson saw no sign of it when they passed by on their way to make the first ascent of *Silver Flow* in January 1994. Perhaps then, the main requirement for good conditions is a close attention to weather forecasts.

A hop, skip and jump technique was needed to ford Cooran Lane without getting our boots full of water, but the Silver Flowe, normally a horrendous marsh full of exhausting tussocks and bottomless slithy pits, proved much easier when frozen and little more than half-an-hour saw us at the foot of *Drainpipe Gully.* This turned out to be an interesting mixed route with much progress made by way of frozen turf, icy slabs and jammed chockstones. It provided a pitch apiece and a great deal of banter for the team as each of us struggled in turn in full view and much to the entertainment of those anchored safely below. A quick visit to the summit of Craignaw was well worth the exertion for its fine winter panorama of Merrick and the Range of the Awful Hand. Northwards, islanded Loch Enoch looked to be iced over and the summit of the Dungeon of Buchan was snowbound. Westwards the gleaming Solway, the Mull of Galloway and even the distant mountains of Ireland could be seen, while to the south, beyond Curleywee, Cairnsmore of Fleet and Screel Hill, layers of blue, each fainter than the last, marked the far off Lakeland Fells.

Though the sun shone brightly out of a cloudless sky, a chill wind soon sent us scurrying for the shelter of some rocks below the summit cairn where we quickly scoffed our sandwiches and then scrambled down steep hillside to the south to regain the bottom of the Spout. From below the view was even more impressive. A band of ice 40ft wide cascaded down the cliff in a series of white stalactites, walls and corners, looking for all the world like a magical staircase leading to some fairy-tale castle. Skating rink ledges were interspersed here and there and clean, grey granite boulders promised good belays.

The first section appeared simple, almost a walk if one felt bold enough, but above, any of those short vertical walls could prove a stopper if it were too steep or too high. At the top the fall narrowed and looked even more sustained. But all of it was in stunning condition, the sort of ice that is so well frozen it sticks to your gloves – or your skin if you are daft enough to let it. It was all old territory for Andrew who had made the second ascent two years' earlier and, having led us up the initial easy slabs and over a short bulge, he pointed me towards steeper territory above. A vertical groove about 8m high appeared to be the only reasonable way up the glittering cascade.

There was little ice on its right wall, but that on the left was reassuringly solid, and a few contorted and ungainly heaves saw me up onto easier ground and running the rope out to a good thread belay. Ian now took over, a big moment for him as this was the first pure water-ice route he had led. Nonetheless, he wended his way efficiently up a series of icy steps and grooves until stopped by a short wall. Picking the thickest part of this, a couple of quick pulls and an instant self-taught lesson in steep ice crampon technique saw him up to a big ledge and a good rock belay to the side of the main flow.

Above the ice grew steeper and narrower before disappearing through a notch in the, by now, darkening skyline – my lead again. Edging back into the centre of the fall, I picked the easiest looking section and stuck my axes high into a vague scoop. A strenuous pull up and I found myself looking into a large hole down which a stream of freezing water was thundering. This was not the place to be! Apart from the risk of getting soaked, the ice felt insecurely attached. A desperate scrabbling two-step bridge out right brought more solid stuff to hand and a few more knuckle-bruising moves attained a good ledge where a splendid nut placement in the right wall calmed me down a bit. Back left, a series of icy runnels and bulges led up through the notch and I gained the top just as the rope ran out. The others followed on as the last dregs of ruby-red sun sunk below the horizon. Before us lay the prospect of negotiating the decidedly awkward descent route in the dark and then navigating across the virtually featureless Silver Flowe. But we couldn't have cared less. What a day, what companions, and what a route.

I returned two days later with Jim Fotheringham and found the Spout in even better condition. Forty-eight hours of freeze-thaw had done splendid work, the sky was blue and barely a breath of wind disturbed the air. So good was the ice that the ascent took us little more than an hour and we were soon back down and gearing up under the deep forbidding cleft of *Silver Flow*. Fortunately, this was nowhere near as serious or difficult as it looked, and three pitches of excellent Grade IV climbing followed, including a new direct finish, followed by another worthwhile trog to the summit of Craignaw and then a long, but pleasant, descent northwards and round under the Cooran Buttress of the Dungeon, the scene of many an enjoyable adventure for both of us in years gone by.

Dow Spout is an easy climb by today's standards, but given a clear day of sub-zero temperatures, it is hard to imagine a finer place to be or a route more likely to be enjoyed by everyone whatever their ability. The arduous approach – miles of pre-dawn motoring, followed by a strenuous bike ride, while all the time suffering that butterflies-in-the-stomach feeling that stems from not really knowing whether the climb is going to be 'in' or not – only adds to the sense of excitement and achievement that is all part of what goes to make a perfect Scottish winter climbing day.

GIVE ME SUNSHINE

(Retrospective on the 1961 JMCS East Greenland Expedition[1])

By Mike Fleming

WHEN a frequent Journal contributor, who may turn out to have more literary talent than judgment, suggested that I write more about the above expedition, the immediate response was "Why?"

"Partly," said he, "to remind people how hard it was to get there."

This rang bells. Today it seems that no-one is much further than a helicopter, boat or lorry ride from one's destination, and, once there, umbilically linked to civilisation by radio, satellite and perhaps even postcard. One can summon support, and for all I know, a delivery from the local takeaway at the flick of a switch. A few years ago an application to the Trust for expedition support quoted 'Bus' as the means of access and 'Guidebook' as the reference to previous exploration. The world has happily become a safer place, but sadly a much smaller one.

In 1958[2], the Slesser/Smart SS pioneered a crossing from North to South Staunings Alps by the Spörre Glacier, Duart/Roslin Col and hence to Schuchert Dal and Syd Kap. Then, in 1960, John Hunt[3,4] pushed a reconnaissance party across this route and into the Bjornbos Glacier region of the South Staunings Alps, climbed two peripheral peaks, and reported "a paradise of unclimbed mountains of alpine stature as far as eye could see". This inspired Jim Clarkson to raise an expedition of six Edinburgh JMCS, one London JMCS and two non-members to blitz the area the following year. Personal recollections of this trip dwell on the logistical and physical difficulties of getting there in equal measure to the delights of the mountaineering challenges encountered. Ship to Iceland then charter plane to Mesters Vig were now routine for East Greenland except that 'Del Boy' Clarkson chartered large Dakota DC4/Viscount planes (in/out) rather than the smaller DC3, then sub-leased seats to two other expeditions at highly advantageous rates to ourselves. Thereafter the problem was to get more kit than could be carried some 80 miles over the Skel Glacier, Schuchert Dal (Valley) and Bjornbos Glacier to our main Base Camp at Concordia, the name given to the confluence of most of the major South Staunings glacier systems and the hub of the whole area. We had arranged to use a mining reconnaissance plane to ferry most of our gear to a small airstrip about half-way along Schuchert, but the best laid plans...; the plane had not yet arrived from Denmark. The Danish Airforce came to our rescue by offering a parachute drop at Concordia as an "exercise" on condition that we retrieved the 'chutes. Howard Brunton and Graham

Hendry, our two geologists, were to fly with them to direct the drop then walk in with light (35lb!) packs. The rest of us would go ahead with the balance. Sounds easy? The balance was 85lb per man.

The next 10 days provoke contrasting memories of horrendous slogging across glaciers, beautiful flower-bedecked country in unremitting sunshine and mosquitoes. The relief, as a novice, of staying on the surface of the Skel snows on ski instead of waist deep without, and the despair of falling off those skis, knowing that a split second later an 85lb pile-driver would hammer one's head deep into said snow requiring at least a two-man rescue. The joy of the mining outpost's hospitality at Malmsberg and the horror of a flowing stream of mud – Jim stepped onto a boulder in the middle; boulder? Jim and load started to sink. Fortunately, Keith Murray was close behind, grabbed his pack and pulled him bodily clear.Probing with ski sticks could detect no bottom. What's all the fuss about carrying 85lb? (You will notice that 1961 was yet unmetricated.) Well, you need help to get it off the ground. You walk for 20 minutes only because you know that a 10 minute break is beckoning. For the last 5 minutes you are scouting for a waist-high boulder to take your pack. If you habitually jump down onto a stepping stone in one of the burns your knees collapse and you just keep on going down into the water. Your feet take terrible punishment and your back and shoulders are raw with pressure sores. How we regretted that the weight of the retrievable parachutes had restricted the amount we could drop.

River crossings were quite dangerous. Keeping ever to the north (mountain) side of the Schuchert river we still had to cross the outflow melt-water rivers from the glaciers, the largest of which, from the Lang Glacier, was a major problem. Late in the afternoon, hip deep and flowing like the clappers, it was totally impossible. But time is almost irrelevant in the arctic, so we camped then tried again at 3am with melt-water at its lowest. Even so, crossing in pairs and roped, the thigh-deep water was still fast enough to rumble boulders along the bottom; bad enough without the beladen exit onto a large snow shelf. The falling melt-water had left a gap between snow and surface of the river which was trying for all its worth to carry you under the shelf. It was here that Gwyn Evans emerged to find that the current had torn one of his boots off his benumbed foot. The amazing man immediately sewed a lump of kitbag onto the bottom of a plimsole and spent the next five weeks on one boot and one gym shoe. He even managed the occasional climb in borrowed boots.

We camped next on the Lang River airstrip – a bulldozed piece of tundra. This was of interest since, optimistic of its imminent arrival, the mining plane had been booked to pick up some of us and much of our gear here in five and a half week's time. A rather loose arrangement involving a "most likely day", a "second choice" (the day before) and a "third choice" (being the day after). The fourth choice I seem to recall was next year. (Pay

attention, there may be questions.) And so on across the snout of the Roslin
Glacier with some pleasant ice and some extremely unpleasant moraine,
then cut the corner to the Bjornbos, and at last we could see up our glacier
to Concordia, and why we had done it all. Peak after peak gleaming in the
crystal clarity that is Greenland and which makes all things appear three
times closer than they really are. A last eight mile day's plod with more
and more mountains beckoning – the pointed ramp that was to be *Pisa*,
the rock tower of *Kilroy*, the ramparts of *Bastille*, and, far up, dominating
the entry to the upper fastnesses of Main Glacier, the snows and cliffs of
the mighty *Sentinel*. Glaciers to the right, to the left; icy mountains, rocky
mountains. All of it ours! Well, apart from the shale bing on the right –
that was Sir John's. So, was it all worth it? Judge for yourself.

The toils of the trek in were compensated by tantalising glimpses of the
Staunings Alps tightening the chest with anticipation. Each day's end was
a real pleasure when we would camp on a patch of hillside, green with
fresh, springy moss set off by colourful cushions of saxifrage, mountain
chickweed, arctic poppies and even Scottish harebells. We would watch
through the mosquito netting as herds of musk oxen lazily grazed on this
abundance – "but don't get too near!"

And once we arrived? – again, judge for yourself. The expedition in the
next three weeks climbed twenty four virgin peaks (even more
impressively, there were seventy three individual man-ascents of these
peaks) and achieved a major trans-Staunings crossing to Alpe Fjord. The
mountains were in the 5,000 – 8,600 ft range with, usually, about 2,000 ft
of ascent from the glaciers. Ascent times were most often four to eight
hours with round-trip times about double, although we did often find
quicker ways down. So we are talking big Nevis ridge to comfortable
alpine day out, not only in length but also in climbing character, up to
mild VS on the hot sun-soaked granite or III-ish on the colder snow and
ice routes. There were significant exceptions though. And all this time the
sun shone round the clock. We had four cloudy days with light snow on
two of them. Our rain gauge was broken in the drop. But it didn't matter.
Nothing would have registered. With one sole exception we climbed *every*
significant peak in an area of perhaps fifty square miles covering at least
five major, multi-branched glacier systems, and including the highest
mountains of the South Staunings. There were notable individual
achievements too. Jim topped the table with thirteen ascents, followed by
Keith on eleven and Ian Douglas on nine. Even bootless Gwyn managed
four. Oh yes, on an expedition scale, absolutely worthwhile. But on a
personal basis? Keep your judge's cap on. My next three weeks involved
an unforgettable ten day journey to Alpe Fjord and back, and a group of
unclimbed mountains including the highest and (separately) my nomination
for the best rock climb in the world. Read on.

The first may not quite have been the best as they say (about mountains?), but an auspicious beginning. Keith and I had spotted a good rock peak on the walk in just below Concordia. So here we were. Released at last from our loads we fairly flew up a 200 ft severe wall onto a fairly easy slabby ridge on good rock if you avoided some looser bits, and onwards past a few harder *gendarmes* for 1,500 ft to a final snow slope. Eight hours to our maiden first ascent. Ours to name. Our euphoric rantings had been of the 'Kilroy was here' on the summit block variety so we decided *Kilroy* was a fine name. The Scottish convention in Greenland was to name after castles; *ergo* we had failed at the first hurdle. However Jim was persuaded that Kilroy was an ancient fortress in nether-Fife, so *Kilroy* it stands in the Bennet bible![5]. Another good peak had fallen that day in the Mars Glacier so the expedition was up and running. Next day, four of us circumvented the impressive cliff behind Base to find a long, fine-looking but rather chaotic ridge which took us, in seven and a half hours of unroped scrambling, to the summit of *Bastille* between the Concordia and Jupiter glaciers. The summit was quite spectacular – a high foot-square pedestal looking straight down the cliff to Base Camp 2,000 ft below. This was a superb viewpoint and we spent an hour or so sunbathing and reconnoitring the wonderful array of pristine summits that would occupy us for the next few weeks.

On the 'morrow I lent my boots to Gwyn who joined Jim, Ian and Ray Tanton on an ambitious assault on a major prominent peak (*Sentinel*) up Main Glacier. They were rewarded by an amazingly easy mixed route by its SE ridge from Pegasus Glacier. The climbing for me was now put on the back-burner since I surprised myself (and the rest of the company) as an obsessive climber – as opposed to walker or skier, by electing to join the Alpe Fjord trans-Staunings party instead of moving up Mercury Glacier for an extra week's mountain-bagging. I'm so glad I made that choice.

Heavy loads on again for Howard, Graham, Ray and myself. Still, 75lb was better than 85, and that included skis which for most of the time at least weren't on our backs. A heavy slog up Main Glacier in by now almost monotonous sunshine. We had a choice of two reasonable cols; one would take us over to the Roslin Glacier and hence to the Duart-Roslin Col and Alpe Fjord by the SS route[2] of 1958. (This was later crossed by a German party in 1966 and named 'Donnau Passet'.) However, with typical courage we chose the very easy one (Main Col) leading to the top of the as yet unexplored Spörre Glacier. A diversion up a small snow peak (*Darien*) north of this col offered wonderful views of both the North and South Staunings and demonstrated that the former were generally an order of magnitude more serious than the latter. For the first time we looked over the shadowed vale of Alpe Fjord to the icecap of Nathorsts Land. But more immediately the northward descent led gently into a marvellous bowl of uncrevassed, unsullied snow which eventually steepened into some seriously crevassed slopes before the confluence of the Spörre with the

Duart Glacier half-way down to Alpe Fjord (or, more correctly, Dammen, which is separated from the fjord by the combined outflows of the Gully and Sefstrom Glaciers.) The next bit from the Col introduced us to a) the most pernicious and b) the most sublimely idyllic of ski mountaineering. We pointed down a gentle slope onto the strangest of surfaces; a thin but hard, bearing crust on top of unplumbed depths of the lightest floury snow. Fine so far – apparently perfect for skiing. Only the crust had somehow formed into gigantic plates overlapping like tiles but with the overlap of several inches facing upwards instead of down. For some distance the skis stayed on top, breasting the overlaps. But then a larger overlap would take the ski tips *below* the crust into a vertical dive and your face was smashed through said crust by a vindictive pack. All hands to the rescue; and you knew it would all happen again a minute or two later. Fortunately, after a quarter of a mile of this, the plating stopped, the crust remained with an inch or two of icing sugar on top and we were in a skiing wonderland. The next six miles were covered in an hour of sheer bliss. We called this basin "The Sugar Bowl", camped therein and were tempted just to stay there and ski. However, on and down through some heavy crevasses to the confluence. We all had our moments with crevasses to remind us we were now one hundred miles out from Mesters Vig and assistance. A particular manoeuvre which really concentrated the mind became commonplace – side-stepping across narrow snow-bridges with both ends of the skis overhanging the abyss and praying that they were precisely horizontal. The big packs came to our aid too. Several abrupt descents into narrow crevasses were forestalled by the pack jamming in the jaws. Another strange phenomenon was a number of clearly 'bottomless' crevasses of just jumpable width full to the brim with jet-black water. The thought of missing the jump and going in with 75lb packs was really terrifying. The lower stretch of the Spörre down to Dammen, now on dry ice with skis dumped, was a totally shambolic icefall; five and a half hours to cover one mile (contrast to the Sugar Bowl). And so to Dammen; five days out from Concordia. We even found a bootprint – Man Slesser? A day's recuperation and sight-seeing. Back the way we came. A detour from the Sugar Bowl to investigate an impracticable col to the Princessa Glacier. A brief pause to shelter from a few hours of our first light snow and down to Concordia. What a trip, and in what company! The chrysalid climber had transformed into a mountaineer. Oh yes, it was worth it!

The glacial scenery at Concordia seemed timeless but there was one salient demonstration of its impermanence. A tent had been left at Base while we were on our various ten day trips to Alpe Fjord or Mercury Camp. On our return it was found to be perched on a two foot pedestal. The glacier had melted by that amount but the shaded tent area had been unaffected. We had also noticed that small pebbles on the glacier lower the melting point and sink whereas large boulders behave like the tent and become raised. This led to an earnest discussion as to whether our bowel movements would be sunken, or reach a critical mass and be raised – stalacturds or stalagturds. Future generations wandering through a forest of stalagturds could be a lasting memorial to our expedition.

Which was going well. The climbing group had had a successful week from a camp on the Mercury Glacier; another five peaks. They confirmed that the deeper you penetrated toward the watersheds, the better the rock became. These high glacier peaks were impressive, yet not particularly hard; good Scottish mixed ridge standard or, on snow, in rather soft condition due to the sun. Fine mountains though. When the expedition reunited, Gwyn decided to take his plimsole and a tent back down to Schuchert Dal and spend the rest of his time *à la* peripatetic Smart[4] wandering those heathy braes. The rest of us moved camp to the Jupiter Glacier system where the highest and finest peaks of the South Staunings are located. Could we match what had gone before?

In the next six days we would climb another thirteen peaks including the highest and second highest in the South Staunings and, separately, my nomination for the "Best Rockclimb in the World." Quality mountains all. First, for me, was a pleasant unroped ascent on snow at first, but mostly by a good, blocky ridge with Jim, Keith and Ian; an all Edinburgh party, so the peak became *Edinburgh*. Next, Keith and I had our eyes on what we had already named *Dinosaur*; a great crenellated rampart of rock jutting into the upper reaches of the Jupiter Glacier where it forked left and right in a T-Junction. The down-glacier face was probably impossible being a 1,000 ft convex bulge with the bottom half actually overhanging, but, moving through the top crevasses and left at the T, we reached easier ground – a delightful Chamonix ridge on top quality cracked granite blocks, laybacking and jamming to our hearts' content at mostly V. Diff/Severe but occasionally mild VS. The exposure down the North Face was terrific without really impinging on our route. A stone lobbed twenty feet out took ten seconds to disappear over the half-way bulge and didn't strike rock before reaching the glacier. Our climb took us only to the lowest (N) of the three towered summits; about one hundred feet lower than the other two, but separated by a steep gap in which the perfectly crystalline red granite suddenly became completely unconsolidated. You could crumble a handful of rock to powder in your hand. There was no reasonable prospect of a safe route onwards so we called it a day and left the true summit unclimbed. The *Dinosaur* ridge also gave us, for the first time, full frontals of a pair of mountains which dominated the end of the left fork (looking up) of Jupiter. These had been glimpsed from time to time from other peaks and were quite exceptional. The left-hand snow-capped mountain had been provisionally named *Tent Peak*. The right-hand one was a jaw-dropper; a massive three-tiered face of Dolomitic steepness twice the height of *Dinosaur's* N Face culminating in a narrow flat-topped tower buttressed on the right by a bastioned complex ridge. Keith and I would have named it Eilan Donan, unaware of Lovat and Bryan's 1958 predecessor[2]. However the alternative unpoetic nickname of *Wedge Peak* was eventually adopted. (Confusion is still likely since a contender called *The Wedge* now exists in the Dalmore Glacier courtesy of Smart's 1968 expedition.) We reckoned that the N Face probably deserved an expedition on it's own, but that the *couloir* between *Tent* and *Wedge* and a series of steep, rock-flanked snowfields could provide a feasible route. The mountain just had to be climbed. But not yet. Another even more compelling priority had first to be attended to. The highest peak in the South Staunings.

Unlike many of its neighbours, this grand mountain stands in almost complete isolation and commands the outlook from Jupiter up the Orion Glacier. It has a massive hanging glacier contained between rock ridges on a rocky base. By now the sun was just dipping below the horizon at night when the summit snows of this beautiful mountain would pick out the last and first rosy tints. *Prometheus*, from he who would steal light from the Gods, seemed an appropriate name. Cyril Levene (our doctor, Lev), Ray, Graham and I set off on the three hour trek to its base (thinking then that it might be second highest in the area). Ian and Keith accompanied us part way *en route* for another fine rock peak (*Blair*) also bounding Orion. After an initial icy couloir then some pleasant slabs and a rock rib we reached the foot of the hanging glacier on the S Face. Good snow-ice brought us in a further 1,000 ft to the final snowfields and the summit. We were overjoyed to find that we were on the highest peak of all – 8,600 ft (2,570m) according to Ray's surveyor's level and aneroid. As an isolated peak the views round the compass were absolutely breathtaking. With the sun low on the horizon and the extraordinary clarity that is Greenland, we not only had highlit panoramas of all our South Staunings peaks, but also uplifting vistas across the North Staunings, Scoresby Sound, out over the iceberg speckled N.W. Fjord and on across the great Greenland icecap. On the descent, Lev and I avoided all rock below the hanging glacier to reach the bottom entirely on crampons. Keith and Ian had also been successful, and with eight peaks already climbed from Jupiter by the Company, Keith and I decided that the time was ripe for an assault on *Wedge Peak*.

And so, together with Jim and Howard who were aiming for *Tent Peak*, we headed once more through the crevasses to the T, turned left past *Dinosaur* and on to our targets. Jim and Howard turned up a snow gully left of the *Tent* and we carried on. The Face loomed steeper and higher till we had diminished to the size of ants. The *couloir*, our chosen line, was, to quote Keith[1], "throwing stones like Gimmer at Whitsun". So, hazarding another look up the N Face, we decided that "Well, we wouldn't get up but it might be fun trying." Stack the skis and cross the bergschrund to a ledge just clear of the snow in the middle of the three-tiered face. I was stale and disinterested – a condition induced by terror. Keith wandered along the ledge for a rightward run-out finding not the vestige of a way up till he reached a clean-cut, foot wide chimney that ascended to eternity. So up it I went. Chimneys are more or less impervious to angle and hence the route of choice up the vertical. Severe with a few more difficult chockstones, but not too bad at all. Depression sloughed off and left at the bottom. Through leads again and again. Height being made. About a Rannoch Wall later –oops; we reached the end of this happy chimney. We stopped (had to) in some confusion. Well, I suppose we couldn't really expect it to go on for 2,000 ft. After some haphazard shuffling up and down the evil, overhanging, verglassed groove that had transmuted from our wee chimney. I took the obvious easy ledge out to the left. We had been trying not to notice this since it led out to a bulge hiding the rest of the wall from view – but we remembered what that wall was like! At the bulge the exposure was heart-stopping – out of the secure chimney to emerge onto that great featureless face. But, astonishingly, *onto* was the operative word, because we were *above* the wall, and the ledge led into some easier-angled icy grooves. (Here we encountered some loose stuff for the only time apart from the two great scree ledges which demarcated the three tiers.) Keith did some nifty work with his slater's pick and we soon emerged onto an enormous sloping scree ledge. The line so far had been more or less directly below the abutment of the great W Ridge with the final tower of the N Face far, far above. The ledge looked as if it might provide an escape route into the now distant couloir; and for all we knew it did. But I hoped not. This route didn't deserve the ignominy of an escape. On the ledge, which was clearly one-way to the left, we looked up at the next tier.

And damned nearly fell off backwards! I've never seen anything so steep. The only escape route offered up there was out of 'this mortal coil'. Dislocating our necks, we looked again. A great vertical pinkish wall with buttressed fringes tapered up for maybe 500 ft to be capped by a huge, square-cut, Cobbler size overhang extending the breadth of the visible face. Gulp. Clearly no way for us up there, so left along the ledge ("Please don't make us traverse off!") till a little welcoming bay was found at the back of which two cracks led steeply left or right. We also appeared to be to the side of the overhung wall. Both cracks disappeared over bulges at 30 feet so it was a lottery. Off I went up the right-hand one because it was marginally more direct to our initial line (I lie; it was because it was marginally easier). Splendid jamming granite crack – great fun – developing over the bulge into a chimney line which was almost a replica of that of the first tier. More marvellous sport in the vertical for multiple run-outs till once again it went blind. No messing this time. Straight out on the easy leftward ledge round the bulge and – oops again; it debouched onto a steep little wall, about 15 ft across, with one detectable small, sloping toe-hold in the middle, leading to another chimney on the other side. Possibly the left crack from the bay might have taken us to this chimney thereby avoiding the traverse which was to be the technical crux of the climb. But I would then have avoided one of the two most cherished moments of my rock-climbing career. (The other would occur further up the Face.) While we were gawping at this wall a distant yodel announced the arrival of the other two at our ski dump after a fine snow and ice ascent of *Tent Peak*. They were somewhat surprised to get a reply from halfway up the Face. We could see them an airy 1,000 ft straight below but they were unable to locate us. We managed to convey to them that we were perhaps halfway up (5 hr; 9:30pm), had no idea how we could get down, and not to expect us before noon on the 'morrow at the earliest. That done, on to the wall. I managed to get a peg in high on the right. With some tension from this and a huge straddle I managed to get my foot on the hold and eventually scrabble my body back to the vertical. Here I could look past my heels to the next focal points which were the twin dots of Howard and Jim on the glacier. A wee touch exposed! On my left foot I couldn't begin to reach the edge of the chimney. It was a change foot job on a sloping toehold on the fine edge of balance on a steep wall so devoid of handhold that, for better balance, I didn't even bother to raise my hands above my waist. Curse, up, off the rock, balletic flail (the grace of which was rather spoiled by the big boots) down on right foot, then that long, long breathless pause while Fate decided whether one would remain attached to the world or not. One did. Thereafter it was a moment's work to friction-straddle the left wall allowing fingers to reach the security of the chimney edge. This chimney also terminated but, this time, an easy 20 feet higher. Keith, with the sack, simply pendulumed across. Somehow we knew then both that we had passed the crux and that we would get to the top - whenever. But there was an even more spectacular pitch yet to come.

Another easy run-out took us to the second (narrower) scree ledge. This time, to restore our direct line, we moved right for Keith to belay a short way from the end of the ledge which terminated as abruptly as a pirate's plank. I went on and looked over the end of the world. I was at the outer edge of the 15 ft horizontal roof overhanging the whole second tier which had forced the earlier diversion. My ledge was the fault line of the roof. Beyond it the whole tier had broken off leaving a void below and beyond. The end of the ledge marked the left-hand vertical fault line which continued upwards as a great 5 feet wide slash through the roof. Just narrow enough to straddle and bridge. But to get in? It was the classic "fall across the gap till outstretched hands reach the other side" move; a bit of a heart-stopper at the best of times – but five feet across the outer edge of a fifteen foot overhang with only space below to the distant glacier! Meanwhile the sun had dipped, threatening clouds were building up, so the scene was further dramatised by a lurid red sunset. I have to confess that I hammed it up even more by then bridging upwards facing out towards the North Pole. It was, I imagine, a sensation akin to free flying. And the ridiculous thing was that it was quite easy! Rough granite with plenty holds at straddling width. Up we went for two pitches, Keith having a moment of pure farce leading a final hard exit where the top of the cleft splayed out and was capped. He needed to mantelshelf onto a small pedestal on the right wall. He did so with great dexterity except that in the last moment he swivelled round and SAT on the pedestal. There he was, like an arctic gargoyle, perfectly safe – and perfectly stuck! Try it yourself – a desperately hard situation to get out of and totally devoid of dignity. The eldritch cacklings emanating from that bloodshot chasm on the upper tower of *Wedge Peak* should surely belong in some wild Wagnerian saga. He finally righted himself to emerge at the junction of the great W Ridge and the Final Tower. When I had stopped laughing I joined him. This Tower was excellent and straightforward; still as steep as ever but multiple run-outs up a proliferation of chimneys, cracks and grooves brought us to the flat tabular summit at 4:30am, an hour after sunrise and after eleven hours of continuously demanding quality climbing. And we were still a far cry from being safely down again.

We were a bit put out to find that the hitherto unseen glaciers to the south were filling with rather ominous clouds and it even appeared to be raining down Bjornbos and Schuchert way. Surely the weather wouldn't break now while we were still atop *Wedge Peak*. (Fortunately the bad weather did not penetrate to Jupiter for another couple of days.) After about an hour for rest and recuperation we headed off for the *Tent – Wedge* col. Easy rock past the first snowfield postponed crampons to the unavoidable second snowfield (70°) leading to col and couloir. But this turned out to be one inch of soft powder covering very hard, very brittle ice. We had two conduit ice-pegs but dared not discard them by roping down and they turned out to be useless for belaying because the ice just shattered. Getting down took an eternity (also invited eternity) and resulted in great plates of this peculiar ice flaking away and threatening to take out your standing step. All highly unpleasant. We ended up by inventing modern technique and going down on front points and ice-axe pick (singular, please note) with ice-pick belays. Eventually the ice became too hard even for this and we were forced to cut down again. We were very tired and this was extraordinarily dangerous. It took four hours to descend that 400 ft icefield to the col – and we had the prospect of 2,000 ft of couloir still to come. But rescue was at hand. The rocks of *Tent Peak* bordering the couloir were unpleasantly shattered – now we saw the origins of the couloir stonefalls of (could it be?) only seventeen hours ago – but relatively easy. We began to lose height at a significant rate. Lower down, the broken rocks steepened dangerously again but the couloir had improved in quality and we were able to romp down good snow-ice to a final glissading leap across the bergschrund to our skis. It was seventeen hours since we had set foot on the N Face.

Down past *Dinosaur* like automatons. Turn right through the icefall screwing up the concentration again to ski the snow-bridges then turn sharply to evade the ensuing crevasses. Down the last slopes to the near level glacier leading to the camp. Here was one last sting-in-the-tail. Trying to make a long stride across a substantial melt-water stream, Keith missed his footing and stepped into a mere foot of water. "Ho! Ho! Ho!" as he started a stately glide down the burn. I watched with glee as this legless torso meandered down the glacier till I realised that his skis were tracked down the centre of a polished, semicircular Venus Flytrap which would inevitably soon plunge into the depths of the glacier. At last he managed to hurl himself at the bank and claw his way out. We finally reached camp ten minutes before our deadline and exactly twenty-four hours after we had left it. I have been reliving those twenty-four hours ever since.

Having swapped tales with the *Tent Peak* and *Kirriemuir* parties we slept the rest of the day away while Jim, Howard and Graham climbed one last significant peak. *Tantalus*, the second highest in the South Staunings, presented a pleasant S Face of mixed climbing from the Orion Glacier. This fine mountain also projects a splendid ridge eastwards to Main Glacier (much admired on our Alpe Fjord trip). With one further day to go and one further peak to climb to complete our total blitz of the area, Jim, Ray, Ian and I set off in lowering cloud. This last was a prominent rock peak terminating the ridge between Ursus Major and Orion, on the Jupiter Glacier opposite *Dinosaur*. It is a sister peak to *Blair*. As we reached it the impending snow began to fall heavily; the second precipitation of the whole expedition. We abandoned the attempt and left it as a crumb for the future. So there it is for whoever wants it. But take a look at *Dinosaur* and *Wedge Peak* while you're at it. So that was it. All we had to do now was get out. Only that?

The plan was for everyone to move out to the Lang airstrip with full loads. Howard, Graham and Keith would go a day early, dump most of their kit at Lang, then race out to Mesters Vig with light packs to liaise with the mine people. Lev elected to ferry his load in two halves and had already gone. He would fly out eventually. The rest of us would pack up the Jupiter and Concordia camps, dump unwanted gear and carry the rest out. Seems straightforward? But this time we were carrying 100lb per man! – 15lb more than the incoming load which we had thought to be on the limit. This was partly due to our commitment to return all of the 10lb parachutes, but largely due to our avaricious reluctance to dump good climbing hardware. Still it was downhill and only three marches. Glossing over the toil of these three days, suffice to say that the Schuchert vegetation,

Bastille cirque with Daldalus behind the climbers, Keith Murray (front); Graham Hendry (back left), Howard Brunton. Tent Peak and Wedge Peak – far right skyline. South Staunings Alps. Photo: Mike Fleming.

Skiing the Sugar Bowl on the Upper Sporre Glacier. North Staunings Alps. Photo: Mike Fleming.

in the last five weeks had gone from Spring to Autumn and was a rhapsody of russet; that we again saw large herds of musk oxen; and that the route over the Roslin snout was much assisted by some large arrows left by the nomadic Gwyn. As we approached Lang our little hearts fairly pounded with nobility; on top of our own loads we had brought out a whole can of raspberries from our luxury mountain rations for poor old Gwyn. What selflessness! At the airstrip was a large encampment. As well as Gwyn's mountain tent were pitched two large canvas things. On one was written "Teahouse of the Midnight Sun." Inside was a replete Gwyn sitting in a nest of packing cases containing *inter alia* cold ham, paté de fois gras, honey, jam, chocolate, prunes, stewed steak, soup and other goodies to the power [n]. He had stumbled upon a 1955 prospectors' supply dump. We didn't even mention the raspberries. Most of the stuff was tinned of course so we wellied in with ptotal disregard of ptomaine ptoisoning. The chocolate was defended by a battalion of maggots, but the more central squares were consumed with great relish. He had also found some powdery material which he thought might be oatmeal. He rather fancied making porridge till he noticed it was labelled "Gummy Dynamite." If he had consumed that our stalagturds and stalacturds would have faded into insignificance. His next movement would have truly made the earth move – with a geological cataclysm to rival the extinction of the dinosaurs. (Might even have levelled our *Dinosaur*.) Gwyn had had a splendid time.

After a day of gorging we were on the eve of our second choice fly-out and still no sign of Lev, so Gwyn and I went off at midnight to search. We chanced upon him still on the far side of the Roslin bivouacked in his parachute. We returned early next morning, turfed him out of his 'chute and told him that we couldn't care less if he caught the plane or not but we were certainly going to see that the parachute went out. The others meantime were off on foot to Mesters Vig. The plane duly came on the next (and first choice) day. After an anxious hour watching the pilot search in the wrong place we managed to attract his attention by burning a redundant prospectors' tent. Then one trip for gear and one for Gwyn, Lev and I. And we were out.

At Mesters Vig our committed isolation in the mountains was brought home to us when we learned that the Bangor party on Lang Glacier had suffered a fatality. They got a message out to nearby Malmsberg. By coincidence a US helicopter was on exercise in the area and took him out. Also the mine manager came to see us. Due to unusually heavy pack ice that year his supply ships were long overdue. It was near the onset of winter, and this was a serious problem. In particular they were very low on diesel fuel. Since we had an empty Viscount coming from Iceland, would we mind if he had it loaded with fuel? "Not at all." As we turned to go – "Would £1000 be alright?" Gulp – "Yes." This meant that our personal contributions were almost completely underwritten. So we had had this

Winter in the North-west Highlands. Ben Mor Coigach and Sgurr An Fhidhleir. Photo: Jas Hepburn.
Suilven from Canisp. Photo: Jas Hepburn.

marvellous trip together with massive amounts of mountaineering and skiing equipment, clothing, even 35mm cameras with accessories, essentially for nothing. The end of a successful expedition? Not quite.

One last sting-in-the-tail and one final sublime experience yet to come. After we and the other parties had boarded our Viscount we lifted off, climbed and circled to some 500 ft – then went steeply into a power dive. We gaped out of the windows with eyes like organ stops. "What's he doing?" "Why doesn't he pull out?" "He's not going to pull out." Then, in unison "Bloody Hell!" He had bounced his wheels on the airstrip runway then roared back up equally steeply. It certainly removed much of my fear of violent death, since there had not been time for shock to transmute into terror. If we *had* gone straight in we wouldn't have known the difference. A mildly apologetic pilot wandered through. It turned out that he had been a Polish fighter pilot in Spitfires during the war and this was one of their celebratory manoeuvres. This was also his last trip after many years on the Greenland run. "So this was not to frighten my passengers; just to say 'Goodbye' to the Mesters Vig boys." In a Viscount for heaven's sake! However, to make amends, he offered to take us back over our mountains if one of us (Howard I think) went into the cockpit to direct him – he was demob happy and just didn't care. We then spent the next hour hugging the glaciers, flying round our peaks below mountain level and popping over the cols. What an experience!

When we at last turned for Iceland my last view over the pack showed the Staunings Alps silhouetted against a finally setting sun. It set on this, my expedition. It also set on the multifarious expeditions of all of the mountaineers on that plane. Because each one had his own story to tell. This was mine.

REFERENCES

1. SMCJ, 1962, XXVII, 239 - 244
2. SMCJ, 1959, XXVI, 311 – 329
3. SMCJ, 1961, XXVII, 124 – 130
4. SMCJ, 1961, XXVII, 195 – 196
5. D. J. BENNET, *Staunings Alps,* The Expedition Library, 1972.

A HARD DAY'S NIGHT

By Alan Mullin

IT WAS another deep and dark December night in the Cairngorms. I was sitting in my car full of the usual anticipation when contemplating yet another solo climb and, as I stared into the blackness outside, I was taken away to another place. Mesmerised by the silence shrouded, freshly fallen snow, I was transported back to my childhood and the winter snowball fights. I could just make out the snowman with his carrot nose and the fun and laughter with my younger brother that I remembered so well.

The cold was biting and brought me sharply back to reality. I had decided to solo a new line which I had spotted in Coire an Lochain the week before. I would be climbing it onsight, solo and in the dark. It was 1am and I really ought to be thinking about moving. I had been increasingly pushing the boat out on my solo climbs, raising the stakes each time. On this occasion climbing alone and in the dark made it harder for me to be successful and that was just how I felt about life back then. Nothing I climbed was hard enough, I was not good enough, and only the highest order of difficulty would give me the feelings of self-contentment and achievement I so desired. But, no matter how difficult the climb, these feelings, feelings I had been searching for most of my life were lost to me and it was this search that was driving me to push myself harder and harder, in some vain hope of finding fulfilment.

I did, on the other hand, have a great affinity with the feelings of fear. The fear of soloing was familiar to me. Throughout my life I had truly felt that fear was my constant companion and I knew all its deepest darkest secrets. I had discovered them long ago at home and in the Army and it seemed I had just forgotten how to understand anything else. However, I was now aware that fear no longer presented itself as the intimidating emotion that I had experienced in the beginning. My sense of it had been placed well into the back of my mind and it no longer represented a great threat. I was not fearless by any means, I just didn't sense the emotion of fear in the same way as when I had first climbed alone and I was becoming aware that with each successful solo ascent, these feelings dwindled more and more. I did, however, know that there were still ways to get my kicks with fear like this.

I left the car and switched on the head torch, the yellow beam guided me over the snow, my footsteps crunching crisply with every step, and with every step the apprehension grew stronger and stronger. These feelings were normal for me and once on the route I knew they would fade into the background, leaving me free to climb as hard as I possibly could. An hour-and-a-half later I reached the Coire and switched the lamp to halogen mode. I looked above and could see my route in the distance. It was on No. 3 Buttress and comprised of a steep rib of rock leading into an overhanging corner, above that lay a steep wall and a secondary corner, which ended on a ledge, common to the route *The Migrant*. I had seen the line the week before when climbing in the Coire with my friend Steve and, on returning home and studying the guidebook, I found that it was not yet a recognized route. It was then that the idea was planted in my mind to solo it. I knew it was risky, as onsight, solo and with no prior knowledge is the riskiest form of winter climbing, but that simply made it more appealing to me.

It was 3am and, as I geared up at the foot of the climb, I pulled my hood up and turned away from the cold and damp that was creeping into every bone in my body. I had been so used to suffering hardships without choices, yet here I was in the bitter cold and damp of my own free will. With the hardships of my childhood and the Army I had very little choice, but here I was my own man, it was my call. I truly felt at home in this freezing vertical world, full of fear and anticipation.

I climbed up the initial rocky rib, immersed in my own little world bounded by the small pool of light given out by my head torch. I was so engrossed in the technicalities of the climbing that I suddenly realised that I had climbed 20m and put no protection in. I heard the clinking of my gear reminding me that I should use it and, when I turned around and shone my torch in the area I had just climbed, I could see my rope hanging free into the darkness below. That I could do without. Now that I desperately needed to protect myself I couldn't get any gear in. I switched to survival mode and calculated every move, being careful to test every axe placement before weighting it fully. I finally pulled onto the small ledge that would be my belay for the second pitch above and rappelled down, did the usual work of removing my two bits of gear and re-climbed to my belay above.

This second pitch would be the crux and it looked fierce and sustained. It was at the kind of angle where having a rest would be impossible and placing gear extremely difficult. I made a short traverse rightwards and reached the foot of the overhung corner where I composed myself as I prepared to tackle the crux. The placements for my tools were thin but I could bridge out really wide and get some kind of balance on this strenuous corner. I couldn't see much in the way of cracks for gear and the only ones I could see were filled with ice. My arms were really aching. I managed to place a small peg and a wire and called them good. As usual I felt as though I was in a state of feud: "It's just me against the route and I am determined not to lose." I clipped the single rope into both pieces and continued up the corner. I was over the worst and now I had to pull onto a slab above and to what I had sworn would be a ledge from below. I got some good hooks for my tools and pulled up hard onto the slabby ledge. Standing now precariously in balance, I became aware that what I thought was a ledge from below was, in fact, no more than a foot rail. I steadied myself and directed the light onto the wall above.

I could see a thin crack that would take a small Rp. I worked it home with the gentle tug that indicates an acceptable placement – relief, I could relax a little and concentrate better on the task at hand. I would have to traverse right, across the wall in front of me and gain a second smaller corner that would lead to the big ledge of *The Migrant*. There was just one small issue, traversing with my solo device was dangerous and awkward. I'd always tried to avoid routes with traverses but sometimes the line that appears logical from the ground is very different when you get on to it. I so wanted to place a high runner but that would create lots of rope drag and thus make it very difficult to move freely on technical ground. I traversed slowly rightwards, immersed in my pool of light, feeling nothing but the tools and crampons working their magic on the wall above. I knew I had to be cool, as I had learned a lot from my other solo ascents. Each new solo climb was like a whole new lesson for me. Slow the breathing, manage the gear methodically, trust the placements, and above all – don't panic, even if it all looks hopeless.

I reached the foot of the secondary corner and could see that the main crack was filled with ice. I would not be getting much gear in there, although I did have a good hook in the corner for my right tool. I forced a peg into the icy crack and smashed it as hard as my adze would let me and clipped it into the rope. I then pushed my left foot off against the wall and crossed through with my left tool, repeating that sequence until I could reach over onto the ledge above and hook some turf. I finally pulled down hard and mantled onto the comfort of the big ledge above. I could then start breathing more slowly again. I had felt quite calm throughout, the feelings of fear being easier to deal with each time I soloed. Once more I rappel and go through the same routine before reaching the ledge for the second time. I was on a ledge common with *The Migrant,* a route I had climbed three years previously and as it was Grade VI ground I could move more freely. I climbed quickly above the ledge and onto the steep wall and snow slope that signalled the end of the climb. I checked my watch, it was 8am and I had been climbing for five hours. It had indeed been, as they say 'A Hard Days Night'.

As I walked over the plateau towards the Ski Centre, the sun was just rising and its golden hue covered the ground before me. These were the moments I had usually taken little, if any, notice of. But, as the years go by, I find myself appreciating the beauty of my surroundings more and more and for once I bathed myself in the sunlight, up there alone where I felt completely at home. I called the route *After Dark* – it seemed appropriate. The climbing felt much harder than *The Migrant* so I settled on *VII.7* and hoped the grade would do it justice, regardless of the fact numbers no longer mattered to me. Once again, no great sense of contentment or feelings of success came. Perhaps that would come with age or something else equally unattainable at this point in my life. I was so familiar with that pattern but I was getting better and better at dealing with it. I had been looking over to my right when on the big ledge of *The Migrant* and could see the fierce overhanging corner of the *Migrant Direct*. I knew it would have to be done, solo of course, but that's another story.

FINNIESTON
Greater Himalayan Traverses and Urban Rescues

By Al Scott

I STARTED climbing around 1979-80, and at that time we didn't have the Glasgow Climbing Centre for training purposes. In fact, in those days to do anything remotely like training was unusual in itself. I had, however, a few friends at the Glasgow University Mountaineering Club at the time who took me under their wing and introduced me to the delights of 'Finnie', the premier rock-climbers training venue in Glasgow (or should that be the rock-climbers premier training venue?) and after a few finger-blistering visits I was hooked.

In the early days, I even had a brush with the Emergency Services – Police, Fire Brigade and the *Sunday Post*. All were involved because of my single-minded dedication to training at Finnie. I was preparing for an expedition to Gasherbrum IV in the Karakorum Himalayas in northern Pakistan. (*Karakorum? – Training? – Finnieston?….hmmm…makes sense*).

It was at the time when they were building the SECC and the area opposite the wall was a massive building site, with a watchman employed to look after the whole area. So, picture the scene – I was traversing the wall, no more than a few feet off the ground and minding my own business. The watchman, across the expressway saw me and assumed that I was in desperate trouble and stuck on the wall. He then called the emergency services to rescue me. Now, I'm not saying that the watchman was thick, but he must have been a few inches short of a builder's bum. That's for sure!

A few moments later – MEE MAW, MEE MAW – the sound of sirens blaring. A fire engine and team of burly firefighters careered round the corner from nearby Trumpton Station. It screeched to a halt and out they leapt with ropes and ladders. I jumped (stepped) down from my lofty perch 2ft off the ground and asked 'Pugh, Pugh, Barney McGrew, Cuthbert, Dibble and Grub' what the problem was, and if there had been an accident? We all had a laugh at the watchman's expense who was doing a Mr Chad: "Wot no emergency?" impersonation over the wall across the road.

After giving a statement to the police back at the station I was back at the wall to finish my greater Himalayan traverse. This was such a big story at the time, that it made the front page of the *Sunday Post*. Hon moots!…it was my 15 minutes of fame, but at least it gave our expedition some publicity. Anyway, that's history, let's get back to the future presently.

The recent outbreak of Foot and Mouth meant a ban on all movements in the countryside. Coincidentally, I believe that the last major outbreak of the disease was in the 1960s, and funnily enough, I think that is when Glasgow's leading climbers started climbing at the Finnieston Railway walls.

Of course, there is no longer a ban on movements at Finnieston, and indeed, I've been caught short a few times myself and I can assure all potential users that there are plenty of trees for cover.

For those interested in a trip to the Finnieston Walls, park your car at the head of Glen Kelvinhaugh in Yorkhill by the Fire Station (Trumpton) and start your trek southwards under the railway bridge. With the help of your GPS Navigation Aid, turn east onto the Expressway. Care is required here as cars and lorries hurtle past at dangerous speeds. There is the occasional *'toot-toot' and* scary *'swerve-screech' from* some bampot drivers who think they know you and wonder why the hell you are walking there. Soon the towering, monolithic sandstone walls come into view, resplendent in the sun, pock-marked with chalk and redolent of diesel and keech.

The area is a naturalist's paradise. Home to giant shimmering armadillos, and the even rarer Big Finnieston Crane seen perching over the jakey and trout-laden crystal clear waters of the River Clyde. To the south there is a panoramic view over the Carpark Savannah to the vast Mirrored Mountains and the sky-piercing Science Tower Folly. There is the roar of trundling juggernauts, the whirring of helicopter blades and the frigging of a Tall Ship's rigging filling the air. Indeed, it is a heady brew. Believe me, this is not a Scottish mountain environment to be missed.

The lengthy approach march (two minutes) will have sufficed for most as a warm-up, though some may like to 'crank some off' on one of the rare Pull-Up Trees that adjoin the wall. To fully appreciate the climbing here, it is best to wear your oldest and tattiest rockboots. I personally use a pair of Calanques, purchased in 1982, and still going strong. Sensitivity on 'micro-smears' is achieved through gaping holes in both toe-caps, with my foot protected by double mountaineering socks.

The climbing, particularly on the shorter left-hand section, is of a strenuous nature, being vertical or even slightly overhanging in places, with plenty of small edges, pockets and good footholds. I have been climbing here for more than 20 years and I am still finding new holds – particularly after 'Scratchy-The-Dry-Tooler' has been traversing with axes and crampons! DESECRATION! I mean to say, how would *he* like it if I put chalk marks on his beloved iced-up V. Diffs. Scratchy – go and practice your foul deeds elsewhere – like some poxy old quarry or the Cairngorms for instance.

The crux is traversing past a 'stick-oot-block' at any of a number of levels, (add a couple of technical grades if a train passes overhead and the wall starts shuddering). As well as traversing there are a couple of 'up-and-doon' bits and plenty of scope for boulder problems. Indeed, a 'Phantom-boulderer' has been at work at various sites, daubing his creations with purple paint. SACRILEGE! Shocking, and anti-social behaviour. Graffiti? – It would never be allowed at Dumbarton Rock, the Boulderers Mecca. Phantom! – get thee to Dumby, and take thy tin of paint with thee.

The longer, right-hand section, beyond a wee buttress, is less steep and is positively slabby in places. The wall here is amply supplied with good holds, with short cruxy sections and some good resting places. There are even some old pegs and metalware *in situ*. I guess these must be relics from the old aid-climbing hard men of the 1960s. I believe Crocket's Hardware Store did a good trade in pegs at the time.

Alas, the 'Greater Traverse' is no longer possible. At one time you could traverse non-stop for about 150 yards, but years of neglect by the climbing youth of today has meant that sections of this wall are totally overgrown and impassable. Napalm, Agent Orange, defoliants and machetes are called for nowadays. Or some more traffic might do the trick.

I recently introduced the delights of Finnieston to an English friend of mine, a top Lakeland climber who was staying in Glasgow on business. He was very impressed and asked where did they get the sandstone from? I told him that it was quarried from a secret Scottish location and that all the scrap boulders and bing-shite was transported down to the Lake District where it became known as Scafell. He didn't seem very pleased with my explanation.

Finnieston Wall, an unspoilt natural wilderness, a climber's paradise right on our doorstep. I urge you to abandon the Church of Latter Day Rock Gymnasts at Ibrox and congregate at Finnieston. The newest of Scotland's National Parks and administrated by Scottish Heritage In The Environment.

THE SECOND SIGHT

By P. J. Biggar

Hamlet: Do you see nothing there?
Queen: Nothing at all, yet all that is I see.
(Hamlet III; iv; 132-31)

CONSCIOUSNESS returned slowly.

A strange calm had descended on the mountains in the darkest hours and he had finally slept a drugged, fitful sleep. Now, over the rough meadows where his tent was pitched, snipe were drumming mysteriously in the half light. For a few moments he felt young and expectant, then memory of where he was returned with the nagging discomfort in his abdomen. Perhaps it was just because he had been so much on his own these last few days, but surely the pain was getting worse? It nagged him constantly. He could feel weakness gaining on him. He shifted uneasily in his sleeping bag, trying to find comfort, but the pain followed his motions. And yet the specialist had said he would probably have 18 months and he had barely had nine so far. The word 'probably' caused unquiet. They couldn't be certain could they? No, not about the time, only about the outcome. He smiled wryly and shifted again, but it was no use, without using drugs he would get no further peace. He caught sight of the whisky flask in the corner of the tent. Why not? And yet he didn't want to. Drink didn't fit with this time of day. Truth to tell he had barely wanted a dram the night before and it hadn't tasted good – not like it used to – but he'd had a drop to give him an appetite. Without food he'd be finished.

Struggling free of the tent he lurched uncomfortably to the boulders nearby and sat down.

The breeze was just starting to pick up again, disturbing the layers of cloud hanging over the hillsides. Winter had gone early, but there were still some big snow patches in the coire. He looked up as a pair of Ravens tumbled out of the clouds and a single distant call came down to him. He had always loved these birds, sometimes his only companion for hours on end on buttress and ridge. He had never found them remotely sinister. He imitated their harsh call and waved an ironic hand.

"Poor bastards," he muttered to himself. "Just like the rest of us, trying to live."

As the breeze shifted the clouds, warm shafts of sunlight came through making the myriad dewdrops sparkle on the spiders' webs. Away down in the valley, smoke rose from dwellings by the river and a small boat moved imperceptibly over the surface of the sea-loch on its round from one orange buoy to the next.

The Primus stove roared among the stones and the water began to steam. Mechanically, because he had always done so, he measured out the oats and the salt for the porridge, set the pan on the stove and stirred it before he sank back onto his boulder with his mug of tea. Now that he had escaped the solitude and darkness of night, the discomfort in his stomach seemed slightly less, but each little activity left him feeling tired. He stretched backwards until his body found a comfortable position and gazed upwards.

* * *

Dr. Jenkins stared morosely out of the surgery window while Sergeant MacPhail's monotonous voice droned on and on. It was always the same at this time of year. The Sergeant would appear with some trumpery complaint when all he really wanted was to talk. He claimed he was afflicted with the second sight and had forebodings of disasters. Outside, the sun was shining and the doctor, sensing an empty waiting-room, was keen to be away to the river. In the bar last night there had been reports of an early run.

"And I'll tell you another thing Dr. Jenkins," MacPhail pronounced prophetically. "There will be more work for the Mountain Rescue Team before very long."

"Do you think so?"

MacPhail regarded him as a missionary might have glared upon an unconverted heathen in darkest Africa. "It is not a question of thinking." He said in tones of gentle reproof. "You just wait and see. This condition is a curse, Dr. Jenkins. Within a week, maybe less, we shall be carrying a man from the hill and," his voice sank to a gloomy whisper, "there will be no life left in him."

This was too much for Dr. Jenkins. "Now, come, come Roddy," he said kindly. "You mustn't let your mind dwell on such gloomy thoughts. People are born and die every day, you know. I think perhaps you are a little depressed. I'll write you a prescription. It's the time of year, you know. We're all run down after the Winter."

He reached for his pad. Dammit all! Why couldn't the man just get drunk like the rest of the village?

Sergeant MacPhail received the prescription with a wan smile and rose to take his leave. The doctor was a good man and he tried to help, but he didn't understand.

As the Sergeant's heavy tread retreated down the passage, the doctor felt his spirits rise. He opened a drawer and took out a wallet of salmon flies. He was deep in contemplation of the size and colour for a falling water when a gentle knock came at the door and Nurse Duncan, the midwife who doubled as receptionist, came in. "That poor man," she said sympathetically.

"Been telling you too, eh?"

"He sees such dreadful things."

"He sees nothing but what you and I see, Morag," the doctor grunted. "It's all in the mind – the man's depressed. It's this awful Winter we've had, nothing but rain and gales. You mark my words, a few weeks of sunshine and MacPhail will be off after the poachers and not a care in the world."

Nurse Duncan kept her own counsel. The doctor was a kind man, but although he had been in the village for 27 years, he was an incomer and didn't understand everything. She herself was an incomer, but from the islands and she knew all about the second sight.

"It may be as you say, Doctor," she said gently. "I've just had Mrs Paterson on the telephone. She says her husband is not at all well and has taken to his bed."

The doctor sighed and closed his fly wallet. "I'll call at once," he said.

* * *

He turned to look back. The tent was now barely visible at the edge of the meadows by the jumble of boulders. It had been an effort to pack his bag and turn up the hill once more. He had been tempted to get his mat from the tent and lie in the sun looking back down the valley, but he wanted to keep going. He had a feeling that time was not on his side. A tune kept repeating itself sonorously in his mind, it began with deep chords, then a scatter of bright high notes like shining jewels was thrown over the rich, dark fabric of the rhythm which was slow and sad and marched at a steady pace. With a last look down at the tent nestling securely in the coire, he shouldered his pack. It seemed unusually heavy and yet each day he had been leaving more and more behind. Now all the sack contained was a map and compass, a tattered scarf, a pair of gloves, his waterproofs, some bread and cheese and a flask of hot, sweet tea.

It was a strange ambition this, to climb all the higher peaks in one's own country. In fact, he had always been rather contemptuous of those who espoused it. He himself had been a genuine mountaineer and looked down on mere 'peak baggers'. It had never seemed to matter a jot to him whether he had climbed them all or not. And yet after he had been to the specialist and learned the truth, he had reckoned up the number of hills he had climbed and been surprised to find that he had only 23 left. Faced with a finite time, it seemed better to choose some possibly realisable goal and try to achieve it. Then, it had seemed a good idea. Elise, his second wife, had been all in favour and she had even accompanied him on the first few excursions. Now, nearing the end of round, he wasn't so sure. Surely this was mere selfishness? What good did it do? Suppose he got to the final summit, so what? The goal was a common one nowadays

– vulgar even – surely he could have done something with the last bit of his life which actually helped other people? But what? It took a special kind of character to do things for other people and he had never been any good at it. He hated raising money for good causes. Part of him distrusted the motives of those who did. He had resisted the idea of getting his last few ascents 'sponsored'. He didn't want a picture in the local paper or half a minute on local radio. He felt, in some ways, very much alone. He suspected that Elise was already making plans for a future which did not contain him. And why not? She was an attractive woman. Like him, she had a family by a previous marriage. His own son was in Canada, his daughter in Australia. He usually heard from them at Christmas.

The sun was now dispersing the cloud round the coire rim. Wearily, placing his feet with care, he moved up the long slope towards the col. The ground was steep, loose and awkward. Sweat started to run down his forehead. Tiny droplets fell on to the lichen patterned rocks. His mind was acute and lucid and yet his body was losing the fight. He found himself pausing more often and leaning heavily on his ski-poles. Occasionally, he felt his heart lurch painfully before resuming its steady rhythm. He forced himself to breathe deeply but each step was becoming an effort. It reminded him of the Alps. He looked up. Not too far now to the col. There the going would be easier and only a gentle ridge remained to the summit. The sun was shining strongly now, its heat reflected by the rock. With exhaustion gaining on him, he moved slowly across the moss covered screes. Sighting an outcrop of rock, he made for it. Sinking down on a patch of dry grass under a convenient boulder he found shade. He let his head rest on his sack and looked out over the deep coire. Before long he was asleep.

Liberated from pain and anxiety he was wandering in great valleys topped by towering snow peaks. At night he rested by crackling aromatic fires and conversed with wise companions. His dreams were full of trees in blossom and gentle showers of rain. In the mornings they would go on in an unhurried way, penetrating farther into this strange country. It might have been a place or a state of mind, he never could decide.

"Excuse me! Excuse me!" A hand was shaking his shoulder. The sun had gone behind clouds and the breeze felt decidedly chill. A young man, really no more than a youth, was bending over him looking pale and concerned. He wore faded jeans, dirty trainers and a red tracksuit top. He had no pack.

"What's the problem?"

"It's my girlfriend, she's stuck!"

"Where?"

The young man gestured towards the far side of the col where a long easy rock ridge led up from the dam on the far side of the mountain. He blabbered out his story, but it hardly needed telling. The girl had failed to make the last step up at the first time of asking. The boy was ahead. When he found she wasn't following, he went back. By this time she had had a good look at the drop and become unnerved. He couldn't talk her up and, of course, he had no rope.

"She saw a dead sheep at the bottom, ken. I think it sort of frightened her.

"What's her name?"

* * *

At the third call a timid cry came up to him. The place was almost a photocopy of the one he had imagined. The difficulties short, the holds perfect, the ledges broad and covered with bilberry leaves.

If only the boy hadn't got too far ahead she might not have noticed the long drop to the coire floor. She was facing in to the rock, gripping a huge flake, fingers white. "Are you the Rescue?"

"No. But your companion's gone for them."

"Will he be long?"

"A couple of hours."

"Oh, God!"

"Sarah, why not sit down and have a cup of tea?"

"I can't!"

"Of course you can."

Gently, he coaxed her into letting go of the flake and taking his arm. She was shaking. She relaxed slightly when she turned away from the rock and saw how broad the ledge really was. He got her to sit down with her back to the mountain and look out over the peaceful valley below.

She had straight blonde hair which covered much of her face, an athletic figure, and she wore pink shell-suit trousers, a pale blue tee shirt and a pair of cheap walking boots. She had no pack, but she carried a cagoule of sorts tied round her waist. From her voice he knew she was English. As soon as she lowered herself shakily onto the ground she began to cry, dabbing ineffectually at her eyes with scraps of tissue. He felt in his pocket and produced a large handkerchief.

"It's clean."

She blew her nose loudly. He rummaged in his sack and got out the flask. He was glad, now, that he'd taken the trouble to brew up that morning. He handed her a cup. She almost spilt it but recovered herself. For the first time she half smiled.

"Were you just out for the day?"

She nodded ruefully and smiled again.

"I'm afraid I'm being a terrible nuisance."

"The only problem was not bringing a rope. It used to say in all the old guide books, 'A rope should be carried unless it is certain not to be needed'. It's good advice."

"We didn't even have a guide book. Darryl got directions from some blokes in the pub last night. It was my fault, I shouldn't have let him bring me up this way. But he was so keen and it was a nice day..."

"I know."

She was looking better now. Her voice was firmer and the colour had come back to her cheeks. He handed her a piece of cheese.

"You know," he said gently, "looking at you, I'd say you could make those moves up there no bother at all with a bit of encouragement. You're fit looking and I'll bet there's nothing wrong with your sense of balance."

"I got scared and started shaking. There's a sheep..." Anxiety showed in her face and her lip started to tremble.

"Yes, I know," he said quickly. "But I expect it was mainly because, the first time, you had no one with you. And then when Darryl came back he couldn't really understand the problem, told you it was easy? Not to make a fuss?"

"Well, he did rather. He meant well, but I kept looking down till I couldn't move. I was sort of paralysed."

"Suppose we did it together?" He could see her shrink back. "I could even give you some protection."

"How?"

"I've got a short length of strong cord. Look, it's the draw cord for my rucksack. It used to be a sling – that's a piece of climbing equipment. You're pretty thin, if I tie this round your waist there'll be just enough to put round my wrist. What d'you think? Should we give it a try?" He could sense that she wanted to, but needed a few moments for the desire to grow into the necessary determination. Looking up, he could see that in a few minutes the sun would come through the light clouds. He poured more tea and let her drink in silence. He felt exhausted and longed to be on his own again, but he struggled hard to overcome his impatience. She seemed a sensible girl. He liked her. She'd only been slightly unnerved. Distant memories of early days in the Lakeland Fells with Janet, his first wife, drifted back fleetingly, but that was in another age.

He could feel her tense up as he tied a bowline round her waist.

"Try to breathe deeply," he said. His own breathing felt none too good, shallow and at times painful. There wasn't really enough cord. But on the most awkward section, he knew that she only had to make two upward steps on slightly rounded rock and her outstretched hand could grasp a satisfying spike. He paused, the looped cord cutting into his flesh, and looked down. She had made one of the high steps and was on the narrow ledge. The next move was crucial. The wind blew her hair in her eyes. Below, steep rocks fell to the stony coire. A fine place.

"One more move, Sarah, then you're safe!" His chest was painful. He wished she'd get on with it then he could sit and rest for a while. She looked up and tried to smile. He could sense the dryness in her mouth.

Her hands scrabbled amongst the heather roots. Through the thin umbilical he could feel that she was shaking. Watching her carefully he tried to gauge just the right moment to pull her smoothly upwards.

* * *

Dr. Jenkins replaced the sheet. He washed his hands methodically and then sat at his desk to write the appropriate official form. In the doctor's lounge where a fire was burning, Nurse Duncan was dispensing tea. Sergeant MacPhail was drinking whisky, he had the telephone in his hand. The young people sat next to each other on the settee.

Nurse Duncan had inclined at first to be severe. ("You young people are not wise to go to the hill!"). But she had soon melted at their obvious distress.

"He was so kind and gentle," Sarah kept repeating. "It was all my fault!" Young Darryl avowed.

Sergeant MacPhail put down his glass and shook his head. "I'm afraid it couldn't be prevented," he said mournfully. "It had been going to end that way since the beginning of Time." His expression was more peaceful now.

"Roddy, you mustn't say such dreadful things," Nurse Duncan admonished him. "You will be frightening our young friends and they have been frightened enough."

The doctor entered the room quietly. "Well now," he said. "It seems that the immediate cause of death was a massive heart attack but," he went on hurriedly, sensing the young couple's contrition, "the deceased was a very ill man. Of course, I haven't carried out a full examination, but it's pretty clear he was suffering from the last stages of bowel cancer."

"The poor man," Nurse Duncan's voice was full of sympathy.

"You could say that, Morag," the doctor said slowly. "But after all, he obviously chose to spend his last days doing something he was fond of, and, at the very end, he was able to do something useful. How many of us are so lucky? Have you any word yet of who he was, Roddy?"

THE FINAL YEAR?
A climber's introspection
By John Steele

Preface:

WHAT follows is a personal account, an examination of a CLIMBER'S thoughts and recollections as he comes to realise that his decades of mountaineering activity are about to change down a few gears, maybe even go into idle. Perhaps he is not alone in his tale.

The observations are loosely based over a year's mountaineering activity, during which time, the CLIMBER has seen that the sands of time, the tank, is running low to empty and the road end appears to be in sight.

Introduction and the 'Round':

Before this happened though, one of the CLIMBER'S main ambitions was to complete 'The Round'.

An extract from that time shows:

"It had been the usual sort of week on the West Coast. The journey northwards through rain-soaked Arran, to fog-shrouded Mull, to gale-swept Skye had left us quite depressed. We then moved onto the mainland and after a restless midge-infested night under Liathach, we were all but for quitting the hills. The final morning saw clouds racing over Torridon, but not a breath of wind found its way onto our damp canvass – Scotland in June. 'Give it one more chance, after all it's light till midnight'. The journey north, past Gairloch and Gruinard through the lashing rain, changed quite suddenly, as the turn east to Dundonnell was made. The ascent of An Teallach that afternoon was truly magical, swirling mist, warm sunshine and numerous spectres, was enough to confirm that ' The Round' had to be completed."

By the following summer, only a handful of Munros remained left to the CLIMBER. The remote summit of Ben Avon and its satellites were traversed on a sweltering Cairngorm day, immediately followed by a long drive to Snowdonia, where he met up with some friends camping under the steep dark cliffs of Cloggy, the Dubh Loch of North Wales.

An extract from that occasion records:

"Flat flats – yes I know where you're at,
snow, wind, rain, (or sheep),
I know you never sleep,
under those steep, steep faces.

I know I tossed your rocks around,
and pressed you with my dusty boots,
but have no doubt your soul remains,
a testament to your glacial roots."

A winchman being lowered from an RAF Sea King search and rescue helicopter. Photo: Jas Hepburn.

Dead Man's Bogey, Ben Nevis. Photo: Ray Sefton.

And so it was, that on a misty day at the end of summer, the CLIMBER compleated.

Ben Lomond was the altar and his thoughts and prayers at that moment were thus:

"The power of Shiva.
The gentleness of Sagamartha.
The glory of the Holy Spirit.
The all encompassing Allah.
Each having watched over me.
This was an endpoint of sorts.
The quest was complete.
But the journey was not yet over."

The descent back to earth was but a glide, a flight down the golden slope.

It was only when the CLIMBER hit the trees at Rowardennan that his plans for the coming year were born.

Contemplation:

He had been thinking hard that winter about how to prolong the journey and continue the adventure. With the Munros completed, it was not however, the thought of new exploits that filled his view, rather memories of past and challenging days on the Scottish hills.

Some examples of these past days were:

"In Winter, getting to the top of a climb on Meggy on a blue sky day only to take refuge in the snowhole at the Window shortly afterwards as a snowstorm engulfed the mountain, a trial on Arran when an ice box climb on a Ben Nuis chimney was followed by a storm-soaked crawl over the A 'Chir comb, or standing in Giants Head on Lochnagar watching the top pitch peal off, after all it was over 70° that day in Ballater in March!

In Summer, tripping over nine ptarmigan chicks on the summit of Lurg Mhor, running from gunfire on a misty Slioch only to return another day and wonder why the cairn was in the wrong place, and blistering his hands in the summer heat on an attempted new route above Coruisk."

This level of adventure, the CLIMBER knew, was coming to an end. His last real rock climb in Scotland had been the one attempted above Coruisk. On ice, it had been a frightening solo venture onto the serpentine ice slopes of Mount Cook's South Face. The game was up. He could no longer be so bold.

The Year in Question:

And this is really where the year begins. With his Scottish sojourn over and his Alpine exploits now curtailed, the CLIMBER had to enlist support if he wanted to continue the journey.

He was given the chance to explore along the Nepalese border with Tibet, then to climb on Everest. Before this though, several weekends of preparation were required and several quick dashes to the hills made, just as the Foot and Mouth epidemic closed in on the mountains. Ascents were done in semi-darkness.

The Salisbury Crags with Edinburgh below. Photo: Alastair Matthewson.

William Wood. Photo: Jim Wilkie.

An encounter of that time records:
"Two lads they were,
quite happy to stand on my hands
and move on past;
but that was low down. High up; ice, mist, darkness, fear,
and then yes, then, they were on my tail not my hands.
Just behind, just enough behind to see my print.
Bowed heads at the boot."

Next came the trip to Nepal. A trek into the Manaslu region involving a circuit of the 8000m peak by passing through a restricted area and crossing a remote pass.

An extract from the trek reads:

"This was a sublime journey, not only were we the second group, but also the first Brits to cross the pass that year. We also took time out to visit the two expedition base camps on Manaslu, the Poles and then the Ukranians, who put up a hard new technical route."

A lot fitter, the CLIMBER arrived in Kathmandu, then set off for Lhasa in Tibet. The initial goal was Everest base camp. His group arrived in a blizzard, took several days rest then set off up the East Rongbuk glacier approach to advanced base camp at 6500m, where he met up with the summit expedition. Several days later everyone was called into the mess tent. The atmosphere was tense.

"We go up tomorrow, all of us, said the leader."

Next morning the CLIMBER set off for the North Col. He struggled through much of the morning to make the col, and on reaching it, collapsed exhausted in the drifted snow. He was not alone, for among the other expeditions established on the col, a number of climbers were already freaked out by the Everest experience. Some retreated in a stupor, others just flailed about among the tents, and they were still 1800m from the top!

The CLIMBER descended late in the afternoon:

"We could only go as far as the col, but still had to get back down before the sun moved behind the NE ridge. Without special gear and oxygen support we could not stay the night above 7000m. Just as we completed the descent down the ice face and moved onto the level glacier below the col, the sun dipped behind Everest. A wind got up and our bodies chilled in an instant. Cold and hungry I kept urging myself to keep calm as my brain was hit by the intense shiver caused by fatigue at high altitude. We all make it safely back to camp that evening. Everest is climbed the following day."

On return, a climbing trip to Antarctica was offered to the CLIMBER. How could he refuse. So by mid-December he was at sea heading due south into the Southern Ocean on the back of a swell, across the icy waters below Cape Horn. A few days later, his first climb was a windswept snow dome which marks the northern most point of the vast frozen continent: "The Ben Hope of Antarctica."

His thoughts at the time are:

"What joy at our very first climb on this magnificent continent. We were lucky. I imagine this point has more days of raging storm in a year than Ben Nevis!"

Several days later and farther south he is again at the sharp end. This time trying a new route on one of the numerous ice peaks that rose from just above the beach. After hours of route-finding and front-pointing, it was decided the climb was proving too dangerous in the difficult conditions, and was eventually abandoned in late afternoon.

On turning round he notes:

"The sleaty view out across the sound was quite surreal, steely blue water, flecked with white growlers, under leaden skies, all of this taken in from a stance on crampon tips."

The weather continued to be fierce. He next came across a tourist ship, which had just run for shelter in the face of a Force 10. The ship he was on slunk past the scarred tourist vessel, then the skipper quite deliberately rammed into the shore pack ice, so the climbers could disembark to try their next snow peak. When the CLIMBER reached its summit, it reminded him of topping out many years ago above SC Lochan, wind blasted, exposed and uncomfortable. His partner now though, had climbed Everest and K2, so he knew he was in good company.

They made a hasty retreat and on reaching the shoreline he recorded:

"Our ship eventually appeared out of the twilight and storm, as we sank wearily through the sea slush of the late spring pack. What a day, or rather what a night, for it was after midnight when we clambered back on board and enjoyed a well-deserved meal. Forget all form of normalcy when contemplating climbing in Antarctica!"

After this adventure, New Year arrived in the UK, with no further plans laid. This did not particularly dishearten the CLIMBER, for he had now completed his three main mountaineering goals, climbing the Munros, climbing high on Everest and climbing in remote Antarctica.

Postscript:

The CLIMBER had reached a point where he thought these achievements would mark the end of a year of personal examination, after all, the culmination of a successful climbing career had been achieved. So, naturally, he thought it was now time to contemplate pursuits other than climbing, pursuits that had been put off for decades. But yet, he was still not certain.

So the CLIMBER took himself away, away up into the hills to contemplate, to make sure that he really had reached the end of his personal climbing exploits. He sat alone amidst the drifted snow and rocks of the Bealach Dubh, watching the frost crystals build on his tent as darkness closed in around him on the remote pass. Eventually, well after dark, he retired to his shelter with a new resolve, that maybe, just maybe, there was one *real* climbing adventure left.

One more tap on the gauge might just be enough.

OLDER, WISER – 40 YEARS IN MOUNTAIN RESCUE

By Terry Confield,
(Team Leader Lochaber Mountain Rescue Team.)

I JOINED Lochaber Mountaineering Club in 1964. This was also the year I joined the rescue team, as the Club formed the backbone of the mountain rescue team in the Lochaber area at that time. It was the club that initiated meetings with the local council, the police and the JMCS to find a source of money for equipment to be used on rescues. The money was somehow found and the 'team' was lavishly equipped with, 12 ice axes, 12 pairs of Robert Lawrie Mk IV boots, 12 pairs of mitts and 12 yellow waterproof jackets (with 'Mountain Rescue' stamped on the back)

Typically, the call-out system in these days consisted of the village policeman arriving at your door at any time of the day or night to alert you to the fact that somebody was in trouble on Ben Nevis. We would then meet at the main police station in Fort William where we would be given the details of the incident or search. In those days the team consisted of members of the Club and a number of police officers.

We would leave from the Ben Nevis Distillery carrying every bit of kit we had, as we did not know how many hours, or days, the rescue might take. The stretcher (Thomas or Duff) and ropes were taken up to the CIC hut and left there until they were required for evacuation of the casualty.

In the early days radio communications, (never mind mobile phones! *Ed.*) were almost non-existent with the only contact with the police station being through the CIC hut radio. The greatest disadvantage of this was that we could not be alerted should the missing climbers turn up safe and sound, and on quite a few occasions we found ourselves on the hill all day, despite the missing party having turned up at 8:30 that morning! On one particular call-out we were tasked to search for an elderly gentleman who had set out to walk from Kinlochleven to Fort William via Wade's Road. He was overdue and it was dark so the team was split into two groups, one lot to go in by Glen Nevis and the other by Kinlochleven. The first group was transported up to the top car park in the police van which then returned to pick up the second party and take them to Kinlochleven. I was in the Glen Nevis contingent and we quickly found the missing person at the old Steall ruin, which meant we needed to alert the other team so that they wouldn't leave (and, more importantly, to get the van to return for us!). Communication to our base was the telephone box at the Glen Nevis Youth Hostel a good five miles away and, because of my youth I was selected to carry the news. I remember feeling quite chuffed walking through the gorge when this apparition jumped over my head. It may have only been a sheep but I took off like a rocket and in what seemed like no time I was at the Youth Hostel phoning the police station. A little slower than radio waves perhaps, but thankfully, still in time to prevent the other party having to start their search.

One of the great benefits of a rescue on the Ben was being able to place the casualty on a trolley on the British Alcan small gauge railway after the long carry down the Allt a' Mhuilinn. This trolley was known to the rescue team (but thankfully not the casualty.) as the 'Dead Man's Bogie'. In all honesty, it would probably have been just as fast to take the casualty down to the distillery, but the long struggle to get off the mountain with the stretcher meant that we could not wait to get rid of it. However, with only one foot brake pedal, it's a miracle that no team member was injured while hitching a lift on the Bogie.

In 1969, Lochaber Mountain Rescue Association was set up to promote a more professional approach to mountain rescue and we became a registered charity to enable us to go out and raise serious funds. A constitution was put in place and a committee was formed to manage the team. The most significant change at this time was the number of rescues we were called out on. Instead of the handful of the past few years, we were now attending more than 40 a year. To assist us the police supplied us with various all-terrain vehicles. First of all a Snowtrack, then a Garron and lastly a VP8, all driven by a police constable. Looking back, we seemed to spend more time rescuing these contraptions and putting tracks back on than carrying out the actual rescue.

Thankfully, help was on the way and the Wessex helicopters that were stationed at RAF Leuchars became available for mountain incidents. This was the start of a beautiful, not to mention successful relationship with the helicopter crews from the RAF and the Royal Navy. I have no doubt in my mind that without their help we could not cope with the number of rescues and searches we are now involved in.

On a modern day rescue there are many differences from the old days, but the job is fundamentally the same. A particularly memorable example was when two climbers were overdue on North East Buttress. We had a full team call-out for first light and had also requested the use of a helicopter. The Royal Navy helicopter duly arrived and went straight to the scene where the crew managed to locate and lift off one of the climbers. The other person could not be found on the face and so team members were deployed on to the summit and in Observatory Gully. By this time the mist had come in and was covering the upper part of the mountain. We tried shouting but got no response.

In the meantime, the team in the gully below came across climbing equipment and avalanche debris. The summit party descended to meet up with the bottom party and a major probing and digging exercise was started. Nothing was found, and because of the first climber's insistence that his colleague must be on the same route we decided to head for the summit via the Arête. We were eventually forced to retreat because of the high avalanche risk and headed back to Fort William.

We had something to eat and then started back up the Ben by Coire Giubhsachan to the summit. One of the team was lowered over the top of North East Buttress where he located the other missing climber below the Mantrap. He was, sadly, dead and encased in snow and ice. The body was pulled up and evacuated off the mountain. The relevance of this rescue is that it is an example of the determination and self-sacrifice required by the members of any team carrying out rescues in the mountains.

To my mind, the greatest change in mountaineering in the last 40 years is in equipment. We now have clothing that keeps us warm and dry (hence the reason we have not had a victim suffering from hypothermia in years), better designs of crampons and ice axes, and, of course, GPS.

So, we have to ask ourselves, what goes wrong apart from the normal accidents? Well, these haven't changed over the years. They are the old classics of not allowing enough time, tackling routes that are too hard or out of condition, and of course, the cost of navigation errors, especially on the summit of the Ben is still as high as ever. Which is why our mountain rescue teams will always be in business.

LAST SUMMER

Rambles in the Rockies and High Sierras

By Cairns Dickson

OH YES, I had been here before, not to Colorado, not to the Rockies, but to that feeling. The feeling that your head is sore, your lungs open but nothing much goes in, your feet drag over the floor. Yes, my first trip to altitude in quite a while and like hangovers, I'd forgotten I wasn't going to do it again.

Here I am at 14,000ft. on North Mount Massive in the Sawatch Mountains of Central Colorado. There are about 56 separate summits higher than 14,000ft. in the Rockies. They have been classified interestingly enough as 'Fourteeners', and yes, people do seem to want to climb all of them – sounds familiar. Surprisingly, we seem to have strayed from the guidebook description and are now ascending some 'Talus', the local name for scree. Yes, I've been on scree slopes before too, so why the hell am I doing it again, It's long, steep and the sharp little stones are very slippy. No, I am not at all happy, The col we are heading for is at least 500ft. higher and I'm tee eye rr e dee.

Last night, we bivied at the trailhead, in the trees at 11,000ft. Why couldn't I sleep, perhaps my body was adjusting to the altitude? No, I didn't need altitude to keep me awake, although it undoubtedly helped. I was scared, scared of bears, black ones, quite common round these parts. "No no, they don't bother with humans and anyway you can just not look at 'em or play dead," so they say. Scared, I was bloody terrified, my first night in Colorado and I couldn't sleep a wink. Every crack, every insect, every rustle in the leaves was to be the start of my life or death struggle with Bruin.

On with the ascent, the scree had done for me and I had just been overtaken by Duncan. Duncan McNeill, my old friend from Perth. He had moved out to Bend in Oregon with his family a few years before. He had just driven to Denver from Oregon through Idaho and Utah in his magnificent Toyota pick-up, (a cross between a transit and a three-toner). It was well kitted out too. There was enough trail mix on board to get from Cerro Torre to Mt. McKinley (excuse me – Denali). A solid 36-hour drive, perhaps Duncan wasn't at his best. He had spent the previous night sweltering in his pick-up, seething with anger that his old pal had failed to turn up on his scheduled flight. He was, of course, concerned: "Where the **** is the useless ****** ****** ", he inquired of Margaret.

"Do you know how much this * * * * * * phone call is costing me."

"No sorry Duncan, I don't know that either I'm afraid," replied my puzzled wife.

Naturally, I was in Cincinnati – well where else would I be, where was Cincinnati anyway? I could have been anywhere, but there I was in my air con cubicle, courtesy of United Airlines. We, that is the airline and I, had failed to make our connection. Thus highlighting my inexperience as a transatlantic traveller in failing to notice the short transfer time. Perhaps I should have paid more bucks for a more direct flight.

Duncan who had only recently stopped working as a professional ski patroller was well rested at the col long before I eventually arrived, on all fours. I think he was too concerned to gloat.

"Hurry up Cairns – y'never ust tae be 's slow is this," says Duncan.

"Relax Dunc what's yer hurry," says I, looking forward to an extended bask on this airy, but comfortable, col a mere few hundred feet below the summit.

"Thunder." That was it, thunder storms in the afternoons are a frequent and unfortunate reality for us ramblers in the Rockies. The weather was changing, colder, sudden gusts, then silent stillness. Feeling as awful as I was, I would have happily buggered off down, but that summit, our first 'Fourteener', was too close. Duncan having not been this high before, at least on a mountain, was keen to go on. Fear of lightning overtook my splitting head and aching lungs as we made the final ascent up a steep boulder strewn ridge. A cursory glance around from this remote summit and I knew we shouldn't be here. Plunging downwards, ever faster into the comfort of that warmer and thickening air, it wasn't long before the hailstones started. Phew! – back to the truck, I'll recover.

Why am I not? Why do I still feel hellish three days on? I suppose the valleys being at 11,000ft. may have something to do with it.

"I'll give it a 100 yards then you'll have to go on yourself," I said to poor old Duncan who had been listening to me moan about my aching chest, my inflamed pleura and my imminent heart attack. We were setting off up Huron Peak, 14,001ft. in the San Juan range, a delightful stroll up through the trees to an enchanting high plateau. To my great pleasure and astonishment the farther I went the better I felt. By midday we were on the summit of our second 'Fourteener'. The silence, the space, the glory of this Rocky Mountain chain was starting to hit me and at three miles with 3000ft. of ascent, it was a shorter day than many a Munro. I felt great.

My sense of wellbeing was short-lived, however, as I fell into conversation with an American who had just arrived. I thought that being a local I should check out his knowledge of bears.

"Bears, you don't want to worry about bears."

I was immensely relieved.

"No no," he continued: "It's mountain lions that you really want to worry about, they'll stalk you for days."

I slunk away to eat my burrito and contemplate this greater menace.

Duncan, unfortunately, was not so hot, he was starting to feel the altitude and his boots were too small.

Handles Peak 14,048ft. in the San Juan range was next, I was on my own. Still, you're never lonely in these mountains thanks to the multitude of tiny furry creatures that are just everywhere, all shapes and sizes from dormice to marmots, not to mention the bears and mountain lions of course. I thought with some sadness how barren Scotland seemed in comparison. Over-population by deer, deforestation and over-grazing by the over-valued sheep are perhaps to blame? Not that any self-respecting animals bother to inhabit the dense conifer monocultures that provide such effective tax breaks for others.

So, it's Mount Sneffels next, (14150ft.) Dunc was trying out his toes but, alas! We parted just above Yankee Boy Basin and I continued alone up this rugged and shapely peak. I knew it would be my last Colorado 'Fourteener'. Duncan could barely walk and our long planned five-week walking adventure was over in just 10 days.

My return flight was from Denver and I could soon be at home, decorating. Little persuasion from Dunc was required though and we were back on the road, 1500 miles, 30 hours, Colorado, Utah, Idaho into Oregon and back to Bend. My son, Finlay, and I had been here at Easter, enjoying perfect skiing on the deserted slopes of Mount Bachelor, a volcano in the cascades, not too far from Mount St. Helen's! Round comes my other old pal from Perth, Brian MacMillan. We first climbed together at Craig y Barnes in 1972 and although Brian has lived in Oregon for the last 17 years we kept in touch.

"Well I suppose we should do something now you're here," says Brian.

Training is very important, so I thought I might visit Bend's 'Alien Rock', and found myself on an intriguing little device called a Roc'n roller. A cross between a blackboard and a hamster wheel, I felt like an idiot, a tired idiot. Two days later we were in Nevada heading for Yosemite and then there I was in Toulome looking way down the valley to Half Dome.

"Hi Torch, ya still here then," says Brian to the warden at Saddlebag Lake. This campground at 10,500ft. is cooler at night and enjoys great views over Mt. Dana (13,053ft.)

"Torch, what a stupid name," says I.

"Yea, he lost a third of his skin in a fire."

I shut up. Torch was a lovely character who had had lots of dealings with wolves, bears etc. we talked a lot and I realised then the importance of not sleeping with your food. Saddlebag Lake was the scene of a desperate struggle for survival in the early 1800s when the wagon trains of the early settlers were caught in the ferocious storms of winter. Many died beneath an unbelievable depth of snow.

Brian was recovering from some ailment or other, which meant he would not be climbing at his best. I was naturally disappointed to hear this, but I had whiled away a few indolent days at Creag Dhubh earlier in the summer with my pals Dave Page and Mike Dougal. I was confident that I could at least get us up something. It turned out not to be that much of a problem as Brian's worst seemed to be substantially better than my best – 5.13c didn't sound like it was going to be in my repertoire and I couldn't understand the grading system anyway. I did have a lurking fear that I would fail to get off the ground on anything that Brian wanted to climb. Toulome at 9000ft. is cooler and quieter than the Yosemite Valley at this time of year.

Our first route was West Crack on Daff Dome 5.9? A couple of delicate slab moves just off the ground then into a friendly crack for 100ft. or so to belay. A short awkward overhang started the next pitch. He was out of sight, I was paying out the rope pretty fast with the odd pause for protection. Eventually, I felt the little tug that told me it was my turn. You could jam fingers and toes in the crack but there were lovely little cubes of quartz studded into the granite all over the place, about one inch wide they were. Wonderful climbing, I was enjoying myself, but where was Brian? Still no sign, my calf muscles were getting that front pointing feeling and this was just the second pitch.

"Well it is a 70-metre rope," Brian explained as I landed on the stance – which was just two of these little quartz cubes. We were basically up the route. Magnificent, what a climb and what a view. I was standing atop a single chunk of granite gazing across at another one, bigger and with an enormous sweep of rock flowing from its rounded summit to the valley floor. This was Fairview Dome and two days later we were on it. The regular route 5.9 (1100ft.) Parallel cracks one metre apart, blind and about one inch deep at an angle of about 75°. Phew! The crux low down. Above lay a series of connecting grooves and cracks. Well protected, outstanding quality and a mantelshelf onto the summit, I was speechless. Two great routes in three days, what next?

A trip down the valley to see the sights and maybe a climb? No chance, too hot, too humid and too busy. We scurried back to Toulome and the cool serenity of Saddlebag Lake.

"The Third Pillar of Dana…no, I haven't heard of it," but this was our next route, 800ft., 5.10c and rave reviews in the topo. Thinking I was on my way up the Allt'a Mhuilinn we eventually emerged onto the Dana plateau at about 12,000ft. Definitely no 800ft. columns of granite round here I thought. The plateau itself seemed to me a lot like the Cairngorms, then it stopped. Over the edge we were looking down to Lee Vining and Mono Lake with the Nevada desert stretching away for ever. Searching for the route we were faced with a mess of broken, soft, awful looking stuff.

"Humm – can't say much for the first and second pillars."

After much ferreting we eventually found the Third Pillar. It certainly was impressive, steepening to vertical on the last two pitches.

"Best 10c in the world, etc. etc," sayeth the book. We were obviously in for a real treat. This solid 800ft. pillar rose out of nothing, the rock baking yellow in the morning sun. Slithering and sliding down the exposed and broken access ridge (maybe the fourth pillar) there we were with nowhere to go but up, it felt very alpine. Voices. Groan. We were not alone, would this lead to problems on the route? Pair one were already well established, pair two got lost on the first pitch so off we went. Running pitches one and two together we were quickly clear of potential cluster problems. More cracks, grooves and laybacks, I felt my climbing was OK, we had already done two fine routes and I had not yet disgraced myself. This was different however, a harder route in a more remote situation, I was a bit worried about how I would perform on the much vaunted 10c pitches at the top. Still, we weren't anywhere near them yet, my feet were on a very steep slab and my hands were too high.

"Ooops," I was off...shite! "Huh , I can do this, let me at it," says I to myself. Ego dented, I thought it best to get up it quick and try to forget this regrettable little slip. Twang, off again. Humm, my fingers are tiring, I'm puffing and panting. This climb is at about I2,000ft. much higher than the Toulome climbs at −9000 ft. Baking hot, dehydrated, rasping breath, I was feeling it. This really was not a good time for me to be buggering about. As I rested I tried to will a bit more energy into my ailing fingers. Would they hold? Yes...yes...yes I was up – that move at least. What a place, climbing now up a large weathered flake, delightful climbing, amazing rock features and what a view. Nestled in a small stance, looking up this steepening pillar it did feel very alpine and hard to imagine we would top out onto a plateau the size of Ben Macdhui.

The pair above were now on the last pitch, it did look impressive if a bit daunting, but Brian seemed to be more bothered by the heat. He had always moaned about 'the heat' and I puzzled why he moved to a place where the summer temperature can reach 100° F.? The pair below were themselves experiencing some difficulties on the slab. The top three pitches were sensational, very exposed and inviting a varied range of moves. I did find the climbing hard, but once I started I suppose it went well enough. Brian seemed to enjoy it too. His climbing was relaxed yet precise, never spending more than 15 minutes on a pitch. I've taken longer placing a runner.

A refreshment at Tioga Pass then back up to Saddlebag Lake to check out recent bear sightings with Torch. The 'Sierra Nevadas', were going down very well, this local brewery had thankfully produced one of the nicest beers I had come across in the whole of America! Unfortunately, my head was not really quite where it was meant to be. We were on our next route. Brian was pretty keen to do this one and I felt I had a duty to tag along after our three previous and magnificent excursions.

We were back on Fairview Dome. Lucky Streaks, 5.10d and 800ft. with another topo description full of superlatives. Maybe I was feeling confident because we'd been doing a lot of climbing or maybe I was still a bit drunk from last night. I was thinking to myself that it didn't look that bad and anyway the first pitch was an easy-angled slab, Brian was already halfway up it. Bloody hell, a testy little balance move, there's no such thing as a free lunch.

"We're goin up there," drawls Brian. PNW (Pacific North West) talk has eventually gotten to this boy from Stornoway. He was pointing to this little crack, vertical, one inch deep and blind. My heart sank.

"One or two little pulls on that one," he calls from the belay 10 minutes later. I didn't like the look of it and I definitely didn't like the sound of it. Gear pulling would be out of the question with Brian overseeing my halting progress from his luxurious stance. So just how much could I stuff my toes into this wretched little crack?

"Well, your shoes are two sizes too big," laughs Brian, with an 'I'm up here and you're down there' sort of a laugh. I was feeling terrible and I was pumped.

"Yes, very fingery," I slumped into the capacious stance.

The next pitch or two, 10c and 10d had their own distinct pleasures and it would have to be said that the climbing was fantastic. Fantastic that is if 5.10 is your sort of grade, not quite so hot if you're really a V. Diff. man. We had surmounted the technical difficulties and were at the bottom of another very long crack. My sugar balance was returning to normal and I had been eating my protein bars. They taste like shit but it's what we rock athletes have to eat.

"We're too high to rap off on one rope," says Brian, getting twitchy.

"What d'yi want tae bale out for, A've only jist got here," says I.

"Weather."

Here we go again. Brian was off, I could barely feed the rope out fast enough. A big pitch, I followed as quickly as I could. Off again, 30ft. runner, large hole (like the one on the Lilly at Aberdour), horizontal traverse 100ft. out left, no protection. Up I go, balance moves, lots of them. Then it starts, the ominous tink and splat of hail on my helmet. It's raining, I've taken the runner out and I'm traversing left. The rock is getting wet, it's no place to linger and no place to fall. It didn't half clear my head. After one or two moments of quiet reflection I arrived at the stance. Well it wasn't really a stance but I was glad to be there anyway, laying away off a 'Friend' with feet slipping off a slab. The deep crack above was running like the drainpipe it was. It was now pouring. After I had had a good bugger about with the rope, (I felt I was due one), I glanced over to a very drookit-looking Brian. He was off again, very much like a rat up a drainpipe. I was worried about the volume of water cascading around Brian and relieved to see him disappear over the top, it was a splendid lead. My fingers were numb but the crack was big enough for hand jams. The climbing was a little easier and haste took over from fear. We were both scared of lightning. Arriving on the top of Fairview we dropped the metalware and scuttled into a big crack. At least we weren't sticking out like sore thumbs. Phew, another Toulome classic – food and beers in Lee Vining then back to camp.

"Cairns!" Why the **** was Brian calling me at 5a.m. The bear was wrestling with our coolbox. I froze.

"Photograph it yerself, am no stickin ma heed oot the tent," he must think am an eedjit.

"Shooo," says Brian from the safety of his pick up.

"You'll have to do better than that," says I, but the bear on seeing the movement shuffled off. I looked out to see the backside of this large furry object ambling off back into the woods. I was gobsmacked, what a creature. Mercifully, it had not been able to get into our armour-plated coolbox. Bears getting access to food leads to all sorts of problems for them and us.

Our next outing took us past the shapely Cathedral and Unicorn peaks to the start of the 6km-long Mathes Crest, an endless knife-edge of rock set in magnificently remote country. That fluffy little white cloud doesn't really look like anything does it? Well does it? Paranoia! We'd been here before too and we were for buggering off. A tremendous walk through wild woods and open spaces led us to the Cathedral Lakes then down the John Muir Trail and back into Toulume.

Next day, we ended up doing a couple of short sport routes on Mendicott Dome having failed to locate 'Middle Of Nowhere Dome' deep in the back woods. We had done OK, but it was time for another long, long drive back to Oregon. Duncan explained graphically how his toenails were removed, acting on the assumption that we would, of course, be keen to know. A few beers in the tub then off to bed. It seemed like I had just dozed off when I was being shaken awake.

"Get out yur bed 'am sellin it."

Duncan immediately removed my bed and put it on the pavement. I was puzzled but this was the Pacific equivalent of a car boot sale and sure enough it was sold while still warm!

A glorious day at Smith Rock, (the local crag made of consolidated volcanic ash) included the ascent of Magic Light at 5.11a . I had failed on this route at Easter and was keen for the rematch. Brian continued with some 5.I3a, indignant at his slow recovery from illness, Farewells with Duncan, Gina and all my other chums in PNW then off to Denver to get my flight. However, Brian was keen to see Long's Peak and visit friends in Wyoming, so back on the road again. The very long straight road through Idaho led us to the City of Rocks National Park at 6500ft. in south central Idaho. I slept on a picnic table and woke up among an arrangement of massive granite boulders the size of cathedrals thrown down in handfuls by the Gods.

It's roasting at 7.00am. Brian is already ranting about the heat and we are ready to start on 'She's The Bosch' 5. 11d , a sport route put up with some help from the famous power tool manufacturer. This was extremely difficult, the holds, scarcely meriting the name, were little metamorphic scabs peeling off a granitic core. I had no compunction about taking the odd aided rest, 5. 11 at 7am, I must be dreaming? On into Utah, through Salt Lake for lunch in Snowville at I05°F. then on again to Boulder in Colorado for breakfast in the 'Buff' – a pretentious local cafe.

Hacking our way through dense scrubland and fallen trees, we were now lost. We were supposed to be heading to 'The Right Book' crag on Lumpy Ridge outside Estes Park. The truly magnificent 'Twin Owls' looked down in disgust. 'Fat City' 5.10c, another classic of the crag, put up by Ray Jardine, pioneer of the camming device. It looked like a walk in the park. The first pitch was a leftward trending crack wandering up a slab. The friction was splendid but turned out to be harder than it looked. Brian was already up the short second pitch, which was the crux of the climb. A horizontal three-foot roof with a three-inch wide crack loomed above.

"Hello, hello, am I missing something," I inquired feebly. I knew it, it had all caught up with me.

I'd survived the 'Fourteeners', Lucky Streaks and even the bears, but I knew when I was beat. Even with Friends for aid and my friend above I still found it hard. The next pitch was decidedly non–trivial but we were up.

"Yes Cairns, its time you went home."

FROM AULD REEKIE TO THE BEN

By Alastair Matthewson

ON JULY 25, 2002 Jamie Thin and myself were climbing the Great Buttress of Salisbury Crags in Edinburgh's Holyrood Park, 100 years to the day after its first ascent by W. A. Morrison, W. C. Newbigging and L. Briquet, a Swiss guide[1]. Of course, making a centenary ascent is more than merely climbing the route in an old set of tweeds with a pipe dangling from your lips. There is that sense of history to absorb and the opportunity to contemplate the characters and ethics of 100 years ago from a closer perspective.

William Morrison was a well liked and respected SMC character. He joined the Club in the same year, 1902, as the Great Buttress ascent and was apparently endowed, with the usual share of delightful eccentricities[2]. "He did not approve of early starts", which perhaps explains his attraction to the short and easily accessible cliffs of Salisbury Crags close to his Edinburgh home. One story recalls how he once urgently cycled to the Crags, clad only in his pyjamas, to carry out the rescue of a cragbound lady climber. The time of day is not mentioned.

It was to Morrison's account[3] of the Great Buttress (originally Eastern Buttress of the Great Quarry) climb that I turned after our own ascent, casually slipped in after work one gloomy and rather breezy midweek evening. The rhythmic beat of the Paul Simon concert wafting intermittently from the Castle, along with the distinctive smell of the breweries, lent a particularly bizarre atmosphere to the whole affair. For us a mere jaunt in the (Holyrood) park, but back in 1902 the old boys' ascent merited an almost full-page description in the SMCJ. Morrison described the crux thus: "The upper right-hand edge of the middle slab is grasped and the narrow ledge above the right-hand white slab is gained by the timely assistance of a finger-hold above." Above, a "balance-pull" ended the main difficulties. The red dolerite has maybe weathered a little further, stabilised by a few more ascents, but that description of a few feet of rock and how to overcome it was exactly what we found 100 years on. The "balance-pull" is now a mantelshelf move of course, (when did that particular terminology arise?).

The Great Buttress is an imposing line on the highest section of the Crags and it was this fact, combined with Morrison's description of the rock as being in "a glorious state of primeval rottenness", which led to the climb's reputation. Indeed, the original description fully admits to a degree of prior top-rope practice or pre-cleaning which seems more in accordance with some modern first ascents: "Several mornings were spent by Newbigging about (the crux) while (Morrison) anchored himself above with 120ft of rope to give assistance if required."

Graded Difficult in 1950s Holyrood Park guidebooks, now Very Difficult, this was however not a climb at the technical limit of its day. Three weeks earlier in the late June heatwave, Harold Raeburn (the original Crags aficionado) had climbed his eponymous 'Arete' on Ben Nevis, now graded Severe. Raeburn, no doubt, had been honing his technical skills on the Crags along with the Inglis Clarks, who were with him on the Ben. He had sooled Observatory Buttress (Very Difficult) two days earlier.

Perhaps news of these Nevis ascents stirred Newbigging's urges for exploration, because, a month after the Great Buttress ascent, he made the journey to Fort William with "a Swiss companion". The description of his 80 Minute Route, just left of Raeburn's Arete, immediately follows Morrison's of Great Buttress in the Journal. The first ascents listing in the current guidebook to Ben Nevis (2002) declines to name explicitly the Swiss gentleman who was sampling the delights of climbing on Britain's highest mountain in 1902 but I can't help but assume that it was the enigmatic Briquet in action again.

References:

1. SMC Climbers Guide *Lowland Outcrops.*
2. SMCJ Vol. 27, p393-94 (1963).
3. SMCJ Vol. 7, p241 (January 1903).

PSYCHELING WEEKEND

By Al Scott

"IT'S like riding a bike – you never forget how to do it," I replied, after being asked how I felt about not having done any winter climbing for around eight years.

I was planning to go away with the Rannoch for a weekend trip up to the Ling Hut in Torridon. It was a somewhat daunting prospect, having spent the last eight years or so playing happy families. OK, I had done some rock climbing (mostly hot Spanish sport rock it has to be said), but this was WINTER furfuxake! – I was going to have to do some serious psyching up for this.

The first thing to do was to go up into the attic and blow the cobwebs off my ice-axes, crampons and double boots. Then it was only the cobwebs in my arms and my head to worry about. Ach! It'll be alright man – *riding a bike* – and all that.

As usual with the Rannoch, plans were constantly changing and then being re-changed. In the light of the diabolical forecast, we decided on a criminally early start on the Saturday morning and a stop-off to climb in the Northern Corrics, before going on to Torridon.

We arrived at the Cairngorm car park at around 8am, and it was getting busy. A myriad of plankers and board-stupids were milling around preparing to be funicularised. Worryingly, there were also several myriads of 'climbing types' about, and I could make out a serpentine of bodies snaking its way towards Coire An t'Sneachda in the murky distance. Hmmm, things had changed a bit since I was last out winter climbing.

After sorting out the teams and the gear, we joined the crocodile and slithered towards the corrie. Colin and Shandboy edged ahead – they probably had something hard in mind. I tucked in behind Bish – *riding a bike, riding a bike* – I had something easy in mind. The crags soon came into view, and it was with a gasp of incredulity I saw there were millions of the buggers! A swift head count revealed it was closer to 150 and a quick look at my GPS 'accent-o-meter' confirmed there were 68 Nigels, 46 Rogers and 32 Simons, and of course us, two Als (one big, one wee), a Colin and a Bish.

It was like looking at a termite mound, there were little black dots clambering all over the place. But wait a minute, there was a route with only one party on it. A swift look at the guide showed it to be *Doctor's Choice (** IV,4)*. OK, that'll do. It was maybe a wee bit harder than I wanted but it was realistically all there was to do. Bish and I geared up and made a zig-zag bee-line for the belay at the bottom, slipstreaming each other all the way – *riding a bike ,riding a bike*. The other party was a pitch-and-a-half up so no problem there But wait, a couple of bandits in a breakaway from the peloton to our right were going for the same route. We had to step up a gear or two before beating them in a bunch finish, and would you believe it, it was wee Al and Colin. "Form a queue lads! Form a queue!"

After losing the toss (I always was a useless tosser), Bish set off up the first pitch, he made it look straight-forward enough and he shouted down he had a bombproof belay. So up I went, full of trepidation and reminding myself – *riding a bike, riding a bike* – and so it was, because my feet were pedalling like buggery all the way up the pitch, and my 'handlebars' were flailing all over the place. Jeezoman! My ego had a big puncture in it by the time I slumped, shattered and shaking, on to the belay.

It was on Pitch 2, the crux, that I realised why I was having such a hard time. My gear-ratio was all wrong – *riding a bike, riding a bike*. My 'gear' was ancient, a 20-year-old Charlet Moser curved axe, a mid-Eighties expedition freebie Cassin ice hammer (rubbish, no wonder they were giving them away) and a pair of old Salewa crampons with the front-points all but filed away.

So Bish was 'in the van' for the rest of the climb, and it was only by the time we got to the final superb, long grade III/IV ice pitch that I finally relaxed a bit in my saddle – *riding a bike, riding a bike* - and actually started enjoying the climbing.

We mingled awhile among the Sauchiehall Street-like hordes on the plateau and struggled back to the car park in ferocious winds by around 3pm. The drive over to Torridon was in appalling weather, so we had made the right choice climbing-wise. After a couple of beers at Kinlochewe we went down to the Ling Hut.

The evening was spent drinking beers, eating curry and talking bollocks – more or less what the Rannoch is best at. The weather outside was still very mild and wet when we crashed out in the late hours, and an early morning inspection confirmed everyone's suspicions that there was no more climbing to be had.

After a long lie and leisurely breakfast we decided on a Ronnie Corbett-bash on Meall a'Ghiubhais by Kinlochewe. In typical Rannoch fashion the day ended up as a bit of a time-trial event – *riding a bike, riding a bike* – with crashes, breakaways, blow-outs, hitting the wall, dodgy overtaking manoeuvres, and sprint finishes – all leading to a very enjoyable day.

I might try a few routes next winter – once I get my puncture sorted. It's just like – *riding a bike* – after all.

DROPPING IN ON FRIENDS

By M. G. Anderson

FOR those days it was your typical boy-girl situation. My interests were him and his interests. My personality was a blank paper waiting for the Xerox machine. I idolised, no that's too soft a word, I worshipped him, and like a squire following his knight, kitted myself out to follow in the pastime he was passionate about mountaineering in Scotland. Where he led, I followed, like Jack and Jill going up the hill, over rock, ice or snow.

It was towards the end of January when we were tramping across the vast bleak wintry Sahara of the Cairngorm plateau, over that crunchy, crusted type of snow that collapses at the last moment, every step teetering on falling over. We weren't absolutely lost, but were lazily hazy about our precise point on the globe. The biting wind kept our hands together with map and compass tight in our pockets. It was getting on for late in the day, when out of nowhere the mist dropped down obscuring everything that might act as a marker. With no rocks poking through the snow to focus on, it became impossible to distinguish ground from sky, as both merged into a grey blur.

We kept stumbling into snowdrifts, but after the first few times were no longer laughing at finding ourselves chest deep in snow. We became increasingly tired and frustrated, even though the snow was too cold for us to get wet, for enough had trickled in through the gaps in collars and cuffs to raise annoying discomfort to the mildest level of misery. With it came the realisation that we hadn't a clue where we were, except that we were somewhere east of the Lairig Ghru. A few minutes later glancing up to my front I saw footprints etched in the peculiar fins of frost that broke up the monotony of the snow's topography.

"Dougie look, we're okay. They'll lead us home."

He looked at them, then me, his eyebrows and balaclava bewhiskered with frost and rime.

"Morag, these are ours. We've been walking round in circles."

He sounded so calm, I didn't feel frightened, at least not until a bit later. He had always been the source of my inner strength. The rising wind was flicking pellets of snow into our eyes drawing painful tears. Reluctantly accepting the inevitable, that we would have to revisit some basic mountaineering skills, we dug map and compass out of frozen rucksack pockets.

"Jean's Hut is that-away." Dougie with the aplomb of the Edinburgh Public School man, pointed a be-mittened paw decisively through the murk.

Jean's Hut, set low in Coire Cas, was, compared to the gorgeous creations erected for the pampered skier, an embarrassing slum. A ramshackle shack providing a welcome respite from the blizzard, for a wee drum-up or a doss for the most indigent climbers. Now, the hut is but a memory, which not even the most nostalgic hillman of the Beatles Era, would wish resurrected. Because I always trusted him, Dougie's self-confidence convinced me, that he would get us home. Using the traditional method of navigation, we attempted to plot a way through the white-out. You know how it is, one of us moving forward in little sorties while the other steered by shouting compass bearings, whipped away by the howling gale, with the wind constantly blowing us sufficiently off our line of travel to reduce our finely calculated course to the level of Blind Man's Buff.

It was my turn in front when I saw the boulders ahead. Thinking to use them as markers, I stepped forward just as the mist swirled away to reveal that my 'boulders', were sizeable crags hundreds of feet below. I was standing on the edge of a cornice! Another step. Well, it didn't bear thinking about. I moved back quickly, then stood leaning on my axe for support shaking with the reaction. The ferocity of the wind was spectacular. At the edge of the precipice, spumes of snow rocketing upwards for about 30ft before being flung away in flat horizontal white jet streamers.

"I think we should rope up, don't you, Dougie?" He nodded, already uncoiling the rope from his sack. After that we travelled roped up in this great white murk, pirouetting around in our traces, torn hither and thither by the gale. Angry flumes of wind-driven snow stung our faces, forcing us to walk with one hand shielding that little area of skin still exposed to the raw elements.

Darkness was now setting in, but we still refused to believe we wouldn't get down before nightfall. My man was grim and silent. I was on the verge of tears but refused to give in to that energy sapping indulgence.

"Hold me!" Dougie screamed, and plunged out of sight. The rope snaked along the snow ripping out its corrugations. I rammed my axe down, whipping a coil of rope round the shaft, and flattened myself on top of the adze to stop being pulled over the edge. The rope went tight and held. I drew breath. There had been no time to feel fear. There was a great howl and then a chorus of curses. The pressure on the rope eased and I wondered if the mist and wind had deceived me.

"Dougie are you all right?" I heard what seemed to be men swearing, with the sibilant flavour of the Lower Royal Deeside.

"Phat the fach are ye daein', mon?"

In a slightly different voice. "Ah'm fachin' aw weet the noo! Ye English Bampot!" To which there was no reply.

Walking to the edge, I peeked over to see Dougie gawping around in astonishment, cosily ensconced between two bulkily clad hillmen, who were wiping snow off their clothes as if they were fastidious diners clearing crumbs from their jackets. The conversation was warm. Like Santa, Dougie had dropped in on their wee bit But and Ben, an emergency snow cave, destroying it in the process. Thinking, oh well, the damage is done anyway, I slid down his chute to land smack on top of one of the cave dwellers. He was screaming blue murder, not at all appreciating finding me in his lap. Then I remembered I was wearing crampons.

Our companions had accepted long before us that they weren't going to reach safety that night and had dug out a snug snow cave in the lee of the slope. Our unexpected First Footing meant they would have to start ain all over again. Luckily, we were now out of the worst ravages of the wind, whose biting, heat-sapping blast was the most serious danger we faced. We could still see its effect above us, for in the half-light, wisps of snow and ice from the broken cornice kept flying into our gully.

The Aberdonians went to work with a will, taking turns at excavating a new cave. In the school for survival you need to be a quick learner, so I set to with my short axe carving out the entrance, while Dougie stood around waving his axe futilely, as if it was a fairy wand. The men from the Granite City let me have a spell inside.

"Wheech lassie, dae a shift doon the pit. You'll be a'richt in thon salt mines, mun, nae doot."

I had to lie flat on my back howking out great blocks of ice to increase the size of our bedroom. It must have been like mining in the old days, my head torch shining on the dull green ice adding to this resemblance. It was warm work, so much better than standing like a snowman out there; so why was Dougie out there? The two Dons came in putting an end to my reveries, by comparing their places of abode and tonight's temporary lodgings.

"Just fancy this in Union Street, Aye?"

"Aye, better than Donnie's hoose tho'."

"Aye, nae hauf, whit a scunner!" They both laughed. I never asked them to explain the joke, just praying never to be invited to tea by Donnie.

"Nae doot about it, hame's best. Ye weet, mon?"

At last they had noticed me, dripping with snow and sweat. I decided to get into the spirit.

"Aye mon ah'm steamin' an aw'." They both laughed again.

"Yer a grand lass, I'll buy you a pint o'heavy."

"Nae doot," I replied with what seemed their catch phrase, and for no reason all three of us began laughing. Dougie joined us, and at once they became sober sides. The Aberdonians drew sleeping bags out of their sacks, all neatly lined with waterproof poly-bags, while we sat watching, doing nothing, just shivering. Everything they did was impressively organised, piling up neat little packages, putting their poly-bags down as groundsheets, laying out their sleeping bags, then finally tucking themselves in bag and rucksack. Besides them we looked like miserable ne'er-do-wells. The one called Jock looked at Dougie and said: "I bet you twae hav'nae sleeping bags."

He was right. Dougie's impetuous approach to mountaineering did not allow for properly arranging logistics.

Jock said: "Well you'd better hae mine." You could tell he was disgruntled because he threw it at Dougie. It was a noble gesture although a bit spoiled by his muttering: "Typical Sassenach! Comin' tae the Gorms unprepared."

He persisted in believing that Dougie was from south o' Tweed, despite the fact that my companion spoke in the patois of Auld Reekie. His pal, Dandy, I think he was called, was fairly reluctant to share his sleeping bag, but it was a matter of survival and he grunted his acceptance as the two of them wriggled together for the double sack race. They were not amused I am sure, although it was difficult to read their expressions blinded as I was by the glare of their headtorches. Five minutes later and it was light's out. For a while we just lay there in the darkness feeling the odd icy drip splashing onto our faces. Since our body heat had raised the temperature just that annoying degree above freezing, our damp steamy bodies in close proximity added to the general discomfort.

Hours passed. I nudged Dougie. "What time is it?" He pretended to be asleep. "C'mon, what time is it?"

"Why do you want to know? Was there something you wanted to watch on the telly? If it's *Coronation Street* I can tell you what happened."

His way of saying I can't be bothered. I persisted and at length, groaning in disgruntlement he caved in and began the lengthy process of extracting his watch from the sack. This consisted of dragging his hand up the whole of our bodies, till the neck of the sleeping bag was reached, from where, to wriggle free he had to squeeze my head against his chin. At last his hand was out and he fumbled about for his torch, the beam revealing steamy breath and the moisture accumulated under the face of the watch making it difficult to read. It was seven o'clock. It was the sort of experience often considered character building, or in this case, as I was to see, character revealing. Jock, who was emerging as the more chatty of our crumpled hosts, asked if we had any food, their's being destroyed when we dropped in uninvited.

We had the usual packets of dried up chocolate biscuits. Jock suggested that we play, 'I spy with my little eye,' and dole out the biscuits for each successful piece of espionage. This little contest gave us something to do and raised our spirits as we flashed our headlights around the cave like searchlights in an ice palace. Under torchlight the cave reminded me of Father Christmas's Faerie Grotto in Binns when I was a child, but of the enchantment I felt when lining up to sit on Santa's knee, the present circumstances were dismally lacking.

All participated except Dougie, shivering and sulking in a corner, complaining of being wet and miserable. Well, who wasn't? When this sport began to pall, which it soon did, there being little to spy on in our spartan surroundings, we scraped together ditties recollected from school, folk clubs, and the wireless. The Aberdonians' contributions were ballads of the Mearns, of ploughboys and their roving lasses, until they ran out of collective memory and had to make do with the *Ball of Kirriemuir*, and other whimsical fantasies of the rugby player's imagination. I like to think I quite outshone them all with my operatic repertoire. Irony of unconscious irony, I started out with, *My Tiny Hand is Frozen*. But sensing this could be bad for morale, switched track to songs of the warm south. Could it have been the first time *O Sole Mio* was sung within the hearing of the Grey man of Ben Macdui? The only sound emerging from Dougie's corner was the chattering of his teeth, which was almost excusable being in rhythm.

With all this excitement, the four of us were dozing comfortably when the sun's early rays turned the dull grey ice bottle green. The steam climbing up from our moist bags must have had an almost hypnotic effect, for we had all dropped off in our glacial squalor. Hours later I awoke with a start. Were the mountain winds   playing tricks? Screams that could have been almost human were merging with eerie, thumping sounds that surely signalled the onset of an Arctic storm. I woke Dougie up. "What time is it?"

"Michty Me!" (He was a great one for the *Sunday Post*) "It's noon! We had better make tracks afore we're caught oot anither night."

The Dons woke from their slumber in time to witness Dougie vandalising their home for a second time. With his axe he smashed down the thin melted wall at our front to reveal the sun shining on a happy holiday scene. A dozen brightly coloured novices in a ski class were gawping at us all in a line. All around there were happy shrieks as fashionably-clad skiers cavorted, slalomed and bounced off moguls in joyful abandonment. We had bivouacked right in the middle of the White Lady, Aviemore's most popular ski-slope.

Above and below us were the gates for the McVitties Chocolate Digestive Ski cup, with the biscuit-shaped banner flaunting its sponsorship, and now we had created a giant crater in the giant slalom course. A child halfway down the line of pupils was the first to recover. "Ma, see those twae bummers cuddlin' up with each other!"

The mother slapped the child but she was evidently incorrigible. "Whit about the wee chappie in wi thon big gowk? Jings it's a lassie. Her ma must be gey strict if she has to go this far for a nicht oot wi' her boyfriend."

The precocious brat was hushed with a sharp slap from the maternal ski-stick. The look Ma gave, told me all I wanted to know about my situation. The student, who was about to snow plough straight into our living room braked goggle-eyed collapsing in a heap just in front of our sleeping bags. No-one laughed. Shamefacedly, we packed up and trudged down the slope. All the way down elegant skiers wheeled in and out of our tattered line. Everyone seemed to know about our escapade, the evidence was as plain as the noses on our faces, since our black hole had howked a massive chunk out of the piste. I dared not look up at the restaurant at the bottom of the slope to see the lines of grinning heads. My cheeks were burning, but not with the fresh air and sunshine.

Just as we were about to make our escape an authoritarian figure stem-christied to a skidding stop directly in our path, spraying us with snow. He was in a fury, screaming, and waving his poles in an alarming manner.

"You're banned, banned, frae this Coire for the rest of your living lives!"

A novel concept, but not one to argue with at this moment. He was in a proper Gaelic tremor: "I'll hae the sheriff on you lot. You've ruined the UK Championship this efternoon!"

Despite our apparent advantage in numbers, no one in our dampened, dispirited group made any attempt to challenge the lone Highlander. We got into our cars sheepishly and slunk away as quickly as was seemly.

Passing the ice floes emerging on the melting Loch Morlich, I tried to make a joke to ease the embarassment. "Are you driving fast in case the sheriff sends a posse?"

He was quiet for a while, then added: "Aye. A few more like him, and Culloden micht have been a different story."

And with you on our side, Bannockburn might have been a different story, I could have added, but kept to myself, as just then Dougie hit a patch of ice and the car fish-tailed across the road, and was skidding towards the Courting Tree at Llynwllg.

STILL LOCHAN ON THE WAY TO AN TEALLACH

Landscape in oils by James Hawkins

By Robert Davidson

Granite sheets, banded gneisses, pegmatite veins
a quartzite glimmer here and there among the hills
reminds you this land was not always as it is now.
The earth ages.

Ruined buildings
the coast
city
your people
all are left behind
the past recedes.
To stray from the path is to risk a thigh-deep plunge
into cold peat.
The land accepts you at a price.

Over the watershed the way narrows
before opening on to a broad, glacial cut that sweeps down
to the mountain's foot, and here
between *the bracken crag* and the high, out of sight
corrie of the son of Farquhar, you find
a lochan.

It is mid-summer, the sun stands high above the defile.
Its light falls near to the vertical.
There has been no rain for days.
Here you rest, pulling off your boots
letting your feet breathe.
You could pass away in a place like this
seep into the ground and be secreted for ever.
Grass might grow through.

Stones for bones.
Prickling forests.
Rivers in place of arteries.
Small mammals resembling all the other lives
that live off your own life.
The eaters of dead skin.

The blood warriors.
The land breathes through its leaves, turns in the heat.
It passes water.

The trickle leaving the lochan halts
its surface flattens and for a moment
becomes completely still.
The light falls straight through.
The bottom becomes so clear there might be no water here at all.
Fish might fly.
This is the silvery eye that raptors circle.
It is where the wildcat waits to kill.
This is where big-eyed hinds come to drink
Centred on it

the towers of rock
the skin of moss
you lie on
all the stones
slowly turning.

You struggle to your feet.
You have to keep moving, to walk through.
If the land has a soul, so might you.

NEW CLIMBS SECTION

OUTER ISLES

LEWIS, The Uig Hills, Hidden Buttress:
Note: With reference to SMCJ 2002, p94, R. Everett notes (with agreement from M. Tighe):
1. Hunting for History is the same as Election Special.
2. Con John follows Election Special for the first 10m.
3. Where Eagles Nest is an independent line for its first half, then it joins Con John.
4. Hidden Treasure was climbed by M. Tighe and B. Newton in June, 1987 but with a runner pre-placed in Election Special which provided a top-rope for the crux traverse. R. Everett's is therefore the first true ascent of the direct line. M. Tighe and B. Newton did climb a less direct line in good style.
5. R. Everett has written descriptions which are available by e-mail and has provided photos for the next guidebook author.

LEWIS, GREAT BERNERA, Geodha Mor (NB 133 386):
A Fiver in the Fickle Hand of Fate 18m VS 4b. K. Archer, S. Armstrong. 3rd June 2002.
Abseil in to the south-facing slab with obvious cracklines well seen from across the geo. The route takes the right-hand crackline. From the abseil, step left to the crack and follow it to the top.

Sgeir Rebrie:
The Moral Low Ground 40m HVS 5a. N. McAllister, P. Woodhouse (alt). 3rd June 2002.
Make a scrambling descent to just above a wave-washed platform with cracked overhangs at the north end. At the bottom of the descent are two grooves, the left being Return of the Absent Friend. This route climbs the right groove. From a notch above the platform, take the right groove through an overlap to a ledge. Take the obvious groove and another overlap (hard but safe), then the wall above trending right.

Part Time Potato Peeler 40m HVS. K. Archer, S. Armstrong. 3rd June 2002.
Take the steep wall immediately right of The Moral Low Ground to a fierce-looking horizontal jamming crack. Follow this to the right arête and pull around this to share a stance with The Moral Low Ground (5a). Take the slab and blocky arête above.

CRULIVIG:
An inland crag just before the bridge to Bearnera. Reported as "fantastic" by the first ascentionists, it may be the same as a crag on which Andy Macfarlane climbed some routes in 1989-1990 (not recorded). If the same, it was reported as lichenous in its top third. It is recommended that, during the lambing season, permission for access is asked from the croft opposite. The most obvious and probably best line is the clean groove and overhang on the left.

Lard of the Pies HVS 5a ***. P. Woodhouse and party. 4th June, 2002.
Trend left up the very steep lower wall on excellent holds, then take the groove
direct, then through the top overhang using a 'bucket' of a jug on the left. Very
sustained and strenuous but the holds are big and it's very safe (if you can hang
around to put the gear in!). This would be a classic tick in the peak.

GEODHA MALADAIL (NB 088 379, West facing):
The headland north of Valtos has a number of good varied crags.
Approach: Park at the side of the road just west of Valtos, overlooking the golden
sandy beach of Camas na Clibhe, just beneath water treatment works. Head north
for about 1km to a long band of clean cliffs extending north on the east side of the
open geo. 20 minutes.

The Main Cliff:
Descent: Abseil from a prominent large block about a third of the way south from
the left side of the cliff, to gain a large tidal platform running along the base.

Just Fantastic! 35m Very Difficult ***. G. Latter, L. Mackay. 10th May 2002.
An excellent route up the centre of the cliff, only marred by a loose exit past
poised blocks. A prominent flake system runs up the left side of the large central
open groove. Start at the left end of a long narrow pool, at the right end of a long
overhang at the base. Foot traverse out left along a narrow ledge to gain the main
groove, then move left and follow the flake crack with perfect holds and protection
to finish.

The next three routes are on a fine 20-25m pink wall of pegmatite 200m further
north. Descent: A 25m abseil from a large block leads to tidal ledges at the base.

I'm Enjoying this! 25m Difficult **. L. Mackay, B. Rose. 10th May 2002.
The fine left-slanting fault at the left end, stepping right to finish by cracks in the
beautiful pink slab.

So Am I! 22m Severe **. L. Mackay, B. Rose. 10th May 2002.
Climb easy juggy rock, passing to the left of a square projecting block to finish up
the short steep crack in the headwall.

This is great! 22m Very Difficult **. B. Rose, L. Mackay. 10th May 2002.
A direct line up the wall, passing right of the block, to finish by a crack up the
right edge of the steeper headwall.

Eala Sheadha (NB 089 382, West facing):
The northernmost point of the headland forms an immaculate 15m off-vertical
wall dropping straight into the sea. In its centre it is capped by a short overhanging
headwall. The base of the wall can be gained at about Severe by descending easy
ground on the north side and traversing in just above sea level, or alternatively a
diagonal fault leads down rightwards, then back left to gain the right end of the
crag – about VS or so.

Wander at Will 15m HVS 5a **. G. Latter (on-sight solo). 10th May 2002.
The arête delineating the right side of the open groove on the left side of the crag.

Diretissima 15m HVS 5a **. G. Latter (on-sight solo). 10th May 2002.
The central line, finishing by a shallow V slot.

Stravaiging 15m E1 5b ***. G. Latter (on-sight solo). 10th May 2002.
The rightmost line, finishing spectacularly on good holds through the overhanging headwall.

AIRD UIG AREA, May Day Geo (near Gallan Head, SMCJ 1998):
Bathtime for Mark 30m E1 5b *. R. Benton, A. Callum. 30th May 2002.
Climbs the crackline in the centre of the north (south-facing) wall of May Day Geo. Start from the tidal ledge under a steep crack, 3m right of the pink quartz band. Climb the crack (crux), then follow flakes rightwards to a good ledge. Trend leftwards easily to the top.

GALLAN HEAD, The Truillich Headland:
The following climbs are located on the headland forming the west side of Geodha an Truillich.

True Grit 30m HVS 5a **. R. and C. Anderson, M. Garthwaite. 20th July 2002.
On the north-west tip there is a crack running up the right side of a fine slabby arête to the left of a black corner. Gain the crack directly, then climb it and the arête, stepping right to finish up a short final arête.

Over the Edge 30m HVS 5a **. R. and C. Anderson. 20th September 2002.
The crack immediately to the left of the slabby arête, climbed direct. Either finish up the top section of True Grit, or easily up the fault.

Slippery When Wet 30m E1 5b *. R. and C. Anderson. 21st September 2002.
The groove immediately to the left of Over the Edge. Climb the groove and crack, cross a small hanging slab, then move up towards the big groove at the back, before going out right across the wall and climbing a crack onto the edge and easier ground leading to the top.

Homerun 30m VS **. R. and C. Anderson. 20th September 2002.
The crack which slants diagonally up left across the slab into the final moves of True Grit.

Dumb and Dumber 25m HVS 5a *. R. and C. Anderson. 20th September 2002.
Left of the abseil corner and just right of True Grit, climb the slabby groove running up the right side of the slab, move up right along a break, then make a few steep moves up a crack and move up right to finish.

Easy Out 25m Very Difficult. M. Garthwaite, R. Anderson. 20th July 2002.
A line up the slabby back wall, right of Truily Madly, left into the corner, then out and up right to finish.

Moby Dick 40m E2/3 5c **. R. and C. Anderson. 17th July 2002.
Just around the edge before the cliff turns the edge to the West Face, start beneath twin cracks cutting through the lower, black wall of a narrow, frontal buttress.

Climb the cracks, continue through an obvious break in the steep grey wall, then step left and finish up slabby grooves.

Minky 40m HVS 5a **. R. and C. Anderson. 17th July 2002.
Just around the edge to the right of Moby Dick, climb a short, wide crack through the lower band of black rock, then its short continuation through the next band. Continue over a reddish slab and climb the centre of the 'tower' to the top.

Bonaventure 40m E2 5b/c ***. M. Garthwaite, R. Anderson. 20th July 2002.
An impressive route up the centre of the imposing West Face. Start in the centre of the face beneath the only obvious break in the lower black wall. Climb this, then move up and left to an obvious undercut flange in the overlap. Pull up right into a groove and from the top of this step left to gain a line leading directly into the upper groove, which is climbed to the top.

Swell 40m E2 5b/c **. M. Garthwaite, R. Anderson. 20th July 2002.
A parallel line just right of the previous route, breaking through the lower band, as for that route, then moving up and right, before climbing back up left to a thin crackline leading over small overlaps to a steepening beneath an obvious short leaning wall with a break in it. Step up left and move right into the break, then pull boldly through the break to gain a blocky feature and finish more easily.

Static Fear 30m E1 5a. R. Anderson, M. Diggins. June 2002.
This and the next two climbs start from a pedestal on the right side of the face. Climb the obvious crackline over a steepening to where it peters out beneath the final eaves, then lurch steeply up right on slightly dubious rock into a shallow groove leading to the top.

Charged 30m E2/3 5c **. M. Diggins, R. Anderson. June 2002.
Climb thin cracks directly to the base of the obvious smooth groove. Climb the groove to its top, then continue a short way before moving up right to finish more easily.

Cool Running 30m VS 4c **. R. Anderson, M. Diggins. June 2002.
Step up right and climb thin cracks just right of Smoothy, which soon widen and lead to a V-shaped groove. Climb the groove then easier ground to the top.

Washing of the Spears 30m E2 5c **. R. and C. Anderson. 17th July 2002.
This climb lies on the continuation face, just around an edge where there is a pedestal at the foot of a slab, seamed with cracks A fine line up the edge forming the left side of the slab, overlooking the West Face to the left. Step up left from the pedestal and climb cracks just right of the edge, staying on the front face to below the final steepening. Climb a left-slanting thin crack to the top.

Gallan Cracks 30m Very Difficult-Severe **. R. and C. Anderson. 17th July 2002.
The area of slabby rocks above the pedestal can be climbed anywhere on fine rock. A central line between the deeper cracks is probably just harder than the cracks themselves.

A short way down and right from the pedestal, almost on the last ledge, is a deep wide crack.

Thinner Better 35m VS 4c **. R. and C. Anderson. 21st September 2002.
Just right of the deep wide crack, climb a thin crack and continue on fine rock always just right of the bigger crack and its continuation.

AIRD UIG, The Gallan Beag Geos:
Two small geos are located on the cliffs just east of the small island of Gallan Beag; Gallan Beag 1 and Gallan Beag 2.

Gallan Beag 2:
The base of the wall has a ledge running along its base from a sea cave on the right to a pedestal on the left. The first three routes start from the pedestal where the ledge peters out.

Every Which Way 25m VS 4c. R. and C. Anderson. 19th July 2002.
From the pedestal go left around the edge, follow a groove, then step down left to a short cracked wall. Climb the wall and continue up the left side of the tower to finish.

Little Boomey 25m VS 5a **. R. and C. Anderson. 15th July 2002.
From the pedestal climb black rock just right of the edge to reach an obvious crack. Climb the crack and then grooves leading out on to the left-bounding edge where easy rocks lead to the top.

Rawson's Retreat 25m HVS 4c/5a *. R. and C. Anderson. 19th July 2002.
From the pedestal step up right and climb a thin crack in the initial short, leaning wall, then continue up somewhat eliminately between Little Boomey and the groove of Jacob's Creek to finish up the obvious groove in the final eaves.

Jacob's Creek 25m HVS 5a **. R. and C. Anderson. 15th July 2002.
From the base of a large groove, climb up and left into cracks leading to a short V-groove. Climb the groove, pull out right, then step back left through the final eaves.

Leftwing 25m HVS 5a **. R. and C. Anderson. 15th July 2002.
The edge left of the large groove. Immediately left of the groove, climb black rock and shallow grooves to beneath the final steepening. Step up right, then pull steeply up left into a crack and finish up this in a fine position.

Rightwing 25m HVS 4c *. R. and C. Anderson. 15th July 2002.
The right side of the large groove. From the foot of the groove climb a V-groove up right, then back left on to the edge. Continue to below the steep upper rocks and make a few bold moves up the edge, then move up and swing left to easier ground leading to the top.

Savage Slant 40m HVS 4c/5a. R. and C. Anderson. 19th July 2002.
The obvious right-slanting ramp. Those of a nervous disposition may not wish to

place any protection under the mass of rock that is perched on the top edge of the ramp!

Aird Uig, The Boardwalk Walls

These walls extend south westwards above a non-tidal shelf, 'The Boardwalk', south of Gallan Beag.

Boardwalk Left (The Black Wall):

This is the area of black rock extending leftwards above The Boardwalk from Chapel Crack.

Chapel Crack (1986) was climbed and found not to be Hard Severe; it is certainly VS and maybe even HVS!

Funky Corner   30m   VS 4c **. R. and C. Anderson. 16th July 2002.
Some 20m left of Chapel Crack is a short thin crack in the lower wall, immediately left of a storm pool. Climb the crack, head up into the slabby corner, which is climbed leftwards, then up to finish.

Disco Fever   30m   VS 4c **. R. and C. Anderson. 16th July 2002.
Just left of Funky Corner, gain a black shelf and follow this up right, then head directly up into a slim groove which leads to steep rock, then the top.

Northern Soul   30m   HVS 5a **. R. and C. Anderson. 16th July 2002.
Follow Disco Fever to the top of the shelf, then head up left to climb a steep crack and groove, then finish steeply up a short wall.

Boardwalk Central:

This is the area extending rightwards from Chapel Crack to a large-bouldered bay.

Groove Armada   15m   E3 6a **. R. and C. Anderson. 26th July 2002.
The wall and steep V-grooves right of Chapel Crack. Scramble up black rock to belay on a shelf below the line.

Shelf Life   35m   E1 5b *. R. and C. Anderson. 24th July 2002.
Start in the large-bouldered bay at the leftmost boulder beside a pool. Move up and left to climb a stepped corner into the base of the crack. Climb the crack and its left edge to the top.

Magic Dragon   35m   E4 6a ***. R. and C. Anderson. 26th July 2002.
The crackline immediately to the right of Shelf Life, gained by a hand-traverse rightwards from the corner.

Divided Fears   35m   E2 5c **. R. Anderson, M. Garthwaite. 21st July 2002.
The obvious crackline in the left wall of the chimney-crack in the big corner. The crack is formed between two distinct types and colour of rock.

-uffing Crack   35m   E4 6a ***. M. Garthwaite, R. Anderson. 21st July 2002.
The thin cracks running up the impending right wall of the big corner, climbed directly all the way.

The RiverKwai   35m   E4 6a **. M. Garthwaite, R. Anderson. 22nd July 2002.
Just around the edge is another big corner; climb this to a common finish with the next route.

A Bridge Too Far   40m   E3/4 6a ***. M. Garthwaite, R. Anderson. 22nd July 2002.
Just to the right is an obvious crackline slanting up left into the top corner taken by the previous route. Start from a boulder in the right corner of the bay, beneath an undercut crack. Move off the ground with difficulty (the vertically challenged will have a problem). Follow the crackline up left in a stupendous position to a steep finish.

Quartzvein Crack   15m   HVS 5a **. R. and C. Anderson. 15th September, 2002.
The steep quartzy crack just right of the arête a short way up the shelf to the right of Shadows in the Sun.

Boardwalk Right (The Point Wall):
This is the west-facing wall at the far right end, just above the sea.

Paranoid   20m   E2 5c **. R. and C. Anderson. 5th September 2002.
On the left-hand section of the cliff, passed beneath on the approach, just before the edge to the right is turned, is a fine, steep slabby wall of grey rock. Climb a thin crack through a quartz patch in the centre of this slabby wall.

Seamed Sane   25m   HVS 5b **. R. and C. Anderson. 15th September 2002.
Just right of the edge is a thin quartz seam running the height of the wall. Climb this quartz seam up and around the edge to finish up a short crack.

Going Spare   25m   HVS 5a *. R. and C. Anderson. 15th September 2002.
Just right of Seamed is a stepped rib of rock, with a corner on its left and a wide crack on its right. Climb the centre of the stepped rib.

Utter Nutter   25m   HVS 5b *. R. and C. Anderson. 15th September 2002.
Just left of the deep chimney-crack formed next to the right-angled corner, is a protruding rib. Climb the centre of this rib, firstly up steep black rock, then up a thin crack.

Bampot   25m   HVS 5b **. R. and C. Anderson.25th July 2002.
The corner running up the left side of the wall, hard up against the face, immediately right of a deep chimney-crack.

Anxiety Nervosa   20m   E3 6a **. M. Garthwaite, R. Anderson. 21st July 2002.
The thin crackline running up the wall just left of the central diagonal crack.

Cracking-up   20m   VS 4c/5a **. R. Anderson, M. Garthwaite. 21st July 2002.
The central diagonal crack.
Black Sabbath   20m   E1 5b ***. R. and C. Anderson. 15th September 2002.
The right-hand crack.

CAMAS UIG, Fiavig Tarras:
Groove is in the Heart   40m   E3 5c **. M. Garthwaite, R. Anderson. 23rd July 2002.

At the left end of the main wall, left of An Dobhrain, is a striking groove/cornerline that terminates at a triangular roof. At low tide traverse the tapering ledge just above the sea and climb to a belay ledge in the corner. Climb the corner and go out left around the roof, then up the headwall.

MUNGARSTADH AREA, Landlubber Geo (SMCJ 1998, p561):
Ceol na Mara (Sea Music)   25m   Severe. F. Macleod, F. T. Macleod. 14th May 1999.
The obvious chimney-crack next to Mutineer's Return and parallel to it.

Screaming Geo:
Port a' Bheul (Mouth Music)   50m   Mild VS. F. Macleod, F. T. Macleod. 14th May 1999.
This is the route referred to in SMCJ 2000, p327 as being marked with string and right of The Heebie-Jeebies. Climb an overhanging cracked orange wall to a roof. Step left to an arête and go up to a ledge with a flake (belay). Traverse left to the exposed arête, go up a wall and finish up obvious left-sloping handrails. Photograph supplied.

Magic Geo, East Face:
Note: M. Tighe notes that Flannan Slab Direct was more direct than the original and that he also climbed the line in SMCJ 2002, p102 and called it the Superdirect (but hasn't claimed it).

Island Fling   25m   VS 5a **. B. Rose, L. Mackay. 8th May 2002.
A spectacular left finish to the slabby corner of Island Life, taking the obvious incut ledge and slanting crack to finish by pulling round the arête in a fine position.
Note: Island Life was thought to be Severe 4a, not VS.

AIRD FENISH HEAD, The Biorach Wall (SMCJ 2002), Slabby Buttress:
On the right of the Recessed Slabs in the centre of the cliff is Slabby Buttress. This contains five routes, the first of which is Dry Roasted (2001), taking the rib overlooking the slabs on the left.

Ready Packed   20m   VS 5a **. R. and C. Anderson. 14th July 2002.
A parallel line to Dry Roasted, starting just up to that routes right. Climb a short wall, then go directly up quartzy rock to finish up the ensuing slabs.

In-step   20m   HVS 5a *. R. and C. Anderson. 13th July 2002.
Start at the highpoint in the centre of the buttress and climb short, stepped walls to gain a crackline, which is followed to the top.
Out-step   20m   HVS 5b *. R. and C. Anderson. 13th July 2002.
Immediately right of In-step, climb stepped walls to an obvious right-angled groove in the right side of a block-like overlap. Enter the groove and continue to the top.

Seaprey   25m   HVS 5b *. R. and C. Anderson. 13th July 2002.
Start beneath the right-bounding arête of the buttress. Climb a groove in the arête and move up until forced steeply up right into the corner, which is followed to the top.

Recessed Slabs:
The following routes lie on the central area of recessed black slabs.

Ready Rubbed 25m HVS 5a *. R. and C. Anderson. 14th July 2002.
The groove in the arête on the left side of the main slab, just right of a corner.

Tight Lipped 25m HVS 5a *. R. and C. Anderson. 4th July 2002.
The thin crack in the middle of the main slab, immediately left of a large crackline.

Close Knit 25m VS 4c *. R. and C. Anderson. 14th July 2002.
The large crackline just left of the slabby corner defining the right side of the slabs.

DALBEG AREA, Solus Wall (NF 231 466):
From Preacher Zawn, walk 8 minutes north, cross a dry stoned dyke at the head of a pebble bay containing an arched split sea stack. On the NW tip of the bay is a mitre-shaped wall. Around the corner facing seawards and protected by a square-cut bookend buttress with windows lies a stepped wall, a roofed recess, projecting prow and blocks. Routes lie from right to left facing inward. Abseil to good ledges.

Solus 20m HVS 4c. F. Macleod, C. Humphries. 9th November 2002.
Climb the wall trending right into the bottomless right corner of the recess/buttress crack.

Dealanach 20m VS 4c. F. Macleod, C. Humphries. 26th October 2002.
The short right-facing corner and crack direct to the left corner of the recess.

An Grian 20m HVS 5a. F. Macleod, C. Humphries. 26th October 2002.
Climb direct to the left side of the blocks. Surmount them and finish up the right corner of the prow.

Rionnag na Maidne 22m E1. F. Macleod, A. Sutton. 30th December 2002.
The sustained direct off-width V-crack before the central arête.

Tigh Solus 22m Mild Severe. A. Sutton, F. Macleod. 30th December 2002.
Start left of the central arête on a low ledge below a left-facing short corner. Climb the obvious fault line through an overhang, finishing across a cracked slab.

Soisgeul 18m Severe. A. Sutton, F. Macleod. 21st December 2002.
The series of right-facing corners direct to the overhang. Step left, climb a short wall to a horizontal break and over an overlap.

PABBAY, Pink Wall:
Paradise Regained 115m E4 ***. I. Taylor, T. Fryer. 12th May 2002.
1. 45m 5a Start approx. 20m right of U-Ei. Climb a crackline through a small overlap to a niche.
2. 30m 5c Trend up and left wards to a hanging corner between two large roofs. Pull left into the corner, then follow cracks to a belay on a ledge below the final corner of U-Ei.

3. 15m 5b Traverse left along a break to belay below the final pitch of Spit in Paradise. Very exposed.
4. 25m 6a The final pitch of Spit in Paradise.
Finishing up the final pitch of U-Ei would give a *** E2.

The Grey Wall:
Mixmaster Snipe   100m   E1 **. M. Davies, P. Newman, G. Latter. 12th May 2002.
A direct line up the left side of the right wall of the recess. Start at the base of the prominent crack system right of U-ei.
1 40m 5b Climb the crack direct through the prominent roof (or easier on the right) and continue in the same line, trending up right to a good ledge.
2 30m 5b Continue up the prominent right-facing corner above, then in the same line to traverse left along a shelf.
3 30m 5b Move left and climb a short steep right-slanting groove, then continue up a crack system, finishing direct.

Bravura   140m   E7 ***. G. Latter, R. Campbell (ground-up). 15th May 2002 (p1); 17th May 2002 (p2-4).
Stunning very sustained climbing up the twin intermittent cracks up the left side of the main wall, just right of the arête. Start at the right end of the sea-level platform, beneath a short blunt arête.
1. 55m 6a Arrange a runner/belay in an obvious deep triangular slot up in the right side of the arête. Make hard moves up the left side of the arête, then pull rightwards and up into a groove. Continue up this, passing an overhung jam slot with interest, leading to easier ground. Go direct up a crack to a platform directly beneath the arête.
2. 25m 6b A stunning pitch. Climb a wide gritty crack up the left side of the arête to the top of the pedestal. Hard moves lead past cams in pockets (Camalot # 0.1 crucial) to a good hold in a crack almost on the arête. Move up right and follow the crack system, eventually transferring to a further crack system on the right which eases to a fine finger-crack leading up into an easier short left-facing corner.
3. 25m 6b From the base of the corner, traverse right along a diagonal crack to gain good holds and protection in the short left-facing groove of Amber Nectar. Finish up this.
4. 35m 5a As for Amber Nectar.

The Great Arch:
Prophecy of Paddling   45m   E1 5b *. I Taylor, T. Fryer. 16th May 2002.
Start 3m left of Customs and Exercise. Climb up the left side of a flake, gain an overhung ledge then pull left round onto a black slab. Climb up the arête above and finish up slabs and blocks.

Sloc Glansich:
The stream that drains westwards from the islands central col flows through this impressive boulder-choked sloc. Rumour has it that this was once the site of an illicit still. The north wall overhangs dauntingly while the south wall is slabby. It is possible to scramble into the east end if the sloc.

The Jaws of Hell 30m E3 5b. T. Fryer, I. Taylor. 12th May 2002.
A serious route on very poor rock. Halfway down the slabby south wall are three diagonal cracks; the left two forming the letter 'A'. Climb up the right-hand of the 'A' cracks, pulling through an overlap at a tottering pinnacle. Stand on the pinnacle, pull rightwards on to the slab above and boldly climb to the top.

Note:
Blo' na Gael – Rockfall has altered the start of this route. Possibly now E3 5c.
Wiggly Wall – Rockfall has seriously affected the start of this route.

EIGG, An Sgurr:
The Nose 90m E8. B. Bransby, A. Long, J. McHaffie. June 2002.
The sensational prow goes free (headpoint style).
1. 30m 5c Follow a vague corner leftwards up the lower wall, stepping left to avoid the band of roofs, to a grass ledge.
2. 60m 6c Traverse right along the large break for 8m before launching up through the roof on large but loose holds. A succession of hollow columns now leads up the wall to the left of the old aid bolts, climbed via fingertip laybacking and long reaches off undercuts (in-situ RURP), to a hard move right to gain the undercut flake and bolts of the old belay. Easier but unprotected ground leads to the top. Belay on the trig point (well back, additional rope required).

COLONSAY:
These lines are on the beautiful west-facing buttresses of Sliabh Riabhach. They are close to and left (north) of the existing route called '367936', and follow obvious natural features. The routes are described from left to right.
    A series of ribs drop down westwards dividing the area into grassy bays as the guide says. The second bay to the south holds the line '367936'. The northernmost bay is bounded on its left by a steep and striking arête pointing north-west which overlooks Glen Raonabuilg. This gives an airy and characterful route. The lower part of this arête is a prominent open-book corner.

Rose Rib 50m Severe *. M. Hudson, A. Hutt. 14th June 2002.
1. 20m 4b Climb up to and out of the steep open corner on sharp incuts. Step right on to a ramp in a fine open position and belay above at a spacious ledge below a wall.
2. 30m 4a Move carefully up on to the reclining heathery slabs and follow the right edge above more easily to blocks at the summit. Descend to the south either down the steep gully by '367936' or down a gentler bay further south.

Crex Wall 30m VS 4b. M. Hudson. 15th June 2002.
The slabby wall forming the right-hand wall of the northern grassy bay, and 25m right of the previous route. A bit dirty at the moment, but quite sound and satisfactory.
Start below a dark slot at 10m. Climb rightwards up the wall past blocks to a slot. Step out left on to the wall and make for the shallow groove in the centre. Good balance climbing follows to a V-notch on the skyline. Belay as for the next route. Scramble to the summit and descend as before.

Blunt Rib   30m   VS. M. Hudson, A. Hutt. 15th June 2002.
The blunt-nosed rib forming the right-hand side of the northern grassy bay 15m right of the previous route, featuring a square white wall high up. Some splintery rock but fun nonetheless. Start below the nose.
1. 20m 4b Take a right-slanting groove up the front of the rib. Zigzag up flaky ground via a delicate overlap on the right of the nose, to a small ledge below the square wall.
2. 10m 4c Climb the steep wall to blocks on the ridge above. A very ancient peg found 5m back from edge denoted earlier activity of some kind. Scramble to the summit.

Note: 25m further right in the back of the next grassy bay lies the existing route '367936' - well worth doing, with the option of finishing direct over the final overhang at Severe).

ORONSAY:
There is a bird ban on Priory Buttress for nesting choughs (March to July). A nearby outcrop with no ban exists 400m away, which can be seen looking west from the Abbey as a plug split on its west face by a deep cleft. Labelled on the OS map at 354 890 as Dun Domhnuill, it can be reached easily from the track back to the crossing. Approaching from the track you first meet an impressive and terminally loose band of overhangs on the south wall, then some better-looking possibilities to the left which run up the steep right-hand side of the cleft on the west face. A couple of short and fairly forgettable lines now exist on the gentler rock left of the cleft - barely compensating for heaving gear over the water. Both by M. Hudson and A. Hutt on 11th June 2002.

Route 1. Start steeply as close to the cleft as you fancy, and finish up the right-hand of the steeper top wall (20m, Very Difficult).
Route 2. Start more easily 10m further left on slabs and finish over the alcove in the middle of the top wall. (20m, Difficult).

MULL, Balmeanach:
Endless Summer   20m   E1 5b *. C. Moody, C. Grindley. 12th July 2002.
Crack, bulge and slab between Mushroom Picking and Glam Rock.

Scoor:
The Cleat   15m   Severe. K.V. Crocket, P.F. MacDonald. 16th September 2002.
A square-cut tower dominates the east flank of the bay (NM 4131 1834). Climb the centre of the west face, overlooking the bay.

Scoor, The Slab:
Splitting Hares   18m   E3 6a. M. Tweedley, C. Grindley. 2nd June 2002.
The thin crack right of Everything Flying By. Wimp on to that route near the top.

Ardtun, Waterfall Wall:
Russian Bustards   20m   HVS 5a. C. Moody, C. Grindley, D. Mercer. 8th June 2002.
Start left of Roadrunner. Climb the crack in the arête and continue up the rib.

Ardtun, The Yellow Block:
Caterpillar 10m VS 4c. C. Moody. 20th September 2002.
A corner-crack right of Midge Shirt.

Ardtun, The Blow Hole:
Mud In Your Eye 14m VS 4b. C. Moody. 3rd August 2002.
Start right of Tarmac Frogs. Climb the right side of the pinnacle, then follow twin cracks above. A bit wet so may be Severe.

Ardtun, The Green Hill:
Spider and Me 7m Severe. C. Moody. 27th August 2002.
The crack round left of No Pyjamas Required.

Erraid:
Most of the following routes on Erraid were on sight soloed by J. Lines. A map and topos were provided.

Upper Tier:
The Round House 10m E1 5c *. J. Lines. 22nd August 2002.
On the left side of the tier, between Pharos and Covenant. Step off the right end of the boulder and make an awkward move to gain a grey foothold. Layback the flake to gain a grey jug and finish on jugs (similar finish to Pharos).

I Hear of the Red Fox 10m E1 5b/6b *. J. Lines. 22nd August 2002.
Start just left of Walls without Balls. Reach, jump, scratch —! for a jug, go up to undercuts and stretch right into WWB for a move to gain a jug, then go out diagonally left to finish though a small crack in the headwall.

Note: J. Lines thinks that Chickenhead should be E2 6a and Covenant should be ***.

The Otter Walls (NM 293 193):
The Otter Walls join on to the Paradise Wall (SMCJ 2002, p124), facing south and on the seaward side. The Longest Yet (SMCJ 2002) is on these walls. The best access is to climb or abseil down The Longest Yet. Routes described from right to left (facing in).

Gourmet Crab Crack 12m Hard Severe *. J. Lines. 20th August 2002.
Cracks to the right of The Longest Yet.
The Otter's Breakfast Table 15m E3 5c ***. J. Lines. 21st August 2002.
Beautiful climbing on beautiful rock. Start 5m left of The Longest Yet on a large barnacle-encrusted boulder (the breakfast table). Climb a slanting groove/crack up the centre of the concave wall. Where it steepens, move rightwards on flakes to reach a large flake on the right edge. Continue up this to a jug and finish at twin cracks and a chokestone hold.

Black Eye Rib 12m E1 5c *. J. Lines. 20th August 2002.
Start on the right side of an obvious rib, low tide necessary. Make crux moves on

undercuts and barnacle encrusted footholds to reach better holds (or start from further right, as per TOBT, and traverse at 5b). Climb the arête on the right, then swing left around the arête to a spike and continue on its left.

Amphibian   14m VS 5a **. J. Lines. 20th August 2002.
Climb the obvious square-cut groove. Low tide needed.

Note: The line to the left of Amphibian has not been climbed. The first half is E1 5b and very good but the second half needs a brush.

About 30m right of Amphibian are some slabby rock shelves about 8m above the sea. This is where the next two routes start.

Tarka   15m   XS 6a S0 (DWS) *. J. Lines. 21st August 2002.
Start at the inland end of slabby shelves and climb down on to a flakey/juggy wall. Move right for 4m to a large granite chokestone. Squirm out above into a roof, slap for a grey nubbin and climb a flake on the right to a big jug. Ramble up a slab to finish.

Ring of Bright Water   XS 5b/c S0 (DWS) **. J. Lines. 21st August 2002.
From the seaward end of the shelves, go down easy slabs with grey nubbins and traverse along the slabs just above the water line (best done at high tide) - interesting and technical in places. Cross the flakey/juggy wall to the chokestone and then rightwards across a square-cut bay, along jugs to where the rock changes direction through 90 degrees and becomes very steep (6a above boulders, so no longer DWS). Here, rock up on to a slab for a rest and then reverse. If done like this, then there is good water underneath for all the way.

Strawberry Pig Slab (NM 290 192, West facing, Alt 20m):
A pleasant 8m slab on the peninsula to the west, with some obvious red intrusions, one of which looks like a pig. All routes J. Lines on sight solo, 19th August, 2002, except Jules' Pistachios (on sight, 21st August, 2002).

1. *Jo's Plums*   8m   VS 4c *. An obvious straight crack at the left end.
2. *Davi's Bananas*   8m   HVS 5a *. Broken cracks.
3. *Strawberry Pig*   8m   E2 5b *. Start at a short crack and make a hard move right to gain the pig, then direct up the slab.
4. *Jules' Pistachios*   8m   E5 6b/c. Start directly below the pig and climb up to a red blotch to the right of the pig. Scratch desperately to the top.
5. *Raspberry Lips*   10m   E3 6a *. Make hard moves to gain an undercut in an overlap. Go right and finish as for Ripe Mangoes.
6. *Ripe Mangoes*   8m   E1 5b/c *. Go up past a red blotch and continue direct.
7. *Rotten Pineapple*   8m   VS 4c. An obvious dog-leg at the right end.

Sunshine Wall (NM 290 192, W-facing, Alt 10m):
Situated about 50m down and left (facing in) of the Strawberry Pig Slab. A small crevasse forms the right side of the crag. Routes by J. Lines, on sight solo on 21st August 2002. Described left to right.

1. *Melanoma* 10m Severe. The initial corner.
2. *Hydrogen* 10m E2 5b. Climb the arête initially on the left via a flake, then on the right.
3. *Daniel's Dihedral* 10m VS 4c *. The off-width corner.
4. *Vermelho Quente* 10m E1 5b *. The obvious arête where the crag changes direction, using the crack on its right side.
5. *Spidery Cracks* 10m VS 4c *. The spidery cracks.
6. *Black Square* 10m HVS 5a *. The crack with the black square.
7. *Sun Spots* 10m HVS 5a *. A crack with a hanging corner and red blotch.
8. *Grey Matter* 10m E1 5b *. A crack and roof with an aerated flake.
9. *Where's Your Tan, Karen?* 10m E1 5b *. Go up to a short corner in an overlap. Pull through and up a hand crack.
10. *Topping up your Tan* 5/10m E1 5b *. Either start from low down by a tongue of flake, or bridge across the void to gain grey footholds. Make delicate face moves using a small ear-type flake.
11. *Anticyclone* 10m E1 5b **. Great climbing into the A-shaped roof and wall above.
12. *Rays* 8m VS 5a. A hand crack through a bulge.
13. *Is this Scotland??* 8m E2 5c *. The centre of the roof via a big hold, then veer left along a diagonal.
14. *Ellipse* 10m HVS 5b. Start right of an arching flake. Move left to a bulge and climb twin cracks to the top past a red knob.

Asteroid Chasm (NM 289 193):
A stunning piece of rock architecture approx. 4m wide, caused by the erosion of a basalt dyke. It has a SW-facing wall, just off vertical and a NE-facing wall, just overhanging. Also a huge block (the asteroid) wedged in the top. There are a few nests so maybe best avoided in the spring. 45 minutes from the car park.

Infinitesimal 8m VS 4c. J. Lines. 20th August 2002.
On the approach to the NE-facing wall from the seaward end, the first line is a tapering crack in a square-cut corner. This is the route.

Passing some amazing looking cracklines, you reach the base of a tapering hanging groove.

Asteroid Groove 22m HVS 5a **. J. Lines. 19th August 2002.
Move left into the groove and climb to its top and a ledge (nest in summer). Move left and continue up the obvious line to finish by the asteroid block.

Milky Way 22m HVS 5a *. C. Moody, C. Grindley. 14th September 2002.
In from Asteroid Groove, the Chasm branches. This route is on the prow beyond the branch; climb the west-facing crack.

Space Traveller 22m E1 5b **. J. Lines. 20th August 2002.
On the SW-facing wall. The central curving twin cracked corner.

Black Hole 25m E1 5b **. C. Moody, C. Grindley. 21st September 2002.
Right of Space Traveller is a right-slanting ramp. Make thin moves to gain the ramp. Follow it to the ledge then climb the steep corner crack. The start is slow to dry and was a bit damp.

Mink Walls:
About 50m north from Asteroid Chasm is the start of the Mink Walls, a red slab with an arching overlap.

The Mink 15m E1 5a *. J. Lines. 19th August 2002.
Climb the right side of the slab, just right of a hairline crack, to gain the start of the overlap/arch on the right. Follow the overlap leftwards to finish up a corner-groove.

The walls extend leftwards for 50m. About 40m left of The Mink is a hanging off-width corner. To the right is a nice flake/groove.

Abby 7m VS 5a *. J. Lines. 19th August 2002.
Climb the flake/groove.

Emma 7m VS 5a *. J. Lines. 19th August 2002.
Just to the right are some flakes going up a slab, the route.

THE GARVELLACHS, Eileach Naoimh (NM 6338 0931):
A landing on The Garvellachs produced a surprising climb up steep limestone rock leading to the mini lighthouse. This island is reputed to be the burying place of the mother of St. Columba, and is well worth a visit in its own right.

Like a Moth 30m Severe. K. V. Crocket, P. F. MacDonald. 17th September 2002.
Start under the light, where the lightning conductor runs down the cliff (avoid this in stormy weather!). Go up then left across the wall to a jutting nose. Continue up then left across a grey wall to ledge. Finish up short wall to belay at light.
Note: C. Orr and M. Slesser climbed a route to the right, following the lightning conductor, probably Severe.

SKYE
SGURR NA H-UAMHA, East Face:
The Crescent 150m (then scrambling) Very Difficult. S.Kennedy, D. Ritchie 21st July 2002.
High on the left side of the east face is a prominent hanging groove topped by an overhanging wall. This is well left of Aslan's Tongue. The face to the left of the groove drops down into a corner and forms an extensive area of slabs. Approach from An Glas-choire and traverse away leftwards along a grassy terrace until directly below the groove. Start in a small grassy bay and follow a basalt fault over a small bulge to gain the right side of a small hanging slab. Climb the slab into the main groove which almost forms a gully in the lower section (45m). Move left from the base of the groove on to a slabby wall. Follow a crackline until below the overhanging wall (60m). Traverse up leftwards to the buttress edge in a fine position. Move up the edge then pull back right to reach the easier upper section of the face (45m). Scrambling leads to the summit.

SGURR NAN GILLEAN, Lota Corrie (NG 473 252):
The following routes are situated on a clean buttress high on the south-west slopes

of Lota Corrie below the south-east ridge of Sgurr nan Gillean. Approach by a diagonal descent from the tourist path on south east ridge across broken ground. The buttress presents a slabby left-hand section and becomes progressively steeper towards the right culminating in a deep chimney. Another steep buttress lies to the right again with a prominent flake crack near the top. The routes are described from right to left.

Arbroath 50m VS 4c/5a **. D. Ritchie, N. MacGougan. 22nd September 2002. Takes the striking line of cracks just left of the deep chimney finishing up a steep upper wall.

Fairy Nuff 45m Severe 4a *. S. Kennedy, A. MacDonald. 22nd September 2002.
Start on the right of a detached pinnacle well left of Arbroath and beyond some steep corners. Climb the left side of the pinnacle to a block. Move out left, then up and back right into an obvious fault running to the top. Follow the fault.

Adamant 45m Severe 4a *. S. Kennedy, A. MacDonald. 22nd September 2002.
Shares the same start as Fairy Nuff. From the top of the pinnacle move out left to the edge then finish directly up cracks and slabs.

Faded Message 45m Severe 4a *. D. Ritchie, N. MacGougan. 22nd September 2002.
A short distance left is a basalt fault which runs up diagonally leftwards. Climb the initial section of the fault into a short chimney/groove at 5m. Step right onto a wall right of a tiny groove. Climb straight up following a short groove at mid height and a blocky bulge to finish.

Ladies Day 48m Very Difficult. S. Kennedy, A. MacDonald. 22nd September 2002.
Climb the basalt fault all the way out left for 25m to the left edge. Climb a groove to slabs then finish up right.

GLEN SLIGACHAN CRAGS, Sgurr na h-Uamha:
Situated on the lower slopes of Sgurr na h-Uamha, close to where Harta Corrie meets the main glen, is a small heart-shaped slabby buttress (NG 487 242).
Hartatak 90m VS 4c. S. Kennedy, D. Ritchie, M. Shaw. June 2002.
Takes a diagonal line from right to left. The slabby buttress has a recessed area in the middle with two small bulges low down. To the right of the bulges are some pale streaks. A narrow grassy ledge runs diagonally left across the slab. From the right side of the slab, roughly below the right-hand bulge, follow a line leading diagonally left, above and parallel to the grassy ledge. A flake-line leads to near the left edge just below a small grassy recess (45m). Traverse back right along a narrow ledge to the middle of the slab then directly up via some short corners (45m).

Riabhach Wall:
Coolin Off 20m E1 5a ***. A. Baugh. 31st December 2002.
At the right-hand side of the wall is a prominent blunt rib. Start at a fault

immediately right of this and trend up and left to reach a horizontal break with poor protection. Make insecure moves to gain better holds above, and then monkey out wildly to gain a huge bucket. Finish up the easier rib left of the corner above.

Taliban Groove 20m E1 5a *. S. Broadbent, K. Wigmore. 31st December 2002.
The shallow corner in the steep headwall right of Kandahar is a bold and technical undertaking. Start as for The Groove but follow the left-hand crack to a small ledge. From here make precarious moves leftwards before finishing up the superbly exposed groove.

Around the corner at the left end of Riabhach Wall, before the North Buttress is reached, there is a small buttress about 10m high. Three corners have been climbed here, all at Difficult standard.

North Buttress:
A short distance further around the corner lies another larger and more intimidating buttress. On the north face of this buttress there are a number of lower grade climbs on immaculate rock. The first of these starts at the extreme right of the wall, just below a steep corner at the foot of the grassy ramp.

Alison's Rib 25m Difficult. K. Wigmore, G. Damerell. 31st December 2002.
Climbs the vague rib to the right of a prominent square corner. The initial few metres are the hardest part of the route, with pleasant easier climbing above.

Electra 25m Very Difficult. S. Broadbent, C. Atkinson, K. Wigmore. 31st December 2002.
The square-cut corner at the right side of the wall is often damp but provides an entertaining and well protected climb.

Venus 25m Very Difficult *. A. Ross, K. Wigmore, S.Broadbent. 30th December 2002.
A good route with sparse protection. Start below ledges a few metres left of Electra and follow the easiest line straight up the blunt rib above.

Warmin Up 25m Mild Severe. A. Baugh, J. Wakeham, G. Damerell. 30th December 2002.
From the large ledge on Venus, make an airy but well-protected step left into the large depression in the centre of the upper wall. Climb straight up this and exit via a small slab above. Good, varied, and interesting climbing.

Faithless 25m E1 4c **. S. Broadbent, K. Wigmore, A. Ross. 30th December 2002.
Follows the vague basalt dyke up the centre of the face. Start just left of a rocky step on the grassy approach ramp. The climbing is interesting and sustained with barely any worthwhile protection.

Mercury Rib 25m Very Severe 4b ***. S. Broadbent, A. Ross, K. Wigmore. 30th December 2002.
A stunning pitch up the blunt arête at the left side of the North Face. The climbing

is superb and sustained on immaculate rock, though protection is worryingly sparse. Start just right of the arête and traverse up and left to gain a prominent niche on the arête itself (crux). Continue up the front of the arête until a large belay ledge is reached. From here the top of the crag is reached by easy scrambling.

Continuing around to the left of Mercury Rib on to the East Face of the buttress the rock becomes steeper and less solid. About 30m along the East Face there is a huge blank slab half way up the wall, with an overhung basalt dyke above. Running up from the left-hand side of this slab there is a tempting rightwards-slanting crack with a small overhang at half height. This is the rather adventurous:

Varsity Crack   55m   Very Severe *. S. Broadbent, A. Ross, K. Wigmore. 30th December 2002.
1. 25m. Follow the crack with relative ease, making several steps right onto the face. Belay in the unpleasant vegetated basalt dyke.
2. 30m 4c. The crack above the basalt is overhanging and often dirty, but does contain excellent holds. After a few difficult and exhilarating moves the gradient eases into pleasant scrambling right to the top of the crag.

High Crag, Black Wall (SMCJ 2001):
Directly below the Black Wall, out of sight from the approach, there is a shorter wall which offers climbs of more reasonable grades (The Lower Tier). The rock is fairly slow to dry, but can offer a number of worthwhile single pitch routes, described from right to left.

Bedrock   25m   Severe. S. Broadbent, K. Wigmore, A.Baugh. 29th December, 2002.
An interesting route that wanders up the walls and ledges at the right side of the crag. Start a few feet left of a shallow broken groove and climb the series of short steep walls above.

Jacob's Ladder   30m   Severe *. S. Broadbent, K. Wigmore. 29th December 2002.
An exciting route following an obvious diagonal line across the centre of the crag. Start up the rightwards slanting basalt ramp and climb up into the steep corner above. Pull awkwardly up the left side of a block before finishing to the right.

Haribo   20m   Very Severe 5a **. S. Broadbent, K. Wigmore, A. Baugh. 29th December 2002.
The prominent right-facing shallow corner provides a well-protected struggle! Reach the foot of the corner via a basalt ramp, and climb it on excellent side-pulls. Arrange protection before racing to the top on good but small holds. An excellent pitch.

High And Dry   15m   Hard Severe. A. Baugh. 29th December 2002.
Near the extreme left of the wall is a corner with two slanting cracks to its right. Climb between these and pull over onto an easier right-trending steep ramp. Romp up this to a tricky and exposed exit.

Pink Umbrella 10m Difficult *. G. Damerell. 29th December 2002.
Around the corner at the left end of the wall is an inviting small slab with an obvious diagonal crack. Follow the crack leftwards and continue over the bulge above.

SGURR DEARG, Coire na Banachdich:
Grey Rib 60m Severe. C. Moody, C. Grindley. 2nd August 2002.
The rib between North-West Buttress and Banachdich Gully. There is a chimney/gully just right of the route. It gets more sun than North-West Buttress but needs some trundling.
Note: Toolie Grooves has had a few failures, VS perhaps HVS.

SGURR THEARLAICH, West Face:
Note: Gully D (SMCJ 2002, p230) was climbed by D. Ritchie and M. Shaw, not N. MacGougan.

SRON NA CICHE, Cioch Buttress:
Rat on a Stick 50m E1. G. Ettle, J. Lyall. 17th September 2002.
1. 20m 5b Climb the crack just right of Stormy Petrel until near its top, then step delicately right and go boldly up to the big diagonal crack which is followed to below a steep wall.
2. 30m 5b Move a short way right and climb a tricky corner up the steep wall, then go easily to the top.
Note: Stormy Petrel was considered VS 5a.

The Nipple: R. Durran felt that the crux move across the top of the groove on the second pitch was at least 5c and that the route was very hard for the grade.

CD ROM 160m VS/HVS. G. Ettle, J. Lyall. 17th September 2002.
An eliminate line, some of which has been climbed before. Start at the stone shelter left of Cioch Direct.
1. 20m 4b Step on to a rib and climb through an overlap by a crack on the left. Follow the edge to a large ledge.
2. 40m 4b Follow cracks up the rib and slabs to belay in Cioch Direct.
3. 30m 4b Follow Cioch Direct for a few metres and go left to climb the corner-crack of Cioch Grooves until possible to break back right across Cioch Direct to a bay right of a steep prow.
4. 25m 5a/4b Either climb the scoop and pull left on to the rib (HVS) or go left up a ramp on to the top of blocks and up the rib to slabs (easier).
5. 45m 4a Follow slabs straight up to the base of The Cioch.

COIR' A' GHRUNNDA:
This route is on the prominent buttress at NG 449 202, left of the route to the Bealach Coir'a' Ghrunnda from the Upper Coire. Its steep profile is seen from well down the coire. It is reached in a few minutes from the lochan. This is possibly the buttress with Stormwatch but if so, the relationship with the route is unknown.

A Walk On Part In The War 50m E3 **. R. Durran, R. Pybus. 6th April 2002.
A direct line up the front face of the buttress. A little dubious rock on the first

pitch, but excellent rock and protection where needed. A superb and sustained second pitch. The most obvious feature of the lower part of the buttress is a large pale right facing and leaning corner. Start on the rake about 8m left of the corner's foot.

1. 30m 5c Gain the steep right-trending broken crackline from the left and follow it, with difficult moves at a small cracked roof and at the bulge above, to a broken ledge.

2. 20m 5c Move the belay about 8m right along the ledge. Above and on the left is an overhanging nose and a final cracked bulge above. Climb a short wall to a break below the nose. Pull onto the wall right of the nose and climb steeply leftwards to the final bulge. Cross this rightwards via the crack with difficulty and finish leftwards.

Alasdair-Thearlaich Cliff:
Stone Shoot Gully 90m Difficult. A. Nisbet. 13th September 2002.
The gully which goes up left from the base of T-D Gap Gully and leads into the scree which is the opposite side of the Great Stone Shoot. Perhaps climbed before but useful in boots as an exit from the cliff to Coire Lagan. Start as for Bower's Climb but soon go left into the gully. There is an obvious independent but harder start.

BLAVEN NOTE:
Several parties have had trouble finding Ecstasis, whose position may not be well described. The Whip (SMCJ 2001, p604) was after a failure to find Ecstasis. C. Dale climbed a route which he thought was Ecstasis, but it took the obvious left-slanting gangway on the wall about 100m left of Clough's Cleft (4c 4c 4b **, p3 being sensationally exposed on the last steep crack).

ELGOL, Suidhe Biorach:
Hairy Mary 35m VS/HVS 4b/c ***. D. McAulay, P. Johnstone. 15th May 2002.
Takes the exposed wall to the right of Fertility Right. The climb shares the start of Fertility Right but moves right to a platform at 10m, then up a wall and crack for 10m to a rightwards traverse along a break to finish up another crack and wall. The uncertain grading is due to a difference of opinion. A great addition to the easier routes here and is much better than the lichenous appearance suggests.

MINGINISH SOUTH:
Stac an Tuil 35m VSL (Very Severely Loose). S. M. Richardson, M. Robson. 21st September 2002.
This spectacular basalt stack is characterised by a huge hole that cuts through its base. It lies between Glen Brittle and Loch Eynort at NG 356 215. It stands 20m offshore below 200m crumbling basalt cliffs. The best descent lies to the north at NG 353 222 where an 80m abseil can be made to a rock platform. From here swim south for 800m to the stack to reach a plinth on the west side. Climb the west ridge via a series of cracks, which becomes progressively more difficult as it steepens and becomes more rotten as height is gained, to the (more solid) summit block. Stac an Tuil is one of the most inaccessible sea stacks in Scotland – it would be cheating to use a boat!

Stack of Ulbster   45m   VS. S.M. Richardson, M. Robson. 22nd September 2002.
Approach the stack (NG 340 416) by swimming 70m to a sloping platform on its
south side. From the west end of the platform climb a series of steep cracks just
left of a deep corner, then trend right along a chimney-ramp to finish.

MINGINISH, Talisker Point, Stac an Fhucadair:
West Ridge Variation   HVS 5a. C. Dale, L. Sell. May 2002.
A middle sized peg (not in situ) helps protect the first (crux) moves. Instead of
belaying on pegs in suspect rock, continue by traversing left for 10m to belay in
good dolerite. Then traverse leftwards with occasional good runners in "islands of
rock", then climb the steep "field" to the summit (peg hammer useful for step
cutting). The rock island of the summit was deemed solid enough for an abseil
descent down the steep south face.

Note: On the Lesser Stack, a 12ft sling allows a conventional abseil to be made.

DUIRINISH, Macleod's Maidens:
Note: C. Dale thought The Old Lady was 75m HVS 4c with p2 as 30m. The
moves past the flake on p3 were the crux, as the flake was potentially very
dangerous. p3 and p4 were best run together. An abseil descent was made from a
horn of rock just below the summit to reach the second stance.

DUNVEGAN HEAD, Am Famhair Sea Stack (SMCJ 2000):
A Peach for the Boys   15m   HVS 4c. R. I. Jones, O. Dewhirst. 22nd June 2002.
Climbs the south-east face of the stack. Climb direct up the middle of the wall and
through the overlaps at the top. Belay above the arch. A more solid and enjoyable
line compared to the north-west face and has a belay!

NEIST, The Upper Crag, Financial Sector:
C. Moody notes that Lottery Live (SMCJ 2002) is a left start to Gammy's Purse
(SMCJ 1999), joining it after 5m but is not as intimidating as the original start.
Jam For Brains (SMCJ 1999) is the same as Worm's Eye View (SMCJ 1997).

The Fin:
The Furry Horse   El 5b. A. Cave, N. McAdie, D. Green. 29th May 1995.
An adventurous route.
1. Climb up the front face of the fin right of centre. Not too hard but has a
committing feel. Belay on top of the fin.
2. Continue along the ridge in alpine style turning towers on the right.

The Lower Crag, Destitution Point:
Come Around to my Way of Thinking   25m   El 5b **. D. McAulay, M. MacCuish.
28th June 2002.
The crack/corner immediately right of Man of Straw. Excellent and well protected
on clean rock.

As seen from the Financial Sector, the next routes are on a small headland to the
north (Destitution Point?), round to the north of the south-facing prow. The climbs
are very short on good rock.

Yan Taylor on the first ascent of Charger the Tiger E2, Raven's Crag, Mull, with Rum in the background.
Photo: Danny Brooks, (Colin Moodie collection).

Neaster's Crack E1 5b (G. Strange and R. Archbold, 30th May 1998.)
An obvious crack, the first good feature on the west wall round from the prow.
Black Groove Hard Severe (RA and GS. 30th May 1998.) A pleasant line a little further north.

Note: Three corner lines were reported by T. Blakemore. They are located by diagram and C. Moody has repeated them. Fine rock, Severe to VS.

The Ramp:
No Access Severe. C. Moody. 24th August 2002
The right-facing corner crack right of Patricia.

An t-Aigeach:
Overcharged E4 6a **. A. Cave, S. Nadin. May 1995.
1. Climb a shaped crack to the right of Supercharger and belay under a bulge.
2. Move up and right in a superb position on good holds until a right-trending crack can be reached. Follow this to the ledge of Supercharger and finish up that route

Conductor Cove:
Vidal Sassoon E3 6a. S. Muir, S. Johnston, S. McBride, M. Saunders. 2003.
The wall 2m to the left of Natural Look, climbed direct with small wires for protection.

WATERNISH:
Caisteal an Fhithich 60m Difficult. C. Dale. 15th May 2002.
This 30m stack is at NG 263 647. Down climb steep grass and rock steps opposite the stack to land on a boulder beach, accessible at all states of tide. Traverse northwards at sea level to gain a grassy ramp line on the seaward face. This leads to the summit. A "rock and two veg" experience, with lots of orchids.
Note: Repeated by M. Hudson on 28th October, 2002 and thought Very Difficult.

Rogheadh (NG 216 602):
The Arches 60m Difficult. C. Dale. 15th May 2002.
At low tide the seaward extremity of a granite-like protruding dyke can be gained. Follow this pleasantly over twin arches and a grassy continuation ridge to finish via a short steep corner. A "rock and one veg" experience.

TROTTERNISH, The Storr:
On the spur leading north from the summit of the Storr, some smaller outcrops of dolerite occur at 500m altitude, above and south of Carn Liath (NG 493 552). For the gentlest and most picturesque approach take the Old Man path from the car park then follow north as for the summit, traversing the bowl of upper Coire Scamadal on a good path to a plateau on the spur 200m south of Carn Liath.

A 10m high band of cliffs extend west for 100m featuring some wet corners of little interest. But some longer possibilities exist on a buttress that runs down the steep hillside below this band of cliffs. It is separated from the higher band by a distinctive square doorway, a collapse between the top of the buttress and the higher band. This buttress actually appears to be a wide dyke about 100m high. Two routes climb the buttress from its toe. Scramble down a gully east or easier slopes west of the buttress to shattered shelves at its foot. An open black chimney takes the centre of the buttress.

North East Outcrops Guidebook Editor Neil Morrison on Family Life, E3 5c, Bridal Cave, Longhaven Sea Cliffs. Photo: John Wilson.

Unswept Chimney 40m Severe. M. Hudson, N. Williams. 28th September 2002.
Follow the black chimney easily to a rightward swing on a blunt beak at 15m.
Continue more easily above until it is possible to step left into a short V-corner.
Finish up this and scramble up the blunt nose to the rock band a little higher.
Traverse off into the east gully or continue easily up the rib, to an abseil descent
into the doorway.

Catwalk Tower 40m HVS 4c *. M. Hudson, N. Williams. 28th September 2002.
The front face of the blocky tower immediately left of the chimney. Marvellous
positions and trustworthy rock. Start as before. Step left out of the chimney on to
the front of the rib. Move carefully up on a series of small ledges (unprotected).
From the left-hand end of the highest ledge, step on to the blunt arête poised over
the gully. Using some rather airy footholds (crux), gain a spacious ledge and
runners. Mount blocks and a delicate wall above with sustained interest to the
same belay as Unswept Chimney. Descent as before.

STAFFIN, Sgeir Bhan (Staffin Slip North), Toy Buttress:
Directly below the scramble descent to Staffin Slip North lies a small crumbly
buttress of rock. Below again lies a wider tier of medium height shrouded by trees
and hard of access due to the legbreaking terrain at its foot. The rock here is some
of the soundest in the area, and the routes have clean finishes on to the meadow
above with good tree belays. This and the slightly gentler angle of 70-80 degrees
makes these routes more leisurely undertakings than the routes on the higher
buttress.
Approach: Drop down either to the right-hand side of the buttress from Frequent
Flyer area, or to the left-hand side from the Earthquake area. Or, for a fuller preview
of the buttress, walk in from below by following the coastline round from the jetty
and cutting rightwards up a grassy strip once level with a pair of huge salt and
pepper pots on the coast.

Hold Music 25m HVS 5a *. M. Hudson, A. Hutt. 30th September 2002.
Five metres left of Above and Beyond past an ivy-filled gully is a slim pillar
capped by a diagonal roof. This is the last-but-one pillar of the whole tier. The line
takes cracks up the face of the pillar to the roof which is passed at its right-hand
end. Surprisingly clean rock with good large to extra-large gear. Climb the steep
jamcrack past a footless section. Step left briefly to a flake-crack and hand traverse
back right under the roof. Fight up through the bulges (crux) to finish.

FLODIGARRY:
A First 25m Very Difficult. D. McAulay, M. MacCuish. 25th June 2002.
This route can be found just south of the main climbing on a clean buttress to the
right of Buoy Racer, reached by abseiling from half way down the arête on the
south of the bay containing Newspaper Taxis. The buttress is just right of a large
corner/zawn and starts from a large block. The line climbs the wall starting at a
shallow scoop just right of a thin crack line and trends left to gain the crack at half
height.

KILMALUAG, Stac Buidhe:
Note: Original Route and North Ridge (Skye guide, p334) appear to be the same
route. C. Dale thought VS 4c and provided a new description.
Stacan Lachlainn:

South-East Face 30m VS 4c. C. Dale, L. Sell. 26th May 2002.
First climbed in the 19th century by local man Lachlann McLeod, this stack is accessible at most states of tide. From the boulder beach which attaches the stack to the mainland, traverse right (eastwards). Once on the SE face, make an ascending traverse rightwards on good solid rock to gain easy grassy slopes. Return leftwards to belay directly above the start.

RUBHA HUNISH:
The Big Breakfast 25m VS 4c. J. and D. Preston. 20th July 2002.
The corner-crack on the mainland cliff directly opposite the narrow gap of Split Stack. Start by stepping off a pointed boulder right of the wide hanging crack. Climb steeply up the corner passing two useful flakey chokestones until a step left can be made. Follow the main crack pleasantly to the top.

Split Stack:
Note: C. Dale thinks that the "easy scramble" approach down the gully is anything but easy and most folk would prefer to abseil.

Forty 30m E3 5c. C. Dale, L. Sell. 29th May 2002.
At the base of the descent gully, at mid to low tide, climb up 5m to gain the rift that separates the two summits of the stack. Climb through the rift seaward and turn left to traverse the NE face of the northern summit on easy ledges. Continue to gain the slender NW face, overlooking the north stack. The route starts here.
  A well protected sustained climb on perfect rock, easy for the grade. Climb the central crack/groove until moves can be made rightwards to gain a ledge on the arête. Climb the steep wall just right of the arête on huge holds to the top of the north summit.
  The excursion can be continued by traversing to the south summit (Severe) and abseiling from here.

BORNESKETAIG, Stack of Skudiburgh:
Note: C. Dale reports that the 'hairtrigger' state of the summit area has been improved. Extensive rock stabilisation has been carried out on the seaward face and summit area. There will inevitably be some small loose rocks on the seaward face route but the route should now be intrinsically solid.

Rubh a' Chairn Liath (NG 364 706):
The Obelisk 60m HVS. C. Dale, K. Grindrod. 10th June 2002.
Park at the slipway and approach via an awkward bourdery hillside and beach westwards to arrive beneath a grooved pillar leading to a land-based pinnacle summit.
1. 25m 4c Climb the cleaned groove to exit leftwards to a ledge and stance a few metres higher.
2. 35m 5a Climb the groove directly above. After pulling through a bulge at 10m, step right and continue up a crackline to finish up the wall right of an obvious but very loose flake.
To descend, a 5m abseil gained the col behind the pinnacle and a 5m wall was climbed to a grass plateau. A return to the base of the climb can be made by a long detour to the west.

NORTHERN HIGHLANDS SOUTH AND WEST
(VOLUME ONE)

KNOYDART, Gleouraich:
Peekaboo Gully   200m   I/II. D. Morris. 16th February 2003.
This climbs the deep gully on the right side of the face leading to the East top of
Gleouraich. The true line is hidden until right beneath the gully where the route
becomes obvious. Climb the gully direct over several steps. The grade can vary
depending upon the snow build-up.

Skinny Gully   100m   II. D. Morris. 16th February 2003.
This climbs the thin gully bounding the right side of the buttress on the north side
of the col between Gleouraich and Spidean Mialach. Climb the gully past a
narrowing at one-third height and continue to the col.

SOUTH GLEN SHIEL, Creag Coire an t-Slugain:
Hourglass Groove   120m   IV,6 *. J. Colverd, E. Gillespie, A. Nisbet. 16th February
2003.
A narrowing groove system on the vague crest between The Triangle and Pioneer
Gully. Start just left of Pioneer Gully and climb an icefall into the turfy groove
system. Climb this to where it narrows into twin shallow grooves and go up these,
keeping left above to reach an easier finishing pitch.

SGURR NAN CONBHAIREAN, West Crag (NH 124 136):
A rather broken crag on the north side of the west ridge of Sgurr nan Conbhairean
(Alt 900m, North-West facing). To approach, start as for the other crags on the
mountain but continue to Gorm Lochan and go up a gully to the col between it and
Drochaid an Tuill Easaich. Go west for 30m and descend a gully on the north side.
The only significant buttress is on the east of the descent gully.

Category Five   100m   II. A. Nisbet. 31st October 2002.
Climb a system of grooves just right of the crest of the buttress.

MORUISG, The Great Grey Slab of Moruisg:
Slapstick   95m   HVS. E. Christison, B. Fyffe, D. McGimpsey, A. Nisbet. 1st
September 2002.
A direct line up the blankest slab available. Start from the same ledge as Rock
Surfer, at the base of the right-rising overlap.
1. 45m 4c Climb up, then go diagonally right above the overlap along a line of
quartz before going straight up the smooth slab left of Rock Surfer to the terrace.
The line could be climbed truly direct but there was a wet streak on the line and a
runner to the right.
2. 50m 4c Climb the easy slab as for Rock Surfer, but then continue direct up the
blank slab right of the corner and between two grassy cracks.

SGURR CHOINNICH, North Face (NH 076 446):
The crag is often in condition. The rock is a variety of rather demoralised schist
that lends itself to form tottering crannies and rather unreliable protection. All this

is irrelevant if properly frozen and the turf is excellent. There are five right-slanting gully lines on the face.

Occluded Ridge 150m II. V. Chelton, N. Harrison, D. McGimpsey. 20th January, 2003.
Start up and right of the long toe at the left-hand end of the main face. From the back of the bay, climb turf up and left into the left-hand of the twin gullies above. Climb two tricky steps then continue up easier ground, moving into the right-hand gully below the top.

Stirling Moss 250m IV,4 **. J. R. Mackenzie, D. Allan (alt). 19th March 2003.
Takes the discontinuous hanging ramp directly below the summit (leftmost gully). A fine line with much variety. Start 40m left of the easier-angled curved ramp line that is the most obvious line on the cliff. The discontinuous ramp is bottomed by mixed ground and ice with a straight snow section which is prominent from below.
1. 50m Climb up to and past the snow section to a little cave.
2. 55m Step left on to thin ice that leads to tricky rock and turf steps which lead to the hidden ramp above (possible belay). Continue up snow to a shelf on the right.
3. 50m Climb pleasant snow and ice steps up the ramp to a tiny cave below a steep iced corner.
4. 45m Climb the fine corner either by ice or turf and continue straight up the ramp to below the steep headwall up on the right.
5. 50m Step right, then move back left and climb past a rockfall scar with some difficulty. Continue straight up steep walls and little ledges to finally traverse left to below a jutting block. Climb past this and up snow to the summit cairn. A complex pitch with some dubious rock.
Note: Also recorded as Baghdad Bypass, III ** by D. Allan.

Chemical Alley 140m IV,4 **. D. Allan, D. Moy. 25th February, 2003.
The second from the right of the five gully lines. It has a steep middle pitch.

The Bow 100m II *. D. Allan, D. Bell, E. Christison, D. McGimpsey. 17th March, 2003.
Climb the long right-facing corner at the right hand end of the main face. It held an excellent 50m pitch of continuous ice on this occasion.

Downhill Racer 150m I/II *. J. R. Mackenzie. 19th March 2003.
This is a Y-shaped and rightmost gully in the centre of the main face. It was descended on perfect neve coated with a thin layer of water ice, was quite steep and had a little ice pitch near the narrows at its base. The gully also has a left-hand exit which looks more or less the same grade.

MAOILE LUNNDAIDH, Toll a' Choin:
The Shiner 80m III,4. P. and G. Robertson. February, 2003.
Takes the wider and less steep icy scoop defining the right side of the Spiral Search buttress (see below). A fine if short climb on more or less continuous water ice.

Hellfire and Brimstone 110m VII,7. G. Robertson, M. Halls, P. Ebert. 4th January 2003.

The steep buttress with Spiral Search (SMCJ 2001) has two obvious gully lines at its left end. This route starts at the base of the right-hand gully and trends up slightly right before tackling the bulging headwall direct. The first pitch may share some ground with Spiral Search. A fine route with some unlikely and strenuous climbing.

1. 45m From the base of the gully, traverse right into a steep groove and climb this to gain easier ground. Continue in the same line then pull on to an obvious right-slanting hanging ramp. Belay at its right end below a very steep groove with a crack in its right wall.

2. 15m Climb the groove to its apex, then make hard moves out right into another groove that leads to a commodious belay in a recess.

3. 50m Exit the recess via a flared chimney on the left then continue up an overhanging groove to below a roof. Pull leftwards through the roof and continue up more or less directly with diminishing difficulty to the top.

FB Gully 100m IV,4. P. and G. Robertson. February, 2003.
Takes the fine narrow gully defining the right side of the Spiral Search buttress. Soloed in perfect conditions, providing around 80m of continuous water ice.

GLAS BHEINN, Creag na h-Iolaire:
Two routes on the section of crag left of Greenhorn Gully.

Frozen Pipes 90m III. A. Matthewson, A. Tibbs, H. Tibbs. 4th January 1995.
Start up a curving gully seen on the approach from Tullich (New Kelso Couloir). Go easily along a terrace to the right until an obvious pinnacle/huge flake is reached (route length from here). The right end of the terrace overlooks Greenhorn Gully. Go up the icefall left of the pinnacle, then easier up a gully to the top.

New Kelso Couloir 180m II. R. Blackburn, E. Blackburn. 4th January 1995.
The curving gully, via its right fork (left fork is hidden on the approach).

BEINN BHAN, Coire na Poite:
Harlequin Rib Right-Hand 265m V,7. C. Dale and party. 12th February 2003.
An ascent of Harlequin Rib by a line suitable for the prevailing lean conditions (2PA). Start a short way up Mad Hatters Gully.

1. Traverse a horizontal terrace leftwards to the foot of a left-facing slabby corner-groove which bounds the extreme right edge of the "steep wall" (the original route turns its left edge).

2. Climb the corner and turfy cracks to a "blank exit" up a smooth slab (1PA).

3. Traverse easily leftwards for 20m.

4. Climb a slabby wall by a central turfy weakness, then continue more easily to beneath the next steep band.

5. Climb this by gaining an obvious right to left ascending traverse line. Follow this to its end, then climb a short groove to a blind and rounded finish. A poor peg was use as a handhold to traverse an undercut slab; continue up the subsequent groove.

6 etc. Continue much more easily.

SGURR A' CHAORACHAIN, A' Chioch:

Rapid Pulse 70m El. G. Ettle, J. Lyall. 12th September 2002.
1. 25m 5b Climb the left-facing corner 10m left of Impulse.
2. 45m Easy ribs and slabs lead to a grass ledge and descent as for Impulse.

Cioch Nose Superdirect VII,8 ***. C. Dale, M. Moran. 5th February 2003.
An ascent was made during winter 1986 by John Sylvester and Dave Toombs but not recorded and it is uncertain what conditions were like. The 2003 ascent recorded pitch grades of 7, 8, 8, 6/7, 6. Five pitches of sustained technical well protected climbing. The party were not inclined to continue up Cioch Corner which in any event was fairly bare of snow. A winter ascent of the combination in a single push would be a grade VIII "tour de force".

BEN DAMPH FOREST, Creag Dubh an t-Sall:

NOTE: At the left (north) end, the crack on a side wall is a short Severe. To its right is a deep chockstoned crack (Very Difficult) which leads to a ledge. Walk right and climb the corner behind a tree to finish. The next prominent feature to the right is a big wet black corner.

Unnamed 10m Very Difficult. D. McGimpsey. 14th July 2002.
Climb the arête to the right of the black corner and the wall above, trending right above a small holly.

Unnamed 15m El 5a *. D. McGimpsey, E. Christison. 14th July 2002.
Two slabby right-facing corners lie 15m right of Bombus. Climb the right corner and step left on to a small ledge. Cross an overlap and finish up a wall. Small RP's useful.

Creag na Speireag:

Unnamed 30m E3 6a **. D. McGimpsey, A. Nisbet. 20th June 2002.
The most continuous crackline in the middle section of crag has a hard but well protected section. A low horizontal break leads right from near the base of One Cog Missing. About 15m right is a pink streak emerging from the left end of a wide section of crack. The crack itself passes a block on its right to pass the right end of this wide section of horizontal crack. Climb the crack past the wide section and steeply above to make a thin move on to easier angled ground leading to the main horizontal break. Pass its capping roof on the left (or direct up the crack, harder), return to the crack and finish up it.

Cuir Tigear Na Do Thanc, Easier Version E1 5b (overall). D. McGimpsey, A. Nisbet 20th June 2002.
Go up the first crack to below its top, then pull out right. Traverse right (crux) to a flake line leading back left to the top of the second crack of the direct route and finish as for that route.

BEINN EIGHE, West Buttress:

Note: A large rockfall in West Central Gully was noted in March 2003.

Creag Mhor (Independent Pineapple Cliff):
Smilodon 100m IV,5. D. McGimpsey, A. Nisbet. 5th January 2003.
By the summer route except that the groove was climbed direct throughout.

TORRIDON CRAGS, Seana Mheallan, Western Sector:
Heather Said Sunshine HVS 5a *. C. Moody, C. Grindley. 10th August 2002.
Just left of Polythene Bag. Climb a short black corner, go over a bulge and follow a crack up leftwards.

Better than a Slap in the Face Severe. C. Moody, C. Grindley. 10th August 2002.
Right of Polythene Bag is a slabby wall topped by a bulge. Climb the left side of the wall, over the bulge using a rib and continue to the top.

Luing Rib Very Difficult. C. Moody. 10th August 2002.
Climb the short slabby wall left of Mr Bean. Go left into the corner to avoid the overhang then back right and continue up pleasant rock right of the edge.

Lap Land 20m Severe *. C. Moody, C. Grindley. 10th August 2002.
Left of Quartz Warts. Take a line through two overlaps to a heather ledge, then a short wall to finish.

KINLOCHEWE, Meall an Ghobhar (NH 026 643)
This route is situated on one of the many crags which border the higher ramp of Bac an t-Sniomha. The first proper crag encountered on the ramp is orange, overhanging and stands above a deep bed of deer droppings. This route lies 70m further up the ramp.

The Blitz 50m HVS. C. Dale, P. and A. Lunn. 30th May 2001.
Start about 10m left of deep tree-filled recess at the foot of a left-facing corner-crack. The route was extensively cleared of blocks on lead but care is still needed.
1. 25m 4c Climb the corner-crack to a ledge system. Move along this for 4m and climb a short steep wall (crux) to gain a short right-facing corner. Climb this and traverse left to the base of a fine right-trending gangway, followed to an eyrie stance.
2. 25m 4b Climb up 2m to gain a ledge system running rightwards into a corner. Follow this to the top.

GAIRLOCH CRAGS, Creag Bhadan an Aisg, Curtain Wall:
Windhover 12m E2 5b. P. Tattersall, J. Buchanan. 19th March 2002.
Go directly up to an alcove with a small tree. A heathery exit.

Hobbyhorse 12m E3 5c P. Tattersall. 10th June 2002.
The widish crackline (second from right).

LOCH TOLLAIDH, Raven's Nest:
BaBa 15m E6 6b. P. Tattersall. 13th April 2002.
A strenuous well-protected line right of Blow-out.

Ming Mong 35m E5 6a *. M. Garthwaite, R. Anderson. 8th April 2002.
Start up MacDonald to the left end of the diagonal overlap. Place a good nut on

the left and make a long move straight over. Follow the overlap rightwards using holds below and above to join, then finish up Feathering the Nest. Micro-wires useful.

Gairloch Wall:
Steer Clear 15m E5 6b. P. Tattersall. 16th July 2002.
The rib between Ageing Bull and The Imposter with a boulder problem start.

Dinosaur Buttress:
Off The Bone 20m HVS 5b *. R. and C. Anderson. 6th April 2002.
Swing rightwards above the roof a short way up In the Pink and climb directly to the top, eliminate.

Reeperbahn 20m E4 6a/b. P. Tattersall. 19th May 2002.
The wall and hanging groove left of Scarlatina.

Ewe Walls:
Right On 15m HVS 5b. R. Anderson, M. Garthwaite. 8th April 2002.
Just left of New Horizons, climb a thin crack to a wide crack, then swing out right and climb directly to the top.

Frozen in Time 20m E1 5a. T. Doe, A. Gorman. 20th August 2002.
The wall right of New Horizons.

Left Out 15m E1 5b. R. Anderson, M. Garthwaite. 7th April 2002.
The obvious left slanting crackline immediately left of Right On.

Peweky 20m E1 5b **. M. Garthwaite, R. Anderson. 7th April 2002.
Climbs the right side of the arête between Incisor and Ewereka.

Hidden Crag:
Monte Cristo 35m E2 5b **. R. and C. Anderson. 6th April 2002.
The thin crackline immediately right of Malpasso and just left of the corner. Climb as for Malpasso to above the grass ledges, then move up right to a steepening and the crack.

Unnamed Crag:
A small crag of fine compact rock, just left of and set back from the top of Hidden Crag. The crackline on the right side has been climbed (HVS 5a with a finish out right just below the top). At its highest point at the base of the crag an obvious wide crack provides a break in the small lower section of the cliff, with an obvious heathery fault slanting up leftwards just to its left. All routes start here.

The Walline 15m E2 5a/b **. R. and C. Anderson. 10th April 2002.
The centre of the wall immediately left of the crackline, passing a small rock scar.

The Nextline 15m E1 5a *. R. and C. Anderson. 10th April 2002.
Immediately left of The Walline. Climb the initial wall and make a few moves leftwards up the heathery fault to a tiny roof, then swing out right and climb the wall to the top.

Fraggle Rock:
Tall in the Saddle   25m   E6 6b. P. Tattersall. 20th July 2002.
The white wall left of Heave-ho. (Toprope practiced)

Top Crag Left:
Poles Apart   20m   E2 5b *. R. and C. Anderson. 8th April 2002.
Just left of Dr Beaker, climb to the left end of a horizontal roof crack, then pull up left into a shallow rising line of weakness and follow this up right to a tiny niche, then swing out left and climb the crack in the wall above.

Top Crag Right:
Nippy Heed   15m   E3 5b. M. Garthwaite R. Anderson. 7th April 2002.
Climb the centre of the wall going up, then slightly passing a thread (wire) near the top. Worthless protection although the climbing does ease a bit towards the top.

Itty Bitty Gritty   15m   E1 5a. M. Garthwaite R. Anderson. 7th April 2002.
The rightward trending line immediately right of Nippy Heed to a ledge, then up the groove above.

GRUINARD CRAGS, The Beach Wall:
Saga of Sewage   10m   E5 6a. P. Tattersall. 29th March 2002.
A thin crackline on the left side of the steep wall at the right-hand end of the crag.

Post Crag:
Instantly Forgettable   10m   VS 4c. A. Cunningham, J. Dale. 23rd May 2002.
Start near the right end of the crag. Climb up steep blocky ground just left of a dirty left-facing corner and finish awkwardly onto the terrace.

Bog Meadow Crags:
Bloody Flake   10m   VS 5a *. A. Cunningham, J. Dale. 23rd May 2002.
The next crag right of the short right-hand section of Bog Meadow Wall is a narrow buttress split by flake cracks. This route climbs the undercut flake corner crack a few metres up left of the toe of the buttress. Start under a chimney crack and swing right and up to the overlap. Climb the corner and flake to its top and continue to the glacis. Possibly done before.

Inveranvie Crag, Lower Tier:
Haywire   20m   VS 4c. A. Cunningham, J. Dale. 21st May 2002.
A route up and left of Temporary Beauty, left of the ivy patch. Start at black streaked slabby rock left of a grassy fault. Climb into a crack in a shallow left-facing corner. Move up and right into a crack in the slab and up to the bulge. Move awkwardly left into a wider crack through the bulge and finish up this.

Optic Wall:
The Saloon of Life   20m   E2 5b **. P. Tattersall, T. Doe. 12th May 2002.
Right of the end of Optic Wall, the crag turns uphill into a sidewall. To the right of a tree filled fault about half way up the sidewall is a fine clean steep prow. This

route climbs a crackline splitting the prow. Start up the slab below the prow and pull right onto it at a flake. Climb steeply into the crack and follow this line direct through bulges and all to the top.
Note: Repeated by A. Cunningham and M. Blyth on 26th May 2002 and named Spit and Polish (same grade).

Inverianvie Crag, Yellow Wall:
Predator   20m   E3 5c. P. Tattersall, A. Tattersall, T. Doe. 16th June 2002.
The groove-line on the left.

Bloomsday   20m   E5 6a. P. Tattersall, T. Doe. 16th June 2002.
The thin left-slanting crackline on the right.

Riverside Slabs (NG 958 890):
These are 20m slabs lying immediately above the Inverianvie river path, just past the turnoff for Dog Crag and with an obvious holly tree at the right-hand end. The climbing is good but the quality is reduced by a degree of mossy rock. There is a left-hand section, a heather filled fault, a main central section followed by another heathery fault and a final rib on the right. Descend to the right.

Pipistrelle Crack   18m   HVS 5a. A Cunningham, A. Fyffe. 9th October 2002.
Climbs the left-hand buttress. Start at the lowest point and climb directly into a pod. Follow cracks left and up to a horizontal break. Move right, climb a short mossy crack and move right again to finish up the crack in the centre of the buttress.

The next routes are on the central section.

Blues Before Sunrise   20m   HVS 5a *. A. Fyffe, A. Cunningham. 9th October 2002.
Start by a thin right diagonal crack at the left end of a low heather ledge. Climb direct to gain thin cracks leading to the base of a left-facing mossy corner. Finish by the obvious left diagonal crack.

Passing Glance   20m   VS 4c. A. Cunningham, A. Fyffe. 9th October 2002.
The obvious crack springing from a recess and lower left-facing dirty corner. Start left of the corner and heather patch and climb cracks in a vague rib to the base of the main crack. From its top move right and up to finish.

Blitzkrieg Bop   20m   E1 5b *. A. Cunningham, A. Fyffe. 9th October 2002.
A right trending line starting from the right end of the low heather ledge. Climb up and through a shallow slot to gain the right slanting crack and up this to below the heather. Trend right and up to finish.

Sunlight Slab   20m   MVS 4b *. A. Fyffe, A. Cunningham. 9th October 2002.
Follows thin cracks in the slab split by a heather ledge. Start by some pale streaks and climb cracks to the ledge. Continue up the cracks heading right towards the edge and finish up a more obvious crack returning left.

Autumn Rib 18m　Severe *. A. Fyffe, A. Cunningham. 9th October 2002.
The rib right of the right-hand heather fault. Climb obvious clean cracks up the rib with a deviation on to the left edge at the top section.

Echolocation 12m　Hard Severe. A. Fyffe, A. Cunningham. 9th October 2002.
The left arête of the block right of the holly tree. Start on the front face and follow the obvious crack over the arête to finish up its left side.

Jetty Crag:
Pikeys Wall HVS 5a. G. Ettle, J. Lyall. May 2001.
Between Buttress Crack and Route 6 is a more direct version of previous routes.
Ascend the dark recess to step left and climb pillar direct.

Carn Dearg an Droma, Weird Crag (NG 974 947, South facing):
This seemingly insignificant and scrappy crag lies on a knoll north of the high point of Carn Dearg an Droma; about 25 minutes walk from parking at NG 981 934 on the A832. It is an unusual sandstone conglomerate with sometimes huge boulders dubiously embedded in a shattered looking matrix. Contrary to first impressions, the rock is solid and runs to jugs and incuts, especially on the more weathered rock, allowing steep climbs at an amenable grade. The crag about 60m long and steadily rises from 8m at either end to a maximum height of about 18m in the middle where it is hugely undercut. The protection is generally very good, as are the views! The crag may be the same as in the following note:
Note from SMCJ 1947 by J. H. B. and P. Bell: A remarkable undercut face of Torridonain sandstone on Card Dearg an Droma, about 1 mile NW of the road afforded a few short climbs.

Near the left end of the crag is an obvious chimney set in a right-facing corner.

Blood Brothers 8m　Severe. M. Blyth, A. Cunningham. 11th May 2002.
Start at the base of the chimney and climb a left-trending crack in the left wall.
Finish straight up.

Clotting Agent 10m　Hard Severe 4c. M. Blyth, A. Cunningham. 11th May 2002.
About 6m right of Blood Brothers is a right-facing corner with a grassy bay near its base. Pull over the bulge and into the grassy bay. Finish up the corner.

Wedgetarian 12m　E1 5b *. A. Cunningham, M. Blyth. 11th May 2002.
About 6m right of Clotting Agent is a thin steep crackline leading through a series of bulges. Climb the crack direct, passing a lichenous jammed block near the top.

Burnt Offering 10m　Severe **. A. Cunningham, M. Blyth. 11th May 2002.
The next obvious feature to the right is a steep right-facing corner with a bulge near the top. Climb the corner moving onto the left edge at the bulge.

Below! 15m　E1 5a *. M. Blyth, A. Cunningham. 11th May 2002.
Start about 2m right of the corner of Burnt Offering. Climb to a handrail leading right to the edge and up this on good holds to a roof. Pull through at a short right-facing corner and easier to finish.

Ban the Burn 18m E1 5b **. A. Cunningham, M. Blyth. 11th May 2002.
A few metres right of Below! is a wide scooped area of rock above a break in the undercut base and a step in the ledge at the base of the crag. Pull left through the undercut and up the scoop via good horizontal breaks to a short roof. Turn the roof on the right, move back left above and finish direct.

At the right end of the crag is a turf fault where the undercut peters out.

Thicker Than Water 10m Hard Severe 4b. M. Blyth, A. Cunningham. 11th May 2002.
Start just left of the turfy fault below a V groove high up. Pull over the bulge, climb up to the V groove and finish easily above.

Charity Crack 10m VS 5a*. A. Cunningham, M. Blyth. 11th May 2002.
Start about 2m left of Thicker Than Water below a crack higher up. Pull through the undercut and move up to the crack. Climb the crack and easier ground above.

Sheiling Crags (NG 992 912 - 991 908, Alt 230m North-West facing):
This is a line of gneiss outcrops descending in a north - south escarpment. They vary in height from roughly 8m to 25m and most climbs will usually require an amount of cleaning to give quality climbing. The quickest access is from car park at NG 003 928 on the A832 passing Loch an Eilich on the east side - 35 minutes.

Corner Crag (NG 992 911):
This is the second most significant buttress encountered approaching from the north, with an undercut wall on the left side and a series of short corners and grooves set into the south-west edge. Descend the gully bounding the left side. The following four routes centre around the short corners.

Basil 10m HVS 5a. M. Blyth, A. Cunningham. 12th May 2002.
The most significant mossy left-facing corner left of the SW edge. Climb mainly on the left wall of the corner.

Laughing Loopworm 10m E3 5c ***. A. Cunningham, M. Blyth. 12th May 2002.
Climb the slim double hanging grooves just right of and overlooking the corner of Basil. Steep and awkward.

Camel Ride 10m HVS 5a **. A. Cunningham, M. Blyth. 12th May 2002.
The left-facing corner crack set in the edge of the buttress.

Wild Goose Chase 10m HVS 5a *. M. Blyth, A. Cunningham. 12th May 2002.
Climb the crack about 2m right of the corner of Camel Ride, on the south-west side.

NORTHERN HIGHLANDS NORTH (VOLUME TWO)

With a new guide (650 pages) containing a lot of unrecorded routes imminent, there seems no point in reproducing routes here.

CAIRNGORMS

LOCHNAGAR, Tough-Brown Face:
Frozen Sorrow 80m X,11. A. Mullin, S. Lynch. 17th November 2002.
The route climbs the second pitch of Crazy Sorrow. Ice forms readilly in this natural summer drainage line. Climb the first pitch of Mort and traverse right to the end of the ledge and the left side of the huge standing block (50m). Climb up to the back of the roof and gain a horizontal crack in the back of the roof. Torque out and hook the lip of the roof. Climb boldly over the lip of the roof and mantle hard on to a small mono hold above. The obvious groove above was climbed mainly on ice, providing good hooks for the tools but scant protection. The top slanting crack was very hard but adequately protected. An abseil was taken from above the second pitch of Crazy Sorrow to gain the ground below.
Note: The grade is as submitted and will not necessarily be used in the next guide.

Coire an Loch Nan Eun, Balloon Buttress:
About 100m left of Whacky Buttress is another steep buttress characterised by a smooth rectangular front face. Approach by climbing steep mixed ground from Loch Nan Eun, or descend from the plateau by a snow gully just to the west.

Feelin' Groovy 40m IV,5. S. M. Richardson, C. Cartwright. 16th March 2003.
The right-angled corner defining the left edge of the rectangular wall. Climb the corner to a ledge and continue up corners and walls to the top.

Slip Slidin' Away 40m V,6. S. M. Richardson, C. Cartwright. 16th March 2003.
The V-groove cutting into the left edge of the wall. Make a difficult pull into the groove and climb it over a bulge to a ledge. Move up and right to the top.

Freewheelin' 40m V,6. C. Cartwright, S. M. Richardson. 16th March 2003.
The fault cutting through the centre of the wall is guarded by a one-metre roof. Climb up to the roof, make a long reach for turf and pull through to the fault above. Wild! Follow this trending slightly right up the centre of the wall to reach easier ground and the top.

The Stuic: North-West Face:
Bonanza 85m V,7. S. M. Richardson, C. Cartwright. 11th January 2003.
This line climbs the right-facing corner system that defines the right-hand side of Millennium Buttress.
1. 40m Climb turfy slabs with occasional awkward steps to where the corner steepens.
2. 25m Step down into the corner and climb it via steep ramps on the left wall. Belay on a ledge under the final headwall at a steep off-width crack. (It is possible to traverse right into Twilight Groove at this point – but don't you dare!).

3. 25m Arrange devious cowboy protection, climb the offwidth (steep, puzzling and technical) and follow the continuation crack through overlaps to easier ground.

Broad Cairn Bluffs:

Call My Bluff 130m III,4. S. M. Richardson, C. Cartwright. 2nd February 2003.
A counter-diagonal to Yoo Hoo Buttress. Start below the broad right edge of the buttress.
1. 25m Climb up and left past a couple of blocky steps to gain the right end of the terrace at the top of the ramp on Yoo Hoo Buttress.
2. 40m Above are two diverging groove-lines, that are separated by a knife-like flake at their base. Climb the left-hand groove-line that opens into a square-cut gully in its upper reaches, to reach a large ledge. A good pitch.
3. and 4. 65m Scramble through blocky ground to where the angle eases. Continue up easy ground joining the upper part of a wide ramp that slants up from the left.

CREAG AN DUBH LOCH, Central Gully Wall:

Snakes and Ladders 150m V,7. G. Robertson, T. Rankin. 11th January 2003.
This climb takes the easiest line up the broad buttress right of Sabre Cut, aiming for an obvious flake crack high up. Start at the base of a prominent right curving groove.
1. 35m Climb the groove for 25m, passing a delicate slab, then pull over an icy bulge to an enormous flake.
2. 45m Move left on to the rib, then continue easily up rightwards to a steep turfy groove leading direct to the steep upper wall. Climb the groove, then a series of steep left-trending steps until forced back right to the base of an overhanging corner.
3. 10m Climb the overhanging corner direct and belay below the flake crack.
4. 10m Pull leftwards, then direct over a bulge to the right end of a long ledge.
5. 50m Follow the ledge out left, then up to the top.
A more determined effort could take the final wall direct but would be very hard and out of keeping with the rest of the route.

COIRE KANDER (Carn An Tuirc):

Wee Gem 120m IV,4. G. Penny, C. Horne. 10th January 2003.
This is an underrated venue in a good freeze with not to much snow to bank out the lines. At the centre of the back of the coire is a burn at NO 185 806 which forms a good ice route.
1. 40m Start at the bottom of a buttress which bounds the lower left side of the ice fall. Climb easy angled ice until the angle steepens.
2. 30m Climb steeper ice to gain a grand ledge.
3. 50m Climb up a broad icefall (steep to start), move up and over bulges to gain the line of the watercourse.

CANNES GLEN:

Where Eagles Dare 135m V,5. N. Batchelor, F. Watt. 9th January 2003.
Climbs the watercourse in the obvious steep depression on the cliffs facing south-east in Cannes glen (south-east of the summit of Glas Maol). The climb only comes into view at the last minute on the walk in. Ice screw protection. Start at the bottom of a gully running up and left under some steep rock. Climb this easily

over ice bulges to an alcove (25m). Cut back right above the overhang and traverse up and right on ice to a cave/alcove (40m). This pitch is technically straightforward, but fairly steep and very exposed with ice screw protection. Climb out of the left side of the cave, then up right on a large sloping ledge to under the obvious icicle (25m). Climb the icicle direct and the steep bulge above to easier angled ice which is followed over short bulges to the top (45m).

CAENLOCHAN:
Have Faith   90m   IV,4. G. Penny, C. Horne. 5th January 2003.
The next watercourse north of The Central Runnel flows over a crag with a distinctive vertical band of red rock. This forms a fine icefall in a good freeze.
1. 40m Climb the steep icefall at the bottom of the crag, then follow the line of the watercourse upwards at a reduced angle.
2. 50m Follow the line of the watercourse to top with a short steeping to finish.

DRIESH, Winter Corrie:
Easy Gully Buttress   130m   II. M. Raistrick, M. Stutter. 2nd March 1998.
Perhaps climbed before. Approach as for Backdoor Gully.
1. 40 m Go left opposite the base of Backdoor Gully, follow snow over short rock steps working up and left until blocked by a steep 10m wall.
2. 30m Move down a few metres and traverse right to gain a steep left-slanting gully and follow this to its top overlooking the right branch of Easy Gully.
3. 15m Move right to climb a short steep chimney (crux).
4. 50m Climb easy convex snow slopes to the plateau.

Coire Brandy:
Smuggler   70m   HVS. S.M. Richardson, C. Cartwright. 29th September 2002.
The impressive buttress of mica schist at the head of the Loch Brandy at NO 339 759.
1. 40m 5a Start below the centre of the buttress and climb a series of steep cracks interspersed with heather ledges to reach a stance by some huge blocks below the impressive buttress headwall.
2. 30m 5a Climb a rib, step left at its top and then move straight up through a scoop (crux) to below a steep wall. Move right into a steep crack that leads to the top of the buttress.

GLEN DOLL, Cairn Damff:
This is the crag with Maud Buttress. This solid crag lies on the eastern side of Glen Doll and has a sunny aspect. Most of the cliff dries quickly, although it is higher and more exposed than the Glen Clova crags. Approach from the Glen Clova track and turn right on to the good path signposted Jocks Road. On leaving the forest, the main crag is the triangular lower buttress of a series of broken crags. Descent is by abseiling from a solid tree above the slab at the right hand side of the crag. The routes are described from left to right.

Dolly Sprint   25m   HVS 4c/5a. K. Milne, J. Ashdown. 20th June 1999.
At left end of crag is an obvious corner facing right. Climb this using cracks and escape left before an overhang. Belay in a large crack up and left. Descend by first scrambling up and across to the abseil tree.

John Ellison climbing on Central Buttress of Coire Mhic Fhearchair, Beinn Eighe. Photo: Scott Muir.

Surprise, Surprise 25m E3 5c *. K. Milne, S. Richardson. 24th August 1997.
Start at the left side of the lowest crag.
1. 25m 5c Climb a short slab, step up and left on to a ledge, then climb up to a steep niche. Traverse right precariously on to a large sloping ledge and belay (old pitons).
2. 25m 5c With a runner in a crack above, traverse strenuously left until it is possible to move up the wall and then bridge awkwardly on to a sloping ledge on the left side of the crag. Finish straight up more easily.

Old Boys' Route 45m E1. J. Ashdown, K. Milne. 20th June 1999.
Based on the finding of pitons, the first pitch of this route has been climbed before, but the previous occurrence of loose rock on the second pitch makes it very unlikely that the route was completed. Start in the middle of the crag
1. 25m 5b Wander over large flat boulders to a short corner crack, then climb up and right to an awkward recess. Move up to a ramp. Climb left up the ramp to a belay (old pitons).
2. 20m 5b Climb delicately up and right along a ramp and swing around a bulge to easier ground. A bit dirty in places.

Long John Silver 40m E2 5b **. K. Milne, M. Atkins. 23rd June 2001.
This route takes a fine line straight up the middle of the slab at the right-hand side of the crag. A full rack is recommended. Starts a few metres right of the lowest point of the crag at a shelf below a niche. Climb surprisingly steeply up into the niche then move around left on to a large ledge. A Friend#4 can be placed on the right before moving up the main slab. Aim for a small overhang (good runner just above). Move left and up (crux) to gain a ramp. Climb straight up a series of breaks following the cleaned line.

Upper Crag:
This is a compact grey crag about 150m above the main crag. It is approached from the right-hand side via grassy slopes. Traverse back in across steep heather.

Between the Showers 30m E1 5b/5c *. K. Milne, M. Atkins 15th September 2002.
Takes the corner line behind a sapling. Steeper than it looks, the corner is climbed with an awkward finish into an easier groove leading slightly left. Step right and then up a slab.

BEINN A' BHUIRD, Coire an Dubh Lochan:
Tearaway III/IV. A. Runciman and party. December 2002.
Climbed on thin but good ice. A good route but banks out unless conditions are lean.

Coire nan Clach:
Bluebell Buttress 200m II. S. M. Richardson. 23rd March 2003.
The broad buttress left of Crocus Gully. Climb Crocus Gully for 50m and follow a left-slanting gully for 50m to reach the buttress crest, which leads easily to the top.

Unknown climbers enjoying superb granite on the 6c pitch 5 of Echec et Marc, Red Pillar of the Blaitiere, Mont Blanc Range. ABO inf. 250 m 6c. Photo: Ross Hewitt.

Garbh Choire:
Elixir   230m   III. S. M. Richardson. 23rd March 2003.
Start 50m left of Alchemist's Route and follow an open gully over two bulges for 180m to enter an amphitheatre topped by rocky walls. Move up and left to enter a hidden right-slanting gully that leads to final snow slope and cornice.

BRAERIACH, Garbh Choire Mor:
Up and left of Crown Buttress, there is a long rectangular wall directly below the plateau. It can be reached by traversing left from the foot of Crown Buttress and climbing straight up easy mixed ground.

Cockade   70m   V,6. C. Cartwright, S. M. Richardson. 29th December 2002.
The next buttress left of Coronet Arête. Start below the left edge of the buttress.
1. 30m Climb a groove and step right to a good ledge below a V-shaped roof.
2. 40m Step back left into the continuation groove and follow this to where it fades. Traverse right across a thin slab (crux) to the right edge, then move up and left up a wide crack to reach the plateau.

Feather Gully   50m   III,4. S. M. Richardson, C. Cartwright. 29th December 2002.
Approximately 50m left of Cockade a hidden right-slanting gully cuts through the long rectangular wall. Climb the gully past a jammed chokestone and continue up the steep exit corner to the top.

Comanche   60m   V,5. C. Cartwright, S. M. Richardson. 19th January 2003.
The next fault right of Cherokee Chimney. Start 10m right of Cherokee Chimney, just left of the start of the right-slanting line of Custer Corner.
1. 40m Climb the right facing corner fault for 25m, then move left across a steep wall to regain a chimney-fault. Climb this to belay below the steep final corner of Cherokee Chimney.
2. 20m Move left across a slab and climb the slab-corner above to the final snow slope.
Note: It is more logical to inter-change the top pitch with Cherokee Chimney pitch 3 to give more continuous lines.

Positive Charge   100m   III,4. D. McGimpsey, A. Nisbet. 31st December 2002.
A mixed line climbed early season and based on the second groove (more of a left-facing corner) right of Phoenix Buttress. Start in the snow bay right of Phoenix Buttress, but climb a groove leading left into the first groove above its steep initial wall. Climb the groove, then return right to cross Forked Lightning Route and enter the second groove. Follow this until it peters out, then make moves right over a rib into another groove which leads to the top.

Coire Bhrochain:
Black Pinnacle Crest   50m   VS 4b. A. Nisbet. 23rd September 2002.
Not "impossible", as the 1960 guide suggested. This is the crest left of Direct Route. Start by an easy wall leading to a band of overhangs. Go up into a corner on the left. Make an airy step out right above a roof (crux), then follow the crest as closely as possible. Some of the rock is hollow, particularly the summit!

Black Pinnacle Direct Route 90m V,6. D. McGimpsey, A. Nisbet. 8th December 2002.
A superb expedition under heavy snow, accessed down Central Buttress Gully and returning down its left fork from the neck behind the pinnacle and back up the right, thereby avoiding all cornices. Climbed by Bell's line. The traverse of the summits under heavy snow is unique in Scotland.

Black Pinnacle Direct Route, Variation 90m IV,4. A. Nisbet (roped solo). 29th October 2002.
The variation was climbed to a ledge overlooking Slab Route (30m). An exposed move back left on to the face was the crux (as in summer), followed by slabby ground to the arête and the outer summit (30m).

CREAGAN A' CHOIRE ETCHACHAN:
Note: K. Milne and S. Helmore climbed a short V,6 with two worthwhile turfy pitches up on the right side of the crag near Stanley.

COIRE SPUTAN DEARG:
Flying Ridge 100m Difficult. A. Nisbet. 22nd August 2001.
Climb the crest of the right leg until beside the easy grassy trough of the upper part of Cherub's Depression. Move right on to a steeper buttress immediately above overhangs and climb a groove just left of the crest to reach and follow the crest to the top.
Winter: IV,5. A. Nisbet, J. Preston. 5th December 2002.
Following the summer route throughout provided an independent finish.

CARN ETCHACHAN, Upper Tier:
Finishing Line 95m III,5. G. Ettle, J. Preston. 14th November 2001.
The first large sloping shelf, below Inside Edge.
1. 30m Climb turf cracks up the slab; move left to belay on Gonaeno Groove.
2. 20m Go up a square fault to an awkward exit left, then traverse left for 10m.
3. 15m Technical grooves up the buttress edge.
4. 30m Easy to the top.

Note: Poison Dwarf (SMCJ 2002) was graded VI,8, with useful ice throughout. Snake Charmer was repeated, easy V,6 and Snake Bite agreed at V,7.

STAG ROCKS:
Gladiator 75m V,5. J. Lyall, J. Preston. 23rd January 2003.
Climbs the left wall of The Amphitheatre, starting 10m below the choice of gully exits. Follow a straight turfy fault to a mossy recess below a roof and turn this on the left. Regain the fault and reach the crest (45m). Follow the crest to the top.

Paraskevidekatriaphobia 65m V,6. J. Lyall, J. Preston. 13th December 2002.
A good sustained route up the narrow fault line 5m right of the right-hand finish to Amphitheatre Gully.
1. 30m Climb up through a short corner and follow a shallow chimney to a ledge.
2. 35m Move up left to follow a groove line to below an impending wall and make a tricky traverse left to finish up the last few metres of the Right-Hand Finish.

COIRE AN t-SNEACHDA, Mess of Pottage:
Pot Doodles   110m   IV,6. J. Lyall, E. Pirie, J. Preston. 19th November 2002
(Upper part has had several previous ascents).
Climb the shallow right-facing corner half way between Yukon Jack and Jacobs
Ladder and lying above the Haston Line. Gain it up the thin lower slabs. Follow
The Slant left and climb the steep crack up the buttress between Frozen Assets
and the chimney left of Yukon Jack.

COIRE AN LOCHAIN, No.3 Buttress:
Note: A free ascent of Daddy Longlegs summer line (see SMCJ 1999) at VII,9 on
7th December 2002 by P. Benson and G. Robertson. The grade assumes the
downgrading of Big Daddy to VII,8.

NORTH EAST OUTCROPS

Cruden Bay, Seals Cave:
Mezzanine   25m   E2 5c. M. Reed, R. Birkett. 23rd March 2003.
The slabs right of Teardrop. Start right of the green chimney just below the short
hanging crack. Go easily up right on the first slab, then back left up a dirty slab to
jugs below a short steep corner. Pull up on good finger locks (crux) then swing
right on to another narrow slab and small black corner below the big capping roof.
Pull out right again to the mother of all jugs and move right along the easy slab to
a comfy belay. Easy ground above to finish.

Arthur Fowlie, South Wall:
Saraman   30m   E5 6a (E4 5c?)   M. Reed, R. Birkett. 23rd March 2003.
The easiest line up the pink granite wall between Incabus and Pink Panther. Start
from the left side, below the Incabus corner. Go up on edges to a juggy small
corner, then up to a bigger corner with a flat top. Stand on this and climb the bulge
(some gwano splattered holds here!) passing a small undercut block with a small
but good runner in the crack (crux). Continue up on bold but easier slabby ground
trending slightly left to join the finish of Incabus near the top. Take tiny wires.

PANNANICH CRAG:
Scottish Tactics   40m   VII,7. T. Rankin, P. Benson. 2nd March 2003.
Basically a winter ascent of English Tactics. It offers two excellent sustained pitches
and is a good choice for a cold stormy day.
1. 25m Climb a thin icefall to the base of the corner. Climb the corner to gain turf
on the left. Use this to swing wildly left around the arête to steep thin cracks,
climbed to grass ledges. Easier ground leads up right, then back left to below the
steep upper crack.
2. 15m Climb steeply into the niche and follow the crack above until forced out
left just below the top. Finish up turf to a tree and abseil.
Note: One fall on pitch 2.

HIGHLAND OUTCROPS

GLEN NEVIS, Buzzard Crag:
Juggernaut 30m E7 6b ***. D. MacLeod. 18th August 2002.
This outstanding line, probably the best on the crag, takes the immaculate wall between Handren Effect and The Monster, featuring fairly well protected but sustained and strenuous climbing. Start up the left facing scoop and step left to the pegs. Launch directly up the wall above to reach a jug (good wire behind this). Move up and left to the deceptive break (RP) and dyno to a good hold directly above (crux). Move left and mantel onto the sloping ledge which gives access to an easy finishing rib on the left.

Whale Rock:
Hold Fast 25m E9 7a ***. D. MacLeod. 16th December 2002.
A death defying line on the pristine wall between Run For Home and Femme Fatale. Start at the right edge of the small ledge (poor skyhook possible). Climb directly up the faint rib through a desperate, technical and sustained crux to gain a tiny finger flake (no protection). Continue with further difficulty to a hard finishing move to gain a line of good edges leading leftwards into Run For Home. Finish up this. Top rope practice used.

The Half Dome:
This micro crag lies 100m up the ridge above the river walls at the top of the gorge. Cross the boulders at the upper edge of the gorge and follow a faint path up the side of the ridge until the crag can be seen. So named because of its resemblance, if not in size to its Yosemite namesake.

Fontindundar 5m E5 6a **. B. Fyffe (solo). July 2002.
This serious micro route takes the shallow groove in the centre of the wall. Move up leftwards to reach an incut hold. Make a precarious rockover and long reach to gain a good edge near the top.

Corduroy 5m E6 6b **. D. MacLeod (solo). July 2002.
This technical route takes the diagonal striations right of Fontindundar. Start at the same point as this route. From the sloping shelf move up and right on thin diagonal edges until it is possible to stand on the shelf and gain a pinch. Keep cool and reach for the top.

MALLAIG CRAGS, Ardnish, Fool's Crag (NM 717 812):
Two crags can be seen to the NNE from Peanmeanach, above the path. The top crag does not warrant closer inspection. The lower is characterised by a large broken boulder slope. This is Fool's Crag. Two lines have been climbed.

The Joker 10m VS 4b. R. I. Jones. 12th May 2002
The clean leftwards slanting slab right of the trees gives good, but unprotected climbing.

The Fool 8m VS 4b. R. I. Jones. 12th May 2002
Slightly further up is slab with a broken left-facing corner. Climb the slab. Loose at the top. Protection is poor.

Wee Crag (NM 701 805):
Beyond the ruins at Glanacardoch are two small beaches before you arrive a much
larger sandy beach at Map Ref 700 806. The second beach has a few 8-10m walls.
The nearest and highest provides the following:

Mulling It Over 10m   Hard Severe 4b. R. I. Jones. 12th May 2002
Start left of the rib and heather at the left end of the wall. Climb through a small
overhang and then the wall above.

Pausing For Thought 10m   VS 4b. R. I. Jones. 12th May 2002
Climb the rib and crack to its top, then the centre of the wall above. Pause, before
pulling on the heather to exit at the top with a good hold for the left hand.

Lizard Rib (NM 701 806):
This is a small 8m rib with a wall on its left-hand side that lies in the gully just
behind Lizard Crag by the large sandy beach. It provides two good short routes.

Persuasive Persistence 8m   E1 5a/b *. R. I. Jones. 12th May 2002
Climbs the left arête. Make difficult moves to get established just left of the arête.
Pull around and on to the arête, taking care of a creaking block at the small break
that crosses the rib. Balance your way to the top.

Evolutionary Delight 8m   HVS 5a *. R. I. Jones. 12th May 2002
Takes the right side of the rib and crack line above. Layback moves get you
established. The break provides excellent footholds to survey the crack above.
Climb this. Good protection.

BINNEIN SHUAS, The Fortress:
In Xanadu 45m   E1 5b *. G. Latter, J. Baird. 13th July 2002.
A direct line midway between Kubla Khan and The Rubaiyat, although a little
close to the former at times. Start on the heather terrace 4m right of Kubla Khan.
Step awkwardly up on to the slab and follow a direct line, stepping out right to
finish up a vague crack where The Rubaiyat foot traverses out right. Belay/abseil
from the thread belay under the huge boulder.

Note: The Rubaiyat was repeated and thought to be E1 5b **.

DUNTELCHAIG, Pinnacle Crag:
A Brazilian 10m   E3 6a. D. Moy. 21st August 2002.
Start just right of Pinnacle Chimney, step right on to the arête and go straight up
this to the top of the Pinnacle. Poor gear and a very bad landing.

No Crack 10m   E1 5b. G. Andrew, D. Moy. April 2002.
Lies between Stepped Corner and Jam Crack. Climb to heather ledge just to the
left of Jam Crack. Go up the wall to a small scoop, then climb to a small step in the
middle of the wall using one good hold to lay off. Bold at the top. A good clean
climb.

Big Nose 10m E3 6a. T. Wood (solo). 19th June 2002.
Start between Jam Crack and Left Bay Groove. Go straight up the prominent arête and the overhanging prow above. Poor gear.

Left Bay Diagonal 5c. D. Moy. 6th September 1998.
Start at Left Bay Groove and go left up a steep diagonal crack, then up to a ledge and traverse off left. Finish up Stepped Corner.

Right Chink 8m VS. D. Moy. 25th April 1999.
Start at the far right end of the crag at a small left-facing corner. Go up to beneath an overhang and step awkwardly on to a slab. Finish straight up.

Notes: There is a Y-shaped crack to the right of the top corner on Stepped Corner – 8m VS 4c. It has been climbed several times but the first ascent is not known. T. Wood has soloed the fin of rock between Left Bay Groove and Broken Groove at 6a on 22nd August, 2002. D. Moy has soloed the diagonal crack just left of Pinnacle Chimney at 5c.

The two routes reported in SMCJ 2002 were done by S. Steer and R. Webb on 20th May, 1999. The grades were the same but they were called Everest and K2. J. Mackenzie had, however, climbed them in the 1980s. A large number of boulder problems have also been climbed around here by D. Moy during the last 10 years including the easier of the two routes.

Dunlichity Crag:
Midgesummer Night Madness 30m E3 5c. T. Wood, D. Moy. 16th July 2002.
A route to the left of the overhanging prow. Go up a line in the centre of a big slab to a ledge below a steep wall. Go direct over a bulge and climb broken rock, working up and slightly left.

Ault-na-Goire (Map Ref 544 228):
Blanched 10m Severe. D. Moy, T. Wood. 15th May 2002.
On the left-hand section of crag. Start at the first left-facing corner and go straight up, passing a small left-facing corner.

Two Left Feet 10m E2 5c. T. Wood, D. Moy. 15th May 2002.
Start 3m right of Blanched below the middle of a bulge. Climb the wall direct to the bulge, pull through the bulge to a good hold and finish up a precarious slab.

Wall and Slab 10m Severe. D. Moy, T. Wood. 15th May 2002.
Start 3m right of Two Left Feet. Go up a slab to the base of a rib and finish up a groove to the left of the rib.

Revealed 10m Severe. D. Moy, T. Wood. 15th May 2002.
This is on the right-hand section of crag. Follow a fault in the middle of the crag to a crack at the top.

INVERFARIGAIG, Monster Buttress:
Note: Monster Magic (SMCJ 2002) was recleaned and led without the preplaced

runner by A. Nisbet, D. McGimpsey, 17th June 2002 at E1 5b **. Dances with Blondes will definitely require recleaning for another ascent.

Nessie 60m Severe. A. Nisbet. 18th June 2002.
Sensational positions for the grade, but some loose rock and vegetation too. Start from the left side of the same pile of blocks as The Monster Mash. Traverse left on big jugs to gain the start of a big ramp leading left. Go up this low angled ramp past a narrowing near its top to ledges. Go over a bulge to a big crevasse (as for The Monster Mash?). Wriggle rightwards up the crevasse, then step down at its far end. Go rightwards up a narrow ramp (crux, more wriggling required) and over a final block to trees.

BEN NEVIS, AONACHS, CREAG MEAGHAIDH

BEN NEVIS, Douglas Boulder:
Note: On an ascent of Direct Route 2 on 16th July 2002 by J. and D. Preston, the "slab just right of the sickle shaped scoop" was very bold. We climbed "the steep upper section direct" at VS 4c on excellent rock with good gear. This bit can be bypassed on the left over towards Direct Route 1, possibly where the route is supposed to go, as it looked the only feasible way at Severe, but not direct. We didn't need to climb a "leaning block" (which again seemed to be away over on the left) to gain easier rock but continued in our line from below.

Pinnacle Buttress of the Tower:
Pincer 200m IV,4. C. Cartwright S. M. Richardson. 15th December 2002.
A good mixed route taking the left crest of Pinnacle Buttress. Start by climbing Broad Gully for 100m to below the foot of the ridge. Climb mixed ground for four pitches just right of the crest to reach the top of the Pinnacle. The final pitch involves a fine 15m-high V-chimney that leads to the summit of the Pinnacle. Continue along the easy angled ridge to the foot of the Great Tower.

Goodeve's Buttress:
The Borg Collective 150m V,6. C. Cartwright S. M. Richardson. 4th January 2003.
The prominent chimney cutting through the centre of the triangular front face of the buttress. Start midway between Goodytwoshoes and Beam Me Up Scotty.
1. 40m Climb mixed ground leading up into the initial chimney (or approach from the right in lean conditions). Follow the chimney to its termination below a steep V-groove.
2. 30m Step right and climb mixed ground to below a steep cracked wall that blocks access to the upper chimney. Climb cracks in the centre of the wall (crux) and belay at the foot of the chimney.
3 and 4. 80m Climb the chimney to its top and continue up easier ground to reach the plateau as for Hale Bopp Groove.

Comb Gully Buttress:
Great Circle 160m VI,7. S. M. Richardson, C. Cartwright. 5th January 2003.
A difficult mixed climb between Comb Gully Buttress and Clough's Chimney.

It follows a natural cleavage line that slices right to left at an acute angle through the buttress.

1. 50m Climb the easy lower section of the buttress to a belay at the foot of Clough's Chimney.

2. 15m Climb the wall left of Clough's Chimney via discontinuous cracks to a good ledge.

3. 25m Continue up the corner and fault-line above to reach a terrace.

4. 40m Move 5m left along the terrace, and climb the left-slanting flake and offwidth cutting through the wall above. Continue left across the ice of Comb Gully Buttress and belay in the groove system cutting through the tower on the left.

5. 35m The groove splits at this point. The right branch is the Annick Exit to Comb Gully Buttress. Follow the left groove to the top of the tower and the plateau.

South Trident Buttress:
Spartacus VI,7. A. Nisbet, J. Preston. 11th November 2002.
By the summer route except that for pitch 2, from the base of the small groove on the right, the wall on the right was traversed to the arête. Slab Route was then followed for 10m until the flake-crack above the overhang was reached. The summer route follows Slab Route for 5m anyway (unless wearing blinkers). The traverse at the end of pitch 3 of the summer description should read left, not right. This and the rest of the summer route was followed.

Notes: J. Preston thought Strident Edge worth VS 4c ***.
1944 Route: J. and D. Preston note that there was definitely some 4b climbing on the second and fourth pitches as described ungraded in the guidebook. Pitches 3 and 5 are 4a, as described. The route is at least Hard Severe, possibly mild VS overall. A good pitch was also climbed from the "large leaning block" of 1944 Route, pretty well straight up and slightly left to the middle ledge, VS 4b, on excellent rock (35m). 18th July 2002. Possibly Eastern Block?

Raeburn's Rib 90m III,4. C. Cartwright, S. M. Richardson. 16th February 2003.
The well-defined rib splitting the upper reaches of Central Gully. The upper crest was first climbed in winter by Raeburn in 1904 by a line further left. Start up and left of the broad toe of the rib in a small alcove, where an icy fault cuts up and right to the crest.

1. 40m Climb the icy chimney-corner passing a tiny pine tree to a ledge. Continue up the continuation fault to the crest of the rib.

2. 50m Follow the crest of the rib to the plateau.

AONACH MOR, Coire an Lochain, Homo Buttress:
Ribbon Development 60m IV,4 **. A. MacDonald, K. Grant. 13th February 2003.
A direct variation of Ribbon Groove, starting as for that route. After pulling out steeply left as per Ribbon Groove, move up right into a narrowing chimney with a chockstone at the top. Climb the chimney (well protected) and pull over the chockstone on to easier ground. Move left to belay at the top of Ribbon Groove (50m). Easier ground leads to the top (10m).

The Ribbed Walls:
Jaws 110m VI,6. S. M. Richardson, C. Cartwright. 9th February 2003.
The pillar between White Shark and Tinsel Town.
1. 40m Climb easily up the right edge of the buttress to a steep wall. Surmount this on the right then move left along a sloping shelf to its end and climb straight up to easier ground.
2. 30m Follow a shallow gully up and right then move up to belay below a vertical V-shaped prow.
3. 30m Climb a shallow groove just right of the apex of the prow and continue up into the "Jaws", the steep chimney-corner above. Continue up this until it overhangs, then swing left onto the arête and climb steep cracks to easier ground.
4. 10m Finish up snow to the cornice.

Barbie Boy 80m IV,5 C. Cartwright, R. Webb. 18th December 2002.
Climbs the crest of the buttress between Easy Gully and Muddy Waters. A narrow chimney splits the crest, starting half way up and broadening as it continues.
1. 35m Start from the toe of the buttress immediately right of Easy Gully and climb the crest, first on the right, then moving left to overlook Easy Gully, up to the base of a ramp that cuts leftwards across the right wall of the gully. Move rightwards into a short, left facing corner. Pull out of the corner and continue to a ledge at the base of the chimney. Belay on a block at the right side of the ledge overlooking Muddy Waters.
2. 45m Enter the chimney (awkward) and climb it, then easy slopes to then top.

Coire an Fhir Dhuibh:
On the front face of the steeper right-hand buttress are two groove lines separated by enormous blocks and compact rock.
Sapience 90m V,5 *. B. Davison, D. McGimpsey. 14th December 2002.
The slim groove near the right edge of the buttress. First pitch on ice.
1. 45m Follow the icy groove to a steeper section, then the thickening smear above to a bay.
2. 45m The ice runs out so traverse out right , then back left and up into the long turfy groove.

Raga Groove 100m IV,5. B. Davison, D. McGimpsey. 14th December 2002.
The lower half of the left-hand groove looks hard but might go with thicker ice. This route climbs a turfy line on the right wall initially, then finishes up the groove.
1. 45m Start right of the groove proper by a ramp and climb turf above, then left along a ledge. Move back right and up on to a flake. Turf leads up and back left into the easier upper groove.
2. 40m Follow the icy groove past one large ledge and go to another large ledge below the final tier.
3. 15m Climb the steep flake and groove above.

Nautical Arête 100m V,6. V. Chelton, D. McGimpsey, A. Nisbet. 29th January 2003.
The left wall of the two-tiered arête left of Easy Gully. Start behind a giant flake and gain the ramp which curves up left on to the terrace (30m, 30m). Left of the edge above is a slabby wall with a steep turfy corner on its left. Belay off blocks

below the wall and climb a slim corner (hidden) near its right edge, then flakey grooves up and left to a ledge; then gain the next ledge - a good bold pitch (20m). Climb the easier arête to the top (20m).

On the south side of the corrie is a large buttress with a rambling north face. On its east face the long gully is an easy Grade I, the rib to its right is also Grade I. Right again, in the bay where the faces meet is a snowy groove with a steep left wall and distinctive slabby right wall:

Roundhead 200m II. D. Bell, E. Christison, D. McGimpsey. 19th January 2003.
Climb the groove, then follow its continuation (a turfy ramp) on to the north face of the buttress. Turf leads up to the crest, which is followed over a few steps to the top.

Bright Side 150m II *. D. McGimpsey. 16th February 2003.
Climbs the north face. A number of turfy ramps and short walls slant up left from the base. This starts up the topmost ramp below the most prominent left-slanting wall. Climb ice steps into the ramp and follow it to its top. Above climb gradually steepening turf steps to the top of the face

CARN DEARG MEADHONACH:
Monox 130m IV,4. E. Brunskill, G. MacFie. 24th February, 2003.
Climb the terrace/ramp in two long pitches until the ramp steepens to form two slabby grooves (100m). Climb the left-hand groove and a crack, then step left and traverse across the steep wall. Climb up and left through bulges to the buttress crest and easy ground.(30m).

AONACH BEAG, West Face, Broken Axe Buttress:
Snake Charmer 150m II/III. A. Kimber, T. Coar, P. Foulkes. 4th January 2003.
Takes the right edge of Broken Axe Buttress and overlooks the deep gully on the right. Ascend broken grooves and cracks in the crest, climbing a distinctive quartz scoop at one point. The last steep pitch goes left on to the final nose of the buttress, before reaching the easy exit ridge.

An Ghaidh Garbh:
Munro's Last Ridge 150m (plus walking) II. D. McGimpsey, A. Nisbet. 9th February 2003.
The ridge left (south) of the North-East Ridge. It angles rightwards towards the top of the North-East Ridge but ends in a new Munro top. The climbing is on the lower section of ridge; the upper is walking and not included in the length. Start just left of a central groove. Move left up a ramp, then traverse left round a nose until a turfy trough leads up to the left end of a ledge (45m). Follow the ledge right into the central groove and climb this to where it steepens (55m). Traverse left to follow snowy grooves to the easy upper crest of the ridge.

High in the north-west corner of the corrie just to the south of the ridge of Munro's Last Ridge is a steep buttress containing a large right-facing corner, the line of Goblet of Fire (NN 198 714). It is well hidden from most directions and the routes only become obvious from below. The routes were approached by descending from the summit ridge at a small rocky outcrop (NN199 713) to the south-east of the summit of Aonach Beag followed by a long traverse back across the corrie to the base of the buttress. Careful consideration of snow conditions should be made as the summit slopes catch the morning sun and are avalanche prone. Large cornices often form. The best and quickest approach is probably by the Gondola over the summits of the Aonachs or for the traditionalist an approach from Glen Nevis. The only previously recorded route, Anabasis, also lies on this buttress and follows a fine looking line of icy grooves up the centre of the face. The easy snow slopes above the buttress lead to the summit cornices (which can be huge) in approximately 200m.

Goblet of Fire 115m IV,4 **. S. Kennedy, A. MacDonald. 18th February 2003. The obvious right-facing corner. An easy initial pitch leads into the corner proper (25m). Climb the corner on ice to a chimney branching off left near the top (45m). Follow the chimney to reach the easy upper slopes (45m). A fine route.

The Chamber of Secrets 135m V,6 **. S. Kennedy, D. Ritchie. 15th February 2003.
An excellent route taking the prominent deep chimney running up the right side of the buttress. Start as for Anabasis up a groove which leads to a cave at the foot of the chimney (50m). Enter the deep recesses, back and foot up into the roof of the cave, then follow the through route to emerge directly above the belayer at the foot of a steep bulging groove. Climb the groove to a fine belay on the buttress crest (45m). Continue up grooves on the left side of the upper buttress to the easy upper slopes (40m).

Hidden Hope 300m IV,5 *. D. Ritchie, F. MacCallum.19th February 2003.
Start 20m right of Anabasis. Climb a right-trending groove, then straight up to belay 10m right of Anabasis (55m). Climb straight up easier angled ice to a rocky alcove (60m). Climb up and right then follow thin ice through the short steep wall above to easier ground. Follow easier snow to the left of some rocky buttresses and break through the cornice to finish directly at the summit cairn.

The following route is found on a small buttress situated just under the summit plateau well above and just left of the previous routes.

Braxton-Hicks 100m IV,6. D. Ritchie, F. MacCallum. 15th March 2003.
A short route following the obvious central groove formed between two large flakes. Follow the icy mixed groove surmounting a short steep wall at mid height to reach easier ground (55m). Easy snow leads to a cornice finish.

High on the south side of the huge eastern corrie is a line of buttresses just under the summit ridge. The following routes are situated on the largest north-west facing buttress which is well seen from the summit of Aonach Beag. The routes are best climbed early in the season before the lower sections bank out. Approach from the level summit ridge between Aonach Beag and Stob Coire Bhealaich by descending an easy gully to the foot of the buttress.

Blockheid   150m   IV,4 *. S. Kennedy, D. Ritchie. 4th January 2003.
Towards the left side of the buttress is a prominent chimney/groove line containing a projecting block near the top. Climb a steep groove to enter the chimney system. Follow the chimney in three long pitches via short ice steps and chockstones. The final projecting block is turned on the left (a through route may be possible) to finish on a narrow ridge. Climbed in thin conditions.

Instant Recoil   200m   III,4. D. Ritchie, D. Sinclair. 9th February 2003.
A rising rightwards-trending line across the face. Start 10m right of Aurora at a right-trending groove. Follow grooves to belay just right of Aurora (50m). Follow a right-trending snowfield past a small pinnacle to belay on Blockheid (50m). Follow Blockheid for 20m then trend right to below an obvious V-corner groove (50m). Follow the groove and mixed ground to the top (50m).

Aurora   185m   IV,4 *. S. Kennedy, A. Nelson, D. Ritchie. 11th January 2003.
Based on the north-east ridge of the buttress. Descend to the lowest point of the buttress. A ledge leads round to the foot of the north ridge. The ridge is bounded on the left by a gully. Start just right of the ridge and follow grooves for 20m before moving up leftwards via ledges until below an open groove right of the ridge crest (45m). Climb the groove and continue up mixed ground to below a wall (45m). Traverse right below the wall to reach another groove close to the crest. Follow the groove passing a large flake, then follow mixed ground to the crest (45m). Finish by the ridge above (50m).

Guilt Trip   120m   II. D. Ritchie, F. MacCallum. January, 2003.
Left of Aurora are two Grade I gullies which join at the top forming an inverted V. This route climbs the small buttress left of and above the left-hand gully. Follow the broad left-hand gully, then move on to the buttress following grooves to the top.

Antipasta   145m   II/III *. S. Kennedy, A. MacDonald. 18th February 2003.
Takes the most prominent left-facing corner line situated roughly in the middle of the face right of Blockheid. Climb the stepped corners in three pitches crossing a broad snow terrace at one third height. Harder early in the season.

BEINN NA SOCAICH   (Grey Corries):
Allt an Leth-chinn Duibh   300m (plus walking)   II.   B. Davison, D. McGimpsey. 15th December 2002.
The frozen burn (at NN 226 737) cascades over slabs for some distance down this rough hillside. A steep and not fully frozen wall half way up was turned by steep turf. Approach as for Coire an Fhir Dhuibh, but cross the dam and follow the opposite bank of the Allt Coire an Eoin.

Another section of crag lies at NN 238 736. Its main feature is a long easy gully.
The Worm   150m   I. D. McGimpsey, A. Nisbet. 27th October 2002.
The gully has two short steeper sections of snow.

The Fox   150m   II. D. McGimpsey, A. Nisbet. 27th October 2002.
Follows shallow grooves in the very crest of the buttress to the left of The Worm. The crux was a steep section with many flakes at half height.
Note: Arguably not the first ascent as a fox took a different line but reached the top first.

STOB COIRE AN LAOIGH (Grey Corries):
White Widow   55m   V,6 **. D. McGimpsey, A. Nisbet. 21st December, 2002.
Right of Spider Man is a deep groove which starts 15m up. Reach the groove by climbing a short clean-cut and undercut corner directly beneath it (15m). Climb the steep but helpful groove (15m). Go up left, then back right above the belay and finish up short steep walls.

Tarantula   55m   V,6 *. D. McGimpsey, A. Nisbet. 2nd January 2003.
A crackline just right of the arête between White Widow and Arachnaphobe. Start up a clean-cut corner about 10m left of Arachnaphobe and just above the left end of a ledge system which leads left from Arachnaphobe. Climb the corner to a ledge, then traverse left to the crackline. Climb the crackline (steep but very helpful) to a huge smooth block (30m). Step right round the block and return left above it to finish up the now vague arête (ie. keeping right of White Widow).

The Epithany   60m   V,6. J. Edwards, G. Hughes. 5th January 2003 (feast of the epithany).
Start at the easiest line in the middle of a bay at the right end of the leftmost buttress.
1. 50m Climb up and move left to climb the left-hand side of the bay directly into a chimney.
Easier ground leads to a belay below an obvious line 5m right of Arachnaphobe.
2. 10m Climb this (unprotected).

The Alternate   60m   IV,5. J. Edwards, J. Thacker. 11th January 2003.
Start just to the right of the bay on the easiest line.
1. 35m Go up and move left along the ledge to the right-hand side of the bay. Climb this, moving right to easier ground.
2. 25m A hidden gully line leads easily back left to the top.

Sloppy Suzie   60m   V,5. D. McGimpsey, A. Nisbet. 16th November 2002.
The left-hand groove in the face right of Loopy Louie. Various deviations right and left until the groove ends at a final wall which was climbed on the right.
Note: On an ascent of Loopy Louie in January 2003, D. Amos and A. Nisbet found that without a build-up at the cliff base, an overhanging wall of about technical 6 had appeared, so they started on the opposite side of the crest and climbed a groove which led into a through route behind the pinnacle to regain the route.

The next two routes are on the left-hand wall of Central Gully.
Choc-a-Block   60m   VI,6. J. Edwards, G. Hughes. 4th January 2003.
Climbs the first fault line on the wall.

1. 25m Climb the steep grassy fault to the terrace.
2. 25m Continue in the same line to the next terrace.
3. 10m Climb up to easy ground.

Chaf Direct 55m IV,6. J. Edwards, J. Thacker. 11th January 2003.
Climbs the second fault/corner line on the wall. Start as for The Chaf.
1. 45m Tricky hooking leads to easier climbing to the first terrace. Continue by the fault/corner line to a spike. Move right and climb up to the terrace.
2. 10m Continue in the fault/corner to the top.

Sleeping Dog 50m IV,5. D. McGimpsey, A. Nisbet. 18th January 2003.
The upper of two faults on the right wall of Central Gully. This is the line wrongly marked as Central Wall in the new guide. The lower fault is Central Wall and has been climbed twice as a mixed route at IV,5. The upper fault was climbed in 3 pitches, each with a short hard section, and ignoring an escape right below the third pitch.

Udder Madness 50m IV,5. E. Brunskill, D. McGimpsey, A. Nisbet. 15th February 2003.
The wall between the faults of Central Wall and Laughing Cow is steep but very helpful. Start centrally and take a line of weakness curving left and up through a couple of terraces to a bigger terrace near the top (35m). Climb the final tier right and back left to pass an overhang.

Laughing Cow 60m V,6. J. Edwards, G. Hughes. 3rd January 2003.
This next line climbs a fault about 10m left of Moo Moo.
1. 25m Climb the groove, then go left and up to surmount a pillar with difficulty. Carry on up the groove until it is capped by an overhang, then go out delicately and boldly up and right to surmount the bulge.
2. 20m Go up and left through a slightly bulging wall with turfy ledges to easy ground. Continue easily to the top (20m).

Cameron's Cooz 55m V,6 *. E. Brunskill, D. Morris, W. Payne. 5th January 2003.
This route climbs the system of thin cracks up the rib between the MooMoo scooped recess and Laughing Cow. Start at the base of the rib at a ledge and step right on to the edge and climb the cracks trending slightly left to an obvious small square chimney. Climb this to a ledge (40m). A superb pitch. Climb the steep cracked wall above to easy ground (15m).

Topside 50m V,7 **. E. Brunskill, P. Greene. 30th January 2003.
A great wee route following the snaking groove line just left of MooMoo. Climb the wall at the left side of the recess to a small ledge, then traverse right to below the groove. Climb the very steep groove through bulges and a flake crack to a small ledge below a roofed groove in the overhangs.(30m). Climb the groove to easy ground.(20m)

MooMoo 50m V,7 **. E. Brunskill, D. Morris. 16th November 2002.
Another fine steep mixed route taking in the crack system springing from the

right side of the large scooped recess left of The Calf. Climb the crack until a large slab is reached just below the overhangs. On the right edge of the slab is a small turfy niche. Climb up and over to this (crux) and go up and right to a ledge (25m).Up and left is a very steep blocky chimney-groove. Climb this and the continuation chimney above (25m). Climb easy ground to the top.

The Calf Direct 60m V,7. D. McGimpsey, A. Nisbet. 12th February 2003.
Follow The Calf along the start of its "crawling ledge" but stop immediately round the arête. Make hard moves up under a roof and right to turf on the arête. Go up on turf to a big chimney behind a pillar. Climb this to pass behind the pillar and rejoin The Calf for a short chimney. A steeper finish right of The Calf was taken.

Cobra Corner 80m VI,6 ***. B. Davison, A. Nisbet. 13th December 2002.
The huge roofed gully right of Calf Buttress. Climb the gully over two steps as for Jammy Dodger (20m). Continue up the very steep corner (the moss is slow to freeze), move right and up turf to a ledge. Traverse right into a groove and climb this to below a steep corner (30m). Climb the corner and its continuation (or move left and climb steep turf) to reach a ledge leading left to easier ground. Go up over steps to the top (30m).

Hoverfly 80m VI,7 **. D. McGimpsey, A. Nisbet. 13th February 2003.
A line up the buttress right of Taliballan. Start at the next groove right of Taliballan. Climb the groove until level with the base of a distinctive cracked smooth wall on the right. Traverse 5m left and climb a shallow corner forming a steep ramp to gain a ledge. Traverse left round an arête to below a corner (30m). Climb the corner to a ledge below overhangs. Traverse the ledge rightwards with a notable step across a gap to reach a bigger ledge with a wide roofed chimney at its left corner (15m). Climb the wide chimney almost to the roof, then use a horizontal crack to traverse left round an arête. Move up, then traverse left again to a sensational position on the lip of a big roof before finishing straight up (35m).

Billy Whizz 70m VI,7 *. D. McGimpsey, A. Nisbet. 11th February 2003.
A line up the same buttress but moving right from Hoverfly. Start as for Hoverfly and climb the groove until Hoverfly goes left. Continue up the groove until level with the top of the distinctive cracked wall. Make a spectacular and strenuous traverse right across the top of the wall until the ledge above can be gained. Climb the left-hand chimney above, then either corner of a square recess to reach the bigger ledge (35m). Climb a narrow chimney with a prominent chokestone (right of the wide roofed chimney), then two steps above to gain an easier groove leading up left to easier ground (35m).

Rampant Jack 60m IV,6. J. Edwards, R. Martin. 15th February 2003.
A mixed route close to Yee Haa. The only difference seems to be that it climbs the chimney for 2m before exiting on the right to reach easy ground after 10m.

At the eastern end of the crag there are a series of grooves and corners above the ramp for Tidal Groove.
Two Stone Groove 55m IV,5. J. Robinson, D. Richardson. 1st February 2003.
1. 35m Start up Tidal Groove and reach a sloping terrace below a grooved

wall. Gain the leftmost groove, recognised by its two chockstones, and climb this with interest to reach a narrow terrace.

2. 20m From the left end of the terrace, climb a shallow gully and short steep rock step to gain the top.

No Stone Groove 60m V,6. D. Ross, K. Neal. 1st February 2003.
A distinctive crack that can be seen clearly from the ground and looks harder that it is.

1. 10m Start up Tidal Groove to the beginning of its traverse right.
2. 25m Climb directly up and right to a distinctive break below two open grooves.
3. 15m Take the right-hand groove, trending slightly left to arrive at a second big break. Traverse 3m left to below an open corner on the right-hand side of a slab.
4. 10m Climb this and pull out left at the top to finish.

MEALL GARBH, Creagan Coire nam Cnamh:
Merciless Mary 60m IV,3 *. C. Wells, M. Twomey. 11th January 2003.
This short but enjoyable cascade lies on a small 70m cliff situated about 200m right of, and slightly uphill of the base of the main cliff.

1. 30m Climb thin ice at around 70°-75° angle for 10m before the ice thickens and lies back to ca. 60 degrees and leads to a large ledge.
2. 30m Traverse diagonally up and left from the ledge on to an ice ramp traversing beneath fearsome-looking ice daggers and umbrellas. Where the ice thins and steepens to near vertical angle, traverse 3m left along a ledge to a giant flake. Surmount the flake and traverse back right above the ice umbrella to finish up easy-angled ice.

CREAG MEAGHAIDH, The Post Face:
The Lost Post 120m VI,5. K. Neal, I. Rudkin. 15th February 2003.
1. 50m Start at the niche as for Post Haste, immediately climbing a right-trending traverse to below a steep icefall.
2. 70m Climb the ice to reach a shelf, traverse 4m left on turf to rejoin ice and then follow easy ground to the top, avoiding the cornice on the right.
Graded VI,5 due to poor gear in lean conditions but might be V,5 otherwise.

Note: M.and P. Cocker climbed a left-hand start to Staghorn Gully in March 1987 (grade III). This has been used as access to Postman Pat but its complete ascent via Staghorn finish has never been claimed despite being marked (wrongly) on the diagram on p302 of the new guide.

STOB POITE COIRE ARDAIR (near Creag Meagaidh), Garbh Choire (NN 436 896):
This north-facing coire held a vast sheet of generally low-angled ice, roughly 100m square, which was not visible on the descent of convex slopes until almost at the coire floor. Conditions were cold and almost snowless; much banks out later in the winter (as a later visit found). In similar conditions there would be no point in carrying anything other than ice screws. The ice sheet formed from a twin watercourse in the centre of the backwall of the coire, east of the stream marked on the map.

La Rive Gauche 150m III,4. A. Nisbet. 20th December 2002.
The line of the left watercourse. Start up a groove at the top left side of a steep lower band to reach the ice sheet. Trend leftwards up this, initially walking but always steepening, to a finish up a 10m wall of 80 degree ice. An escape left below this would reduce the grade to II.

Mer de Glace 200m III. A. Nisbet. 20th December 2002.
Start up ice right of the groove to reach the ice sheet. Trend right up this to finish up a shallow gully (stream bed) in the rocks above.

CARN LIATH, Coire nan Gall:
Lurgainn Groove 90m IV,4. S.M. Richardson, C. Cartwright. 2nd March 2003.
The obvious line of zigzag grooves on the right side of the steep front face of No.4 Buttress. Start by climbing snow slopes up and right from the toe of the buttress to where a turfy break cuts left into the face.
1. 40m Move easily left along the break, then right and left again to gain the right side of a huge pointed triangular flake. Move up and right across a short steep turfy wall to gain a narrow V-groove. Pull into this (crux) and continue to a stance on the right of the buttress.
2. 50m Climb the slabby turfy wall on the left to gain an easy corner-ramp that leads to the top of the buttress.

BEN ALDER, Garbh Coire Beag:
McCook's Gully 300m III. I. Small. 16th February 2003.
A parallel gully to the left of Left Gully's start and right of Alderwand. Cross a snow terrace and continue up a left-slanting gully line containing an ice pitch. The gully ends on a buttress crest which leads to the plateau. No cornice problems on the day.

Bheoil Pfeiler 300m IV,4. S. M. Richardson, C. Cartwright. 23rd February 2003.
A good mixed climb up the right side of the triangular buttress between McCook's Gully and Left Gully. Start by climbing easy icy grooves right of McCook's Gully, first trending right then straight up, to gain the wide snow terrace crossing the face. Continue up to the right edge of the triangular buttress. Move left 10m and climb a 5m mixed wall and follow a left-trending corner-ramp past a cave to an excellent stance below a steep corner crack (40m) Step back right above the cave and continue up mixed ground on the right side of the buttress for three pitches to the top.

MONADHLIATH, Loch Dubh Crag:
Lumpy Mixture 100m II. J. Lyall, D. MacDonald. 20th February 2003.
Roughly 100m right of Wee Team Gully is a straight narrow gully, climbed on thin ice.

Youth in Asia 55m II. J. Lyall, D. MacDonald. 20th February 2003.
An ice sheet high on the right end of the crag.

GLEN COE

BUACHAILLE ETIVE MOR, Slime Wall:
The Appraisal 30m E2/3 5c. I. Taylor, B. Sheddon. 6th August 2002.
Left of Bloody Crack is another wider crack. This route climbs the wall to its left.
Climb directly to gain a thin crack, which leads to a small roof. Pull over the roof
and continue more easily.

Cuneiform Buttress:
Long Chimney Direct 220m VII,6. E. Brunskill, S. McFarlane. 12th December
2002.
A sustained and serious direct version of Long Chimney. Climb Ordinary Route
to the big ledge (60m). Climb out right from the ledge into a steep groove and
continue straight up (Ordinary route goes up and left) to a cave recess formed by
a blocky undercut groove (30m). Climb up right on to a small rocky ledge and
step delicately down and right to another capped groove; climb this for 5m and
make delicate moves right into another groove. Climb this to a small ledge (35m).
Climb the continuation chimney line until a flat easy section of the shelf is reached
(45m). Continue in the same line up another chimney crack and above this, make
a desperate and serious traverse right for 10m to the obvious ledge below two
large detached flakes (35m, a very serious pitch). Climb the flakes and wall above
to easy ground beside the descent path to Great Gully (10m).

Cuneiform Buttress Right-Hand Start 60m IV,4. M. Hind, R. Webb. 2nd January
2003.
Climb the obvious right-hand fault to reach the central ledge on the buttress. Slightly
harder but better protected than the normal (left) way.

Central Chimney Direct 135m V,7. M. Hind, R. Webb. 8th January 2003.
Climb the summer route, probably a much better winter route than a summer one,
especially the final chimney.

BIDEAN NAM BIAN, Sron na Lairig:
Trickle 200m III. A. Spink and party. 8th January 2003.
A deep stream with ice bulges between easier sections which lies NE of the bealach
(741m) and SE of Sron na Lairig at about NN 166 533 and between the 450m and
650m contours. Normally banked out.

Lost Valley Minor Buttress:
Note: The Nipper (SMCJ 2002) is the same as Men o' War in the new Glen Coe
guide.

STOB COIRE NAN LOCHAIN:
Scabbard Chimney, alternative finish (Celtic Connection) 45m V,5. N. Bullock,
M. Tweedly. January 2003.
From the abseil point on Scabbard Chimney, there is a buttress straight ahead to
the right of the Scabbard Gully. Climb the centre up grooves to a obvious jutting
roof. Climb left on to a wee wall and pinnacles.

Scabbard Chimney, alternative finish   25m   VII, 7 ***. M. Garthwaite. January 2003.
Climb the obvious thin crack on the left wall of Scabbard Chimney just after the sentry box. Well protected and very steep.

Micro Rib Direct   70m   IV,5. E. Brunskill, P. Greene. 11th December 2002.
This route climbs the crest of the rib in two pitches with the tower half-way up providing the crux.

Central Buttress:
The Douglas Pebble   50m   V,7. J. Edwards, G. Hughes. 1st February 2003.
A hard and well protected alternative start to Original Route. Climb the overhanging corner and into the snow field, then takes the right-hand chimney.

Church Door Buttress:
Fundamentalists   100m   E4 6a ***. G. Latter, P. Craig. 15th September 2002.
The crackline at the left side of the face, just left of Lost Arrow. Start at the block belay as for that route.
1. 25m 5b Move up leftwards on to a ledge, then up left over blocks. Step right and climb a wall above a block to belay on the right, as for Lost Arrow.
2. 25m 6a Climb the slab on the left into the base of a grey corner. Step right into a crack with difficulty and follow it past an old PR to a small recess just right of the prominent square-cut roof.
3. 20m 6a Undercut left and pull spectacularly round the roof. Climb a crack above to a good no hands rest on top of the huge block forming the roof. Continue steeply on good holds to a ledge. A superb pitch on impeccable rock.
4. 30m 5c Move diagonally up left and climb a short arête on its front face. Continue trending leftwards to a deep corner crack. Step left and climb a short finger crack with difficulty to a ledge above. Scramble to finish.

West Top of Bidean, Bishop's Buttress:
Ambush   VI,7. B. Fyffe, D. Hollinger. 23rd January 2003.
By the summer route. Although short, it packed a fair punch with the first 50m being very sustained, and the gear a bit poky.

Hourglass Groove   60m   III. S. McFarlane, A. Clark. 16th February 2003.
Start half way up Hourglass Gully and 10m right of Surely at a groove below a notch in the skyline.
1. 40m Climb the groove trending slightly right (runners) then back left to a ledge beneath a large groove.
2. 20m Climb the groove above to the top.

Beinn a' Chrulaiste (see SMCJ 1998):
College Daze   300m   II/III. A. Spink, S. Johnston and party. 1st February 1996.
A stream bed at approx. NN 238 560 over slabby ice for many pitches. It finished a way to the left of the summit of Beinn a' Chrulaiste, almost 1km away from the summit.

Surf and Turf III. A. Spink, S. Johnston and party. 2nd February 1996.
The longest stream bed with 7 pitches over nice steep bulges, approximating the
line of grid square 240, again finishing way to the SW of the summit.

Note: A. Spink and party followed a frozen watercourse further to the right (which
may coincide with the highest gully?) on 10th January, 2003 at grade II for six/
seven pitches.

GLEN ETIVE, Glen Ceitlein Slabs:
Viagra Falls 35m IV. A. Cave, P. Carol. February 1996.
Directly opposite Patey's Old Man, climb an icefall direct to reach the main slabs
and continue up these

GARBH BHEINN:
Hare Course 200m II. R. Milne. 15th February 2003.
The buttress between Winter Buttress and Pinnacle Buttress, not mentioned in the
guide.

Garbh Choire Slabs:
Jerking Crocus 110m III. S. Kennedy, A. MacDonald, D. Ritchie. 3rd February
2003.
Generally follows the corner bounding the right side of the main slab in two long
pitches. Climbed on a wild day when the slab was plastered with a thin layer of
snow ice. Approximates to a line just right of the summer route Lodestone.

GLEN TARBERT, Meall a' Bhraghaid:
Note: *John West* (Coe guide, p.353) - A revised description from C. Moody:
Scramble to the base, climb 50m to the overlap, then another 30m to the top.

GLEN GOUR, Indian Slab Crag:
Mullenium Direct Start 50m Severe 4a ***. G. Latter, J. Birkbeck. 16th August
2002.
A logical entry, the integral providing four excellent full length pitches. Start at
the very toe of the crag, down right of the shelf at the base of Indian Slab. Move
up right over initially broken ground to gain the superb smooth slab and follow
this, taking the cleanest line trending slightly right to gain the base of the original
route. Poorly protected, but straightforward, on superb rock.

Note: (C. Moody):
North facing, belays are usually good. Mullenium might be Very Difficult. First
ascentionists: Outrider – L. Brown, P. Brown Easter 1972
Indian Slab – I. Davidson, L. Brown Easter 1972
Time Change – I. Davdson, L. Brown, J. Mitchell
Other routes – C. Moody, C. Grindley 2000

(G. Latter): The approach description (page 315 of new guide) is inaccurate. The
track from Sallachan extends for 3km (not 10!) to the sheep fank, and, even with
the use of mountain bikes as far as the sheep fank (rough going), the approach to
the base of the crag took a little over 2 hours (not 1hour 10 minutes!) Furthermore,

the crag faces north (not south!), though being easy-angled, does receive a fair amount of sun and dries remarkably quickly.

Descent: From the large heather terrace at the top, traverse left and across the stream bed, then down the slope just to its right (east), re-crossing the stream lower down to slant down left to regain the base.

Paleface   30m   VS 4c **. G. Latter (on-sight solo). 16th August 2002.
Obliquely up left from the base of the main cliff, on the opposite side of the open gully, is an obvious pale slab with a prominent thin crack. Climb the crack, finishing by an easier ridge at the top. Descend down the right side of the crag.

ARDNAMURCHAN, Beinn Gheur, Ranald's Buttress (NM 667 709):
The crag lies on the flank of Beinn Gheur, east of the road from Acharacle to Doirlinn. Approaching Doirlinn the road leaves the River Sheil and cuts through a steep-sided forested wee glen. Parallel buttresses rise above the tree line. The triangular shaped crag lies to the left of these and a wide open gully. It provides two walls split by the arête – 10 minutes walk. The buttress has a heathery air to it, but this does not detract from the good rock in between.

Ranald's Claim   25m   Mild VS 4c. R. I. Jones. 11th May 2002.
Climb the cracks left of the centre of the wall left of the arête. Climb the slab above and through the overlap 2m left of MacGillivray's Grip (crux) and then direct to the top.

MacGillivray's Grip   30m   VS 4c. F. and C. Templeton. 13th August 1999.
Climb the initial bulge in the centre traverse right to the arête and continue up to an overlap. Traverse left to a double niche breaking out left at its top. Move rightwards and follow the edge to the top, a pinnacle (the niche taken on the right is also 4c).

The True Line   25m   Mild VS 4b/c. R. I. Jones. 11th May 2002.
This is an almost direct ascent of the arête. The technical grade depends on how direct you make the start (crux). Start just left of the undercut arête, pull through this (a long reach helps). Climb the wall/arête to the top.

Makalester   25m   VS 5a. R. I. Jones. 11th May 2002.
Good and enjoyable climbing up the thin crack just right of the arête to join it at 5m. Initial layback moves lead to more delicate moves to gain the arête. Continue to the top.

A Sure Thing   25m   Mild VS 4c. R. I. Jones. 11th May 2002.
4m right of the arête two cracks split the centre of the wall. Climb the centre of the wall direct to gain the arête at 9m at the overlap. Climb this and the arête to the top.

Lord of the Isles   20m   VS 4c *. R. I. Jones. 11th May 2002.
Start 5m right and just left of a small left-facing corner topped with heather. Difficult

moves get you established to enjoy the fine climbing up the wall above to finish left of the small trees.

General Persuasion   20m   Severe 4a. R. I. Jones. 11th May 2002.
Climbs the wall further right to finish right of the small trees.

Two hundred metres further up, the gully levels out. Centre left is an obvious buttress split in to a higher and lower section with a crack down its lower section, topped by a small tree.

Contemplative Solitude   20m   VS 4c *. R. I. Jones. 11th May 2002.
A fine line on excellent rock. Climb the crack to the tree. Traverse left and upwards to the next buttress. Climb this to the top.

To the left of the higher section is a short wall with three micro routes, by R. I. Jones on 11th May 2002.

Busy 4b: Climb just right of the left end up onto the arête to finish.
Bumble 4c: 2m right up into a small niche.
Bee 5a: 3m right again.

ARDNAMURCHAN, Garbhlach Mhor (NM 418 654   Alt 50m   WSW facing):
The climbs are on the short upper cliff over looking the sea. The clifftop forms a flat area of rock which is easily seen walking along the grass. The rock is a red and grey gabbro with horizontal breaks similar to some sandstones. Access is easy down either side. The lower cliff might give some more adventurous climbing on different rock. Routes climbed by C. Moody and C. Grindley on 6th April 2002. S. Abbott and M. Tighe have climbed routes south of these.

Free Nelson Mandela   25m   E1 5b **.
Just left of the lowest point of the cliff base is a rib. Start left of the rib and climb straight up to a grass patch. Move right to the rib, make a thin move up the rib, then move right and up on immaculate rock.

Stop The Corry Bill   25m   VS 4c *.
Follow the previous route to the grass patch but climb the flake line above. Possibly HVS.

Disband The S.P.G.   22m   VS 4b.
Left of the last route is a corner-crack; left again is a huge flake which runs half way up the cliff. Start just right of the flake and climb straight up with an awkward bulge near the top.

There is a short cliff at the left end of this face. The corner is Moderate, the crack 3m right is Severe with some loose rock near the top. 3m right is a fine wall E1 * (E2?) starting up a short right-facing corner.

ARDNAMURCHAN, Sgurr nan Gabhar:
Acting Soft E2 5c. M. Howard, T. Carruthers. 18th April 2003.
The hairline crack between Ozone Layer and High Plains Drifter (no touching allowed!).

Meall an Fhir-Eoin, Summit Buttresses, Upper Tier:
Barbarella 20m E4 5c **. J. Lines (on sight solo). 4th June 2002.
The beautiful square-cut gritstone style arête. Start from the left to gain the arête, climbed to a break. Pull through a capping overlap and continue easily.

Fear of Flying 40m VS 4b **. S. Kennedy, R. Hamilton, P. Harrop. May 2002.
A good route in a wildly exposed position for the grade. Follows parallel cracks running horizontally left above the overhanging wall just left of Pyroclast. Climb the initial corner of Pyroclast before pulling out left into the parallel cracks. Traverse horizontally left along the cracks to the edge. Continue left a short distance then directly up to finish.

RUBHA CARRACH:
Gun Fhiamh 30m E5/6 6a. S. Crowe, K. Magog (on sight). 3rd August 2002.
Start just left of a small triangular cave above head height. Climb on good pockets following a faint hairline crack until the dolerite band. Step left here to finish boldly up the final headwall. The name means 'without fear'.

ARDNAMURCHAN POINT, Left Wall Area:
No Mucking About 8m E1 5a. R. I. Jones (unsec). 6th April 2002.
Takes the very thin crack line up the middle of the wall left of Muck Climb. Start 3m left of the start of Muck Climb. Take the small overlap at mid-height on the left.

Tidal Wave 15m E5 6a. K. Magog, S. Crowe. 4th August 2002.
Right of the roof and left of the black corner is a steeper wall. A good route with reasonable climbing for the grade but relies on small wires and micro cams, which are difficult to place. Start up a short groove beneath the roof and step right to gain the steep wall. Climb the narrow groove on side-pulls and undercuts to the small roof (micro-cam on the left). From here reach right to gain good crimps on the blank-looking wall above and follow these to a powerful last move at the top of the prominent diagonal crack.

Rum For Your Money 15m HVS 4c/5a. R. I. Jones, S.J. McNaught. 6th April 2002.
The corner left of E-numbers. Climb the corner taking care to avoid loose rock on the right near the top.

On The Cusp 15m Mild Severe. R. I. Jones, S.J. McNaught. 6th April 2002.
Climbs the line at the far right of the Left Wall and just left of the Chimney. Steep moves lead to a right facing corner at mid-height and easier ground to the top.

Becalm 15m E2 5b. S. Crowe. 4th August 2002.
A bold right to left traverse of The Left Wall. Traverse in to the twin cracks of

Incoming Tide along a prominent low-level break. Climb up the twin cracks to gain a higher-level traverse that leads boldly into the black corner. Continue to traverse up the diagonal break to finish with a powerful but well protected move.

Main Wall Area:
Diamond Days 5m VS 5a. K. Magog, S. Crowe. 4th August 2002.
Good crimps and edges up the wall right of The Chimney. Take care with the last move.

Open Book 6m Difficult. R. I. Jones, 6th April 2002.
Between the Chimney and Home for Tea is an obvious open book corner.

Whale Watching 10m E1 5b. S. Crowe, K. Magog. 4th August 2002.
A small groove right of Home for Tea leads to beneath the roof. A powerful move soon leads to better holds and protection.

Hmmmmmm 15m Severe 4b. K. Magog. 4th August 2002.
Good holds up the arête lead to the ledge. Finish up Westering Home.

Whoosh 5m VS 5a. S. Crowe. 4th August 2002.
Climbs the narrow V-groove at the right-hand end of the crag making full use of the left arête at the start. The most westerly recorded route on the British mainland!

Plimsoll Line 30m VS 5a. S. Crowe. 4th August 2002.
A right to left girdle of Main Wall starting up Whoosh and finishing up Diamond Days.

Beinn Na Seilg, Hebrides Wall:
The Intrepid Mountain Elephant 35m Very Difficult. W. Sweeney, J. Kimber. 29th December 2002.
Scramble halfway up the triangle of grass leading to Gabbro Slab. On the right there is a prominent corner. Climb this (or the slab to its right) until it steepens. A thin move up to the right leads to a comfortable ledge. Climb the slab above this to another corner. Step left onto an arête here and finish up to the summit. An enjoyable route on very clean gabbro with good friction. The finish up the arête feels wonderfully exposed.

SOUTHERN HIGHLANDS

MULL OF KINTYRE, Campsite Crag:
Rainy Day 25m VS 4c. B. Davison, A. Nisbet. 7th June 2002.
Between the hanging groove of The Tablet and Campion Crack is another hanging groove. Start up the face of a detached flake-pinnacle. From its top step on to the face and move up to an overlap. Move right and up into the groove. Follow this to the top.

Inhouse Crag:
To the right of Hooded Groove is a blunt arête climbed at E1 5b (7m) and the

wall to its right starting at a small rock at its left and trending right to an overlap at VS 5a (7m). Both B. Davison and A. Nisbet on 8th June 2002.

Ballinamoill Crag:
Silver Surfer   30m   E1 5b. B. Davison, A. Nisbet. 8th June 2002.
The spectacular undercut arête. Start up Cresting the Wave and where that moves up into the groove continue left to the undercut arête. Climb this on its right side to the top.

Bay City Roller   25m   E1 5b. B. Davison, A. Nisbet. 8th June 2002.
The arête between the two parallel grooves. Start up Rites of Passage until it is possible to move left above the lower roof. Ascend the wall moving diagonally left to the arête. Climb the wall just right of the arête to a final bulging section. Climb just left of the arête to reach the huge capping roof. Traverse right under the roof to finish at the same point as Rites of Passage.

Between Outhouse Crag and Wee Half Dome but about 200m uphill is a small steep wall with a prominent arête at its right side (The Arête, 6m, VS 5a, B. Davison, 8th June 2002). The left side of the crag has a large steep flake crack which sounds loose. To its right is a wall containing two hanging grooves. Route 1 (8m, E2 5c, B. Davison, A. Nisbet, 8th June 2002) takes the first groove with an unprotected start and lichenous rock. Route 2 (8m, VS 5a, K. Kelly, M. Powell, 8th June 2002) takes the right-hand groove. To the right the arête and wall gives Route 3 (8m, VS 4b, G. Gatherer, K. Kelly, 8th June 2002) while the next wall right of the corner gives Route 4 (8m, VS 4c, B. Davison, 8th June 2002) with The Arête and the end of the crag being another 6m further on.

GLEN CROE, Upper Crag:
Tick Tock   18m   E6 6b ***. D. MacLeod. July 2002.
The stunning and bold arête right of The Sharp Kiss features a bouldery crux with a serious finish. Climb easily to a jug (wire behind this). A hard move gains incuts on the arête. Make a long reach from here and finish on improving holds.

The Fugue   20m   E9 6c ***. D. MacLeod. 16th October 2002.
A very serious and hard climb with sparse protection, taking the very steep wall left of Short Sharp Shock. Start just left of this and climb a short groove to good holds. Place an assortment of dubious gear behind the soft jug on the right. Step left and launch up the overhanging wall with increasing difficulty to a desperate crux move from a small undercut. Move left to a jug at the lip and in a serious position, reach rightwards through the bulge to twin finger pockets (wires in the left hand pocket). Climb the steep wall above direct on crimps to a good finishing jug. Very powerful climbing (F8a+) with groundfall potential. Top rope practice used on the first ascent.

Independence Crag:
Imposition   10m   E4 5c *. D. MacLeod. 10th May 2002.
This short but pleasant solo takes the left end of the bulging wall. Start below a small groove. Climb this and move right along a handrail. Pull over the bulge

(crux) moving right to good holds. Climb the easier finishing slab leftwards to good finishing holds.

THE COBBLER, North Peak, South Face:
Note: The bolt runner on Whither Whether is no more (broke off Sept 2002).

Cat Crawl VI,7. A. Clarke, M. Garthwaite. 3rd February 2003.
A winter ascent of the summer line in snowy conditions.

Centre Peak Buttress:
Note: M. Garthwaite notes that Turftastic (SMCJ 1999) is a winter ascent of Lobbydosser, bypassing the wide crack mentioned on the right.

BEINN AN DOTHAIDH, Creag Coire an Dothaidh:
Cool Riders 170m IV,5 **. D. Redpath, D. MacLeod. February 2003.
An amenable line through the steeper left-hand section of the cliff left of Beelzebub. Start below a large easy left-slanting ramp, directly below a band of roofs high above.
1. 60m Climb the ramp for 8m, then break out right to a flake. Step down and traverse awkwardly round a nose to gain a turfy bay. Move diagonally right to gain a line of turfy grooves and climb these until level with the big roof on the left. Traverse left over a nose to a a short steep corner.
2. 30m Bridge up the steep corner (crux) and follow a ledge/ramp system leftwards to past an awkward step to gain a large expanse of easy angled slabs.
3. 60m Climb directly up the easy slabs to reach the headwall.
4. 30m Walk right along the big ramp (as for Professorial Seat) to finish.

BEINN UDLAIDH, Coire Ghamhnain:
Three long watercourses are seen at the head of the coire. The right-hand one is an easy Grade I. The central one is an open series of icefalls.

Coput 200m III. J. A. Sumner P. Gibson. 2nd February 2002.
Takes the central watercourse. The first 75m is climbing a series of short icefalls separated by snow bays. The upper section has a fine 40m stepped icefall.

BEN CHUIRN:
Goldmine Gully 180m IV. A. Cave, R. Hutchby et al. March 1996.
1. Before the waterfall of Eas Anie, climb up left to the foot of the goldmine (jutting railway tracks).
2. Climb out of the mine entrance on the right-hand side (mixed) until a snow bay is reached.
3. Traverse left to reach a thin icefall. Climb this direct (crux).
4. Follow the line of weakness leftwards on turf and a steep rocky exit.

MEALL NAN TARMACHAN, Creag an Lochain, Coire nan Easan:
Tote Gully, Icicle Entry III,4. R. Simpson, A. Reid. 13th January 2001.
This classic line first climbed in the snowy 80's can be difficult to enter these days. One solution is to scale the 6m icicle which drools from an overhang on the left, then lunge for the first bulge of ice in the gully.
Note: Fragile Fall (SMCJ 2001) should be grade IV,4.

An Caisteal:
Sleepless (M)ice 70m   IV,4. G. Nicoll, R. Simpson (alt). 12th January 2003.
The conspicuous icefall which forms on the lower tier of An Caisteal offers
continuous ice for two pitches with two vertical sections. Finish by climbing the
buttress or Y-gully for 100m.

Cam Chreag, Forgotten Buttress:
Forgotten Buttress, the wide face to the left of Fan Gully, is poorly described in
the guide. It is bounded on the right by the diagonal Fan Gully (with a left-hand
branch low down, normally grade I but can be harder) and on the left by the open
Cam Gully (grade I). On the left-hand (upper) side of Forgotten Buttress (close to
Cam Gully) are two distinctive short gullies, Chimney One and Chimney Two.

Fan Buttress:
Note: M. Mckenna and A. Percival climbed a more entertaining finish to Clark's
Gully on 15th February 2003 at Grade II (Clark's Commandos). They climbed the
shaded turf and rock wall left of the finishing gully to below a large rock pinnacle
at the top of the buttress.

ARRAN

BEINN TARSUINN, ConsolationTor:
Note: Consolation Arête (SMCJ 2002) is the same as Draugen (SMCJ 2001).

LOWLAND OUTCROPS

GLASGOW OUTCROPS, Craigmore:
Note: The route Craig's Wall reported as first being led in 1997 in SMCJ 192 was
soloed by A. Ford in May 1989.

THE GALLOWAY HILLS, The Tauchers:
Dragonslayer 30m   E3 *. C. King, S. Reid. 4th September 2002.
1. 20m 6a The sustained crack left of Dungeonmaster leads to a grass ledge.
2. 10m 5b Traverse horizontally right under the upper groove of Dungeonmaster
to a second slimmer hanging groove which is followed to a ledge.

Smaug 30m   E2 5b. C. King, S. Reid. 4th September 2002.
The right-hand groove (right of Dungeonmaster) gives a rather grubby pitch with
a worrying feel. An extra-large Hex is useful to protect the crux.

Dungeon of Buchan, Silver Slab:
This clean slab up and right from Dungeon Buttress, and above the descent ramp
from Cooran Buttress, provides some good climbs in the lower grades.

The Scrieve 50m   VS 4c **. J. Biggar, S. Reid, C. King. 26th October 2002.
Start at the lowest point of the slab and follow the rib and twin cracks of The
Slanter until just below the grass ledge where it is possible to move left into a

scratch-like crack in the slab. Follow this with interest to a good flake and then continue directly through bulges, crossing The Wee Slanter, to a bold direct finish. A good pitch.

The Wee Slanter 55m Severe 4b *. J. Biggar, L. Biggar. 26th August 2001.
1. 25m Start at the lowest point of the slab, just right of a large overhang. Climb a crack in a rib to a horizontal grass ledge, then follow the obvious large twin cracks to the left end of a larger grass ledge and belay below a large flake.
2. 30m Climb the flake above on good holds, steeply at first. Make an airy step left at the top to finish up the easy angled rib on the left.

The remaining routes start from the large grass ledge that cuts in from the right at half height, or can be reached by climbing the first pitch of the Wee Slanter.

Sprauchler's Groove 30m Severe ***. J. Biggar, L. Biggar. 16th October 2002.
Climbs the obvious thin dogleg crack in the upper slab. An excellent route with some unusual climbing for the grade. Follow the second pitch of Wee Slanter for 4m, then step right to the foot of the crack. Climb elegantly up the crack or sprauchle your way to the top.

The Big Smirr 30m Mild Severe 4a *. J. Biggar, C. King, S. Reid. 26th September 2002.
Only Very Difficult except for one tricky move early on. Start 3m right of the left-hand end of the grass ledge and below the central crack in the upper slab. Climb rightwards, then back leftwards, past a good flake, to reach the crack which is followed to the top.

Unnamed 30m Severe. L. Biggar, J. Biggar. 2002.
Start at the lowest point of the grass ledge on the right hand side of the upper slab (a poor pitch has been climbed up the slab below). Climb the obvious little staircase, cross vegetation leftwards, and then climb the thin crack in the slab above with a choice of three finishes. The right-hand crack (hardest), ledges on the slab on the far right (easiest) or the left-hand crack. A good climb apart from the heather in the middle.

Cooran Buttress:
Snakes and Ladders 110m E1 *. S. Reid, C. King (alt). 1st September 2002.
Four good technical pitches though little in the way of a line. Start just right of Traitor's Gait where two ragged cracks spilt the sidewall of the buttress.
1. 25m 5a Climb the right-hand crack to a large ledge stance on Traitor's Gait.
2. 25m 5b Climb the short crack on the back wall to a rib on the left and follow this boldly to a ledge which is traversed past a spike to a block in the gully. Climb the crack system above, moving left to the arête near the top, and belay at a wide crack at the back of a commodious grass ledge.
3. 30m 5a Climb the crack to a footledge and traverse this left to a crack in a rib which is followed to grass. Scramble up a few metres to a square tower. Follow a groove on the front face to a ledge on the left then step right on to the slabby upper face and go up to belay in a paddock under an attractive blocky grey pillar.
4. 20m 5a The pillar.

Unnamed   120m   Mild VS. S. Reid, C. King (alt). 12th October 2002.
A reasonable route with a very good top pitch, but some vegetation on the first pitch. However it is very quick to dry and all the difficulties are short and well protected. Start just right of Cooran Buttress Original Route at an obvious left-slanting jamming crack with a wedged spike at its base.
1. 55m 4c Climb the crack (Friend#3.5) and the vegetated rib above for a few metres, then step left to the base of a steep buttress (possible belay). Climb up this, moving left to cracks which are followed through a bulge to easier ground and a belay on a terrace by a huge leaning block.
2. 30m 4c Climb the slab on the right of the block for a metre or so, then traverse right to a prominent spike at the left end of the shelf. Move right along the shelf to a hidden groove and climb this to a terrace. Scramble up to the base of a clean narrow slab descending from the left-hand end of the overhang.
3. 35m 4c Climb the centre of the slab to a thin crack that just skirts the left end of the roof. Follow this with assistance from the wider crack on the left (all about 2m right of Traitor's Gait Direct), to an easier groove and finish up this.

Castles in the Air   130m   HVS *. S. Reid, M. Cundy. 5th May 2002. Climbed direct on p1 by S.Reid, C.King, 13th September 2002.
A fine series of variations on Monkey Puzzle. Start as for The Highway Man.
1. 45m 4c Climb a shallow groove to the central crack but quit this at 6m for a left-slanting crack system (this may also be reached rather unpleasantly direct from below). Follow the cracks up and left to an impasse below a smooth slab. Either climb this direct (5b), or traverse left along a ledge 3m and climb up a blocky gully to easy ground. Scramble up and rightwards up heather to belay at an obvious wide crack (P2 of Monkey Puzzle).
2. 25m 5a Climb a slim right-slanting groove just right of the crack, to step left on to a slab. Go up to flake cracks and pull up these to the right-hand end of an overhang. Scramble up heather to the obvious crack in the short wall above.
3. 30m 4c One metre right of the crack is a line of jugs up the wall. Follow these to a slab and more heather.
4. 30m 4b Left of the finish of The Highway Man are some fluted cracks leading to a perched block. Climb the wide left-hand crack almost to the block, but then trend up leftwards into a crack 2m to the left. Finish up this with interest.

High in the centre of the area to the right of Cooran Buttress is a prominent hanging arête which is best gained by traversing from the top of Cooran Buttress. Buchan Arête (20m, HVS 5a *, S. Reid, A. Gillies, 2002) takes a crack in its left side, passing two large blocks with care.

The Lion's Head:
This is the old name for the area of slabs that until this year only contained the classic E2 Saddle Tramp.

Aughty Star   115m   E1 **. S. Reid, C. King (alt, via direct finish). 10th October 2002.
C. King, S. Reid, 17th October 2002, as described.
A fine series of sustained pitches, with the option of a fiercesome finale on the third. Start at the right-hand side of the initial slab of Saddle Tramp.

1. 40m 5a Climb easily up rightwards to gain and follow a thin crack up the right side of the slab to grass. Follow the continuation crack in the upper slab, overcoming a bulge with difficulty, to belay on the bilberry ledge on the right below the lower of two diagonal cracks.

2. 20m 5b Make a rising traverse rightwards along the crack to a shallow niche. The awkward crack above leads to an easy left-leaning scoop and a rib on the left which is followed to a large ledge.

3. 45m 5b Ignore the final pitch of Saddle Tramp above left, and follow the ledge leftwards, with interest where it narrows, to join the twin right-slanting cracklines of Horns of a Dilemma. Make a very puzzling move up the left hand one, exiting leftwards and follow a leftward-rising ramp to a crack on the left. Climb the crack to an overlap and step down and right to belay on a slab.

4. 10m 4a Overcome the overlap directly to finish up slabs. Alternatively, continue to follow the narrowing rampline leftwards (5a).

Direct Finish: 15m E2 5b *.

On gaining the ledge at the top of pitch 2, belay on a flake over to the right, below an overhanging offwidth that cuts through the left end of the impressive roof of Aslan. This skin-rasping cleft succumbs only to the most masochistically determined. A Friend#5 is a useful booster of determination.

To the right of the Lion's Head is Dungeon Stone Coire, an atmospheric area containing several interesting looking crags. However close approach reveals these to be of the shrinking and broken variety, and the only route recorded is Brishie Buttress (25m Mild Severe, S. Reid, C. King, 17th October, 2002) which climbs the longest area of rock on the crag at the very far right-hand side of the buttress, just below the crest of the ridge.

Craignelder, Craig an Eilte:
Although these routes are short, nowhere more than 20m, they are very quick to dry and on excellent rock. All were climbed on 30th August, 2002 by C. King and S. Reid. Thirty metres to the left of Eilte Gully (the gully to the left of Eilte Tower) is Hind Gully. *Snozzle* (VS 4b) climbs directly up the rib on its right. *Slab-u-Like* (HVS 4c) boldly climbs the centre of the slab on its left via a fluted scoop to finish just right of a poised block, and *Slabadabadoo* (VS 4c) follows cracks on the left, via a dodgy block to finish just left of the poised block.

Flowers of the Forest 45m III,4 **. A. Fraser, I. Magill. 10th January 2003.
Great positions and fine climbing. One metre left of the initial chimney of Gloom is a rock groove. Climb this, then continue up the mixed ground above (as for Gloom) to the neck of the tower (25m) The next pitch heads rightwards across icefalls to exit from an icy niche. While the exact line will depend on the build up of ice, the FA took the following line. Move 2m down right to a split flake. Step off this and climb the thin wall above to gain turf , then a ledge with block. Traverse 3m right into the icy niche and exit this on the right (20m).

Gorm 25m III. A. Fraser, I. Magill. 10th January 2003.
Short but meaty. Some 500m down and right of the main cliff, is a deeply recessed bay. This route climbs the back of the bay, the lower bulge being climbed by steep

ice, just right of centre. A walk of 150m uphill from this climb leads to a 20m grade II/III icefall.

Eilte Tower:
In the Hall of the Mountain King   40m   VS 4b *. S. Reid, C. King. 30th August 2002.
A pitch of some character following the obvious line of weakness via niches up the centre of the wall. Start at a crack with a stalactite hold about 6m left of the cave and 3m right of the open groove of Kerb Crawler. Climb directly up to a narrow ledge, then make a rising traverse to the right up stepped holds to a flake crack which leads to a huge slabby niche. Traverse left across this and gain a rib on the left which leads back right to a steep groove. Go up this to a grass ledge and continue up a crack and bulging ledges above until it is possible to step left onto a large sloping ledge and make a puzzling finish up the hanging arête.

Some 100m to the right of Eilte Tower are a pair of similar but lesser towers. Minas Tirith (VS 4c, S. Reid, C. Bonington, 17th August 2002) is the left-hand and better of the two and gives a good steep 25m pitch following the undercut rib up into a blocky niche from the top of which a hand-traverse right gains a V-groove splitting the top of the tower. Minas Morgul (Severe 4b, C. Bonington, S. Reid, 17th August 2002) on the right is longer but more broken. The blank upper wall is avoided by a crack on the right.

Craigdews:
Up Perisgoat!   50m   VS *. S. Reid, J. Biggar. 31st October 2002.
Good climbing via direct variations on the first two pitches of Das Goat, starting as for that route.
1. 20m 5a Follow Das Goat via the short rib to the white scoop. Make hard but well protected moves up rightwards from this to a bald slab, then follow the crack above, finishing boldly up the juggy wall. Traverse left to belay at the end of the thin grass terrace.
2. 30m 4c Traverse 2m right, then take a rising line rightwards up the wall until it is possible to step down left onto a large patch of heather. Leave this via its left rib to gain the obvious central groove which is followed to an exciting exit and a scramble to the terrace. Traverse right to descend via the Ramp.

Craignaw, Shot Cleugh:
The Sleigh Team   120m   III,4 *. A. Fraser, I. Magill. 5th January 2003.
A satisfying mixed climb, better than appearances suggest. The difficulties are largely on frozen turf and snowed-up rock and it does not require a build up of ice. High on the crag, some 75m left of Shot Cleugh, and immediately above a tree, is a chimney line. Start down and slightly left of the chimney, at a small gully. Climb this over a bulge, then move up and right across easy ground to the foot of the chimney (45m). Climb the steep chimney above by excellent torquing (30m). Continue up the chimney, taking the right-hand of two steep sloping cracks at the top (45m).

Goat Track Gully   II. J. Biggar, S. Reid. January 2003.
The right-hand of the "three gullies", followed by the Direct Finish (IV, 4)

Broad Gully II. J. Biggar, S. Reid. January 2003.
The gully between the three gullies and Shot Cleugh.

Shot Cleugh, Left-Hand Start II. A. Hinkes, S. Reid. 8th January 2003.
A thin ice gully.

Shot Cleugh Right Hand Start II. S. Reid, A. Hinkes. January 2003.

Hidden Chimney IV,5 *. S. Reid, A. Hinkes. 8th January 2003.
A good pitch of steep ice with a rock overhang, situated half way up Shot Cleugh
Left-Hand finish.

Secret Sliver IV,3. A. Hinkes, Prior. January 2003.
An ice/turf smear to the right of Hidden Chimney.

Shot Cleugh widens into an easy basin in its central area. The main gully is the left
fork, which is easy and a reasonable descent to the next route.

Full Metal Jacket 60m II/III. I. Magill, A. Fraser. 5th January 2003.
This takes the right-hand icy gully, which springs from the central basin of Shot
Cleugh. A fine icefall leads to an easier upper gully.

Loch Grannoch Crag (NX 535 686):
It consists of four groups of slabs lying in a splendid position on the hillside above
the sandy beach at the southern end of Loch Grannoch. However although the
rock is good, the shortness of the climbs together with the long approach means
they are unlikely to prove popular except with instructors based at the Loch
Grannoch Lodge. Park as for Clints of Dromore, then continue on the track, turn
left and take a forest track past Meikle Cullendoch. Then take the next left and left
again to the lodge (one-and-a-half hours but much quicker by bike). Follow a
vague path through woods to the crag (a further 15mins). Some routes were
recorded in 1981, the remainder in 2002, though some, particularly on Lodge
Buttress, had obviously been climbed before. Please note that there is a ban on
climbing on this crag from 15th February to 30th June due to rare birds nesting.

Lodge Slabs:
The lowest slabs on the right. The left-hand slab is climbable anywhere at about
Diff., but the right-hand slab is more interesting. *Spike Slab* (V. Diff) gains and
climbs the ramp above the big spike. To the right, *Wall Left* (Severe 4a) takes a
vague crack, *Wall Centre* (VS 4b) goes via a niche and *Wall Right* (H. Severe 4b)
take a crack to ledges and a wall. Just right again the striking right-slanting diagonal
crack is taken by *Diagonal 1* (VS 5a) which crosses the obvious central crack line
of *Centre Crack* (V. Diff) before finishing up slabs on the right. Just right again,
Diagonal 2 (HVS 5b) gives a hard start up a faint line of tiny flakes before crossing
Centre Crack and then finishing up the upper of two diagonal faults. *Diagonal 3*
(H. Severe 4b) starts at the foot of Centre Crack and follows the lower fault in its
entirety, and *Diagonal 2.5* (E1 5b) climbs boldly and slightly artificially up the
slab between the two faults. All the routes are 10-15m long.

M Slabs:
These are 60m up the hillside above Lodge Slabs and gives some very clean but
short (8m) routes. The centre of the white left-hand slab is taken by the very bold

Kid's Stuff (E2 5c). *Kids R Us* up the arête to the left is V. Diff and *Kid You Not* (Mild Severe 4a) climbs the short wall to the right. The remaining routes lie to the right of the vegetated central groove. *M1* (VS 4b) takes the thin wiggly crack on the left and *M6* (VS 4c) the excellent right-slanting diagonal crack starting at the same point, whilst *M62* (HVS 5a) follows M6 until it is possible to step left into the upper crack and boldly follow this. Right again, *Bypass* (HVS 5a) takes an unlikely line up the blank-looking slab, and at the far right, *Detour* (Diff.) follows the clean cracked slab.

Goat Slabs:
These are 50m to the left. *Stemlines* (E2 5b) gives a sustained pitch up the thin triple crack system on the right of the main slab, whilst *Goat Slab* (Hard Severe 4a) climbs the unpleasantly vegetated left-hand side to finish up the wall/arête. The inaptly *named Goat Grooves* (Mild Severe 4a) starts up a subsidiary slab on the left, before crossing heather to finish up the pleasant upper slab. All these routes are 25m long.

Madman's Slabs:
Situated 200m to the left again, at the far side of an open gully. *Black Ball* (25m Severe 4a) gives rather vegetated climbing up the centre of the large dark convex slab on the right. To its left are two prominent clean ribs. *Right Rib* is an 8m Diff., while *Left Rib* (10m V. Diff) starts up a steep crack then more easily follows the rib above. Up and right of the ribs, *Shortie* (Severe) is a pleasant if heathery 12m wall leading to the foot of the upper slab where *Captain Madman* (VS 4c) gives a good 25m pitch up the thin right-slanting crack just right of the vegetated crack.

First Ascents: Left Rib, Shortie, Captain Madman, Goat Grooves, Goat Slab, Kid's Stuff, M1, M6, Bypass: D.Gibson, A.Fraser, April 1981.
Spike Slab, Wall Left, Wall Centre, Wall Right, Centre Crack, Diagonals 1, 2, 2.5, and 3, Kids R Us, Kid You Not, M62, Detour, Stemline, Black Ball, Left Rib: C. King, S. Reid, 19th September, 2002.

Clatteringshaws Crag:
There are no climbs recorded in the unattractive quarry opposite Clatteringshaws Dam, but on the hillside above this lie the easy angled vegetated slabs of Clatteringshaws Crag (NX 549 754) which is best reached by taking the first left turn 100m down the Raiders' Road and then striking directly up the hillside. The sole climb is *Dam It*, a pleasant 25m Moderate which takes the rib formed by fallen blocks on the left of the crag (S. Reid on 7th November 2002).

The Merrick, Black Gairy:
The Lang Scots Mile 155m IV,4 **. A. Fraser, I. Magill. 5th February 2003.
A fine long ice route. 150m right of the Black Gutter (50m left of the icicle of Interstellar Overdraft), at mid height on the face is an overhanging square black wall. Start below the right end of this, mid-way between a shallow groove and a large spike at 3m. Climb iced walls directly to beneath a short steep chimney. Ice screws needed for runners and belay (30m). Climb a bulge to the left of the chimney, then easier ground to below the square black wall.(25m). Climb the icefall corner on the right of the wall, then continue up the hidden gully above (50m). Continue by icefalls to the top (50m).

Swatte Fell (near Hart Fell), Upper Coomb Craig, Right Coire:
M.W. Holland and J. Blackford climbed two possible new routes on 11th January 2003 after an extended freeze. The routes are escapable on to turf on either side and may bank out with more snow, but were good in the conditions. The routes were on good water ice and frozen turf to the left of the grade II central gully mentioned in the Lowland Outcrops Guide.
1. 160m III. Starting from the left-hand side of the second bay left of the central gully, 30m of stepped water ice was followed by an easier gully line. The left-hand fork of the gully was taken for the second pitch.
2. 140m II. Starting approx. 40m left and higher than the previous route, a stepped water ice pitch was followed by further easier angled water ice in the gully as it dog-legged back right. After the gully, turf was followed up and left to the top.

Moffat Valley:
Broken Cleugh 500m II/III. S. Mortlock, J. Lawrence, C. Barr. 11th January 2003.
A frozen burn with several short pitches on the north-facing (south) side of the valley opposite and 800m above Grey Mare's Tail. On the day, Grey Mares Tail was very wet. Also climbed by an another party the same day.

THE DUMFRIES OUTCROPS, Clifton Crag:
Main Wall Girdle 110m HVS. S. Reid, W. Hurford. 13th February 2002
Artificial, but with some good exciting pitches. Climb Jeune Ecole, or any other pitch to the top of Hollowstones Wall.
1. 30m 4c Follow Gramercy until just below the mantelshelf, then traverse right along the flake and step across Dirl Chimney. Descend down rightwards with difficulty and traverse the lip of the roof, to gain the crack of Gibbon in Wonderland. Use this to gain a platform up on the right, and traverse right to the top of the groove of Tour de Force. Descend this for 2m, and step right awkwardly on to a heathery ledge.
2. 20m 4b Traverse rightwards across a slimy slab into Owl Chimney, and step out right on to a platform. Descend the crack of Lipstick for 2m, then follow the rising traverse of Stiff Upper Lip to a huge block at the right hand side of Main Wall.
3. 35m 4c Descend slightly the corner of Ratten's Rest, and traverse the break under the roof taking care with loose blocks to pull out at the top of The Groove. Descend halfway down the Esplanade, then make a slightly rising traverse across the mossy wall, and go up to a small oak tree, just left of Red Slab.
4. 25m 5a Cross the red slab to join DIY and finish up this. Alternatively, continue the traverse to an awkward finish up Nebula (E1 5b).

CENTRAL OUTCROPS, Cambusbarron Closed Quarry:
Grangemouth High Grooves Hard Severe 4b. N. Tait, S. Tait. 24th September 2002.
As you walk in, stay left against the small cracked wall as it rises and follow this until it gets about 8m high. Just before a blocky corner, and after a small block which makes a wee 1m roof, there is a groove system which is followed to finish on small blocks.

Daniel Can Walk! E1 5b. N. Tait, S. Tait. 24th September 2002.
Continue beyond the above route around a leaning/hanging corner and start at the bottom of a steep slab, just right of an arête. The first few moves are a well protected crux on clean rock, using the arête to layaway, then easier but poorly protected.

LIMEKILNS, Gellet Block:
Note: A. D. Robertson notes that The Struggler can be climbed independently of the neighbouring E2 by climbing the wall direct (slightly left, then right) to the peg at about 5m (E3 6a but harder than the original). Recommended. Iron Fist has now lost two crucial jugs and is much harder than the current grade. Certainly 6b, E5 suggested.

EAST LOTHIAN, North Berwick Law:
Note: M. Raistrick has led the slab which is top roped occasionally by groups at 15m, Severe.

THE FAST CASTLE SEA CLIFFS, North Brander Bay:
Whalers Crack   15m   VS. A. McKay, M. Raistrick. June 2000.
On the striking shark's fin-like pinnacle, a few hundred metres north of Crimpanzie Fin and the Souter. Tidal. Approach as for Souter. Follow solid twin cracks for 10m, then move right to a wee friable rib which is followed to a ledge near the top of the pinnacle. Scramble off the back.

Brander Slabs:
Mince and Tatties   50m   Difficult. M. Raistrick. September 2000.
Start opposite the end of Brander Slab across the Geo.
1. Follow an attractive corner with a slabby left wall for 15m to a steepening.
2. Follow cracked slabs more easily to belay at a col on the ridge that leads to Brander Slab.

Fatlips Crag:
This crag is composed of dolerite and not of sandstone as indicated in the current guide.
Fatlips Rib   35m   VS 4b. G. E. Little. 12th May 2002.
Start just to the left of Fatlips Corner and climb slabby rock to a diagonal, left-trending stepped overlap. Follow it up and left to its end, then move up and step right on to a clean rib. Climb the rib to its top at a big detached flake and finish on slabby rock.

THE CHEVIOT, Hen Hole, Peake's Buttress (Map Ref 887 202):
Although this north-facing buttress actually lies in England (about 300m from the Scottish border), it is most conveniently accessed from Sourhope or Cocklawfoot in Scotland in just over one hour.

Muzzlehatch Arête   70m   II. G. E. Little. 11th January 2003.
This is the right-bounding edge of the crag. Start at the lowest point of the crag. Gain the arête from the right (or more directly by an obvious rock groove, III,4), then follow it to a blunt rock nose. Bypass the rock nose on the left, then move right on to a platform. Continue on easier angled but slabby ground just left of the edge to the top of the buttress.

Prunesquallor Gully   60m   III,4. G. E. Little. 11th January 2003.
This is the obvious central gully that does not reach the foot of the crag. Start up and left of the fall line of the gully at a short groove. Climb straight up to a ledge, then traverse right to gain the gully. Climb a short pitch, then go up to below a steep constriction where the gully bends to the left. Surmount this (crux) and climb to the top of the buttress.

MISCELLANEOUS NOTES

The W. H. Murray Literary Prize.

As a tribute to the late Bill Murray, whose mountain and environment writings have been an inspiration to many a budding mountaineer, the SMC have set up a modest writing prize, to be run through the pages of the Journal. The basic rules are set out below, and will be re-printed each year. The prize is run with a deadline, as is normal, of the end of January each year. So assuming you are reading this in early July, you have, for the next issue, six months in which to set the pencil, pen or word processor on fire.

The Rules:

1. There shall be a competition for the best entry on Scottish Mountaineering published in the *Scottish Mountaineering Club Journal.* The competition shall be called the 'W. H. Murray Literary Prize', hereafter called the 'Prize.'

2. The judging panel shall consist of, in the first instance, the following: The current Editor of the *SMC Journal;* The current President of the SMC; and two or three lay members, who may be drawn from the membership of the SMC. The lay members of the panel will sit for three years after which they will be replaced.

3. If, in the view of the panel, there is in any year no entries suitable for the Prize, then there shall be no award that year.

4. Entries shall be writing on the general theme of 'Scottish Mountaineering', and may be prose articles of up to approximately 5000 words in length, or shorter verse. Entries may be fictional.

5. Panel members may not enter for the competition during the period of their membership.

6. Entries must be of original, previously unpublished material. Entries should be submitted to the Editor of the *SMC Journal* before the end of January for consideration that year. Lengthy contributions are preferably word-processed and submitted either on 3.5" PC disk or sent via e-mail. (See Office Bearers page at end of this Journal for address etc.) Any contributor to the SMC Journal is entitled to exclude their material from consideration of the Prize and should so notify the Editor of this wish in advance.

7. The prize will be a cheque for the amount £250.

8. Contributors may make different submissions in different years.

9. The decision of the panel is final.

10. Any winning entry will be announced in the *SMC Journal* and will be published in the *SMC Journal* and on the SMC Web site. Thereafter, authors retain copyright.

The W. H. Murray Literary Prize (2003).

THE winner of the 2003 W. H. Murray Literary Prize is regular Journal contributor, Peter Biggar, for his short story *The Second Sight*. As his previous work has shown, Peter is very much at home with this genre, an opinion borne out by judge Terry Gifford's comment: "This writer has learned from good storytellers some of the tricks of the well-crafted tale."

In creating a work that addresses myth and mortality, the author evokes, if not past times, then certainly gentler and unfortunately passing ones, where one inhabits the world of the primus and real porridge oats as opposed to Trangias and energy bars. Having said that, the introduction of a pair of "pink shell-suit trousers" is perhaps indicative of the way the author moves freely and seamlessly between points of view.

His ability to create a sense of place with a deft choice of language is excellent, as evidenced by passages such as: "As the breeze shifted the clouds, warm shafts of sunlight came through making the myriad dewdrops sparkle on the spider's webs. Away down in the valley, smoke rose from the dwellings by the river and a small boat moved imperceptibly over the surface of the sea loch on its round from one orange buoy to the next."

Three other articles could be said to be runners-up in terms of the attention and comment they attracted from the judges.

Dave MacLeod gave us a well-written piece on just what lies behind a major first ascent at the very cutting edge of today's rock climbing scene. In describing his new route which fills in a blank space on the Chemin de Fer face at Dumbarton Rock, Dave produced, in the words of our new President in his first term as a W. H. M. judge, a piece which was " very focused (as befits a climber at this level) and well written." The Ian Nicolson of his generation as far as 'Dumbie' is concerned anyway.

Stephen Reid produced a well-written piece about what must be an ever more ephemeral pastime, that of ice climbing in the Galloway Hills, *Dow Spout* which the President found to be, "in many ways a model climbing article – informative, evocative and conveying the exhilaration and satisfaction of a good day on the hills".

A final mention goes to M. G. Anderson, again, as last year, in the position of bridesmaid with his humorous piece *Dropping In On Friends* which I feel may well be a cross genre work, best listed under the heading 'Faction.'

Terry Gifford commented that this piece would "delight readers of the Journal, especially with its use of the Royal language of Lower Deeside." (perhaps that should be the Lower language of Royal Deeside!). Derek Pyper has kindly offered his services as translator for any of our more southerly-based readers who may experience difficulty with this one.

Congratulations again to Peter Biggar, and to the other contributors and all you budding authors out there, there's always next year. The winning article as well as appearing in this year's Journal can also be read in full on the SMC Website.

Charlie Orr.

Scottish Mountain Accidents

DUE to the death of club member John Hinde, (obituary appears elsewhere) who compiled the Scottish Mountain Accident statistics for over 20 years, there is no Accidents Section this year. The Scottish Mountain Rescue Committee has appointed a successor but, due to the vast amount of work involved, in what for John was undoubtedly a labour of love, it has not been possible to manage a seamless transition. The Club, and indeed, the wider community is indebted to John for his meticulous recording of these valuable statistics over the years.

MEN, MOUNTAINS AND ADVENTURE

By Walter Bonatti

(Address to The International Festival of Mountaineering Literature – Leeds University 2002)

I have only one aim when I talk about my experiences – to remind you what wise men have always pointed out as the correct path to follow. They say that each of us must be the author of his own story as it unfolds throughout the course of his life. From this precept it is easy to conclude that if you wish to build your own spiritual identity, your basic need, your only goal, should be to assert yourself and grow. This calls for a commitment which demands passion, perseverance and integrity concerning the sound principles one must accept. This will have excellent results – you will feel stronger and firmer and as a result will feel like a winner. We therefore should never wait for anything to come as a gift from others, and still less for so-called 'luck'. Our 'lucky stars' are merely what we manage to create for ourselves – step by step, year after year, experience after experience. Everything must be paid for with our own hides. This then is not luck, but continuing growth. To reaffirm what I have just said, I offer the experience of an entire lifetime – my own life.

I am not a mountain man by birth, but became wedded to the mountains by pure passion after growing up in the flattest part of Italy – the plain of the Po valley. I will say at once that my adventurous instincts, which were to become the driving force of my life, were undoubtedly produced by curiosity, an abiding curiosity which little by little became ever more associated with fantasy, with dreams, with the insuppressible need to give concrete reality to all this. But a hard, difficult adolescence also contributed a great deal to the development of my character, formed not only by the defeat of Italy in the Second World War but also by the resultant sudden collapse of human values and the lack of any real prospects – totally absent in my country at that time. This happened to a lad who just then was facing the realities of life.

As a repercussion, such precedents could have been transformed into moral degradation for the poor in spirit, or to the exact opposite in those with positive potential. Fortunately, this latter alternative was what happened to me.

While still very young – only 18 years old – I began to practice mountaineering at the highest level, and this led me, in less than a year, to repeat the most difficult climbs achieved up till then by my predecessors. But doing extreme climbs was for me not so much a flight from the daily round (however understandable that might have been), nor rebellion against the misery of the all too unexciting society of the time, it was rather above all, an obstinate and irrepressible need to succeed over and over again.

From that time, for the next 16 years, I travelled in the Alps and the other mountains of the world, following my dreams as a means of fulfilment – going always a little farther. I believe that only when you dream with open eyes can you conceive things that represent the limits of your sensitivity. In fact, my exploits always started to exist from the very moment they first took form in my thoughts. To transform them into reality was no more than a logical consequence off that first thought, that first idea. When I first imagined what would eventually become my most significant ascents, I found myself in a peculiar state of mind – I would say almost unreal – when anything seemed possible, even normal. To then achieve the climb itself was no more than the natural and inevitable consequence of that idea, certainly no more real than its conception. It is when you are imagining things that you live intensely and it is only when you believe in yourself that you are able to really develop concepts. So, up there, as exploit followed exploit, I felt more and more alive, free and true to myself. I was also able to satisfy that innate need of every man to test and prove himself – to know and to understand. I add and underline that I have always followed my emotions – let alone my creative and contemplative impulses.

Right from the start, mountaineering for me was adventure – it should not and could not have been otherwise – and I always wished to live adventurously to the measure of man, with due respect for tradition. Soon, however, this became a fascinating way of living and knowing myself and it was also helpful to my physical and mental well-being.

I have always admired mountaineers of every epoch but I have never regarded any of them as a model. So I read their books, saw, heard and evaluated many mountain men, but only to create my own self, not to copy them. I am convinced that mountaineering improves only those who improve themselves – it certainly doesn't improve the apathetic or the arrogant. It isn't being a mountaineer that enriches a man – indeed, as I have already said, what he carries inside himself grows in a particular way if he has integrity.

All my climbs have been equally important to me, leaving aside the difficulty and commitment they demanded. I remember them all in the same way, with satisfaction, because they were all imagined, wanted, sought after, experienced, delighted in and they have all been cut to my measure and so were right for me at the moment they happened. Everyone knows that great trials either toughen you or annihilate you – this is the story of life. It follows from this that each of us is the sum, the end result of his own experiences. Mine have made me grow and so my limits have expanded.

It was by practicing traditional alpinism that I was able to enter into harmony with Mother Nature, but it was only solo climbing – I mean at the highest level – that released the deepest inborn energy of my being. In this way I was able better to know my motivation and my limitations, moreover, I learned how to make crucial decisions for myself, to judge them by my own measure and, naturally enough, pay for them with my own hide. In brief, solo climbing was an effective, formative school for me, a precious condition, then a real necessity at times. So I reaffirm my conviction that in a climb there is nothing more profitable than solitude and isolation to sharpen your sensations and amplify your emotions. It was really thanks to the preliminaries just set out that I was able to complete every time a fascinating internal voyage of discovery, the better to examine and understand myself but also to understand other people and the world around me. I can say now that I know myself better, know what I have achieved and what I want from myself and others. As far as others are concerned, naturally I fight against ill-will if it arises, but I can accept criticism – it can be helpful if it is constructive, whereas destructive criticism is like the air to me, it doesn't affect me.

One could say I have been lucky but I don't believe in luck, nor in fate. Fate then, I repeat, is what we knowingly create for ourselves (with the sole limitation of the unforeseeable). Many years have passed since the time of my climbs but the mountains have left within me, still vital and indelible, the imposing images of their architecture, of their superb severe outlines suspended in the sky – alien at times to the measure of man and certainly far beyond his limitations. With the eyes of the mind I can still recall those freezing, silent heights in every detail and, as before, my thoughts fly in a constant circuit from things to imagination and back again, liberating new perceptions, unknown dimensions which constantly slide away from any attempt to explain them. How true it is that by understanding beauty we possess it.

This and more besides, is what I described in my book *Mountains Of My Life* about my experiences, chapter after chapter, until the day of my winter ascent of the north face of the Matterhorn in 1965. It was really then that I concluded my climbing career. I realized then that after this adventure of mine, achieved by classical, fair means, I would not have been able to push on farther without accepting the compromises inherent in the new climbing techniques with its whole armamentarium that I had always disdained.

And here, even so many years after the epilogue of my mountaineering career, I wish to set out some concepts, perhaps debatable according to some people, but drawn from what were my motivations in mountaineering. What makes me speak of them is the ever more obvious derangement that nowadays compounds and disturbs the mountaineering world, making orphans of the values it regards as outmoded while, at the same time persisting in the laboured search for alternative incentives in which to believe.

Granted that we all are free to believe whatever we wish, to adopt whatever rules we find are most convenient for our aspirations, free also to climb in our own way. I too, for the same reasons, chose a mountaineering philosophy to my own tastes and measure, consistent with my ideology. So I repeat – it was traditional methods that inspired me right from the beginning. This habitual, classical way of climbing is an alpinism that, in the act of measuring your limits against the great mountains, puts your whole being to the test – physical endurance, principles and moral values, with nothing whatever held back. And this, which I define as 'greater mountaineering' becomes especially austere and demanding precisely because of the limitations put on the technical means we choose to accept in confronting the mountains. But greater mountaineering is still more fascinating and gratifying if we keep in mind its historic and ethical values, quite apart from aesthetics. Personally, I have never been able to separate these three elements nor choose between them, since for me they are fundamental. To this end, I committed myself and conformed to the mountaineering methods of the Thirties – obviously adopting the essentials, not to mention the elementary and limited equipment used in those times.

But why would I have chosen limitations so 'anachronistic' in relation to my own times? Certainly not because of masochistic perversion, but rather so I could conserve an unchangeable measuring rod for comparison – a sort of Greenwich Meridian, unalterable by time or conditions, to be precise the only reliable constant that could allow me to reach an impartial judgment about things and also about myself.

So that is what I believe are the just, fair rules of the game I had chosen, rules which I imposed on myself right from the beginning and which I would still choose today, really to guarantee myself a bond and a sure means of comparison with the past to which I had always referred. Committing myself to my summits in this way, I repeat, I have been able to test myself to the depths by comparison with those who went before me and I have also been able to remain in harmony with the physical and psychological conditions involved in the exploits of the past. I have also been able to evaluate objectively the importance of what I had managed to achieve compared with what was known to have been done before.

If we ignore the past and refer only to the present in making judgments about mountaineering – an ever more technological present, ever more liable to remove from a climb its peculiar difficulties, its unknown problems, even its impossibility, a present in which a mountaineering exploit, most times, has the sole merit of confirming the success of the technical equipment used – well then, I believe we will never be able to formulate just and clear criteria which will allow us to understand what mountaineering really is and this will be because we have never really understood what its limits and motivations were in the past.

Experienced in this way, the mountains have given me more than I could ever have hoped for. This despite the fact that I realized I had been 'also' a mountaineer till then, but not 'just' a mountaineer. Actually, as the years passed I had come to understand that my true character was driving me always more to experience adventure in its widest universal expression. So I had to broaden my horizons through the entire 360° of a world which at that time was still almost unknown to me. I was then transferring my extreme mountaineering, with all its psychological components, out of its vertical surroundings and putting it into an adventurous context which was just as extreme but, for the most part, as yet unknown. I therefore had to trust the instincts of my life in an even vaster multi-dimensional cultural world, where the real space in which I was travelling would be, above all, that of the mind. In short, I felt that I was embarking on a period of personal growth. After the great mountains, a huge world now awaited me. From then on I went everywhere, and came to grips with forests, deserts, lost islands, the depths of the sea, volcanoes, icy and tropical latitudes, not to mention primitive peoples, wild animals, and the remains of ancient civilizations. But everything I did provided me with the most beautiful, significant and richest of sensations because, as before, I used to intensely long for every one of these experiences before living through them.

I had the chance to become a journalist, a special correspondent of the then great Italian weekly journal *Epoca* (published by Mondadori) and had *carte blanche* to produce, where and when I wished, my 'extreme journalism' and 'introspections'. But how did it start, this new adventure? First of all, I revisited my childish fantasies and the books I had read as a boy concerning the things I use to dream about so much. At a certain age we all dream about what we read, I was now able to give life to these dreams and made from them the motive for my travels. At that time, in the Sixties and Seventies, there were almost always some difficulties, few people had been to those places and very few knew anything about them. I must say too that in the experiences I encountered I tried never to fight with anyone or anything, whether people or fearsome animals were concerned – on the contrary, I was seeking a point of contact with the savage world in order to know it better, assimilate it and transmit this world to others by means of words and pictures. This is what I wanted to do, developing my own variety of journalism, making the reader understand that behind the notebook and camera was a mere man, full of curiosity and alone with his emotions.

It is now clear to everyone that I am instinctively attracted to and fascinated by primordial nature. Because of this I climbed down into active volcanoes and I went into those smoking craters above all to see how the world was made when it began, to imagine how things would have looked the day after its creation if anyone had been there to see. One can therefore imagine how much emotion, surprise and admiration was aroused in me by an episode of that sort.

I can certainly say that what drove me on and sustained me in all those situations I lived through – in every experience I had after I had given up mountaineering – were the same motivating forces which had thrust me on to 'impossible' mountains. Nothing had changed. But in all this, my intention was always to know and to consider, to try myself out and test myself, entering as far as possible into conditions that were able to awaken those modes of thought, those endowments from other times which certainly still exist in all of us, even if they are somewhat dormant nowadays. Moreover, I wanted to experience to the full the freedom of knowing myself to be absolutely detached from any sort of technical, organized support which if necessary would have helped me, supplied me with provisions or even saved me if I got into trouble. Naturally, the places and situations I chose offered all those ingredients which could give life and logical sense to my adventure as I envisaged it.

In this way, detached and far away from all that one might regard as the developed world, I can say that on most occasions I came to know a world still untouched from the time of its origin. On my travels I encountered all manner of wild animals, and also primitive tribes whose mode of dress had remained unchanged for millennia. In those places sun and rain, birth and death remained the only reality, which regulated their lives; their survival was torn tenaciously from a miserable environment hostile to life; they were ignorant of the rest of the world, which ignored them in its turn. But then, in those far-off lands, huge and without history, where nothing changes, everything repeats itself in an endless cycle. I experienced fears and hopes, discomfort and exaltation. There I listened to absolute silence, to hurricanes, I inhaled the vapour of volcanoes, the smells of the jungle and during dark nights my merest glance encompassed a plethora of stars. With my mind floating I have wandered, dreaming of impossible horizons, giving human proportions to the infinite, until I have lost myself in the universe. Now more than ever I am convinced that a man's life makes sense only if it encompasses everything he has within his being. It is there, in the mind, that real spaces are created.

However, although on my new travels in the six continents there was no lack of great mountains, Mont Blanc has remained the one I have most assiduously explored again and again by all its ridges and valleys. I have done this much as a man returns to his own father, to converse together with all the affection and memories a son looks for in a parent.

Would you like to know what conclusions I have drawn from my intense wandering life? Well, I have never been sated by dreaming about far off lands – my imagination has always been captivated by their intense silence.

Translated by Robert Marshall.

SCOTTISH WINTER NOTES

THE winter of 2002-2003 will not be remembered as one of the great Scottish winter seasons. Although there was early snow in October, and it was consistently cold from November onwards, the season was too dry for consistently good winter climbing. The West in particular suffered from a real lack of snow, and at the beginning of January, Number Four Gully on the Ben was just bare scree – something that I have never witnessed in winter before. Inevitably, the lean conditions significantly reduced new route activity. Although there were a respectable number of new climbs, many were variations or very short routes. There were some good additions nevertheless, and this report summarises a selection of the significant new routes.

Some of the most rewarding new climbs were those that follow natural watercourses and drainage lines. Andy Nisbet was most adept at combining his encyclopaedic knowledge of the Highlands with an accurate assessment of the best type of climbing on offer. In January, he visited Foinaven with Dave McGimpsey and climbed Moss Ghyll (IV,5), an impressive frozen stream bed in Lower Corrie Lice, and a line he had first spotted in the late 1970s. They soloed the first three pitches, and then roped up for an imposing barrier icefall. Fortunately, wind had made the ice form in a contorted structure that allowed the pitch to be climbed with relative ease giving access to easier ice above. Nisbet and McGimpsey were also responsible for the other major addition in the North-west when they climbed a 300m ice smear on Ben Mor Coigach in the company of Erik Brunskill and Malcolm Bass. This fine discovery lies just left of Consolation Gully on the North Face and gave an excellent Grade IV outing. Farther south, Andy Nisbet visited Stob Poite Coire Ardair just east of Creag Meagaidh and soloed two icefalls he had noted several years ago. Mer de Glace and La Rive Gauche are both fine Grade III climbs and the first recorded routes in the corrie.

Creag Meagaidh came into good condition in February after one of the heaviest snowfalls of the winter. The gullies on the Post Face saw many ascents, and Kevin Neal and Iain Rudkin made a good addition to the left side of the face when they made the first ascent of The Lost Post (VI,5), a fine two-pitch icefall just right of Post Haste. South of Loch Laggan, Colin Wells and Mary Twomey visited Coire nam Cnamh on Meall Garbh where they found Merciless Mary (IV,3), a two-pitch icefall to the right of the main crag. Farther west in Coire an Lochain on Aonach Mor, the lean conditions exposed a considerable quantity of ice to the left of Easy Gully over an area that is normally banked up by snow. Gareth Hobson, Julia Baron, Ed Hartley, Rachel Wilson and Tim Fairbrother took advantage of the settled weather over the New Year period and climbed five Grade III ice routes. These lines provided good ice climbing through the season, and being less exposed to the late winter sun than the routes farther right, they proved popular until the end of the winter.

One of the finest ascents in the Cairngorms was the first ascent of Tearaway (III/IV) on Glaucous Buttress in Coire an Dubh Lochan on Beinn a'Bhuird by Alex Runciman and partner. This buttress often ices up well early in the season, and it is somewhat surprising that this classic VS line had remained untouched in winter conditions for so long. In the centre of the massif, Steve Helmore and Keith Milne visited Creagan a'Choire Etchachan where they climbed Infidelity (V,6), a series of steep, blocky corners cutting through the upper right-hand side of the crag near the summer route Stanley. Dave McGimpsey and Andy Nisbet had a wild day in Coire Bhrochain on Braeriach when they made the first ascent of Bell's Direct Route on the Black Pinnacle. A blizzard, ferocious winds and limited daylight made this a particularly hard-fought V,6. Farther south on Creag an Dubh Loch, Guy Robertson and Tim Rankin climbed Snakes and Ladders (V,7) on the buttress to the right of Sabre Cut, and Chris Cartwright and I polished off Bonanza (V,7), one of the last remaining lines on the North-West Face of The Stuic. The most interesting Cairngorms climb was the first ascent of Where Eagles Dare (V,5) by Neil Batchelor and Fiona Watt. The route follows a frozen watercourse with a steep icicle crux and is the first recorded climb on the cliffs at the head of the Canness Burn in Glen Isla.

The North-west suffered from limited snowfall throughout the season, which severely limited exploratory activity. The most difficult new route was climbed by Guy Robertson, Matt Halls and Phillip Ebert on the remote Maoile Lunndaidh to the south of Glen Carron. Hellfire and Brimstone (VII,7) takes a very steep direct line over an overhang up the buttress climbed by Spiral Search. Robertson returned a few weeks later with his brother Peter to climb FB Gully (IV) on the left side of the buttress, and The Shiner (III), an icy scoop on the right. In Garbh Choire Mor of An Coileachan in the Fannaichs, Andy Nisbet and Dave McGimpsey took advantage of a heavy fall of snow in January to make the first ascent of Triffid (VI,7) a steep line up the right side of the steep buttress climbed by Venus Fly Trap. The same pair also visited Coire Ruadh-Staca on Beinn Eighe and made the first winter ascent of the short but good groove-line of Smilodon (IV,5) on the right side of the crag. Dave Broadhead and John Mackenzie added several new climbs to the Strathfarrar crags including Sleeping Beauty (IV,5), a good route to the right of Red Campion on Sgurr na Fearstaig.

Andy Nisbet and Jonathan Preston took advantage of early snowfall on Ben Nevis when they made the first winter ascent of Spartacus (VI,7) on South Trident Buttress. This makes a fine companion to The Slab Climb climbed by the same team at a similar grade two winters before. Chris Cartwright and I made a couple of successful early season visits to Coire na Ciste. Pinncer (IV,4) takes the unclimbed north ridge of Pinnacle Buttress starting a little way up Broad Gully. Four varied pitches with a final squeeze chimney led to the summit of The Pinnacle leaving us rather surprised why such an obvious feature had been overlooked for so long. Farther right we climbed the prominent fault-line on the front face of Goodeve's Buttress to the right of Goodytwoshoes. The Borg Collective (V,6) was a surprisingly amenable climb with a chockstone runner whenever the going got steep. The following day we climbed The Great Circle (VI,7) on Comb Gully Buttress. This left-curving line takes the wall left of Clough's Chimney before climbing an awkward offwidth and finishing up the tower left of Comb Gully Buttress.

Nisbet and McGimpsey continued their development of Stob Coire an Laoigh in the Grey Corries with Black Widow (V,6), the deep groove right of Spider Man, and Tarantula (V,6), the crack-line to its right. They also climbed Sloppy Suzie (V,5), the left-hand groove in the face right of Loopy Louie, Sleeping Dog (IV,5), the upper of two faults on the right wall of Central Gully, and Hoverfly, a wild line with a very exposed traverse along the lip of a big roof right of Taliballan. They also teamed up with Brian Davison to climb Cobra Corner (VI,6), the huge roofed gully right of Calf Buttress. Erik Brunskill and Dafydd Morris visited the cliff after the first prolonged cold spell in November when the crag was thick with rime. They headed straight for the impressive crack-line on the left side of Calf buttress and climbed MooMoo (V,7) which turned out to be sensational – incredibly steep but highly amenable, and with very good protection. Their second new route, Cameron's Cooz (V,6), which takes the unlikely looking cracked wall just left of MooMoo epitomises the climbing on the cliff with hook after hook and big blobs of turf where required. James Edwards and Gareth Hughes made a productive visit to the crag in January and came away with a good haul of routes included Laughing Cow (V,6) the fault about 10m left of MooMoo, Choc-a-Block (VI,6), the first fault line on the left-hand wall of Central Gully and The Epithany (V,6), the easiest line in the middle of a bay at the right end of the leftmost buttress. A week later, Edwards was back with James Thacker to add The Alternate (IV,5), the fault to the right of The Epithany and Chaf Direct (IV,6) to the right of Choc-a-Block.

Farther east, Iain Small could not resist the diagram of Ben Alder's Garbh Coire Beag in the new Ben Nevis guide that shows a prominent unclimbed gully up the centre of the cliff. The resulting climb was a fine Grade III named McCook's Gully. The finest addition in Glen Coe was Long Chimney Direct (VII,6) on Cunieform Buttress on Buachaille Etive Mor by Erik Brunskill and Stuart McFarlane. This is a sustained and direct version of Long Chimney, stepping right from groove to groove with a serious traverse to reach hanging flakes to finish. Over on Bishop's Buttress of Bidean, Blair Fyffe and Dave Hollinger made the first winter ascent of Ambush (VI,7) – a route that packed a fair punch into its 70 metres. Farther south there were some good additions to the Bridge of Orchy crags. Dave MacLeod and Dave Redpath visited Creag Coire an Dothaidh and found a line left of Beelzebub to give Cool Riders (IV,5), and Eddie McHutchison, Chris McDaid and Raymond Wallace climbed Off the Beaten Track (III/IV) on Beinn Udhlaidh, which takes a good line up ice right of Ramshead Gully. Andy Clarke and Mark Garthwaite visited the North Peak of The Cobbler where they made the first winter ascent of Cat Crawl (VI,7) the obvious fault left of Direct Direct.

Over in Coire an Lochain on Aonach Mor, Chris Cartwright and I put a long-standing problem to bed with the first ascent of Jaws (VII,6), the well-defined buttress between White Shark and Tinsel Town. I first attempted this line in 1989 with Roger Everett, but the rock is more compact than elsewhere in the corrie and it requires ice to enter 'the jaws', a hanging groove slicing through the final tower. Farther left, Jose Bermúdez and M. Gray found Is This the Way to St Louis? (IV,4), the icy groove left of Back Street Boogie, and David Brown and Fiona Murray, climbed a new Left-Hand Finish (III) to Spider Rib, which provides a longer and more interesting continuation to the original route. Nearby on the West Face of Aonach Beag, Alan Kimber, Tony Coar and Peter Foulkes found Snake Charmer (II/III), a good mixed route on the right side of Broken Axe Buttress.

The vast east face of Aonach Beag saw one of the most interesting ascents of the season when Andy Nisbet and Dave McGimpsey climbed a long Grade II ridge-line to the left of the classic North-East Ridge. Remarkably, this led to an unrecorded Munro Top. Andy Nisbet explained later that the "face is so huge that the easier upper section of the ridge contained a large rounded summit with as much of a drop as some of the smaller Tops. Now named Munro's Last Ridge, it might see lots of ascents from folk updating their Tops. We'll have to get it in the next edition of the Munro's Tables!"

Who said exploratory mountaineering in Scotland is dead?

Simon Richardson.

100 YEARS AGO . . .

THE Club Year began with the Annual Meeting and Dinner in the Carlton Hotel, Edinburgh, on Friday, December 5, 1902, with President Ernest Maylard in the Chair. The Treasurer, Robert Napier, reported a 'healthy' balance of £176 4s. 6d, and Secretary Willie Inglis Clark announced a total of 152 members. Archie Robertson boasted about the success of the Slide Collection, now numbering 700 slides. President Maylard then gave way to the new incumbent Sheriff William C. Smith.

At Dinner – a French menu of 13 courses – after the President's Toasts, Sandy Mackay toasted the Alpine Club (reply by Cecil Slingsby), Frederic Squance toasted the Visitors (reply by David Christison) and Professor Ramsay proposed a most unusual Toast – 'Our Dundee Members' (reply by Harry Walker of Ardvreck, Perth Road).

The New Year Meet, at Killin, was visited by deep snow, hard frost, dark misty weather and a lady guest, Jane Inglis Clark. A gully somewhere on the Cam Chreag crags of Tarmachan was mastered by the very miscellaneous cordée of Mr and Mrs Clark, their small son Charles, the Reverend Robertson and an indeterminate individual identified by the pseudonym 'Ben Alder'. On Sunday, when the mass of the Meet had departed, Harold Raeburn and the Walker cousins struggled up to Creag na Caillich through the drifts, and made short work of the arête bounding the Great Gully on the right. The Walkers (Charles W. and Harry) were, of course, two of the recently-toasted Dundee members, if Newport may be counted a part of Dundee.

The Easter Meet, one of the most extraordinary gatherings of the Club, took place in Skye, in rotation and counter-rotation between the comforts of Sligachan Inn, Camasunary Lodge and Glenbrittle House. A number of grand traverses were accomplished in the thoroughly wintry conditions which obtained. One of the most impressive was executed by Willie Ling, Raeburn and the Walkers, who took only 12 hours to traverse Druim Hain to Coruisk, and the Dubhs, the Tearlaich-Dubh Gap, Alasdair and Sgumain to Glenbrittle! Secretary Clark contrived a logistic triumph in which all beds in the three residences were kept full, and everyone moved to a new residence each day.

In June, the Clarks drove in their magnificent new motor to Kingshouse where they were joined by Raeburn (delayed by yacht-racing), who reached Kingshouse by old-fashioned methods at 5.45am on the 14th (night mail from Edinburgh to Tyndrum, then bicycle). The party then made the second ascent of Crowberry Direct. Raeburn used *kletterschuhen* to surmount the crux, belayed after a fashion by Frau Clark, and photographed by Clark 'standing on [his] head' in order to use a 12-inch tripod. On the following day the party attacked a portion of the snowy Chasm, dropping into it from the North Wall perhaps just above the 100-foot pitch, though the description is none too clear, and escaping below the Cauldron to the south *via* a forgotten Buachaille feature, the Lady's Pinnacle.

In early July, Raeburn and Reverend Robertson visited Ben Nevis, making 'the first descent' of Observatory Ridge in torrential rain and returning to the Summit Hotel in two hours *via* the North-East Buttress. On the following day they repeated the Staircase Climb.

The summer season saw Club members at work in various parts of the Alps. However, the more enterprising ascents were made elsewhere.

Two Willies, Garden and Douglas, visited Western Canada, and climbed a number of peaks in the Rockies and the Selkirks. The most notable ascent was Douglas's first ascent of the North Ridge of Mount Assiniboine with the guides Christian Hasler and Christian Kaufmann.

In the Caucasus, Tom Longstaff made a number of ascents with Lancelot Rolleston, the most noteworthy being the West Peak of Shkara by its South Ridge (see 'The Finest Climb' in *This My Voyage*). John H. Wigner, another Dundee member, made the first ascent of Shtavler then joined forces with Oskar Schuster to climb a number of Caucasus peaks, several being first ascents. Schuster was part of the large German expedition led by Willy Rickmer Rickmers (who joined our Club in 1904), and was one of the party of four which made the intrepid first ascent of Ushba's South peak that year.

In Norway, Ling, Raeburn and Howard Priestman enjoyed good weather in July and made a number of fine new climbs in the Söndmöre group, including the huge south-west face route on Slogen from Oye (Ling and Raeburn). Raeburn once again had recourse to his trusty *kletterschuhen* in overcoming the difficult sections, and they reckoned the route as "the biggest rock-climb they has ever had the luck to be on". At the end of the month the pair moved south to Turtegro, but encountered bad weather during the remainder of the trip. Meanwhile, Norman Collie, with Slingsby *père et fils* and R. Northall-Laurie, was in the Lofoten Islands. The party made the first ascents of both peaks of Rulten, young Will Slingsby playing a decisive role in these successes.

In October, William Newbigging made the first ascent of D Gully Buttress on Buachaille. This "gave good sport under the very wet conditions, assistance having to be given to the leader at two points". At the end of the month, Raeburn and the Walkers explored Creag Meagaidh, climbing the gully below the Pinnacle Face and the Centre Post, avoiding the big pitch by a leftward excursion. The party reached their base at the Loch Laggan Hotel by cycling 15 miles in the moonlight from Dalwhinnie – a traverse which moved Raeburn to stray from his usual dry reporting style.

"There is a great charm in this kind of cycling, in the dark on a good, but unknown, road...Every sense is keenly on the alert, sight and hearing appear to become abnormally acute. The eye ranges the contours of the hills, faintly silhouetted against the lesser darkness of the sky, in the endeavour to recognise some familiar outline. Back again to the road in front, in the attempt to pierce the darkness ahead of the swiftly shifting patch of light formed by the rays of the lamp. The sudden cry of a plover, rising from the slopes below, shatters the outer silence of the night with almost painful loudness. The murmur of a distant fall is now heard, now lost, as we sweep round the hollows and over the shoulders of the moor. The whisper of the night breeze through the heath and sedge is scarcely audible above the soft rush of the wheels on the smooth damp sand, and clicking 'purr' of the ratchet as the leader 'frees'."

While returning in similar fashion to Kingussie, the party stopped to fight their way up two gullies on Creag Dubh.

The Club Journal, besides recording the events described above, published the first guidebooks to Arran, Monadhliath, and all the Cairngorms. Norman Collie (with Stutfield) published his *Climbs and Exploration in the Canadian Rockies*, and Cecil Slingsby published his *Norway, the Northern Playground*.

In what was otherwise a productive year, particularly abroad, there were, remarkably, no routes recorded on Ben Nevis or Skye.

Robin. N. Campbell.

Campbell Steven.
Hal Taylor.

GARRICK'S STAIRCASE AND MACROBERT'S SHELF

THE Shelf Route on Buachaille's Crowberry Ridge has a rich and interesting history. Most of this history is well-known. However, there is a part of it – the earliest part – which has disappeared from our guidebooks. The purpose of this note is to provide a reminder of this first encounter.

The Easter Meet of March 24-28, 1910, was spread over four locations: Kinlochewe, Dundonell, Kingshouse and Inveroran. According to the reporter G. L. Collins the Meet enjoyed "the best weather since 1894" (*SMCJ*, xi, 103). Howie's well-known view of the south side of Beinn Eighe from Loch Coulin, taken at the Meet, shows good tidy snow cover. The Kingshouse party included Harry MacRobert and Arnold Brown and on Monday 28, they "had a long day on the Crowberry Ridge of Buachaille Etive – being roped from 9.30 to 6.30, but did not succeed in gaining the summit. Arrived at Abraham's Ledge they had a very difficult traverse to the right, and then climbed up to a point near the tower, but were cut off by slabs and ice, and were forced to retreat by the same route. It was found impossible to regain the ridge owing to the rocks being badly iced, the west side of the ridge being of course in shadow all day." This laconic report by Brown (*SMCJ*, xi, 111) hardly does justice to what was a tremendous feat of ice climbing, involving a difficult ascent, at the absolute limit of the standards of the time, and a perilous descent without benefit of adequate anchors or abseil devices.

So far as I can tell, neither MacRobert nor Brown gave any fuller account of their interesting day until April 1924, when MacRobert added a note to J. A. Garrick's article *The North Wall Variation of Crowberry Ridge* (*SMCJ*, 17, 1-10). This is, of course, the account of what Garrick took to be the first ascent of the route by himself and D. Biggart in May 1923. MacRobert's description (*ibid*. 9) is as follows: "On Easter Monday 1910 Arnold Brown and I, after a Sunday of torrential rains, followed by a night of keen frost, set off for the Crowberry Ridge. It was, as we expected, badly iced, and the 100 feet of steep rock below Abraham's Ledge took us over an hour to negotiate. It took another hour to descend the little chimney on the right and cross over to Naismith's route. This was sheeted in ice, and so we tried the more broken-up gully to the right (Garrick's route). After a further strenuous four hours we had reached the final difficult pitch referred to by Garrick. Here the take-off was badly iced, and the second man had neither secure stance nor hitch. The place completely beat us, and we turned at 3 pm. The descent of the ice-pitches and the glazed rocks took some time, and it was not till 6.30pm that we got off the rocks on to the snow slope between the foot of Crowberry and Curved Ridges."

Neither Garrick nor MacRobert refers to the route as a 'shelf'. Garrick describes it as a gully, but adds that "the gully would be more accurately described as a gangway, or staircase, with three flights and two landings. It slants up the north wall of the ridge in much the same way as an emergency fire-escape staircase on the wall of a building".

According to MacRobert: "The gully is really a ledge or rake running up the steep bounding wall of the deeply-cut Crowberry Gully. On its left the wall rises steeply to the Ridge, shutting off all access thereto, while on its right the climber looks down into the dark rift of the Crowberry Gully".

Nevertheless in his 1934 *Central Highlands Guidebook*, MacRobert refers to

John Hinde. Photo: Roger Wild.
George Chisholm. Photo: G. Scott Johnstone.

the route as "The Crowberry Shelf Route" (p. 56) and "Garrick's Shelf Route" (diagram, p. 52), and the latter name came into common use. The route is not mentioned in the *SMCJ* in the intervening period of 10 years, so it seems likely that this name must have been coined by MacRobert.

In fact, the route had first been climbed by Fred Pigott and John Wilding in September 1920. They reported their discovery in the *Rucksack Club Journal* (4, 190), but this was evidently not known in Scotland until much later. Alex Small's *Crowberry Commentary* in 1940 (*SMCJ*, xxii, 190) doesn't mention Pigott and Wilding's ascent and – so far as I am aware – it is not until the publication of Bill Murray's *Rock Climbs – Glencoe and Ardgour* in 1949 that there is explicit acknowledgement of their primacy.

It was Murray and Bill Mackenzie who recorded the first winter ascent of the route (*SMCJ*, xxi, 244) in March 1937, but in December 1936, together with Archie MacAlpine and Kenneth Dunn, they had been defeated by the Shelf, in much the same manner as MacRobert and Brown nearly 27 years before, by icing on the exit pitch. However, due to an excessively late start, and the short December day, the retreat was a much less orderly affair than MacRobert's, consuming some 12 hours of dire struggle. Although Murray's account of this heroic battle (*ibid.* 237*ff.*) didn't refer to the 1910 defeat, the Editor (Bell) added a footnote about it. It is therefore curious that Murray didn't include mention of it when he revised his account for inclusion in *Mountaineering in Scotland*. Moreover, his acknowledgement of MacRobert's effort in the 1949 guidebook (p. 145) is only a perfunctory note "Previous attempts, April 1910, J 17.7", buried in the general entry for Crowberry Ridge.

Whatever one makes of the neglect of MacRobert and Brown's brilliant failure, it passed out of the guidebooks from that point on. So the route's history is doubly ironic: it was once named for Garrick, who didn't make the first ascent, and became famous for a valiant defeat, but for the wrong valiant defeat! Since 'Shelf' is probably MacRobert's name for it, I suggest that we personify the thing again, and call it – in the tradition of the Douglas-Gibson Gully of Lochnagar – MacRobert's Shelf.

Robin N. Campbell.

JAMES ROBERTSON'S MONADLIATH TRAVERSE IN 1771.

THE name of James Robertson is well known to those with an interest in the history of mountain exploration in Scotland.

A protégé of Hope, Professor of Botany at Edinburgh University, Robertson worked as an 'assistant gardener' in the Botanic Gardens and was educated by Hope to carry out surveys. Though these were funded by the Commissioners for the Annexed Estates, they were not direct surveys of those estates, rather, a general survey of Scottish flora was the aim. The commissioners granted Robertson £25 a year, later raised to £50. After his surveys, Robertson was in debt, so in 1772 he joined the British Navy, and eventually ended up in Bengal, returning to buy an estate at Balgarvie near Cupar in Fife in 1789.

He built a new mansion house, costing £14,000 and died in 1796. (Details from *A Naturalist in the Highlands, James Robertson. His Life and Travels in Scotland*, 1994, ed. D. M. Henderson and J. H. Dixon.)

According to D. B. Horn in *The Origins of Mountaineering in Scotland – (SMCJ)* XXVII, 1966) – Robertson climbed Ben Hope (1767) Ben Klibreck (1767) and Ben Wyvis (twice, 1767 and 1771) as well as Scaraben and Morven, both in 1767.

In 1771 he climbed Mayar and Ben Avon as well as Ben Nevis (all first ascents). It is doubtful if he ascended Lochnagar, as stated by Horn and later by Campbell Steven in *The Story of Scotland's Hills* (1975). Robertson does not mention an ascent, just the mountain itself. (*A Naturalist*….p155). He may have traversed the Sgoran Dhu/Mor Range "I traversed the mountains which ly(sic) South of Invereichy" (*A Naturalist*…p168), though this could just as easily refer to the Corbett range west of the Feshie, not the Munro range to the east. Additionally, Cairngorm was climbed by Robertson, but this was a repeat ascent. However, I am now convinced that Robertson's claim to another first ascent has been overlooked.

Campbell Steven (*The Story*…p66-7) mentions Robertson's crossing of the Monadliath on June 26, 1771, and his being caught in a severe thunderstorm with huge hailstones, and steering by map and compass. He does not hazard a guess as to the route taken. In my own *Scotland's Mountains before the Mountaineers* (1998) I state: "Robertson ascended a Monadliath summit on his 1771 tour, but the evidence is too scanty to determine which one." (p76.) Mea Culpa. A re-examination of his accounts of his traverse allows for a fairly informed calculation to be made of the route of the crossing and the summit(s) ascended – though Robertson himself mentions no names.

Travelling from Pitmain near Kingussie in Badenoch to Strath Dearn (the Findhorn) Robertson mentions "crossing the mountains that ly(sic) at the head of the water of Findhorn." (*A Naturalist*…p170), but without naming any. He started at Pitmain and he stayed at the former hotel near today's Pitmain farm, not the eponymous lodge. "About 9 o'Clock in the morning…I set out from Pitmain towards a very high hill situated North West from it…Between 11 and 12o'Clock I was at the foot of the mountain." (p171).

A'Chailleach lies five miles from Pitmain which tallies with the two to three hours taken. He sheltered from a violent thunderstorm for possibly three hours and he tells us that when it passed: "I ascended the mountain and reached its top about 4 in the afternoon." (It would take one to two hours to climb A'Chailleach from its foot). Hence directions and times combine to argue that the mountain Robertson climbed from Pitmain was probably A'Chailleach (930m.) and/or its Carn Sgulain outlying peak at 920m.

We can confirm this by Robertson's next moves. "Having fixed the rout(sic) by Map and Compass I advanced towards Strath-Dearn which tho' 10 miles distant is the nearest inhabited place."

Between nine and 10 miles from A'Chailleach's summit, in the glen of the Findhorn (Strath Dearn) lie the ruins of an extensive settlement named Coignafeuinternich. Robertson reached "the nearest inhabited place", soaked and exhausted, in six hours from A'Chailleach: six hours for those nine or 10 miles would seem reasonable. The next day, the 27th, Robertson attended a wedding and he said the wedding party marched to "the church which is nine miles distant" (*A Naturalist*…p174). Coignafeuinternich lies approx. that same distance from Tomatin where the church for Strath Dearn was, and still is. On the 28th, Robertson travelled down the glen: "I proceeded down the valley by Dalmagachie" – to Speyside – and the first clachan down river from Coignafeuinternich is Dalmigavie.

Distances times and locations all indicate that Robertson climbed A'Chailleach or Carn Sgulain – or both – probably by the Allt na Beinne from Pitmain; then he took a bearing which posibly led him across another Carn Sgulain (812m) and Carn Icean Duibhe (805m) and proceeded down the Allt a Mhullin (or Alt Fionndairnich) to Coignafeuinternich. This was important enough to have a mill, and the wedding appears very well attended, so it was a considerable centre of population in 1771 and logically, the one he would have headed for. Crucially, and finally, A'Chailleach lies "at the head of the waters of the Findhorn" – where Robertson states his mountain lay.

I considered the possibility of Robertson having followed the road by Carn an Fhreiceadain marked in Roy's map of 1755 (*Scottish Hill Tracks,* SRWS p114-5), which would have been an easier traverse of the Monadhliath, but the details do not tally. Carn an Fhreiceadain is (a) due north of Pitmain (Robertson specifically says he went north-west) and (b) the summit of Fhreiceadain is but six miles from Coignafeuinternich, not the nine or 10 miles from Robertson's ascended summit and (c) Fhreiceadain is at the head of the Dulnain River not the Findhorn.

Probably, Roberston was not the first to reach the summit of Lochnagar, but in all probability he was the first to ascend a Monadliath peak, A'Chailleach, showing a high degree of mountaineering skill and endurance in the process. Amend your records.

Ian R. Mitchell.

The International Festival of Mountaineering Literature 2002

A CHANGE of venue for the Festival this year, occasioned by refurbishment work at Bretton Hall, took it into the city centre and Leeds University's main auditorium which, while being acoustically perfect, was a bit too big and a bit too cold. Apparently, someone had forgotten to clock the heating on!

These however, are minor details and once again Terry Gifford and his team provided an excellent event which was tailored around the appearance of the legendary Walter Bonatti. Anyone who has any doubts about the status of the Leeds Festival need only ponder that Bonatti rarely gives presentations of this type, his last being at Buxton 19 years ago, (It probably says a lot about Terry's powers of persuasion as well).

The undoubted highlight of the event was a very polished simultaneous translation presentation, the text of which is reproduced in full elsewhere in this Journal, by a very fit looking Bonatti belying his 74 years. This was based around the publication of his book *The Mountains of My Life* which covers much more than just climbing. It seems strange to think that Bonatti's last great ground-breaking climb, the solo winter ascent of the Matterhorn was in 1965, nearly 40 years ago.

A second highlight was our own Douglas Scott's unaided slide presentation (no mean feat at 91 years of age!) of his 1938 Himalayan expedition with Bill Murray, Tom Mackinnon and Tom Weir, as related in Murray's biography *The Evidence of Things Not Seen*. The quality of the slides was superb given their age and the technology of the day and it was clear from his delight in the recalling and retelling of these events to a captivated audience, that Douglas's memories of these great pioneering days have dulled not a bit.

This year's Boardman/Tasker award went to American Robert Roper for *Fatal Mountaineer* – his biographical account of the life of Willie Unsoeld. It was probably unfortunate that on this occasion the chairman of the judges, Mike Vause, was also an American, who in his address referred to Murray's book as "probably the best mountaineering book he had ever read". Judging from the winning author's own reading of his work, followed by some ill-prepared ramblings on it by a visiting American professor, perhaps Mr Vause should have followed his instincts. (*conspiracy theorist-moi!* Ed.)

Colin Mortlock's presentation on his book *Beyond Adventure* (reviewed elsewhere in this Journal) was certainly one to get the audience thinking. His subject is just what it says on the tin, trying to see beyond the outdoor experience as a mere extension of the gymnasium that it has become for so many. If I were in charge of classification at Waterstones I would definitely place this book in the Philosophy section. Homespun it may be but, then again, so was Aristotle's.

Jim Curran was next up with his usual shambolic, but one suspects well rehearsed, absent-minded professor routine. On this occasion his remit was to talk on *20 years of The Boardman Tasker Award*. His view however, was probably somewhat coloured by his having been shortlisted no less than five times but being always being the 'Bridesmaid.' I liked his account of how this particular Shiny Prize is adjudicated – That the judges are full of praise for the runners-up, the shortlisted writers get savaged and the one who gets savaged the least is the winner! – Well if you will put your head above the parapet.

A regular that I look forward to at these things is Ian Smith's reading of the winning entry in that other Shiny Prize 'The *High* Mountain Writing Competition.' In recent years though, I feel that this has been more to do with Smith's performance than with the quality of the material he has had to work with. Happily, this year saw the two coming together with a fine piece of writing *Bolt Hangar* by Jon Sharrat. I think we will be hearing more from him.

The next Festival will be delayed until March 2004, due to building work being behind schedule at the Bretton Hall Campus, so although it is only a delay of three months it will mean that there will be no event in 2003. The main man, already booked for 2004, is Royal Robbins – he of White Cap on El Cap fame – so it should be a good one.

Charlie Orr.

THE NATIONAL MOUNTAINEERING EXHIBITION

MANY of us will have memories of wet weekends in Keswick when once you'd been round Fishers a few times, the pub was the only option. And even then, if it was after two o'clock in the afternoon you were snookered.

Well, things have changed, the main focus of Fishers it now seems, is to fulfil the role of a coffee and clothes shop where the leisured, four-wheel driven, middle classes can be relieved of their disposable income in a sort of 'Four-Wheel Drive meets Harvey Nicks' kind of way. The only remnant of how things used to be is a small nook, housed discreetly, so's not to cause offence perhaps, in the basement of this multi-storey paean to the ravages of market forces.

You do, of course, now have the option of visiting the other 38 'outdoor' shops in the town, all selling the same stuff, at the same price and be pestered by the same earnest featured youngsters wanting to know, "what exactly does sir want to use the sock for?" The only exception I found to this general rule was NeedIsports. It's the one painted a sunglasses required yellow. It's still a climbing shop.

But all is not lost. The saviour is Rheged, that is the Rheged of Arthurian legend, The Village In The Hill. And what, I hear you say, has this got to do with climbing? Well – I'm not one for visitor centres and the like, but this – this is different. You know when you turn right at Penrith off the M6 (or left if you come from south/middle England) to head for the Lakes, well, over to your left, (I think that's right, right that is as in correct not as in the opposite of left, right) totally invisible from the road and built into the side of a hill is Rheged, home to the Helly Hansen National Mountaineering Exhibition.

It's a huge, airy, cavernous place infused by natural light from a huge glass frontage, built between walls of natural rock, and portals in the roof, which is at ground level. There is a theatre showing IMAX films of Everest, Shackleton and the like, cafes and restaurants and, joy of joy, a few shops where long-suffering spouses can do their thing while the lads enjoy what, for the likes of us, is the meat of the place, the National Mountaineering Exhibition. (My lack of PC and what might be perceived as stereotyping of women in that last sentence was purely a matter of frivolous levity, just in case Heather, Ann and the rest of the ever-growing band of female members, all of whom climb better and harder than me, decide to get together and take retribution, let's face it, they probably wouldn't even need to get together these days!)

I digress – to the Exhibition. The days when exhibitions of this nature were simply a matter of looking at labelled exhibits in glass topped cases is a thing of the past and Rheged employs the cutting edge of technology in its use of video, sound and interactive programming to breathe life into what is a fascinating account of our abiding passion (I always hesitate to call it sport) from it's inception up to the present day. I must admit to being a bit sceptical when I found out that the role of interactive video guide to the exhibition was entrusted to that well known non-mountaineer John Peel (di ye ken fa ah mean?) but, with his dry self deprecating sense of humour, he actually comes across very well and there are substantial video interview contributions from well respected figures in all the climbing disciplines to give the Exhibition the required weight of authority.

The whole thing is set out in a logical progression or 'Time Line' leading the visitor on an 'ascent' through various 'Camps' taking them from the 'Golden Age of Alpine Climbing' in Camp 1 to 'Climbing Today' in Camp 5. It was rather disconcerting when my wife (newly returned from the shops!) noticed that some stuff on display, somewhere between Camp 3 and 4 was the same as some of the gear in my cupboard at home!

If I have one criticism of the Exhibition it is that the Scots could, and indeed should, have been more strongly represented. We do get a mention at several points but I feel that given the contributions of the likes of Smith, Marshall, Patey, Raeburn and others, we don't get our full slice of the cake. But hey, we're all Europeans now anyway, so didn't let a minor detail like that stop you from going.

I think the best thing I can tell you about Rheged, and the National Mountaineering Exhibition in particular, is that I, a born sceptic, always wary of such projects, would quite happily spend a full day here – albeit, preferably a rainy one!

Charlie Orr.

SCOTTISH MOUNTAINEERING TRUST – 2002-2003

THE Trustees met on September 26, 2002 and February 20, 2003.

During the course of these meetings support was given to the National Trust for Scotland; Scotland's Mountain Heritage Project; the Jonathan Conville Memorial Trust Winter Courses 2002-2003; the Mountaineering Council of Scotland Upland Path Advisory Group; the Alpine Club for the Alpine Club Library; an expedition to South Georgia 2003; an expedition to Baffin Island 2003; footpath work on Ben Rinnes.

John Gilmour CA ,of Hardie Caldwell, Chartered Accountants, Glasgow, attended the meeting of the Trustees on September 26, and gave advice on regulations affecting charities relative to the trust accounts.

Douglas Anderson having retired as Convener of the Publications Sub-Committee of the Club also retired as Trustee ex-officio of the Trust. The Trustees recognised the services which Douglas Anderson had rendered to the Trust since 1991, when he took over as Convener. His contribution is greatly appreciated.

Bryan Fleming retired as Chairman of the Trust at the end of 2002. Bryan has been involved with the Trust as Treasurer from 1988 to 1999, and more recently, as Trustee for 1999 and 2000 and then as Chairman of the Trust for 2001 and 2002. He has played an enormous role in guiding the Trustees with expert financial advice on Trust affairs since 1988. His steady approach and input into Trust meetings will be much missed.

The present Directors of the Publication Company are R. K. Bott (Chairman), K. V. Crocket, W. C. Runciman, M. G. D. Shaw and T. Prentice (Publications Manager).

The present Trustees are K. V. Crocket (Chairman), P. MacDonald, R. W. Milne, C. J. Orr, R. K. Bott, G. S. Nicoll, M. G. D. Shaw, G. E. Irvine, W. C. Runciman and A. Tibbs. R. K. Bott. W. C. Runciman and M. G. D. Shaw are Trustees/Directors and provide liaison between the Publications Company and the Trust. J. M. Shaw is the Trust Treasurer. The Trustees wish to record their gratitude to P. W. F. Gribbon for his services to the Trust as Trustee until recent retirement by rotation.

The following grants have been committed by the Trustees:

General Grant Fund:

National Trust for Scotland, Scotland's Mountain Heritage (£4000 per annum for five years)	£20,000
Jonathan Conville Winter Courses 2002/2003	£1014
Mountaineering Council of Scotland, Upland Path Advisory Group	£250
Alpine Club, Alpine Club Library	£500
South Georgia 2003 Expedition	£500
Baffin Island 2003 Expedition	£250
Ben Rinnes footpath work	£5000

James D. Hotchkis,
Trust Secretary.

MUNRO MATTERS

By David Kirk (Clerk of the List)

Another buoyant year of hill going has taken place and I thank everyone who has written to me to register a Compleation, or to amend their original entry. I continue to be amused at and touched by the anecdotes your letters contain. The total number of new Compleaters for the last year is 192.

The Munro Society is growing and developing and Iain Robertson, the Society Secretary has produced a report at the end of *Munro Matters*.

I urge everyone on the List to dig out an old final summit photograph of yourself, and send a copy (or the original along with SAE) to – Ken Crocket, Glenisla, Long Row, Menstrie, Clacks. FK 11 7EA – so it can be part of the SMC Website, Munroist Section, and be recorded for posterity.

As before, the first five columns are number, name, Munro, Top and Furth Compleation years.

2693	Alan Steele	2002		
2694	Deanne Steele	2002		
2695	Helen L. McLaren	1992		
2696	Peter Bibby	1992		
2697	Peter Baines	2000		
2698	Alan Whatley	1987	1987	2002
2699	Gordon Booth	2002		
2700	Stanley Stirton	2002		
2701	Kay Lloyd	1998		
2702	Billy McIsaac	2002		
2703	Colin Goldsworthy	2002		
2704	Melanie Nicoll	2002		
2705	Deryk Mead	2002		
2706	Mark Bull	2002		
2707	Gillian Duncan	2002		
2708	Jeremy Martin Wright	2002		
2709	David Rutherford	2002		
2710	Louis G. Skinner	2002		
2711	Norman Barker	2002		
2712	Philip Brown	2001		
2713	Doug Clarke	2002		
2714	Gillian Webb	2002		
2715	John Kennedy	2002		
2716	Mike J. Perry	2002		
2717	Iain Lambert	2002		
2718	Iain F. Macdonald	2002		
2719	Doug Hughes	2002		
2720	Kenny Duncan	2002		
2721	Nigel Walsh	2002		
2722	Alan Maude	2002		
2723	Gerald A. Davies	2002		
2724	Robin A. Campbell	2002		
2725	Alexander M.G.Campbell	2002		
2726	Ian H. Cameron	2002		
2727	Colin H. Campbell	2002	2002	
2728	John Potter	2002		
2729	Mike Gill	2002		
2730	R. G. Mahaffy	1987		
2731	Douglas Johnson	2002		
2732	Jim Johnstone	2002		
2733	David Underdown	2002		
2734	Elizabeth Swain	2002		
2735	Rita Gallie	2002		
2736	Margaret Sinclair	1996		
2737	Rod Mumford	2000		
2738	Paul Exley	2002		
2739	Catherine Exley	2002		
2740	J. K. Dale Smith	2002		
2741	James T. Christie	2002		
2742	Chris J. Cleare	2002		
2743	Anne Jago	2002		
2744	Michael Brian Webb	2002		
2745	Anthony George Bladon	2002		
2746	Robert J. Forsyth	2002		
2747	David J. Bryan	2002		
2748	Ben MacGregor	2002		
2749	Raymund Johnstone	2002		
2750	Peter Goodwin	2002		
2751	Jean Veitch	2002		
2752	Alister Macdonald	2002		
2753	Jan Rumsey	2002		
2754	David Flatman	2002		
2755	Robert Sparkes	2002		
2756	Joy Biggin	2002		
2757	Paul Biggin	2002		
2758	Stewart Fraser Knight	2002		
2759	Helen K. Morgan	2002		
2760	Alan Morgan	2002		
2761	Pamela Black	2002		
2762	Brian Griffiths	2002		
2763	Sheana P. Griffiths	2002		
2764	Donald F. M. Stevenson	2002		
2765	Derek Beverley	2002		
2766	Christine Taylor	2002		
2767	Robert Taylor	2002		
2768	Robert Bingham	2002		
2769	Mr W. P. Reed	2002	2002	
2770	Douglas Flynn	2002		

2771	Alex Stobie	2002	
2772	Dennis Latham	2002	
2773	Ranald N. Macinnes	2002	
2774	Howard Jones	2002	
2775	Irene McCulloch	2002	
2776	David McCulloch	2002	
2777	Andy Scott	2001	
2778	Peter Barclay-Watt	2002	
2779	Gordon Nuttall	2002	
2780	Colin Ballantyne	1991	
2781	John P. Moir	2002	
2782	Terry Shaw	2002	
2783	John Bishop	2002	
2784	*Reg Pillinger	2002	
2785	J. Reynolds	2002	
2786	Iain Ellis	2002	
2787	Vince Mason	2002	
2788	Murray Tosh	2002	
2789	Janet MacDonald	2002	
2790	Hugh MacDonald	2002	
2791	Jonathan Ridge	2002	
2792	Susan Sharpe	2002	
2793	Moira Finlayson	2002	
2794	Rigby Russell	2002	
2795	Maria R. Hybszer	2002	
2796	Willie Munro	2002	
2797	George Flint	2002	
2798	Carol Flint	2002	
2799	David Wharton	2002	
2800	John Ormerod	2002	
2801	Richard T. Daly	2002	
2802	Caroline Thompson	2002	
2803	Jamie Brogan	2002	
2804	Brian Whitworth	2002	
2805	Heike Puchan	2002	
2806	David M. M. Wilson	2002	
2807	John G. Moncrieff	2002	2002
2808	Barry T. Shaw	2002	
2809	Ian Matthews	2002	
2810	Anne Matthews	2002	
2811	Jim Bremner	2002	
2812	Helen Bremner	2002	
2813	Peter Woolverton	2002	
2814	Jean Philips	2002	
2815	John Blair	2002	
2816	Iain Alexander Blair	2002	
2817	John Meldrum	2002	
2818	Geoff Carson	2002	
2819	Robert Copeland	2002	
2820	David M. Russell	2002	
2821	Alfred McGhie	2002	
2822	Alan Smith	2002	
2823	Fred Ward	2002	
2824	David Tolmie	2002	
2825	Ian C. Smith	2002	
2826	Julie Dundas	2002	
2827	Michael Johnson	2002	
2828	Susan Mossman	2002	
2829	Alan Mossman	2002	
2830	Alistair Reid	2002	
2831	Peter Simpson	2002	
2832	Richard A. Lloyd	2002	
2833	Pamela Manning	2002	
2834	Jack Brindle	1999	2002
2835	Keith Slinger	2000	
2836	David Nunn	2002	
2837	Steve Bonham	2002	
2838	Ian S. Roy	2002	
2839	David E. Minnikin	2002	
2840	Rob Mackean	2002	
2841	Neil Jones	2002	
2842	Gerrie Somerville	2002	
2843	John Brian Rhodes	2002	
2844	Norman Keith Fraser	2002	
2845	Alan Green	2002	
2846	Roy Miller	2002	
2847	Michael K. Taylor	2002	
2848	Marian S. Larson	2002	
2849	James T. Watters	2002	
2850	Valerie Scott	2002	
2851	John Steel	2002	
2852	Robert Allan	2002	
2853	Douglas Clark	2002	
2854	Ian McNeish	2002	
2855	Janet Munro	2002	
2856	Miss S. D. P. Gould	1989	
2857	Keith Harold Bennetto	2002	
2858	Allan W. Taylor	2002	
2859	Graham Galloway	1986	
2860	Cath McCaul	2002	
2861	William S. D. Mill	2002	
2862	John Edward Casson	2002	
2863	David Dickson	2002	
2864	Iain Forrest	2002	
2865	John Duncan Beaton	1993	
2866	David Harrison	2003	
2867	Leslie Robin Mackie	2002	
2868	Tom G. Hall	2002	
2869	Ben McGinn	2001	
2870	David Kidd	2002	
2871	Peter Hamilton	1992	
2872	Alan Don	2002	
2873	John E Barnett	2002	
2874	Anthony Dyer	2001	
2875	Jackie Butler	2002	
2876	Christopher M. Martin	2002	
2877	Marion Gibson	1999	
2878	Alan Mitchell	1999	
2879	Sheila I. Nicoll	2002	
2880	Alex Findlay	2003	
2881	*Richard 'Rusty' Bale	2002	
2882	Clive Summerson	2003	
2883	Harold C. Smith	2003	
2884	Martin Bott	2002	

This year, we have had the unusual situation of two people registering for the first time, having compleated two Munro rounds. They were: Colin Ballantyne (2780) and Peter Hamilton (2871). Their first round compleation years are recorded on the previous page. Both their second rounds were compleated in 2002.

As ever, the tales of the various triumphs and antics of this year's Compleaters make interesting reading.

Stories of large groups on summits featured often this year. David Harrison's (2866) final summit party of 11 friends had to wait at the bottom of Schiehallion as he had to return to Pitlochry for his boots. It proved a bonus, however, as they saw a Brocken Spectre near the top. Mark Bull (2706) and Gillian Duncan (2707) managed to get 25 people, aged between eight and 72, to their Compleation on Ben More (Mull). David Underdown (2733) got 22 up Sgurr an Lochain on the Clunie Ridge, including his companion from his first Munro who'd flown especially from Paris. Marion Lawson (2848) also managed to get 30 folk on Devil's Point. When Susan (2828) and Alan Mossman (2829) compleated together, it was a true family occasion, as their children, Paul and Fiona, also climbed it as their first Munro. Their party included more than 30 on the summit of Sgurr na Lapaich.

The largest group of the year goes to father and son Robin (2724) and Alexander Campbell (2725), on Sgurr a Mhaoraich in June 2002. They managed more than 40 in their group and enjoyed champagne and smoked salmon on top. They also managed some path repair work during the day. Robin has the unusual hill claim of having found a toothbrush in his boot following a hill day above Glen Etive. Since they wrote to me, more of the Clan Campbell have been in touch about their round. Colin Campbell, (2727) compleated both Munros and Tops, finishing on Sgurr Dubh. He compleated "anything which had ever been anything" since 1974, hoping to avoid being caught out by a later revision – there's a challenge for you Mr Bearhop!

Father and son Compleations are not uncommon. Like the Campbells above, John (2815) and Iain Blair (2816) also compleated together, on Carn nan Gobhar. John had started his Munros 51 years earlier on Cairn Gorm before there was "a road up it".

Doug Clarke (2713) finished on Bidean in 2002. Although he did not compleat with any of his children, he did do a lot with them. They all had a total epic due to a slab avalanche on Stob Coire Sgriodain in 1990 and Doug enclosed his children's log pages giving very interesting reading from different sides of the story.

Filing a contender for *Primiere Munroius Youngus,* David Bryan (2747) reports that during his round, he managed to get his two-year-old daughter, Natasha ,up Carn Aosda 'unassisted', He wonders if this is a record?

Husband and wife teams feature a lot too. Brian (2762) and Sheana Griffiths (2763), who compleated on Ladhar Bheinn were rewarded for having introduced their son, Duncan, to the mountains – he became a climber and was able to help them on the Inaccessible Pinnacle. Paul and Catherine Exley (2738 and 2739) reported eagles soaring below them on their final summit ridge of Ben More (more of this popular final hill anon). Hugh (2790) and Janet MacDonald (2789) climbed all hills as a husband and wife team, however Janet, I am told, touched the final summit (Slioch) first. At the opposite end of the spectrum, David Rutherford (2709) left his wife in Broadford Hospital while he compleated alone on Sgurr Mhic Choinnich – she had damaged her ankle the day before on Sgurr a Mhadaidh. Indeed, Pamela Black's (2761) husband found a great solution to the yearly problem of a suitable birthday present when he gave her, "the Aonach Eagach ridge, guided".

Eight years later, in 2002, she compleated. Tales of epics in the mountains feature a lot in the letters that I receive and a fair proportion of these involve Skye. Dennis Latham (2772) did the Skye ridge in May 1972 as some of his earliest Munros. He had two days of sunshine, but effectively got the ridge in full winter conditions, with snow up to his armpits in places. You don't get winter conditions in May on Skye much these days! Ben MacGregor (2748) reports that the Inaccessible Pinnacle was the only summit he had a companion for – the rest were done alone. Howard Jones (2774) also did all of Skye first, then finished with another island – Ben More on Mull. Iain Forrest's (2864) most memorable Munro, Ben Macdui, also gave him his most terrifying moment in the hills. He did it on a wet autumn day by way of Crystal Ridge. In the conditions, he found the ridge a greasy gearless slab.

By far the greatest (worst!) epic that was described to me however, was from Bob Sparkes (2755). Bob had a break in his bagging after falling off the Corbett, Stob Dubh, in 1995. Lochaber Rescue Team and the SAR helicopter team took six days to find him, and the search and subsequent rescue became headline material. He took two years to recover, but went on to continue his round.

A standard section of *Munro Matters* seems to now concern Ben More on Mull, and this year is no different. Deryk Mead (2705) intended playing his bagpipes on this, his final hill, but the wind in May meant he needed a tin whistle instead. David Flatman (2754) also completed on Ben More and claimed the honour of being the first 'Flatman' to complete the Munros. His name, he explained, originated in Norfolk. Gerald Davies (2723), another Ben More compleater, was impressed by the improved relations between walkers and estate staff during his years in the hills. One estate worker in Attadale invited them to stay at the local estate bothy.

Largest multiple Compleation of the year goes to Ian (2809) and Anne Matthews (2810) and Jim (2811) and Helen Bremner (2812), who all compleated together on October 5. Yes, you've guessed the hill!

Munro logs are often sent to me, and along with the other letters, these go on to form a part of the Scottish Mountaineering archives. Iain Ellis (2786), then later, Ian Smith (2825) and Alan Green (2845) supplied these. Barry Shaw (2808) also supplied a log, detailing his three-year round, which he compleated after he celebrated his 60th birthday (climbing Kilimanjaro). Barry recorded 37 hillwalking trips to Scotland from Cheshire in one 42-month period.

Speaking of records, Gordon Booth (2699) is an ex-over 60 British Marathon Champion. He ran a lot of his summits, including Ceannaichean and back in two hours from Gerry's hostel on New Years Day, aged 57. Also with an impressive finish was Mel Nicoll (2704), who was six months pregnant for her final Munro (Beinn Liath Mhor from the Ling Hut). She now feels she has served her Scottish mountaineering apprenticeship.

This year's *Munroist Longius* must go to Reg Pillinger (2784*) who quotes more than 50 years between starting on the Buachaille and finishing on Schiehallion. And this year's political summiteer was Murray Tosh MSP (2788), who is, as far as I can tell, the first MSP to compleat. Murray finished on Ben Hope. Most supplied information of the year goes to Richard Daly (2801). Thanks, Richard for your short story concerning your Assynt trips. The escape from the house fire in your holiday home was definitely not the usual type of epic I hear of. Terry Shaw (2782) has the West Highland Way to thank for getting him hooked on Munro-bagging. He decided that it was too much of a West Lowland Way, so took in several hills including the Stob Ghabhar to Meall a'Bhuiridh group.

Humour always forms a good part of the letters I receive. I was highly amused by the names of the hillwalking clubs founded by John Casson (2862). These were the 'Conquistadors' and 'Wazeks.' And like myself, Ian McNeish (2854) attributes his original interest in the hills to Poucher's *The Scottish Peaks* – that, and being able to see the Ochils from Brockville football ground! My thanks, however, for probably the funniest article of the year goes to Peter Smith (2831). Peter's satirical article concerning his trips with his walking companion, Richard Lloyd (2832), left me in stitches. Despite Peter's statement to the contrary, they sound like the best of friends.

It is becoming quite common for people who are arranging Final Munro Celebrations to ask for certificates in advance, to present the Compleater on the day. Stan Stirton (2700) was presented his, by his daughter, Sheila. Along the same lines, Channel TV (from Jersey) planned to make a film about Norman Barker's (2711) final Munro. His daughter's partner (a Channel TV employee) requested a certificate in advance to present at the occasion.

AMENDMENTS

The following have added to their entries on the List. Each Munroist's record is shown in full. The columns refer to Number, Name, Munros, Tops, Furths and Corbetts.

Number	Name	Munros	Tops	Furths	Corbetts
1441	Jim Bryce	1995	1995		2002
2637	Christopher J. Horton	2001	2001	2002	
375	Robert H. MacDonald	1984		1989	
		1987			
		1990			
		1992			
		1995			
		2002			
1801	Lindsay Boyd	1997	2002		
		2000			
		2002			
1991	Pat Hay	1998		2002	
1992	Alan Crichton	1998		2002	
1239	Roger C. Henshaw	1993	2001	2002	
336	Stephen T. Ramsden	1984		1989	1993
		1993			1999
		1996			2000
927	Dorothy Spencer	1991	1991	1997	2002
781	Norma Sutherland	1990	2002	1991	
		1996			
152	Erlend Flett	1977			2002
2561	Andrew Hyams	2001	2002		
1100	Christopher Bantoft	1992		2002	
1920	Ernie Potter	1998	2002		
202	H. Thomson	1979			2002
1401	Alan Bellis	1995			2002
1397	Douglas R. MacLeod	1995	1007	1998	
		2000	2002		
668	Ian Henderson	1989		1989	1994
		2002			
290	Kenneth J. MacIver	1982		2002	
		2000			

No.	Name				
1240	Michael Atkins	1993	2002	2002	
2230	Rod Crawford	1999		2002	
1691	George W. Graham	1996			2002
2172	Ian Clark	1999	2002		
2173	Alan Clark	1999	2002		
2058	Alan Stewart	1998	1999	2002	
1308	Audrey M. Litterick	1994			2002
2475	Alan Sewell	2000	2002		
555	Robin Howie	1982	1984	1987	
		1984	1987		
		1987	1992		
		1990			
		1992			
		1995			
		1999			
		2002			
1406	Charles D. M. Black	1995		2002	
832	Les Rothnie	1990	1990		2002
1213	Andy Whitehead	1992			
		2002			
1067	Frank Malloy	1992			
		2002			
225	Alan L. Brook	1980	1980	1078	
		2002	2002		
2628	Rob Pearson	2001	2001	2002	
2629	Margaret Pearson	2001	2001	2002	
1331	John Mackay	1994	1994	1997	2002
700	Terry McDonagh	1989	1990		1995
		1998			
		2002			
832	Les Rothnie	1989	1989		2002
1477	David Claymore	1995	1995		2000
1478	Graham Jackson	1995	1995		2000
825	Bernard Smith	1990	2000	1979	
23	*M. Hutchinson	1955	1955	1970	1992
		1992		1998	
		1998			
1611	Alex Smith	1996	1999	1999	
		2003			

Those who wish to register a Compleation or an Amendment and who would like to receive a certificate (either for Munro or Corbett Compleation) should send a letter with a second class SAE (A4) to me at: Greenhowe Farmhouse, Banchory Devenick, Aberdeenshire, AB12 5YJ.

If a certificate isn't required, and an e-mail address is given on a received letter, I can speed up return of information, by e-mailing back. My e-mail is: Dave.Kirk@greenhowefarm.fsnet.co.uk.

Dave Kirk.

Iain Robertson reports: The Munro Society is one year old in April 2003, a new group within the Scottish mountaineering community and one that is still defining its role and pre-occupations. Membership is drawn from the ever-expanding cohort of those who have compleated a round of the Munros. That part of the cohort which is recorded by the Clerk of the List seems likely to exceed the innately significant number, 3000, during 2003, though the actual number of compleaters must be above that figure. Membership of *TMS* is a more modest 135, but there has been a 50% increase in members since the inaugural meeting. Within the membership there is neither a preponderance of recent compleaters, nor those of longer standing, which suggests the Society has broad appeal.

On the social side, both the inaugural meeting in Dundee and the first dinner in Fort William were well attended and enjoyable events. The numbers participating are not insignificant as members of the Society live throughout the UK and abroad.

The first annual meeting, to be held at Stirling University, is yet to come and this will be followed by the inaugural Munro Lecture given by Sue Harvey of Harvey's Maps. The Munro Lecture is open to the public and it is intended that this be an annual event. In addition to social events the Society has responded to members' wishes by establishing an archive which is housed in the A. K. Bell Library, Perth. While in no way wishing to restrict the nature of items deposited, particular stress has been laid on securing the personal records of Munroists and also matters of interest concerning particular Munros. Those wishing to deposit relevant items need not be members of *TMS*.

One of the fundamental ideas endorsed by members of *TMS* is that the Society is a means by which they have the opportunity to give something back to the mountains. Given the number of organisations already concerned with mountains and the mountain environment, the Society is still intent on finding the niche in which it will be most effective. But it is determined to establish itself as an organisation recognised as being both independent and knowledgeable on matters affecting Scottish mountains and the Munros in particular.

All communications should be addressed to: Iain Robertson, 28 Fairies Road, Perth, PH1 1LZ.

IN MEMORIAM

WILLIAM M. MACKENZIE j 1937

MOUNTAINEERING was Bill's major leisure-time interest. He participated and competed successfully in many sports and recreations and was blessed with a natural talent which we all envied. In addition to mountaineering he achieved high standards in golf, in football, in skiing and in fishing.

From what he himself described as 'minor mountaineering' in his native Moray in the 1920s, he became the leader of the group who were climbing new and harder routes in both summer and winter in the 1930s, firstly as a member of the Glasgow JMCS and from 1937 as a member of the SMC. He was never a member of the Alpine Club, probably because he considered he was already a member of Britain's premier mountaineering club. He was, however, a member of the UIAA, a vice-chairman of the BMC and the first president of the MC of S which had arisen, phoenix-like, from the ashes of the ASCC. Nevertheless, he took greatest pride in his election as president of the SMC in 1966.

Most of Bill's climbing was in Glencoe, on Ben Nevis and in the Cuillin of Skye, but his first contribution to the Journal described a new route, climbed in 1935, on the Braeriach Pinnacle in the Cairngorms. Between 1935 and 1939 the climbs log book from the CIC Hut records his climbs there. His regular companions at that time were Kenneth Dunn, Archie McAlpine, Tom Mackinnon, Bill Murray and Douglas Scott.

Bill's name was invariably listed first – a sure indication that he led most of the climbs. One entry from February 1938, records an ascent of Observatory Ridge/ Zero Gully which took 14 hours from the hut to the summit. A note reports that there was much windslab on the ridge and much ice in the gully, the latter requiring step-cutting by torch-light! Another entry describes a variation to Rubicon Wall which Bill described as steep and exposed – and that they carried both socks and boots – perhaps bare feet are better than rock boots.

Bill was once asked: "Did you climb with Bill Murray?" His terse reply was: "No, Bill climbed with me."

In the hills his mountaineering skills were matched with skis, particularly for touring. He took up this sport in the 1930s when it was not wholly acceptable to the climbing fraternity. Nevertheless, he pursued it with his usual vigour and encouraged others to participate. In 1936 he joined the Territorial Army and at the Munich crisis was called up for a short time with French Alpine troops at Chamonix. Later, during the war, his climbing, ski-ing and mountain survival experience led to his being attached to Special Forces and he saw service in various mountain warfare training establishments including Achnacarry, Iceland, the Rocky Mountains and Alaska.

In the years following the end of the war Bill was an active climber and skier. In Europe he climbed in Chamonix, the Pennine Alps, the Bernese Oberland, the Bernina area and the Dolomites. He also led ski-touring parties to Norway, accompanied among others by Hamish Hamilton, Tom Weir and Bill Bennet. In 1946 he became a member of the Alpine Ski Club and was elected an honorary member in 1986. He was also, for a time, secretary and treasurer of the Scottish Ski Club.

Bill contributed a substantial article to the Journal in 1946, *Bad Weather and Bivouacs,* which drew on his wartime experience and included advice on mountain clothing and bivouacs. A second article in 1947, *The Snow and Ice Climbs of Glencoe,* reviewed the winter routes climbed up to that time. In 1958, following years of climbing in the Cuillin, he was author of the new climbers' guide*The Cuillin of Skye.*

Bill enjoyed a full life with his many friends. He climbed in his 70s, skied in his 80s and golfed and fished in his 90s. His philosophy is summarised by his own quotation: "The one thing that matters among mountains is that we enjoy them."

Bill Wallace.

CAMPBELL R. STEVEN J. 1934.

IN MAY 2002, I received a copy in the post of a book from an old friend and fellow SMC member – Campbell Steven. The book was his latest, and, as it happens, his last, as one month later he died at the good age of 91. He had enjoyed good health right to the end and there was no illness.

Many outside of the club may well have come across Campbell's writings in the past, especially through a book called *The Story of Scotland's Hills.* This is probably out of print, but is well worth finding in a library, being a very readable account of various aspects of our mountains – their names, heights, scenic attractions, climbing history, scientific connections and so on. Over the years I have found it to be a useful basic source of material as well as being a good read.

I first met Campbell in 1978, when he was updating one of the SMC guidebooks, *The Central Highlands*, and he was needing a primer on the latest climbing exploits of younger climbers. He was a mild-mannered man, a true gentleman if you will, and over dinner in our home in Glasgow happy to listen to my outpourings of the stories of the latest horror climbs being done in Glen Coe and other areas. I was then fully engaged in writing a new edition of the Glen Coe Climbers' Guide.

We since then visited him and his wife Maisie, herself an author, at their home in Aberfeldy. Maisie pressed upon us a copy of her book *the Good Scots Diet - what Happened to it?* She was a nutritionist, and it may not be too idle speculation to ascribe her husband's long, healthy life to her cooking!

Campbell was born in 1911, in Helensburgh, and his earliest memory was of watching the liner *Aquitania* moving down the Clyde, having been recently launched from John Brown's Clydebank works. He was then three years of age.

Happy early years in Helensburgh led to more sporty times at school and university; rugby, golf (at competitive levels) and others. The collection of birds' eggs is confessed to, which led to a healthier life-long interest in ornithology. The mountains arrived almost unbid, and in 1934 Campbell joined the SMC. He was proposed by George Todd and seconded by I. G. Jack. His application form began its list of routes and hills in 1927, with an ascent of Braeriach. Many of his early walking was done in company with his younger brother, Colin.

In September 1934, when he submitted the form, he listed a traverse of the Cobbler peaks, Right-Angle Gully, Spearhead Arete and Jamblock Chimney, possibly solo, as no other names are mentioned for these routes. Increasing experience led to Alpine seasons just before the Second World War broke out, when he served in a ski battalion raised to fight in Finland.

Campbell joined the Commandos, as a climbing instructor, and was also active in small boat reconnaissance. There are many tales of the usual military mix-ups, but

Bill MacKenzie. Photo: Mary MacKenzie.
Andy Wightman. Photo: David Stone.

essentially, Campbell made it through the war unscathed. Times then became hard, as they were for many following the war. Campbell, although blessed in many ways, had his share of personal tragedies, including the loss of his first wife, Helen, through illness, and the death of an older brother Douglas, also through illness.

As an indication of how short of money one could be in these days, Campbell, although a member of the Alpine Club for 20 years, resigned when their annual fee rose to the giddy height of four guineas!

Meanwhile, Maisie, who was to become his second wife, was also experiencing the hand of fate, though in a very different way. She was, in June 1962, a lecturer in nutrition and dietetics at Queen's College in Glasgow (long and affectionately known to Glaswegians as *The Dough School*). She was due to enjoy a foursome with two friends and her fiancé Jock, on Jock's yacht *Suva*. This was to be a sail in the Firth of Clyde. At the last minute, some changes at the College meant that Maisie felt obliged to attend a dinner party for one of her pupils. Faced with the choice, Maisie did as duty told her and attended the dinner, leaving the three on the yacht. That Saturday night, a fierce storm hit the West Coast. *Suva*, moored off Millport, had her anchor chain snapped. The yacht broke up and foundered in the Firth. On the Sunday, Maisie heard the news on television that the three bodies had been washed ashore near Wemyss Bay.

When I read this, I thought how unusual it must have been to experience such a storm in June, and in the perceived shelter of the Firth of Clyde. A week later, in June 2002, I helped John Peden sail his yacht across the Firth of Clyde, from Troon to Brodick, on Arran. We made it in a Force 8, jib only, with the wind and waves crossing our beam from the south. I have never heard the rigging make such a noise, a threnody, a constant scream. At the time I had no real fear – there's too much to do anyway – steering as good a course as you can, adjusting the tiller for the odd, random big wave, hanging on with one hand when the angle increases. Both of us were pretty tired when we finally picked up a mooring in the shelter of Brodick Bay, and John had been exhausted to begin with, having just finished the Scottish Three Peaks' race. After that, I wondered about June storms no more.

Three years after that disaster, Campbell met Maisie for the first time. They were married the following spring. Over the years, Campbell had been collecting a series of brief notes – special quotes which had appealed to him. This collection grew and grew, until he began to think of publishing them, perhaps in some sort of Christian context. They were quotes which had helped him deal with the personal tragedies which he had experienced. In all it was to take some 26 years' of work before the collection was ready to publish.

Finally, after many trials, *An Anthology of Hope* saw the light of day. You should have no problem in finding it, and hopefully, it may raise any sprits which are downcast, as it did for Campbell over the years. He was the author of another eight books, including *The Central Highlands* already mentioned, a history of the Glasgow Fire Service and *Enjoying Perthshire*. For many years Campbell had a regular monthly column in *Scottish Field*. Campbell's last book, *Eye to the Hills,* subtitled *A Scotsman's Memories of an Outdoor life*, is as the title suggests, autobiographical.

The hills were always a source of pleasure for Campbell and his wife who survives him, and to whom we pass on our thoughts. There are many stories in his last book which you will enjoy reading. It's a neat encapsulation of his life. There's no big expedition story, no rock or ice climb at the forefront of technical difficulty. It's a series of tales from a long life well spent, and what's wrong with that?

Ken Crocket.

John Bickerdike. Photo: Colwyn Jones.
Oliver Turnbull. Photo: Dick Allen.

RIGHT up to the very week of his death, aged 91, my father Campbell Steven's enthusiasm for adventure remained undimmed. Plans were still being hatched for a cycle expedition over Ryvoan pass, maps were inevitably brought out and suitably easy Munros for the 90-year-olds pondered over. Indeed, the last Munro that he and his wife, Maisie, climbed was A'Bhuidheanach Bbeag in 2001 at the age of 90.

He was already hooked by the mountains at the age of 16. As with so many, it was the lure of the Caimgorms that was the original inspiration for Campbell's love of the high tops. Braeriach of the wide skies, hidden lochans and sudden plunging corries remained high on his list of favourites, long before the days of made footpaths, funiculars, or even a surfaced road to Loch Morlich.

There is a wonderful freshness of new discoveries in Campbell Steven's descriptions of climbing in the early 1930s. Routes that have become mountaineering household names, such as Shadbolt's North Chimney route on the Bhasteir Tooth, Window Buttress, Collie's Climb on Sgurr Alasdair, Clachaig Gully, have all the excitement of recent discovery. The people he met, too, read like a *Who's Who* of the early pioneers – Norman Collie, Shadbolt, A. E. Robertson, Glover, Ling and Rooke Corbett, to name but a few.

In the early 30s Campbell and his brother Colin, companion of many climbing adventures, joined the JMCS, and then in 1934 he became a member of the SMC. He describes the qualifications for entry in these days, somewhat modestly perhaps, as "good sound familiarity over several years with the Scottish hills, summer and winter, with rock and snow experience to match". But always the emphasis was on all-round competence and genuine love of' the hills. Campbell's qualities admirably fitted the bill, for it was this deep love of the hills in all weathers and seasons, rather than any tigerish first ascents that characterises Campbell Steven's mountain career. Not that he was a slouch in respect of hard rock routes in those early days, as his list of routes in the company of such climbing companions as Graham MacPhee, Norman Tennant, Bill Murray, and Theo Nicholson would suggest. It was with Hamish Hamilton, George Roger and Torn McKinnon that he made the first ascent of Chancellor Gully in Glencoe.

The summer of 1938 and 1939 saw Campbell aspiring to the high Alps. In spite of somewhat mixed weather, ascents were made of the Fletschhorn, the Laquinhorn, the Weissmiess, the Rimpfischhorn and Monte Rosa in 1938, and in 1939, the Schreckhorn and the Finsteraarhorn, which he said: "Stand out brilliantly as dazzling peaks to remember." Four weeks later war had begun and Alpine expeditions were brought to an abrupt end. However, a brief and somewhat hilarious time spent with the 5th Battalion seconded to join the Chasseurs Alpins at Chamonix extended the alpine season

In 1943, Campbell was able to put his mountain skills to good use by joining the recently-formed Commando Mountain Warfare Training Centre. After initial training in Lochailort, he was stationed first in Wales, and then at St Ives, Cornwall, where he trained units in rocky landings and cliff climbing from small boats. Having to turn out in all weathers and climb with serious deadly intent, I think somewhat blunted his passion for rock-climbing, and he often spoke of the cliffs at Sennen Cove with a shudder. Ironically, the action for which he was decorated was not in the mountains, but below sea level on the island of Walcheren.

After the war, as a man deeply committed to his family, Campbell put Alpine adventures and hard routes behind him, concentrating rather on discovering the full potential of the Scottish hills. Campbell was a true all-round lover of the hills, and this is vividly expressed in his writing. He had eight books published, including the SMC Central Highlands Guide (1968). His wide knowledge of the history and background of the mountains is described in *The Story of Scotland's Hills* and *The Glens and Straths of Scotland,* but it is his sheer love of adventure and originality that shines through his first book *The Island Hills* and *Enjoying Scotland.* Crazy exploits of a true original who had the imagination to discover Scotland's hidden potential. Some of these unlikely exploits included being stormbound on Ailsa Craig, sunbaked on the A'Chir Ridge, boating by moonlight over Rannoch Moor, and traversing the Cairngorm Plateau on skis as a relative novice

Campbell completed his Munros in 1976 choosing Fionn Bheinn near Achnasheen as a suitably easy and accessible top, but Campbell was never a fanatical Munro bagger. Mountains were to be enjoyed and delighted in. Another great passion was bird watching and often specific outings or long detours were made to see a peregrine's nest or to spot a dotterel near the cairn or to find a crested grebe on a lochan. In his Eighties as the hills became unaccountably steeper, the bicycle became his favoured mode of reaching mountain terrain, and with Maisie he traversed the Gaick and the Corrieyarraick. Sitting listening for the grumble of the ptarmigan, battling blizzards above the corries of the Fannichs, bothying and bivvying in Fisherfield, Arran or Jura, all of Scotland was his playground and his joy.

As a deeply committed Christian, Campbell rarely climbed on a Sunday, as church always took precedence over the hills, but it is this reverence for life and the glories of creation that was the mainspring of Campbell's love of the mountains. He truly lived life 'in all its fullness' and has left us a rich legacy. As Campbell's daughter and a member of the LSCC, I feel privileged to have this opportunity to express my gratitude for that legacy.

Helen Steven.

JOHN HINDE j1963

JOHN died suddenly at home in Findochty on June 28, 2002. He had just spent a week walking in the Cairngorms. He had been based at Muir Cottage in Braemar, a favourite haunt of latter years, in the company of good friends. He had had a great time, loving every new experience with his usual exuberant enthusiasm. His diary record extends to the day before his death. It does not, however, cover his last hill. On his last day, on his way home, he climbed Bennachie with a friend.

From the days of childhood exploration from his home in Staveley, to the day of his death, John's life was dominated by his love of the hills and the great outdoors. Born on December 21, 1927, he kept a detailed record of his adventures dating from his 14th birthday. His logbooks provide a fascinating account of a life rich with the joy he found in the hills and the interest he took in his companions. He started exploring the hills of Derbyshire at the age of about 11, at the beginning of the war, inspired not by friends or family like many of us, but by Frank Smythe's *The Spirit of the Hills.* He did not know any climbers and to the best of his knowledge there were none in the town.

He would head off by bus or train, with or without his bike, with or without a companion, into the apparent wilds of rural Derbyshire. Being from a working class background, there was never much money about but he seemed to exist on a diet of bread, butter, boiled eggs and cocoa in those schoolboy jaunts. He was an early member of the YHA. His hostel card of 1941 records destinations long since forgotten or even flooded by the encroaching waters of the reservoirs of the Derwent valley.

An early diary entry of May 1942 records a weekend spent exploring the area around Edale. He caught the bus into Chesterfield on Sunday afternoon and there bought a return rail ticket for Edale. He details his wanderings across the moors between Edale, Castleton, Buxton, Chapel-en-le-Frith and back to Edale.

At the tender age of 14, he writes: "After crossing the Nick I ascended to the summit of Mam Tor which is known as the Shivering Mountain. Then I descended the steep grassy slope by zigzags until I came to Greenlands Farm and I followed the path by easy stages into Edale where I caught a train home after waiting in the warm sun on the station for a half-hour. This has been one of the most pleasant weekends I have had despite the fact that I have been on my own."

This gives a flavour of the passion that inspired this lad to a lifetime of enthusiasm for the hills. He was born in an area of strong mining tradition. His father was a lorry driver and his mother worked in a local factory. Widowed when John was only five years' old, his mother was left to bring up John, his older brother Frank, and his sister Beth, alone.

John was a pupil at Netherthorpe Grammar School from 1938 to 1943. At 15, he followed his brother, Frank, into the RAF as a boy entrant, and for a while he was its youngest recruit. At about this time, based in Halton, a Christmas card he sent to a friend reads: "Thinking of the day we spent together on Bleaklow, reminded me of the passage we read in Edale. 'And in the darkest hours of urban depression I will sometimes take out that dog-eared map and dream awhile of more spacious days, and perhaps a dried blade of grass will fall out to remind me that once I was a free man on the hill.' I hope we spend many more days as good as that together."

Trained as an aircraft engineer, he worked on engines for the first 18 years of his RAF career. Posted to Kinloss for the first of three times in 1948, his association with RAF Mountain Rescue, and his intimate knowledge of the Scottish mountains, began.

At age 33, John's mountaineering experience was recognised and most of the remainder of his 30 years' service career was spent as leader of RAF mountain rescue teams. In 1961, he took over the Kinloss team, responsible at that time for the north of Scotland and most of the islands. This at a time when there were very few civilian teams, and even less use of helicopters. Rescues often involved protracted searches and long stretcher carries. John remained at Kinloss throughout the Sixties, managing to wangle consecutive three-year stints, unheard of in normal service life. During this time he was awarded the BEM for services to mountain rescue. A joint services expedition took him to Mount McKinley in 1962, and another to the Himalayas to climb one of the Dhaulagiris in 1965. During his time at Kinloss, the idea of multi-Munro bagging trips was conceived. He was involved in an east-west route in 1966, from Sgurr na Banachdich to Mount Keen, with 14 days walking and covering 30 Munros, and a north-south journey from Ben Hope to Ben Lomond in 1968, including 48 Munros.

A posting to lead the team at RAF Akrotiri in Cyprus in 1969 gave the opportunity for more exotic adventures: Alum Kuh and Demavend in the Elburz, Kuh-i-Dinar in the Zagros mountains in 1972, Mount Kenya and a holiday trip to Mount Etna. There was also a trans-Iceland trip in 1972.

It was during his time with the RAF that John gained the Mountaineering Instructors Certificate, the civilian qualification that was to form the basis of a major career move. Posted back to Kinloss and back to his trade in 1972, his appetite for adventure was whetted by an advert for Chief Expeditions Officer on the schooner *Captain Scott,* built in Buckie, at the Herd and MacKenzie shipyard. Buckie was the family home of his wife, Betty, and since the schooner was to operate between the Outward Bound establishments of Moray Sea School at Burghead and Loch Eil Centre, near Fort William, its appeal was so much the stronger.

The job was his, and without more ado, he resigned from the RAF after 30 years' service. The adventure courses run on board involved a month-long sail and land activities for young people in which they sailed the ship all around the west and north of the Highlands and Islands, with three land-based expeditions organised and led by John, that gave access to wild country from the sea. Using his words: "Three adventurous years doing this were probably the best years of my life." The photographic record of this era illustrates his pleasure in that lifestyle.

With the decommissioning of the schooner, John became an instructor at Outward Bound Loch Eil, teaching sailing, canoeing, rock and snow climbing, general mountaineering and organising the Skye Treks. During this time he touched the lives of countless folk, young and not so young, and their many letters, included in his diaries, bear witness to this. He worked with Outward Bound for 20 years.

A great admirer and friend of the late Ben Humble, and a long-term member of the Mountain Rescue Committee of Scotland, John eventually fell heir to his predecessor's work as its mountain rescue statistician. The compiling and recording of this information has provided an invaluable service to Scottish mountain rescue for more than 20 years and gave John a great deal of satisfaction. He continued with the task until his death.

Since their retirement from full-time work about eight years ago, John and Betty had spent more time than ever before in each other's company and obviously thrived on it being as active and adventurous as ever. At home they were stalwart members of the local rambling group, exploring the wonderful countryside of Banffshire and the surrounding areas and abroad they roamed the hills of Canada, Spain, Cyprus, Tenerife, Portugal and Poland together. John had taken up Scottish country dancing in recent years. He realised that he couldn't beat Betty's love of it, so he had to join in too. Together they had some great fun and made many new friends. As recently as 1998, aged 70, John helped organise a reunion trip to the Himalayas. Targets varied with age, fitness and enthusiasm, but true to character, John had a great time and was delighted with Kala Pattar as his achievement.

His irrepressible enjoyment in the hills knew no bounds. He had been out walking every day of 2002, his last week in Braemar a culmination of all he loved best. To those of us who knew him, climbing companions and youngsters on his courses, he was a true inspiration and a great friend. He will be sorely missed by a multitude of hill-goers of all ages and backgrounds.

John is survived by his wife, Betty, son Neil, daughter Fiona, and four grandsons.

Fiona Wild.

WILLIAM LINDESAY WOOD

BILL WOOD was born in Aberfeldy on Christmas Day 1912. He joined the Customs and Excise Service after leaving St. Andrews University, and was initially posted to Stornoway. His career as a mountaineer took off when he transferred to Skye as His Majesty's representative at the Talisker Distillery, a dream posting, where he promptly went native.

He regarded the West Highland way of life as "the only one worth a damn", and his refreshingly irreverent attitude towards the authority that he himself represented became legendary in the island. Wood anecdotes of the 'now it can be told' variety are legion. His prowess with a stalking rifle earned him the sobriquet of 'the Duke of Kinlochainort', where as captain of the Skye Home Guard he put his arsenal of weaponry to its only constructive use. His sergeant, who happened to be his bank manager, was the troop's recognised expert on angling for salmon with hand grenades. Bill was on the fringe of official action on the Whisky Galore affair; as at Talisker, his very reasonable attitude was that "nobody gets his dram until the exciseman's had his". There is a wonderful and very accurate pen-portrait of him in Elizabeth Coxhead's novel *A Wind in the West*.

He also features in Benny Humble's classic book on the Cuillin of Skye. As a resident on the island, and very largely his own boss, he had every opportunity to do all the famous routes at his leisure when the weather was optimal. There is a spectacular photo of him standing upright on the late lamented gendarme on the West Ridge of Sgurr nan Gillean.

Being small of stature, albeit larger than life in character, he liked climbing with me, because I could often manage the salvation hold that was beyond his reach. He was intimately friendly with the great Professor Norman Collie during the latter's retirement at Sligachan. In fact, under wartime conditions, Bill Wood was the only mountaineer present at Collie's funeral. He related to me how, before tackling the Window Buttress, he asked Collie how difficult it was, and how Collie replied in his squeaky voice: "I can't remember much about it except that I've taken hundreds of women and children up it." Since Bill had naturally done the complete Cuillin ridge several times, he proposed – years later, after he had left Skye – that we should attempt the first winter traverse. However, we never got the right weather conditions at the times we were free, and eventually another group beat us to it.

From Skye, Bill transferred to Oban, then to the distillery in Dumbarton, and finally as exciseman in the Singer factory at Clydebank. Our main stamping grounds by then were Arrochar, and above all, Glencoe, where we did most of the classic routes of the day in summer and winter, very often meeting up with other SMC members like J. H. B. Bell, or Myles Morrison with his antique Rolls-Royce. I never managed to climb with Bill in the Alps after I moved to Central Europe, and to the major peaks around Innsbruck, Zermatt and Chamonix, but I went out with him every time I could get home. We had several years of an Indian summer with Frankie Milne in the bothy of Alice Campbell's Cuillin Cottage at Glen Brittle. My last Cuillin climb with Bill was the southern half of the main ridge out to Sgurr Dubh Mor on a day of glorious sunshine with the Hebrides laid out at our feet.

With time getting on, Bill went over to Munro-bagging, and was on his second round when the blow fell. In the winter of 1981 he had a stroke while driving on the A9 at Dunkeld, with the result that he went off the road and lay for 12 hours in the snow before he was discovered. In response to his anxious question when he regained consciousness, the neurologist replied: "Oh yes, you will be able to climb again, but you won't enjoy your dram as much" – a fate that Bill regarded as worse than death. I and my 12-year-old son managed to get him up Ben Lomond the following year, but that was his last Munro. He let his SMC membership lapse, but for some years continued doing some modest hillwalking around Dumbarton in company with a young woman doctor. With his powers failing, he spent the last years of his life in hospital in Dumbarton, where, as a great-great grandfather, he died on September 1, 2001 in his 89th year.

Jim Wilkie.

HARRY F. W. TAYLOR j.1986

HAL TAYLOR's climbing and hillwalking life began in 1943 or 1944 when he was a member of the Lancashire Caving and Climbing Club – a small, but active, club based in Bolton. He was a participant in monthly meets, caving in the Yorkshire Dales or climbing on Peak District gritstone and crags in the Lakes or Wales. His involvement with Scotland began in 1947 when he and his wife, Joan, hitch-hiked to Skye from London and did most of the Cuillin and the Pinnacle Ridge of Gillean. They were back in Skye in 1949 when the weather conditions were very different. A route-finding error enforced a long and very wet return to Glenbrittle from Coruisk. Near the end of this Hal collapsed with hypothermia, only being saved from an untimely end by some nearby campers.

These visits marked the start of an attachment to Scottish mountains reinforced by climbing trips to Glencoe and Ben Nevis. Torridon, and especially Liathach, were favourites as were the Cuillin where he twice did the Main Ridge traverse. He completed the Munros with Ben Wyvis in 1976; but Hal cast his mountaineering net widely and became a dedicated alpinist, finishing all the 4000m peaks of the Alps with the Aiguille Blanche de Peuterey in 1985.

The first Alpine visit was to the Dauphine with Joan in 1950. With very limited experience and guidebook in hand they did some easy peaks. In this self-taught manner was experience gained. Having joined the Climbers Club he attended several of their Alpine meets and began to notch up some 4000m summits. In the Seventies he set himself the target of doing all 61 of them.

A frequent companion was Peter Edwards who lived in Switzerland. He remembers: "The Scottish hills were something of a yardstick for him. For instance he liked to translate the names of Alpine peaks into Gaelic and often referred to Mont Blanc as Beinn Bhan. When he was staying with us on his trips to the Alps, Hal was really obsessed with the hills and climbing them. He could think and talk of little else. I used to ration his access to books, photographs and so on but, when not occupied with these, he would listen to radio reports and phone various sources for the latest conditions and weather prospects. Once we gave ourselves the go-ahead, Hal more or less steam-rolled us to the top and back. His determination was extraordinary. He didn't care how rough we slept or whether we ate or not, as long as we were moving towards our goal."

He was not a hard climber, but was a man of remarkable willpower which often meant he would overcome obstacles or adverse conditions which seemed to be beyond him.

Hal Taylor was in the Chemistry Department of Aberdeen University from 1953-1983, being head of department for four of those years. He became a world authority on cement chemistry, a subject for which he had a similar fixation as he had for mountains. His expertise was used by a number of cement companies and if he went abroad for them, or for scientific reasons, he was usually able to fit in some mountain activity.

After he retired Hal enjoyed a kind of second youth, doing a great deal of climbing all over the place and of all kinds – Scottish winter with ice tools, Nevis, Glencoe, Meaghaidh, Lochnagar, the North-east sea cliffs, Arran, the Lake District, Pembroke, Cornwall, Gritstone edges and farther afield to North America, Kenya and New Zealand. He went on climbing courses in Glencoe and met some young enthusiasts who went on to become guides and took Hal on various trips. A frequent companion was Tony Brindle with whom he returned to the Alps for an ascent of the Meije and also did Mount Aspiring in New Zealand. It was in this period that he joined the Club, membership of which he valued highly.

I only got to know Hal Taylor fairly late in his career and much of the detail in this account has come from Peter Edwards and from Joan Taylor herself. Hal would sometimes speculate on whether the mountains or science would last him the longer. It was in doubt to the end. He had to stop climbing after an operation six years ago but was up Bidean nam Bian in May, 2002.

However, in November he attended a scientific meeting in Denmark but died while returning to his home in Cumbria.

W. D. Brooker.

JOHN BICKERDIKE j.1996

JOHN BICKERDIKE died tragically on October 23, 2002 near his work at the premature age of 53.

John was born on February 1, 1949, in Newton Heath in Manchester. He was the youngest of five children enjoying the care and attention of his mother and three elder sisters, especially his sister Marjorie. His father had served in the First World War and was a brass moulder making armaments and serving in the Home Guard during the Second World War. His mother worked for British Avros building Lancaster bombers. Soon after the war his father was unable to work as the toxic fumes of smelting brass had chronically damaged his chest and he died when John was nine years old. His mother was the breadwinner working from 4am each morning cleaning local offices while his sister, Marjorie, got him ready for school.

John attended Briscoe Lane Primary School, and being a bright child, got into Grammar school. However, his education might have stopped there if a benevolent primary teacher had not arranged for a loan from the education department so his mother could buy him a school uniform for the best local Grammar school, Openshaw Technical College. John never forgot the sacrifices of his mother.

Despite the dangerous transport of a BSA Bantam and never seeming to study, he did well at Grammar school and went on to study Civil Engineering at Nottingham University where he met his wife, Barbara. He got a taste for potholing when first at university and at the insistence of his mother he gave it up, but he became a climber!

He was vice-president of Nottingham University mountaineering club in 1969 and succeeded in what may have been the first and only free ascent of the laundry chimney at Nottingham University. Using the bolts placed by the builders for protection, John and others forced an ascent under cover of darkness but were dismayed to find a security guard waiting when they abseiled down. Taking the situation in hand, John explained that they were doing a health-and-safety inspection of the chimney and that they always did them at night to avoid alarming passers-by. The reason why the guard had not seen one before. They eventually departed with the promise that they would be back next year for the annual inspection.

British Aerospace was where John was an apprentice in engineering. It was here that he crafted a lot of his own climbing equipment from locally available aviation grade aluminium. It reflected his attention to detail and art, perfectly engineered to a level of precision not found in commercial climbing equipment. Last winter, a snow belay device called a deadman which had been in use for all these years, was still in excellent condition. The quality of build and raw materials was unmistakable.

His daughter, Alison, was born when he worked in Northampton for the council where he designed and built a public toilet, before moving to Largs in Scotland to work for ICI in the mid-Seventies where his son, Robert, was born. He was even the harbour-master at the ICI plant for a time and worked there until his death.

John had an ultramontane approach and did a number of first British ascents in the Alps. The North-east Spur Direct of the Droites in 1975 with Martin Wragg was probably their best alpine ascent. The worst was the first British ascent of the North Face Direct of the Grosshorn. The lower face was hard ice and the middle section dramatically bad rock. When John was leading, a large pillar fell and shattered Martin's helmet. Later, they could not descend from the summit because of the snow conditions and had to bivouac, enduring a night of continuous thunderstorms, where the only thing to be seen was the zipper of his sleeping bag faintly glowing with static electricity.

John climbed many other Alpine routes often with Barbara. The harder routes included the Kanzelgrat (Rothorn), Gervasutti Pillar, North Face Piz Badille, Eiger, Aiguille de Blatiere. He also visited North America climbing in Yosemite where he reached the Stove Leg bivi on El Cap before deciding they couldn't haul the gear any higher. He did climb The Headache in Zion, Exxon Direct on Grand Teton, Canyon Lands Supercrack, Pingora in the Windrivers, Casual Route on the Diamond Face of Long's Peak and perhaps the first British ascent of Sabre in Estes Park. In 1978 he became an aspirant member of the Alpine Climbing Group proposed by Pete Boardman and seconded by Paul Braithwaite.

Across Scotland he climbed widely including King Kong on the Ben, Dragon and Gob at Carnmore, Rhino and Skydiver on Arran, King Rat and Blue Max at the Dubh Loch and the Old Man of Hoy. One successful ascent of Left Edge route of Gardyloo Buttress was almost stopped as the way was barred by the perpetual snows of Observatory Gully. Only the chance finding of a plastic boot complete with crampon, which John clipped to his fell running shoe, allowed the team to successfully cross the snow to reach the foot of the climb.

Living in Largs in Ayrshire, sailing was another passion for John and he combined sailing and his love of the mountains doing the Scottish Islands Peaks Races many times, sailing and running up the mountains of offshore west coast islands. His determination was clear as the team won the all-rounders trophy almost every year they competed.

I first met John in 1994 on a trip to Chamonix where we spent the time skiing and climbing with Tim Pettifer and my partner, Ann. We had a superb week, out every day no matter what the weather, which was typical of John. We were also on a modeling assignment. I wonder how many people knew that John had been a male model. When we came back to Scotland, John and I climbed regularly in winter. Astral Highway and Minus One Gully on Ben Nevis being the hardest but including most of the classics. He was an accomplished downhill skier and ski-mountaineer and we occasionally used skis to ascend to the CIC hut for the weekend.

Many people felt safe climbing with John, he took many of us to places we could not have reached on our own, even when we didn't want to go there! I had the pleasure of proposing John's membership to the SMC in 1996. Tim Pettifer, Ian Angell and Bob Richardson seconded his application. Contrary to the usual system he later joined the Junior Mountaineering Club of Scotland in 1999 and was an active member.

More recently, John took part in two Scottish Mountaineering Club expeditions to the Stauninys Alps in Northeast Greenland. The main achievement was the first ascent of the South Ridge of Hjornespids. It was a serious rock climb which would never have been completed without John's cunning, nerve and strength.

The new peaks climbed in Greenland John named after his two children. Giving a new peak someone else's name is a unique and rare gift and was John's way of saying how much he loved Alison and Robert, trying to give them immortality.

His climbing was not without incident as he broke an arm in the US. He also broke both of his ankles at the Quadrocks near Largs. Although he described them as "cracked" and was soon back on the hill well before the orthopaedic advice suggested he should be.

John was a very private, powerful, caring man, with a steely determination and a surprising lack of fear. At his funeral he was described as a catalyst, promoting change in all those around him, while remaining unchanged himself. The change he catalysed in other people was to bring them happiness. He once flew out to South Africa to a surprise party for his brother's 60th birthday. He was also very gentle and caring with a great propensity to worry. Climbing was his escape from the pressures of life and work, and he excelled as a climber. His premature and tragic death is a painful loss to his family and those who shared the pleasure of his company on the hills, crags and on the open sea.

John is survived by his two children, Alison and Robert and his partner Pat Grant.

C. M. Jones.

JOHN LOGAN AIKMAN j1928

LOGAN AIKMAN was born in Glasgow on September 5, 1902, the son of Patrick H. Aikman. He was educated at Glasgow Academy and Fettes College. He lived in Novar, Tannoch Drive, Milngavie for more than 30 years, commuting by train to Glasgow. In 1963, he and his wife, who predeceased him in 1989, moved to a small cottage in Station Road, Balfron. He lived the last eight years of his life at Dalnair House, Croftamie, where he died on November 1, 2002, in his 101st year.

His interest in climbing began on leaving school when he was training to be a chartered accountant, and working in the family firm of Aikman and Glen in St. Vincent Street. After the early death of his father in 1924, he took his place in the business and ran it almost single-handedly during the war, as well as being in the Home Guard – which necessitated many sleepless nights on duty. The firm was later taken over by a larger company and he retired in the early 1960s.

He was at his most active in the hills in the 1920s and 30s. He kept a regular mountaineering diary for the years between 1924 and 1930, which covers the period of the formation of the JMCS (he was a member of the Glasgow Section from January 1926) and his first years of membership in our Club, which he joined in 1928.

The diaries are a very full record of his mountaineering, running to 1854 pages. Although he climbed all over the country, there are frequent accounts of visits to Ben Nevis and to Skye, and it is plain from the enthusiasm of the writing that these were his favoured haunts. He was particularly fond of the Ben Nevis Hut, and stayed in it even before the official opening. He enjoyed a memorable encounter with A. E. Robertson there, and recorded a wonderfully racy vignette of Robertson huffily presiding over 'his' Hut, which was recently published in *The Munroist's Companion*. He arranged special Dinners at the Hut for his friends, garnished with decorated French Menus, and followed by lengthy Toasts and Speeches. His only substantial contribution to the Journal (*Joys of the Hut,* 1937, 21, 163-4) was a piece deploring the low levels of use of the Hut by members – only 22 of 300 members used it in 1936. The later diary expeditions were assisted by his Austin 7 named Beckmesser after the character in Wagner's *Mastersingers,* who sings badly!

Although many of his friends, such as Norman Mowbray, Gordon Robinson, George Williams and the Speirs brothers, were active rock-climbers, Aikman's diaries record few climbs – he seemed content to climb the hills, and to be as happy with a repeat ascent in good company as with a new mountain. Perhaps for that reason, despite his excellent start (93 Munros on application in 1928), he fell a few short of completion. His last Munros were climbed in the late 1950s with his daughter, Patricia. The diaries, together with much other interesting material, were donated to the Club in 1997 – thanks to the generosity of the family – and are now in our National Library archive.

In 1931, Aikman was recruited by George Sang as Assistant Secretary, and appointed to the Club Committee. He assisted Sang until 1935, then took over the Secretaryship, which he held until 1946 when Ian Charleson succeeded him. His office coincided with the efforts of Arthur Russell, Percy Unna, James Wordie and others to bring about the various Glencoe purchases for the benefit of the nation in 1935-37. The Club was at the centre of this process, and it must have been exciting and exacting work for a young Secretary, new to the job. In 1938 he undertook the task of organizing the enormous, and very successful, Jubilee Dinner in Glasgow. During his time as Secretary he was a regular attender at Meets and was also involved in rescue work, at that time often carried out by Club members recruited by the Club Secretary at the request of the police. Aikman's distinguished tenure of the office of Secretary was marked by a short, but fulsome, appreciation in the Journal by Alex Harrison and J. W. Baxter (*SMCJ* 1947, 23, 446).

I am indebted to Aikman's daughters, Patricia Knutson and Morag Maddy, for their generous assistance in preparing this obituary.

Robin N. Campbell.

OLIVER TURNBULL j 1987

OLIVER TURNBULL's passion for mountaineering began during the Second World War, when his uncle, Professor Herbert Turnbull, a past President of the club, took him walking in North Wales. Later they attended the Club's Easter meet 1949. His uncle, who was Professor of Mathematics at St Andrews, also introduced Oliver to golf and he soon had a handicap in single figures.

Oliver was born at Bowden, near Altrincham, Cheshire on August 8, 1933, the youngest child of the Reverend Peveril and The Lady Jane Turnbull (née Grey). He was educated at Marlborough, where he learned to play the oboe, and there developed his three great interests in life – literature, mountains and music. It was these wider interests that made his holidays almost a cultural experience. Poor weather in the Dolomites and he would point towards Verona and an opera in the Roman Arena. After a hard climb on Mont Blanc he would relax in Aosta in an ornate rural church listening to an organ recital.

After completing National Service, when he was able to continue hill walking and take up rock climbing, he instructed, for short time, at the Ullswater Outward Bound School admitting that he had to learn quickly to keep one step ahead of the students. Later in life he became chairman of the school and took a great interest in the young.

In 1957, Oliver joined the Wayfarers' Club and climbed in the Alps for the first time with club friends. This was the first of more than 20 seasons in the Alps – many with Charles Warren, Iain Ogilvie and myself. He also climbed in the Canadian Rockies and trekked in the Himalayas. It was these members who reintroduced Oliver to SMC Easter Meets as their guest in 1977. After continuing to attend these meets for almost 20 years, he was pleased, when we returned very late from a day on the hills, to hear that a past President had commented: "You don't want to worry about those two." His friends Charles, Iain and Ivan Waller encouraged him to apply for membership of the Club. He was told, by John Fowler, that it was important to enjoy "gadding about in the hills" – a phrase that described Oliver's approach so very well.

Oliver took great trouble choosing which areas to visit and his anticipation and enthusiasm were infectious. He would quietly pour over maps and guidebooks for days looking up references in his climbing library before telephoning with a firm, but thoughtful, suggestion. On one occasion he spent hours with his friend, Ivan Waller, planning his 'Ultimate Challenge' route across Scotland. His friends often said when he was planning these trips that you could see his 'tail wagging'.

He was delighted to have climbed North East Buttress in winter and the Long Climb in summer, both from Fort William, but most of all he loved to wander the Scottish hills (accompanied by his lovely dog 'Widge'). His active interest in the club and his enthusiasm for the Easter meets culminated in his taking on the role of Meets Secretary. The meets had declined in popularity but Oliver's first meet in 1996 at Tomdoun Hotel was a huge success with wonderful weather, ice on the loch and the largest turnout for several years.

After working for a timber importer in Finland, Newcastle and Liverpool, he moved to Lancaster to work for Courtaulds before settling in Kendal where he owned and managed Titus Wilson, publishers and printers. The company merged with Dixon Printing and Oliver concentrated on encouraging local authors and the production of antiquarian book catalogues – a job he loved. He had a natural charm and gained the trust and respect of his colleagues and clients, many of whom became friends.

He frequently searched through second-hand bookshops, and on one occasion, found the original CIC hut book on a Kendal bookshelf, which he bought and returned to the club. His collection of mountaineering books was auctioned shortly after his death comprising 180 lots and described as 'A Fine Collection collected over 30 years including Charles Fellows's own copy of his book *A Narrative of an Ascent of Mt Blanc,* a unique copy, arguably the most desirable work on Alpine Mountaineering to be offered for sale in recent years'.

Oliver didn't talk openly about his climbing plans. He preferred to keep his options open. He only once let a thought slip – the Matterhorn. In the hut, after good climbing days, he would talk of other routes and mountains and he frequently commented that he didn't want to climb the ordinary route on the Matterhorn jostling with the crowd. So an ascent had to be by a good route, in good style.

The Zmutt ridge was in poor condition so we walked to Cervinia from Zermatt. Next day we climbed to the Carrel hut on the Italian ridge. Out well before first light the next morning we set off up the ridge with its fixed ropes and rope ladder; the sun rose as we climbed. We had the ridge to ourselves and were alone on the summit. It was Oliver's 60th birthday. We descended the Hörnli Ridge, mostly on the East face avoiding the crowds as they ascended, reaching the hut seven hours later. Tired but elated, Oliver's first thought was to phone his wife, Viv and the children – Lucy, Clare, Sarah and Harry. He was extremely proud of his children and grandchildren.

Oliver had many varied interests and an inquiring mind. When travelling a plan would emerge; go and look at a grand house; visit an art gallery, or call on an interesting friend. Even rainy days could be a great adventure.

After he and his wife moved to Suffolk in 1998, he returned to golf and took up a new interest – silver making. Oliver, who had a classical education and maintained he wasn't good with his hands, created many lovely gifts for his family. He was quietly proud of his newfound talent. He frequently returned to Kendal for business and pleasure and would delight in walking along the High Street greeting old friends and colleagues on the way.

His trips to Scotland continued until the last months of his life and he attended Robin Campbell's Skye meet. Along with others we set out from Allt Dearg House to climb Pinnacle Ridge. Oliver was in two minds but was encouraged by Iain Smart to continue and at the abseil on the last pinnacle Oliver produced a thin line that he had carried for many years. "This rope is just the right length." Much to the amusement and heckling of those above we then proceeded to struggle down this rope. On returning to the house the rope was carefully measured and only then did Oliver admit, with a wry smile, that it was "a bit short".

It is hard to imagine, that less than a year before he died from cancer, he walked more than 100 miles in the Pyrenees, in both snow and sun. But we will all remember the vibrant enthusiastic man who shared his wide interests with so many friends. He was always great company, especially on the hills.

Dick Allen.

ANDREW WIGHTMAN j. 1960

DURING the mid-1950s Iain Haig and I escorted members of the Edinburgh scouting fraternity over a few Easter hill weekends. On one of these I first met Andy as a slight, quiet, youngster (fortunate for him) for my part was to burn off the aggressive lads while Iain nurtured the others along at a sensible pace – a technique which successfully endowed the latter group with new-found confidence in comparative abilities.

He later appeared at University as a six-footer (I was unaware of the past connection till he let on) and fell in with some of the most dynamic climbers hitherto grace the Scottish climbing scene.

By the early 60s he joined the Currie lads labouring on our self-build house; in between wild goings-on, extensive climbing weekends and final-year studies, he patently lived life in the fast track.

Given his grasp of the subject matter he was unhappy about the finals result, but when he moaned about a 3rd, we all gave him a hard time, calling him a 3rd class citizen which possibly led to his eschewal of chemistry, opting instead into the high-tech revolution. We thought this was rejection in the extreme but it proved to be an astute move and led to a very successful career of world-wide service with IBM.

In mountaineering terms, Andy was brought up hard, and endured the rigours of old-style climbing well. One weekend we were to rendezvous at the CIC, I didn't have a key, wrongly assuming that someone would be in residence, but on arriving in a healthy blizzard had to force entry by the 'wee door'. In following up Andy missed the snow plastered hut and ended up in an unscheduled bivouac under an old army cape in Coire Leis. I was awakened at first light by his energetic assault on the front door, but fortunately, saved the place from destruction with a loud hail from the temporary 'door'.

A good breakfast saw him to rights and we spent the day achieving nothing, dodging avalanches etc. but enjoying the wildness of our situation.

His middle man role on the 'nightshift' ascent of Zero Gully has passed into history, but prior to the Eiger, he and Dougal tried a bold winter attempt on Route II which certainly impressed Andy for Dougal took a slithering fall from high up under the overhangs onto a baby nylon runner with little else of a belay between them.

Retreat from the Eiger can be misconstrued as failure whereas in reality, getting safely off any big mountain in storm condition is the ultimate test of climbing competence. Our pair had almost succeeded but on the home stretch Andy tripped and tumbled, only arresting his fall just before the abyss.

He suffered enormous pain from a smashed ankle but his tenacious courage plus the super endeavours of Dougal and two selfless Italian rescuers returned him to safety and a future life.

His post-Eiger life was greatly enriched in marriage to Mary, his alter ego and equal and despite nagging discomfort from the ankle injury, they regularly enjoyed sorties on home hills or farther afield.

Having only recently resettled in Edinburgh, we all anticipated entertaining social interaction to follow, but fate intervened as Andy fell victim to cancer where once again he displayed the courage and determination of his earlier days, but sadly, to no avail.

Regrettably, Mary succumbed to the big C within a year of Andy's demise.

J. R. Marshall.

EDINBURGH University in the early 1960s was a daunting place for a young climber. Smith, Haston, Wightman and Holt were all at the height of their powers and those of a more modest ability were left in no doubt as to their station.

To Smith we were 'Boy Scouts', to Haston 'hangers on'. Andy regarded this hierarchy as something of a joke. In particular, he viewed the Teutonic posturings and ambitions of the young squirrels as totally hilarious! Andrew simply loved the outdoors and would walk or climb with anyone who shared his enthusiasm – regardless of their abilities.

After the Eiger incident, especially, his gregarious and social nature came to the fore and there was no more popular member of the EUMC. He was relaxed and humorous and always first choice for any student party. His friendship and subsequent long and happy marriage to Mary Paine, a fellow EUMC member, came as no surprise to their friends.

As a student of Nuclear Chemistry, he was the first to agree, (he found out) the going was hard and like most of us he survived, rather than enjoyed, what he claimed was the toughest course in the world! Nevertheless he was quietly pleased with his hard-won Honours degree, and the same qualities of determination and hard work carried him through a demanding and highly-successful career in business.

Of his many qualities, he will be remembered particularly for his generosity. As a young man he would do anything to help a friend. On my own first trip to the Alps he loaned me his rucksack, his crampons and even his Lawries 23Rs – surely greater love hath no man!

This generosity of spirit endured and grew throughout his life. Mary and he were never happier than when providing hospitality for friends, be it in Edinburgh, London or North America.

Andrew's love of mountains and the open spaces remained undiminished by time or failing health. He discovered ski-touring fairly late in life and, despite a busy professional life, he made time for an extended trip to the Fann Mountains in Russia. Less than one year before his final illness he joined a group of friends for a testing 10-day trip in the Pyrenees. He was his usual cheerful, self-deprecating self. His last painful weeks were borne with immense courage and dignity an inspiration and example to all. We mourn our loss.

Paul Brian.

GEORGE T. B. CHISHOLM j. 1954

WHEN George Chisholm died on August 27, 2002, at the age of 87 after a lifetime of service to the community and devotion to the Scottish hills, most of the then members of the SMC would only remember him as a regular attender at the AGMs and less frequent participant in the Easter Meets for the past 20 years. His climbing record would probably be unknown to them and many would have been surprised to learn that although no 'Tiger of yesterday', neither was he a 'pussycat' and had a list of climbs, both at home and abroad, that many would be happy to attain today. Although his climbing career ceased in 1978 after the death of his regular climbing partner Fred Mantz in a scrambling accident on B buttress on Aonach Dubh, George continued to go on the hills winter and summer until three years before his death. His last winter Munro without the aid of mechanical uplift was in 1996 when he climbed Spidean Mialach on the Tomdoun Easter Meet. His first recorded Munro was Ben Lomond in 1936 – 60 years earlier! He was among the first 100 Munroists.

He had walked with his wife, Olive, from the time of the Ben Lomond ascent (they were married in 1941) and his first 'Rock or Snow' climb in his application for the SMC was also with her – Ben Lui's Central Gully in 1946.

He joined the JMCS, which in those days was almost a pre-requisite to SMC membership and was President of that club in 1947-48. His application records the usual selection of climbs for the period up to V. Diff standard – par for the course – and he joined the SMC in 1954. While he climbed with many present SMC members of subsequent high reputation, his usual companion was Fred Mantz who only came to the SMC in 1971 and led him into high grade climbing.

As a Primary school teacher, George had no holiday problems and went to the Alps nine times, again with the more experienced Fred as leader. Among notable ascents were the Jagigrat – a quality rock climb above Saas – three ascents of the Matterhorn including a traverse in poor weather conditions, most of the major peaks of the Valais, the Piz Bernina and Piz Palu. Apart from the Alps, George walked and scrambled in the Drakensburg during wartime service in South Africa. His last rock climb was Eagle Ridge on Lochnagar in 1977, led by Fred, in a day trip from Edinburgh.

Like George, I continued climbing with friends, other than Eastern District SMC, until about 1980, so I only knew him by rather casual acquaintance until then. From that time onward however, we formed part of the Eastern District walking group, loosely organised after the death of Ken Macrae by Bill Myles. This became a regular Saturday outing and, thanks to Bill's driving, we covered Scotland from the Cairngorms to Criffel and Misty Law to Hartfell. George was an excellent walker and repeated many of his earlier Munro ascents, although chairlift was used if available to make days feasible. Even after he recovered from a cardiac arrest he could still manage good days and his last Munro was a worthy one without mechanical aid. It was deliberately intended as a final gesture, which it was.

Latterly, his days on the hills were somewhat curtailed by the need to assist Olive during a severe terminal illness, but he managed to get out for short days for several months. He made arrangements to cope with the situation with several Highland hotels that they formerly patronised, which no doubt revived old memories of happier times.

George was a teacher all his working life in several schools in the Tynecastle area of Edinburgh and when he retired he was Headmaster of Burdiehouse School in the city. To judge from appearances he must have been well liked as he had a long list of correspondents who had been pupils and several came to visit him when he was in a nursing home before his death as a result of a stroke. Indeed, it sometimes seemed that the Scottish hills were populated by ex-pupils or church friends as we were constantly meeting them on the paths. It must be said that George, as an inherently friendly soul, was a great talker and he often lagged behind chatting to his friends but usually managing to be not too far behind at the summits.

He and Olive were dedicated churchgoers and he was organist at Gorgie and Stenhouse Baptist Church from the age of 30 where they took part in much of the associated life of the Church. His two sons follow in the tradition of public service. Iain, the elder, is a senior Civil Servant in Whitehall, while Malcolm is at present Minister of Health in the Scottish Parliament.

G. Scott Johnstone.

Jason Currie on the Grand Traverse of the Rabada-Navarro (ED-) on the West Face of El Naranjo de Bulnes, Picos de Europa, Northern Spain. Photo: Adam Liversedge. (Jason Currie collection).

PROCEEDINGS OF THE CLUB

The following new members were admitted and welcomed to the Club in 2002-2003.

David Adam, (46), Artist, Brechin.

P. John Armstrong, (??), Mountain Guide, Carrbridge.

Colin M. Bell, (33), Environmental Consultant, Innerleithen.

Erik W. Brunskill, (28), Network Analyst, Glasgow.

Martin Cooper, (33), Youth Worker, Musselburgh.

Nicholas L. Cruden, (29), Doctor of Medicine, Edinburgh.

Christopher Dale, (41), Mountain Guide, Penrith.

Blair Fyffe, (23), Mountaineering Assistant to SAIS, Aviemore.

Joanna M. George, (33), Designer, Ballachulish.

Kathryn Grindrod, (37), Mountaineering Assistant to SAIS, Coniston.

Ross I. Jones, (34), H. R. Consultant, Edinburgh.

Michael R. Lates, (36), Mountain Guide, Broadford.

Derek Morley, (32), Chartered Water Engineer, Motherwell.

David J. Pritchard, (39), Medical Research Scientist, Scone.

Mark Robson, (33), Information Systems Manager, Throsk.

Euan J. M. Scott, (38), Company General Manager, Edinburgh.

Iain G. Small, (36), Mountain Footpath Contractor, South Queensferry.

Ian W. Taylor, (38), Retailer, Edinburgh.

Michael L. Watson, (54), Physician, Edinburgh.

Colin Wells, (42), Writer and Ecological Consultant, Dyce.

The One-Hundreth-and-Thirteenth AGM and Dinner

PITLOCHRY and the Atholl Palace – the safe choice and an overdue change from the West Coast. The weather, however, showed no improvement, which guaranteed a respectable turn out for the afternoon slide shows where Hamish Brown, Tom Prentice and Simon Richardson described varying styles of our sport in distant places.

The AGM was a parochial affair – some more chairs might have helped – with issues such as the annual loss, the colour of our Journal cover, hut access rights, subscription levels and the future of the slide collection exciting members. And on to dinner where a record 189 members and guests attended table, including Annie Haston, whose late husband, Dougal, our former member, had that afternoon been introduced into Scotland's sporting Hall of Fame.

As for the meal, I remember the slick service and the haggis parcels – or rather the absence of haggis parcels due to a menu mix-up. But no-one complained.

The hotel's reluctance to move its concert grand piano left the entertainers with a problem, but they did their best with the Club song. The President recited a list of members' climbing achievements – phew! – to be followed by a brilliant Toast

Scott Muir topping out on Pema M9+ in the Haston Cave, Val Savaranche, Aosta, Italy. Photo: Scott Muir collection.

to the Guests by Charlie Orr – a memorable highlight (I didn't write this but I wholeheartedly concur – *Ed.*). Chris Bonington provided the response with a polished performance and finally, Peter Macdonald accepted Raeburn's axe with the normal modesty to commence his Presidential stint.

Many said afterwards it was a great Dinner. Was it due to the food? Unlikely. Or the famous guest? Perhaps. Or the location? More likely. Or the members themselves? Almost certainly. And so we're taking a great risk – going back. Clear your diaries for November 29.

J. R. R. Fowler.

Ski-mountaineering Meet 2003.

Members present: Dick Allen, Donald Ballance, Richard Bott, Ewan Clark, Colwyn Jones, Ann MacDonald, Peter Macdonald, Chris Ravey, Bob Reid, Bill Wallace. Guests: Gordon Clark, Bill Shaw, Nick Walmsley.

The participants arrived at Mar Lodge throughout Friday evening, renewing auld acquaintances and planning for the weekend ahead.

On Saturday 8, February, DB, CJ, PM, CR, BS, and NW ascended Glas Maol via Meall Odhar, mostly on skis. There was soft, patchy snow and the Meall Odhar café was closed. After a swift lunch on the summit we returned via the Sunnyside ski run and the open fire at the Fife Arms.

During the above expedition Chris demonstrated the strengths and weaknesses of his new GPS. One strength was that it guided us to within 30m of the summit in whiteout conditions, this despite our indirect route attempting to find patches of snow to string together. One weakness of GPS is that shortly after arriving the batteries ran out and Chris had to revert to map and compass to guide us off the hill.

One guest said: "I had long looked forward to my first experience of the sport under the watchful eye of this internationally well known group of exponents of the genre. My head was soon reeling with the technicalities of skinning, partial release, high stepping and so on. As we trudged up the line of a non-functional t-bar, however, I could begin to see the possibilities of the freedom to roam that this technological and financial investment might achieve.

"The clamber to the summit, much the same as walking up (only less elegant), soon gave way to appreciation of the diversity of a day out like this. I counted 23 different changes from skin to ski, 117 binding adjustments, several disputes of direction, and the thrill of walking down a boulder field with my skis cleverly mounted on my rucksack to catch the wind in the manner of a windsurfer sail. Determined to substitute enthusiasm for my lack of experience, I was excited to see how my companions threw themselves into the snow in a series of spectacular car boot sales, and had no difficulty in matching their flair. In short, this is a sport for everyone seeking an alternative day on the mountain."

Another member said: "Within the company present on this year's ski meet I consider myself a mere junior to the sport. It was with eager enthusiasm that I set out with five of the finest of these wilderness mountain explorers on Saturday. You can imagine that I was a little taken aback when the car stopped at the local ski resort.

"However, on skinning up a steep hill my confidence was restored that a fine day witnessing perfect turns on virgin snow lay ahead. I was a little shocked on entering the cloud to find that my companions were happy to follow a little device, which apparently talks to satellites. It must be the modern way I thought and followed their lead. I must say that I was shocked when they proceeded to use mechanical means later in the day.

"In fairness, it had been a long adventure under less-than-ideal conditions. Worse was yet to come. At the top of the long and daring descent back to the glen all five of my childhood heroes paused, fumbled with their bindings and, shock, horror, clipped in their heels. Please my friends restore my faith in you. Free the heel and free the mind. It is the only way."

SYSTEMS TESTING: The Clarks and Reid recorded on digital camera cycling with skis on. Truly this is a sight to behold. Various techniques were employed including rucsac mounted skis, crossbar mounted skis and variations on both these themes. Directional diversions tended to occur to the crossbar-mounted set-ups as wheels pointed one way and skis pointed another. Ski boots were carried or worn to various effect. Bow legged-ness ensued.

SYSTEM FAILURE: This occurred following a cycle from Mar Lodge Stables along to the Linn. Intentions on the Derry Lodge track failed after 60 enervating metres – Ewan Clark getting farthest through the difficulties. These it has to be noted were the result of 25 cm of frozen slush recently compacted by a vehicle known as an Argocat (a more sensible means of transporting skis).

Bikes abandoned, skins put on skis and a modest tour up Sgor Mor via Sgor Dubh ensued, but the summit was not reached owing to rain, wet snow and absence of lead in pencil.

BW, DA and RB looking for the maximum snow with the minimum carry to it, headed for the fleshpots of the Glenshee Trois Vallees. Greeted with mist, mud and squalor they carried on south to the old iron bridge. From the lay-by they were able to ski non-stop to a large area of heather and gravel high on the south ridge of the Cairnwell, followed by another similar area. The summit of the Cairnwell is an abomination of masts and tin sheds. The air-conditioning of the buildings on the summit spoke volumes for the expected conditions at the top of one of Scotland's premier ski resorts. They had a fine run down on almost continuous snow and were back at the car so early that they had to kill time in the shops of Braemar before showing face at Mar Lodge again.

Ann enjoyed a birthday that evening. Champagne, roses, presents and best wishes sung in true SMC style with harmony and much revelry – but thankfully, no *Old Hobnailers.*

Sunday dawned with more promising weather and everyone headed along to Linn of Quoich for an ascent of Carn na Drochaide. With our President to the fore, we skinned up the patches of snow as the cloud cleared and the sun shone from a clear blue sky. The views were superb in all directions over Ben Macdhui, Beinn a' Bhuird and Lochnagar. We finally heather-hopped our way to the summit to enjoy a light lunch in the lee of the summit cairn. However, the breeze cooled us sufficiently not to dally overlong and we skied from just below the summit to just above the cars at Linn of Quoich. This Corbett is an excellent viewpoint and was an excellent choice on an excellent day.

There only remained handing in some skis at the hire shop and the customary cup of tea before heading for home.

C. M. Jones.

JMCS REPORTS

Perth Mountaineering Club (JMCS, Perth Section): The year got off to a good start with a well attended meet at Milehouse, during which no fewer than 21 members plus one prospective member (aged six months) put in an appearance at one stage or another.

This was the start of a typically active year with 11 weekend meets and 10 day meets. The club membership continued to climb slightly to 105.

Those taking part in an unusually popular day meet to Glen Lochay in December were rewarded with a superb temperature inversion. Above the clouds there was almost perfect visibility in all directions.

The New Year started with the usual social New Year's Day walk at Birnam Hill. Later in the month the atrocious winter weather was exemplified by a weekend spent in Glen Etive. There was some respite from the gale-force winds and sleet on the Saturday, but by Sunday, thunder and lighting added to the overall menace and no-one ventured out.

February's CIC hut meet was convened by Mark James who climbed Comb Gully and No. 2 Gully Buttress in rather less than perfect conditions.

The February meet to the Smiddy at Dundonnel was a victim of its own popularity with an overflow party having to be accommodated at a local bunkhouse. This, in spite of a rather uninspiring forecast, which turned out to be accurate.

In contrast, an equally dubious outlook for the Ling Hut meet in March turned out to be overly pessimistic, and the Saturday was fine, enabling three members to traverse the Black Carl pinnacles on the Beinn Eighe ridge in Alpine conditions.

A select group ventured into deepest Aberdeenshire in April to the Allargue Arms bunkhouse at Cockbridge. A new venue, with interesting new route possibilities in the eastern Cairngorms, was enjoyed with the first sign of spring weather on the summits.

The year's most successful meet was arguably the camping meet to Glen Brittle in early May. No fewer than 27 members and guests took part, and 16 climbed a dry and sunny Pinnacle Ridge on the Saturday. Had we realised then that this was about the last decent weather we would get all summer, perhaps the perfect conditions would have been savoured even more.

The annual backpacking trip was to the Knoydart peninsula. Being the 'Jubilee weekend' the area was mobbed and in some instances by people who were rather alarmingly unprepared for a visit to remote country in poor conditions.

The year was rounded off with a September family meet – now becoming a regular fixture.

The Wednesday evening rock-climbing was a washout. Only a few evenings early on in the season were graced with anything like summer weather – most were too wet to contemplate going out.

The Club now has another Munroist with Melanie Nicoll climbing her last few over the summer while expecting her second child.

The Annual Dinner was held at the Cultoquhey Hotel at Gilmerton in November.

Officials elected: *President,* Phillip Taylor; *Vice-President,* Karen Campbell; *Secretary,* Sue Barrie, Glensaugh Lodge, Laurencekirk, AB3O IBH. Tel: 01561 340673; *Treasurer,* Pam Dutton; *Newsletter Editor,* Des Bassett; *Meets Convener,* Beverley Robertson; *Committee,* Dave Prentice, Mike Aldridge, Melanie Nicoll and Carolann Petrie.

Sue Barrie.

Edinburgh Section: Membership is currently 95 – including a number of aspirants.
The section continues to hold mid-week meets at the Heriot-Watt climbing wall during the winter months and various crags around Edinburgh during the summer. Traprain and Aberdour feature regularly, but there are also visits to Dunkeld and Kyloe. Particularly dedicated members also meet on Monday nights at Alien Rock. For those more partial to less strenuous evening entertainment, the section meets on the first Thursday of the month at Kay's Bar in Jamaica Street.

Weekend meets in winter have tended to be better attended than those in summer, mostly due to last summer's unsettled weather. The Lakes have been a popular rock-climbing destination, and some members were at Stanage in June. In Scotland, a meet at Jock's in August saw parties climbing at Creag Dubh, Kingussie and Duntelchaig.

The January meet at Muir of Inverey cottage was memorable for some great weather on the Saturday that saw members visiting Creag an Dubh Loch, Lochnagar and Corrie Kander for winter climbing. Others went ski-mountaineering around Glen Shee. Unfortunately, a thaw set in on the Sunday and those that ventured out went hill walking. Mild conditions also affected February's meet at Invercroft in Achnasheen, and the only climbing done in the area was the traverse of A'Chioch. Conditions improved for the March meet at Blackrock Cottage in Glen Coe while the winter ended with a visit to the CIC Hut for such staples as Comb Gully, Tower Ridge and Good Friday Climb.

Club trips abroad have taken in a variety of destinations. Rock climbing in the sun is proving popular, with Spain and Italy being the favoured locations. Various groups visited the Costa Blanca and Sardinia during the winter months. The Alps continue to be widely visited during the summer months, with members climbing around Chamonix, Zermatt and the Dolomites. A small party spent some time in Chamonix in February for some winter alpinism and valley ice climbing. Farther afield, other members visited the US, Canada, Norway and Greenland.

The Annual Dinner took place at the Atholl Arms Hotel in Blair Atholl. An excellent meal was followed by an entertaining speech from Doug Lang. Doug recounted tales of first ascents in summer and winter, including the ever-popular Ardverikie Wall on Binnein Shuas and Slav Route on the Ben. The only complaints related to the non-availability of the hotel's specially brewed beer at the bar. This will be rectified in time for our intended return in 2003.

The section's huts have continued to prove popular with both members and other clubs. Jock's was the venue of a couple of memorable meets for new members, and Hogmanay at the Smiddy is as popular as ever. Comfort levels at the Smiddy have increased with the purchase of mattresses, and bookings have increased.

The Joint Eastern Section SMC/JMCS slide nights have continued to be interesting events with speakers on a wide-range of subjects associated with climbing and the hills. The slide nights take place at 7:30pm on the second Tuesday of the month from October to March at Edinburgh University Pollock Halls.

Rab Anderson kindly agreed to give an additional lecture and slide show in October on the subject of Scottish winter climbing. Many of Rab's new routes were featured as well as classics such as Mitre Ridge and Poachers Fall. The evening was also an opportunity for members to hear first hand about developments at the Ratho Adventure centre.

Officials elected: *Hon. President*, John Fowler; *Hon. Vice-President*, Alan Smith; *President*, Helen Forde; *Vice-President*, Sally Dipple; *Treasurer*, Bryan Rynne; *Secretary*, Neil Cuthbert, 25 Plewlands Gardens, Edinburgh (cuthbertneil@netscape.net); *Web Master*, Douglas Hall; *Smiddy Custodian*, Alec Dunn, 4 King's Cramond, Edinburgh; *Jock Spot's Custodian*, Ali Borthwick, 2 Aytoun Grove, Dunfermline. *Ordinary Members*, Patrick Winter (Meets Secretary), Stewart Bauchop.

Neil Cuthbert.

London Section: After the quiet year imposed by Foot and Mouth restrictions of 2001, we have made a concerted effort to infuse new vigour into the club.

The meets program has had an increased number of meets at the club cottage which has helped attract a dozen or so new members.

It may be of interest for other clubs to know that most (if not all) inquiries to the secretary were from enthusiastic walkers who wanted to develop into mountaineers and climbers. They were looking for clubs to provide training, coaching and opportunities to develop the necessary skills safely and in enjoyable company. Most of the interest has come by word of mouth and we have had one inquiry as a result of our new website!

The club has made substantial improvements to the cottage in Bethesda, including a new drying room, repaired flat-roof and new bedding. This is part of the longer-term plan to make better use of the cottage and improve the overall quality of the JMCS experience.

In response to requests from new and prospective members we ran a series of introductory, beginner and improver weekends aimed at inspiring and coaching new-comers to the sport. These proved very successful and suited those people who like to plan their development rather than our traditional 'have a go' style. The highlight must be the group of four 30-somethings who were surprised to find themselves outpaced and intimidated by a retired Civil Servant who took them swimming in a series of pools and cascades by Snowdon's Watkin path on our introductory weekend! I don't think they expected to be quite so immersed in the experience. Other first-timers went climbing on Milestone Buttress and ended up on the Adam and Eve stones of Tryfan – an instant buzz and they want to join.

As a well-established club with several mature members, 2002 saw many self-contained expeditions to various places. Our best year yet I feel.

Chris Comerie and Gordon Dalgarno had an interesting trip on the Gervasutti Pillar when they couldn't locate their stash of gear for the overnight bivi. But it didn't stop them going on to take a party up Mont Blanc.

Tony Buj took Geoff Howes, Jamie Ward and Andy 'Paz' Parrish to the Alps for their first time and he also did Mont Blanc, as well as the Monch and the Mirroire d'Argentiere – the three Ms. Congratulations to the Alpine novices.

Peter Stokes spent a few months taking his yacht to Greenland exploring the fjords, icebergs and mountains of the West Coast.

We have had other meets where members arrive by sailing boat – a growing interest within the club with several members acquiring qualifications and experience of different levels.

We would be interested to hear from other climbers with sailing interests with a view to linking crews to boats, organizing mini-expeditions and creating a general 'community' of sailing mountaineers.

All these exploits and more are recorded on the new website www.jmcs.freewire.co.uk

The finale of the year is as always the Annual Dinner and the annual meeting which was again at the Giler Arms on the outskirts of Snowdonia.

Usually, great mountain biking conditions pertain and the new 'Marin' trail at Betys-y-coed must be the best bike route in the area – well worth exploring for anyone with three hours to spare on a wet weekend in Wales.

All in all, a healthy year for the club.

Officials elected: President, Marcus Harvey; Vice-President, John Firmin; Meets Secretary, Roy Hibbert; Treasurer and Hogwash Editor, Dave Hughes; Secretary and webmaster, Chris Bashforth; Hut Custodian, Rod Kleckham; Hut Works, Pete Turner; AGM/Dinner Secretary, Geoff Deady.

Glasgow Section: Club membership is 106, including 13 female members. Several new members have joined this year.

Fortnightly pub meets are popular, and serve as a good point of contact with prospective members. Members can now be found at the climbing wall on at least two nights of the week

Weekend meets have been mostly well attended, but numbers as always are subject to the weather forecast.

Twenty-three weekend meets took place, covering most of the mountaineering areas of Scotland. A whole club meet in Arran in May was well attended by Glasgow and London sections, but they unfortunately, never met due to the distractions of climbing. Members have also made trips to the Lakes, Pembrokeshire, and the Peak. As usual, the AGM and Dinner in Glencoe was well attended.

Activity abroad included a ski-mountaineering trip to the Pennine Alps by Colwyn Jones and Ann MacDonald, climbing Flucthorn, Rimpfischorn, Briethorn and Strahlhorn. They also climbed Mount Olympus on a separate trip. Vicky Stewart spent several months in South America, and climbed Iskinka (5545m) in Peru. Autumn saw Davie MacDonald and Neil Marshall visiting Sardinia for some bolt-clipping, followed by Colwyn and Ann a few weeks later. Other trips by members have included climbing in Spain and walking in China.

Officicials elected: President, Scott Stewart; Vice-President; Ann MacDonald; Treasurer, Scott Stewart; Secretary, Vicky Stewart, Coruisk Hut Bookings, John Fenemore; Coruisk Hut Custodian, Alex Haddow.

Jeremy Morris.

SMC AND JMCS ABROAD

Greenland
Alpine Club/ACG Lemon Mountains Expedition

GEOFF COHEN reports: Yesterday, had been a long day. We left 'advance base camp', a tiny tent, in the midst of the vast Frederiksborg Glacier and skied for many hours up to a col. We were aiming for the North Lemon Mountains, a group never before visited, at latitude 68° in East Greenland. A previous attempt, a week earlier, via a different col, had been thwarted by a steeply crevassed glacier descent – impossible to take pulks over. From our new col, Dave had led us cleverly through the crevasses by huge gentle curves till we reached a broad highway running south-west, with the spiky peaks that we had seen in the distance when we first landed on the ice-cap now hidden from view. Finally, as we got once more into a crevassed area and the glacier prepared to flow over steeper ground down to a major junction, we put up our tent and retired for a well-earned rest.

Now we were embarking on a reconnaissance. With light sacks we would go down the icefall to the junction and see if we could establish a camp within striking distance of a soaring mountain of classical sharp triangular outline that had dominated the distant view. This was the day I enjoyed most. In spite of the slushy ice on the lower glacier and the inevitable zig-zagging when finding a route for the first time, we had the thrill of exploration in an entirely new area, with untold magnificent mountains on every side and without the mood-altering heavy loads that so often numb the experience of exploration.

We first outflanked the icefall by a dirty gully on the right bank, then walked with ease for a mile or so over a flat glacier past the junctions with two inflowing tributary glaciers. Not all the mountains looked pleasant to climb. One that we dubbed the Nesthorn had a repellingly steep snow face, another, on the opposite side of the main glacier, had few safe lines apart from a ridge with a large gendarme which would require some down-climbing. Still, with a greedy urge to omnipotence, my imagination ranged over ascents of them all. I wanted to penetrate each of those glacier recesses, wending couloirs, complex icefalls and rock towers fitfully betraying their sharp secrets by their shadows. My body would certainly not be up to such a programme and, of course, we had little time and only food for a few days, but it was wonderful to dream, especially with easy walking in such a dramatic setting.

After a few hours we ascended a short icefall, had a brief hiatus in a maze of crevasses and then found an excellent campsite on dry ice with running water nearby and a full-on view of the major peak, later dubbed 'Spear.' It was about 2500m high, rising 1200m above the glacier. Its north-west face was steep, compact rock, a 'big wall' far beyond our aims or capacities. But the north-east aspect was a steep snow/ice face with a broken rib seaming its centre. Rising below this face was a narrow glacier with a jumble of icefalls bordered by a steep couloir. Obviously, this was our challenge, whether we would get the weather and have the strength to do it remained to be seen.

We returned to our ski/pulk camp and next day brought food for a week over to the Spear camp. The weather remained excellent, for the first time on this expedition. The trip, ably organised by Roy Ruddle of the ACG, comprised eight Alpine Club members. We had been dropped on the Sorgenfri Glacier 10 days previously at a point about 12 miles from our intended base camp on the Frederiksborg.

Four of the party, with Salvationist tendencies, had decided to ski some easier mountains before proceeding to the Frederiksborg, while the more Ultramontane half of the party had hastened towards the spiky Lemon Mountains that lie south of the Frederiksborg. Roy and Robert Durran (SMC), definitely the A team, had gone to attempt Mitivagkat, a formidably steep and rocky objective at the north-east corner of the Lemons, while Dave Wilkinson (SMC) and I had gone to our first col and climbed a Skye-like rock ridge and a Cairngorm-like snowy plateau *in lieu* of descent to the North Lemons.

Now, after a rest day, we were all set for a 9pm departure to our major objective when, all of a sudden, we saw figures in the distance. Surely, another party could not have come to this same never-visited mountain group? My mind flitted through various unlikely possibilities. We had seen no-one for about 10 days – sure enough the obvious answer was the right one – Roy and Robert had followed our tracks over the col, having endured even worse weather than we in the preceding week. Full of enthusiasm they planned an ascent that same night, but decided not to accompany us, so we set off as planned.

The first part of our route followed excellent snow-ice in an avalanche couloir. All seemed to be going well till we met a vast bergschrund, the other side of which formed an overhanging ice wall at least 60ft high. The crevasse was big enough to park a dozen lorries in. Fortunately, we were able to outflank it by a long descending traverse, only to encounter more of the same above. The next lorry park, however, provided a comfortable ice grotto with a fine icicle curtain and a jumble of blocks enabling us to pass onto the upper slopes of the approach glacier. Finally, after about four or five hours of climbing we were at the foot of the face.

Initial apprehension, faced with a steepish ice gully from an ice-axe belay in the deep soft snow of the upper glacier, gave way to steady progress as we found excellent belays on the rock rib and the lower ice pitches were replaced by snow at a forgiving angle. Though we rose steadily, as on many an Alpine route, the pinnacles far above seemed never to get closer. Finally, after about 16 rope lengths we debouched onto a ridge and a dramatic window onto the peaks to the south-east. Thereafter, we were presented with more mixed climbing, but by weaving between buttresses, never encountered anything more than Scottish Grade III. We approached a fore-summit that had to be bypassed by a traverse on steep snow, then more mixed ground, rock flakes and short steep icy sections as the bright weather of the morning gave way to thin layers of cloud.

About noon we reached a little rock shelf below the summit. Two rock pinnacles, about 25ft high, rather like Tryfan's Adam and Eve, constituted the highest point, and necessitated taking it in turns to stand on top, belayed from below. This was the only pitch where we had to remove our crampons. All this time we had looked forward to a view out to sea, and especially to a neighbouring peak which we suspected was the point marked 2600m on the map, and presumably the highest in the group. But tantalisingly, the wreaths of mist rose continuously from below preventing us from getting more than the briefest of glimpses. After about half-an-hour we gave up and began the descent. The summit ridge had to be pitched and provided almost as much route-finding perplexity in descent as it had on the way up. It was nearly 5pm by the time we had descended the nine pitches that took us to the point where we had to leave the ridge. Tiring by now, after being on the go for 20 hours, we stopped for a brew. Dave wrapped himself in his duvet, but I found that, even with all my layers on, I was far too cold to sleep. Soon we continued the descent, laboriously kicking down pitch after pitch. It was not really steep enough to abseil, in any case we didn't have enough gear for that option and the rocks of the rib would probably have caused a lot of rope jams. It was interesting to observe, as though in another person, the extraordinary contortions the mind went through to try and stay awake, memory, speculation, longing. Bed, far more than food or drink, was what I craved.

By perhaps three in the morning we had descended the 16 pitches of the face. Only the last involved an abseil, as I decided to entrust myself to a piece of ice that seemed well adhered to the base of the rocks. Then there was a tortured, and doubtless unsafe, descent of the glacier – moving together around those huge crevasses while the exhausted mind made feeble attempts to keep the rope coils in order and provide a semblance of mutual protection. From the avalanche couloir we gave up with the ropes and each painfully front-pointed down. From time to time, at an easing of the angle, I would face outwards or sideways, then feeling too insecure in both mind and body, would be forced to face in again. Somehow, the endless passed, we reached flattish ground and found that Roy and Robert had very kindly left us a bottle of drink by our ski-sticks. Enveloped in thin cloud we traced our way back, mesmerised by the strange sastrugi and barely able to detect up from down on this gentle glacier. We were back at the tents by about 8am after nearly 36 hours of continuous climbing.

After recovering and waiting out several cold, wet days we were fortunate to get fine weather for two hard and long days of skiing back to the air drop point. The Salvationists had completed an excellent tour and climbed about a dozen hills, but the A-team had been very unlucky with the weather and had had to restrict themselves to skiing over snowy domes. A final couple of days were spent enjoying some fine Arctic sun, eating copiously and feeling relieved that we would never have to ski the ice cap.

IAIN SMART REPORTS: In 1999 and 2000 John Hay and I made boat journeys in East Greenland to the area north of Mestersvig. For both journeys we had the use of an Avon inflatable with a hard keel driven by a 40hp engine which allowed us to get up on the plane and proceed fully loaded at speeds of up to 20mph with food for two weeks, fuel for 250 miles and a spare 15hp motor. Both journeys were made during the second part of August when the mosquitoes had gone and the autumn colours were in full splendour.

The plan for the 1999 expedition was to travel south down the coast of Liverpool Land to Ittoqiarmiut, the Inuit capital of North-east Greenland. The distance is about 150 miles. In good conditions it would take three days in bad conditions it cannot be done. From Mestersvig the first part of this journey crosses open bays 10 miles across with laid-back mountains. After 50 miles the north end of Liverpool Land is reached. The coast here is exuberantly indented with bays and narrow fiords which cradle glaciers at their heads. The mountains are rocky, steep and serrated and descend to the sea. (See Slesser's article in *SMCJ,* 2001,192, xxxvii, 731-735).

If the conditions were right we would climb what we could *en passant.* The greater part of the proposed journey was exposed to the open coast with its stream of moving ice. Most years this coast is blocked by heavy pack and even landfast ice from the previous winter and impossible for navigation. Some years the ice is open and ornamental and opens up access to some remote, little-visited country and if you are caught by a sudden return of the pack you can always find your way eastwards on foot to the airfield at Constable Point or Ittoqiarmiut. It is essentially an opportunistic journey: if the conditions are right then go for it, if not then best not try; it could be a trying experience. 1999 turned out to be a bad ice year not only along the outer coast but also in the inner fiords; Kong Oscar's Fiord, for example, was plentifully supplied with ice. We could see most of the route as we flew in and it didn't look good.

To give the ice time to go out we decided to go north from Mestersvig where the ice was lighter and to re-explore Alpe Fjord, the site of the memorable 1958 expedition. We camped for the first night in the solitude of the second Menander's Island 10 miles from the airfield. That morning we had left Iceland and the night before Glasgow and now we sipped our goodnight dram of Lagavuillin below the jagged Stauning Alps with the midnight glow over Ella Island and the immensity of the open fiord and the distant skyline of Traill Island at our backs. It is good to be lucky but doubly fortunate to actually know you are lucky and able to extract a double dose of the aesthetic content of one's surroundings.

The next morning we went to the head of Alpe Fiord. It took us a few hours to get there with our powerful rig. In 1958 the journey had taken many days to relay the eight of us in a heavy 10ft wooden pram dinghy driven at walking speed by a 5hp British Seagull outboard. The head of Alpe Fjord is an impressive place. The immediate approach is guarded by the tongue of the conjoined Gully and Seftstrom Glaciers which extends across the fiord leaving a narrow navigable channel between its terminal ice cliffs and the steep screes of the opposite shore. The water in the channel is muddy and strewn with sub-surface boulder, dangerous for propellers.

Once through this hazard the head of the fiord is a magic place, steep and girt with mountains and glacier tongues. We tried to find the site of the base camp of the 1958 expedition but without success. Solifluction seemed to have altered the landscape. All we could find was a rusted Crawford's biscuit tin on a nearby hillside. We went up to the Seftstrom Glacier and sun-bathed for an hour as we viewed the derring-do peaks of 50 years ago. At the very head of the fjord we could see the jumbled end of the Sporre Glacier the route Malcolm and I had followed to cross the southern Staunings to Syd Kap almost 50 years ago. A feature of the extreme head of the fiord is a long stripe of snow high up on the mountain running for a mile or more across buttresses and gullys. It must represent a geological continuity of some kind, a broad terrace or ledge hopping from one mountain to the next.

We returned to the outer fiord, turned left into Forsblad Fiord and camped near its head then returned to the hunter's hut at Kap Petersen where we found a note from the Simpsons who had passed by a couple of days before on their way south. There was still a lot of ice around which did not bode good for the southern voyage. We crossed over to Arwidsson's Island – one of the bigger islands at the mouth of 'Royal Swedish Yacht Club Fiord' the clumsy name of the outer part of the Alpe Fiord system.

Two things of particular interest happened there. One day we watched an iceberg calve over a mile away. It was small as icebergs go and it was not a particular large piece that fell off. The fjord here was wide open and so exerted none of the throttling effect you get in confined waters. We watched with interest wondering if the wave would even reach us. The noise when it reached us was not particularly loud. Then to our dismay a few minutes later the wave arrived about a metre high. Only the bow of the boat was drawn up on the shingle. We couldn't do much about it and had to watch the heavy boat being tossed in the air and swamped. No damage was done as the boat was empty. This episode highlights one of the main dangers of navigation among icebergs. You are safe enough when you are out travelling as a decent boat will ride a smooth wave nae bother, but when the wave reaches the shore it is forced to dissipate its considerable energy in a second or two by running up the beach against gravity and finally bursting into turbulence. In enclosed waters even a small berg calving can send a wave several metres farther up the beach than you expect.

For safety a boat must be hauled well above the high tide mark unless in a small land-locked harbour with no bergs in it. Anchoring offshore is not a solution as you can never really get the boat anchored far enough out as noted in *SMCJ,* 1995, 186, 773. In any case, floating ice can snag a boat anchored offshore. Things are not so bad if there is a lot of pack ice around or even if other bergs lie between you and the one that's calving as they absorb much of the kinetic energy before it reaches you. The moral is: choose a landing in unconstricted water well away from bergs and haul the boat up on rollers, farther than you think you will need to, particularly if you are leaving it for any length of time.

While we are on the subject of icebergs it may be worth mentioning that when travelling in open water they provide shelter from the wind. As we all know, most of an iceberg is underwater like an ice cube in a glass of gin and tonic to use a familiar example. An iceberg is a floating hulk with an enormous underwater hull and a relatively small sail. They are therefore more subject to the grip of the dense sea than the thin air. When wind and tide move in opposite directions the greater grip of the sea pulls the iceberg through the wind. This configuration is intimidating but it at least provides a lea in the berg's wake where a small boat can shelter.

When both wind and tide are in the same direction the lea side is the bow-wave and there is less shelter. All in all, you are better not being out in conditions like that. The bergs we encountered north of Mestersvig were fairly sparsely scattered, and as they were old and had come a long distance, they had become beautifully sculptured over the years. Although some were big, with the above water part about the size of St Giles's Cathedral, they do not compare with some of the ones in inner Scoresby Sound. Many bergs in this part of the Arctic are pieces of glacier, maybe a kilometre or more square, that have floated off complete with crevasses. They are ancient wrinkled parts of the Inland Ice that have embarked on their last cruise. These crevassed plateau bergs are noted for building up internal tensions and then comprehensively splitting asunder. As their fragments collapse into the sea gigajoules of energy are released and generate waves of commensurate size. When they hit the shore enormous energy is dissipated. It is better not to be there. Nevertheless, if you are prudent and choose landings with care, travel among icebergs is a whole lot safer than driving up the A9 or along many a winding Highland road on a Saturday night. Sorry, I seem to have got distracted.

Meanwhile, back on Ardwidson's Island at the end of August 1999 we emptied the water from the boat hauled it well up the shore where it should have been in the first place. We now had our camp on a little shelf well above the grasp of an enterprising wave. As we sat in the gloom of a sort of a twilight-of-the-Gods evening enjoying our goodnight dram of Lagavuillin five adolescent hares wandered into the camp. They were unsophisticated and unwordly. After inspecting us closely then scratching a bit they wandered off, skipping and hopping as if they lived in Disneyland when in reality they were off on a dinner date with a fox or gyrfalcon.

The weather continued in a windless mode. There was still a lot of ice around which did not bode good for the southern voyage. So we crossed the 20 miles of open fjord through widely scattered pack to the continent-sized Traill Island and explored for a bit. The weather changed to winter drizzle and cold. We sought refuge in a Sirius Hut. Then the weather turned into dramatic mode with layers of cloud and sunshine and banks of mist. We climbed up to the top of some cliffs and sat in the warm sunshine enjoying the vast landscape. We saw about a dozen ravens cavorting around in the air with a provocative gyrfalcon. Truly spectacular aerobatics, all the participants seemed to be enjoying it. On the way back John saw a lone figure! We eventually identified a tent near a hunter's hut at the head of the bay. We visited it the next day. Two delightful French scientists were there studying predator-prey relationships using state of the art radio-collars. They entertained us hospitably with good coffee and rich chocolates.

Finally, we crossed back to the mainland and pushed south. This was an empty gesture; there was no hope of going very far. We got just south of the Pictet Bjerg before the leads gave out. Honour was satisfied. Nevertheless, it was tempting…it might be better just a little farther on… Very sensibly we turned back. We camped on Archer's Island, a red basalt formation about a square mile in area, surrounded by loose pack. We enjoyed here a period of calm weather with dramatic cloudscapes, changing light and autumn colour; the midnight period was particularly haunting.

In 2000 we used the same boat but were indebted to Douglas Anderson for supplying the engines and petrol/oil mix. He and his family had spent the previous six weeks exploring northwards beyond Ella Island. In that year floe ice was practically absent. Our plan was to proceed northwards beyond Ella into the outer reaches of Kaiser Franz Joesef's Fiord and then turn north to reach Geolog Fiord where we had heard a rumour that a volcanic vent might exist. According to my informant it had been seen once from a distance. A line of geothermal activity does extend up the East Greenland coast so it was not an impossible sighting.

Once again we arrived at Mestersvig one midday towards the end of August and the same evening found ourselves camped on Menanders Island amid the usual, but still overwhelming, glory of a fine evening. Thereafter we proceeded north in generally fine weather reaching Maria Island on the next night and the foot of the Devil's Castle, an enormous ziggurat on the west side of the outer, northern arm of KFJ fiord We had a plan to climb it and tried to get into Leonora Bay to land at its foot. The bay, however, shallowed rapidly and it was difficult to get ashore through the mud, and when we did the ground was rough and disagreeable.

So we did a rethink. We were running out of fuel. We only had enough to get us back the 100 miles or so to Mestersvig, allowing enough spare for detours around ice. Geolog Fiord was out of our range. We decided to cross to Ymer's Island on the east side and spend a few days exploring rather than travelling. Blomster Bay where we made our base has been described elsewhere – *SMCJ*. It is a good base for exploring some very textured country, We spent some happy days there. John carried out an inspection of the local wild life, especially the numerous musk oxen while I climbed the Chocolate Mountain and was rewarded with spectacular views. We then returned to Maria Island where we camped for a couple of nights while exploring the island. My main memories are of a sudden windstorm that flattened the tent, the discovery of a wartime German fuel dump with oil drums stamped with 'Deurtshe Wehrmacht' and 'Kriegsmarine', and a memorable evening of approaching night and a big crescent moon reflected in a shimmering loch.

We then crossed to Ella Island to the Sirius sledge patrol base. As we approached two men came from the base hut to meet us. We landed at the jetty and shook hands. They had no idea anyone was to the north of them. We had applied for permission late and our permit had not reached them. After a pause one asked tentatively: "Where is the rest of the expedition?"

A couple of old men arriving unexpectedly and unsupervised from the wild uninhabited north required some explanation. There was none beyond a sort of mild eccentricity on our part and a civilised tolerance on the part of the authorities in distant Nuuk. We had our faxed permission with us so bureaucracy was satisfied and we all relaxed. They offered us floor space in one of the huts and an invitation to join them for supper. We brought a bottle of good French wine we had kept for a special occasion. They had an even better bottle so it was quite a pleasant evening.

Dinner with good wine, good company and good conversation sitting by a window looking north over the Arctic sea towards a spectacular sunset is better than the anything an expensive restaurant in some millionaires' ghetto can provide. For that all you need is money: for dinner at Ella you need something more than money. The sledge patrol people were picturesque types. The C-in-C was half-Danish half-Japanese, his 2-in-C was a romantic who wore a pistol in a holster and had his hair tied behind. They had stopped a huge Russian icebreaker full of tourists some time in the summer in order to assert Greenlandic Authority by examining their papers. The icebreaker took a long time to realise that this little inflatable with two men aboard required them to stop and be inspected.

The next day we went to climb to the top of the island, the massive Bastion. It is a plateau girt with 4000ft cliffs, a long climb but with spectacular views as it stands at the confluence of five fiords. Dinner that night was a big party as another four of the sledge patrol had arrived in a big launch from the south. They were discussing plans for the coming winter. We had to head south. Nevertheless, we had two further days of good weather and ended up with another final night on Archer's Island – this time gloomier than the year before – the landscape was in a forbidding mode.

As PART of an Anglo-American expedition, Graham Little and Scott Muir, spent two weeks in the Kangikitsoq Fjord area of south-east Greenland (access via Aappilattoq).

Despite the unwelcome attention of millions of mosquitos and black fly, they made the first ascents of four peaks, including the 'inaccessible' Sgorr a' Ceo (2001m) at N6025 W4413.

They also made, a bold, but futile lightweight attempt on the huge South Buttress of Titan I (1736m). This peak, together with its higher neighbour Titan II (1811m), offers vast scope for high standard rock climbing on an array of 1000m high walls and buttresses.

BILL WALLACE REPORTS: A relatively new hut accommodating up to 12 now exists in the very attractive and scenic mountains north of Tasiilaq (formerly Angmagssalik) in East Greenland. The plan was to use this hut as a springboard for ski-touring at the Karale Glacier.

Included in our group of 13 were Dick Allen, John Hay, Iain Smart and Mike Taylor; also David and Mary-Lucy More (Edinburgh JMCS) and two Norwegian telemarking friends from Tromso.

Almost from the outset problems materialised. On arrival in Reykjavik our Icelandic agent advised that all our food which had been sent in advance via Copenhagen was still there. Fortunately, this turned out to be untrue and all but one carton was awaiting us at Kulusuk. At Reykjavik airport the following morning we were told that the plane was full and there was considerable excess baggage. All passengers were asked to leave behind some non-essentials. We left our skis – we had to have camping equipment.

As it happened, the weather in the mountains prevented helicopter flying for four days by which time our skis had arrived. The fifth day dawned clear and sunny and a French Trans-Greenland Kite Expedition was airlifted to its starting point with our lift promised for the afternoon. By that time the weather had again deteriorated. As there were now insufficient days remaining to follow even part of our original plans, re-appraisal resulted in our taking the scheduled helicopter to Tasiilaq and basing ourselves in the middle of Angmagssalik Island where we had seven days of excellent weather and ascended all the peaks within reach.

We then returned to the airstrip on Kulusuk Island where the weather again turned bad and for six days we waited, becoming increasingly frustrated, for a plane to fly us out to Iceland.

BILL WALLACE REPORTS: Because of the poor weather we experienced in the Tasiilaq region of Greenland in 2002, we (six of us) decided to return to the Roscoe Bjerg at 71° N in 2003 where good weather is more likely.

The party included Dick Allen, Peter Macdonald and myself. We assembled at Glasgow airport on April 25, stayed overnight in Reykjavik and flew on to Constable Point airstrip the following day. Access to the Roscoe Bjerg from Constable Point is by the helicopter based there. We flew to site three of our planned five camp sites, left a dump of food, fuel and whisky there and flew on to site one.

The manager at Constable Point had told us that prior to our arrival a 'Pitorak' (a warm gale force south wind) had been blowing which had firmed up the snow in the mountains and this, combined with two inches of new powder snow, gave ideal ski-ing conditions throughout our two-week stay. We occupied each camp site for two or three nights and ascended many peaks on ski, some new and others which we had ascended on previous expeditions. The highest peaks are 1300m-1400m and consequently, the glaciers are of manageable size.

Unlike the previous year, everything went according to plan. All members thoroughly enjoyed themselves and some are anxious to return in 2004.

South America.

ROB MILNE reports: New Year 2003 found me at Casa Piedre, the end of the second day of the approach walk for the Polish Glacier side of Aconcagua, Argentina. At 6869m (22,800ft) it is the highest point of the South American continent. Although we were enthusiastic to celebrate the New Year, the evening was windy and cool, so we celebrated the Ukrainian New Year during dinner (7pm local time), then the French New Year at 8pm local time. My climbing partner was Louise Trave-Massuyes from France who provided the appropriate champagne. By Scottish New Year we were settled in our tent for the night, but managed one last celebration.

The previous two days had been spent walking up the wide river valley, starting at Punta de Vacas. In general, the surrounding peaks were covered in scree and not interesting, but the river valley provided constant new views as it turned this way and that. The wind was ever present and we seemed to always be going uphill over an alluvial fan and then losing the height gain again.

On January 1, we crossed the wide river on mule back and enjoyed a leisurely walk to the base camp, Plaza Argentina at 4000m. We even found a great boulder for some climbing fun to break the walk. The Amara agency had transported all our gear on mule back to here and welcomed us with tea and cakes in their cook tent. We were well catered for at base camp, with steak most nights and even pizza cooked in an oven that the mules had carried up. Base camp was full of groups, some coming down happy, but most anxious about what lay above. We fitted in the latter category.

Our first carry to Camp 1 was more fun than work. We had our first exposure to the Penitents. This unusual snow pattern creates great fields of snow spikes. Since the sun is almost directly overhead, the sides of any small pinnacle get shaded and don't melt. The gaps between the small pinnacles then melt down, leaving spires as high as eight feet. They were great fun to weave between and across, for an hour. Another hour though and it was all getting to be like hard work. Luckily, the path was mostly on scree across a glacier. The final pull to Camp 1 was up a broad snowfield, proving a torturous introduction to 16,000ft. I'd like to say the view was great, but the way ahead was mostly scree at the head of a wide valley.

After another day of rest, it was time to finally move up to Camp 1. We needed the day of rest for the endless discussions of what gear to take and what to leave. How cold would it get? How much of the medical kit do we need? Will we really eat all the food our agency provided? Do we really need all those socks? Hours and hours of discussion packing and repacking filled the day. I barely had time to sharpen my crampons. Dulled from many Scottish mixed routes, they didn't seem to stick in hard glacial ice any more.

The final move to Camp 1 was fine. Although the packs were heavy, we were getting much fitter and more acclimatised and, so far the weather had been blue skies and virtually cloudless. But the wind never stopped and this put a big dent in my sunbathing time.

Settled in to Camp 1, summit fever started to grip us. The normal plan is to carry to Camp 2, followed by a rest day before moving up. Our local mountain guide and cook, Matias, thought we were strong enough to do a half carry and then move up quickly. Luckily, for us, his agency had other groups on the mountain with enough leftover food at the high camp that we didn't need to take more up. However, he always seemed to have another bundle of food for me to carry. I am

The West Face of Mount Gilbert in the Canadian Coast Mountains. The West Pillar climbed by Chris Cartwright and Simon Richardson takes the centre of the barrel-shaped buttress directly in line with the summit. Photo: Simon Richardson.

sure I carried up everything we actually ate! We were pleased that so far we had been fully healthy, with no headaches or eating problems. It seemed most groups were losing at least one person to altitude sickness. We just made sure to move very slowly and drink lots and lots. Unfortunately, the side effects of drinking a lot were not always welcome with the ever-present high winds.

It was a slow move to Camp 2. Although we were feeling acclimatised, walking at 18,000ft is always hard work. Louise, being much smaller couldn't carry much weight and the winds were around 50mph. Sometimes I could twist in such a way that the wind would give me a boost up the endless scree slopes. Needless to say, we were ready to crawl into our tent when we got to Camp 2 at 19,000ft.

Our original plan was to climb the Polish Glacier Direct. But this was an icy year and so far, no parties had done it. It seems that the organised groups only do it when it is mostly snow. This year there was a lot of bare and brittle ice. Like many groups, we easily gave in and agreed to do The Traverse.

The night at Camp 2 was dominated by the wind. It arrived like a freight train. You could hear it a minute before charging around the mountain, getting louder and louder until it slammed into the tent. The tent would shake for a couple of minutes and then all would become quiet. A few minutes later, we heard the next gust coming. We felt for sure that it was going to be too windy to go for the summit.

At 4am, Matias had not wakened us, so we assumed he agreed. At 5am, I could hear him shouting my name. I shone my torch at his tent to make contact and he screamed over the wind: "We go." The plans of a rest day to explore the base of the Polish Glacier disappeared as we started the rush to get ready.

Dawn had broken by the time we were ready to move and it was very cold. Our position was similar to sleeping on top of Kilimanjaro (highest mountain in Africa) and then climbing Ben Nevis (highest point in the UK) so that we get to the highest point in South America. But, all of this offset to 5km up into the atmosphere.

Slowly, we worked our way up the very boring path. The views were great and as we turned onto the north side we could see the full width of the Andes stretching north. The wind was a steady 30 to 40mph and although it was −10°C, we were comfortable. As always, the trick is to go slowly enough so you never get out of breath. Of course ,at 20,000ft, this can mean pretty slow.

At the ruined Independencia Hut, Louise dropped her pack. She was doing fine, but the pack was just too much. We cached some gear and I took what was left. The crux of the climb was next, the Windy Col. It is just a wide smooth col and an almost horizontal path. But the wind funnels up it and can be very strong. On Matias's previous trip, they had to turn back here, unable to cross in the wind. We were more fortunate, and although it was hard work, it was no worse than a windy day in the Cairngorms (but at 6000+ metres).

I felt good up to the lunch break at the base of the Cannaleta, the final broad scree gully to the summit. Twenty paces after we re-started, my legs became very tired. Time to cache more gear. Luckily, we could follow snow for most of the final climb, rather than the loose scree. There were three other groups ahead of us, not to mention the solo Japanese climber we passed as he was sleeping on the trail.

All of us arrived at the summit at the same time, breaking into a quick celebration. The views north and south were great and the usual photos seemed to take up the

Spear, 2500m, climbed in the summer of 2002, North Lemon Mountains, East Greenland. Photo: Geoff Cohen.

time quickly. It was 3pm and we had enough time to descend, but not much extra. It always seems strange that after a year of planning, the summit passes so quickly.

The descent to Camp 2 was fine, although we were all pretty tired. Dinner was pretty minimal, although we desperately needed to rehydrate. We had summited a day ahead of schedule and not used any contingency days, so I was ready to hang about and explore some. But like most trips, we bolted for the roadhead. The next day was spent descending with very heavy packs to Base Camp. I didn't mind, it was all downhill. Beer was waiting for us at base camp, followed by a superb steak dinner. Or was it from the slowest mule?

The normal return to the road takes two days, but Matias was keen to get back. So, we did the 30-mile walk in one 13-hour day, longer than the summit day. This is not recommended, especially as we had been accompanied by Matias's fiancée. She had little hiking experience, and found it a very hard introduction. Although a professional dancer, her legs weren't designed for this. Ah well, at least she found out what her future husband's job is like.

Celebrations, showers and a soak in the natural hot spring marked the end of my fourth Continental summit and the start of the plans for my fifth one.

Canada

ALISTAIR ROBERTSON REPORTS: Squamish on the west coast of Canada about 40 miles north of Vancouver is one of the world's finest granite rocking climbing areas. The main attraction is the Stawamus Chief- a granite monolith that rises 2000ft above the Howe Sound fjord. The most famous route is probably *The Grand Wall* which is an ultra-classic and one of the great long 'free' (there is a short A0 bolt ladder) climbs of North America. I had wanted to do this route for years, and finally, in August this year the opportunity arose to visit the area and, hopefully, realise this dream. My climbing partner for the week was Scott Rietsma, a friend from when I had lived in Boston a few years ago. Scott is an excellent climber but the arrival of fatherhood had slowed him down a bit the last 18 months and he was keen to climb some stone again.

We had arrived pretty late the night before and were both feeling pretty tired and jet lagged – the eight-hour time difference from Scotland takes a few days to get over. The weather, however, was perfect, blue skies and a nice breeze, so the desire to get on something reasonably substantial overcame any weariness we were feeling. We settled on one of Squamish's most famous face climbs on the Chief, *Cruel Shoes,* six pitches long with every pitch being British 5b or 5c and worth E3 overall. Scott led the first pitch, an immaculate 35m E2 5b layback crack with the crux near the top. It was just brilliant, this was why we had come here.

The next pitch was probably the crux and proved a real baptism of fire for me. Beware, my experience has discovered that North Americans are extremely good at climbing thin face routes and they have a tendency to feel pretty thin for the expected British grade. I managed to wobble my way up the steep slab and belayed to a very solid two-bolt anchor, you don't get those at home on the Dubh Loch. The route continued for another four pitches winding a logical, yet slightly cunning, path through the lower walls to the tree at the base of the *Split Pillar.* This 40m incredible corner-crack is one of the most famous pitches at Squamish and the start of the Grand Wall proper. It was tempting to continue but instead we decided to call it a day and opted for three long 50m abseils back down to the sacks. We had climbed six long pitches and yet hadn't reached halfway up the face – what a crag.

The forecast for the next two days suggested the chance of a shower, then perfect weather for the rest of the week. The main objective of the trip for us both was the Grand Wall, but we were really keen to do it in good style and not have to bail out because of the weather. So, the next day we went to Murrin Park, about five miles south from Squamish and home to a selection of single pitch crags, the most famous being the Petrifying Wall – a 30m plum vertical crag with mainly sport climbs ranging from mild 5.11 to 5.13b+. We started off with the easiest sport route *Pleasant Pheasant,* 5.11a (F6b+) which gave exhilarating climbing on mainly big holds with the crux quite high. Next up was *No-Name Road,* 5.11b, which felt really stiff for the grade, but excellent. The highlight was the final four-foot roof at the top, a real stamina test. We then did the crag classic *Burning down the Couch,* 5.11d, which also felt pretty full on for the grade but is a real must-do. Harder routes such as *Flingus Cling* 5.12b also look brilliant, but by this point we were getting tired and after doing a 5.9 trad route called *The World's Toughest Milkman* we headed back to the Howe Sound Brew Pub where it was half-price fish-and-chips night.

Day three, and the boys were feeling a bit stiff after only two days cranking. As the weather forecast was still excellent for the rest of the week we decided to take a rest day, with an aim at attempting the Grand Wall the following day. We went to Vancouver and made the must-do trip to Mountain Equipment Co-op which is a gear freaks' paradise and very reasonably priced.

What amazes me is how they can sell British-made gear 20% cheaper than at home. My major purchase for the day was 5m of tape, out of which I made some basic home-made etriers, not bad for $5 or £2. We then drove back to Squamish and sorted our rack out for the next day, the Grand Wall beckoned. Dinner at the Howe Sound Brew Pub was becoming routine. Although re-marketing itself as the Outdoor Recreation Capital of Canada, Squamish is still very much a working town with little in the way of exciting nightlife (do not come here for all-night raves). However, the brew pub offers a range of in-house ales and a good selection of food. Do not miss out on the all-you-can-eat salmon buffet on Sunday nights – only $10CDN (about £4). There are other places, but we just ate at the Brew Pub every night as it was hard to beat.

Next morning at 6 am, the alarm goes off. We wanted to get an early start to avoid the heat and crowds. A hearty breakfast of pancakes liberally covered in maple sauce and a couple of mugs of strong coffee at the Mountain Burger House – Squamish's equivalent of Pete's Eats in Llanberis, and we headed off to the Chief. There were a couple of other cars in the car park but a brief conversation with the pair parked next to us revealed that they were off to do *The Angel's Crest* another of the Chief's long area classics – great, no competition. We racked up, stuffed one waterproof, two litres of water and a handful of energy bars into our small communal sack and headed off through the trees and boulders to the base of the route. The lower section of the Grand Wall is most commonly climbed by either the layback cracks of *Apron Strings* followed by *Merci Me* a run out 5.8 or *Cruel Shoes.* As we had done *Cruel Shoes* on Sunday we opted for the *Apron Strings/Merci Me* combination. We started climbing at 7.45am, not quite an Alpine start but early enough. I was not completely over my jet lag so it didn't feel that early.

The first pitches went very smoothly – a couple of pitches of laybacking with some moderate crack climbing led to *Flake Ledge*. Above, run-out, but positive climbing on the slabby dykes of *Merci Me* led to an exposed belay and some large roofs. The next pitch had a tricky traverse right under these roofs before rising rightwards to the tree at the base of the *Split Pillar*, where *Cruel Shoes* comes in from the right. This pitch features three points of aid up an A0 bolt ladder and provided an opportunity to christen my home-made etriers. I had never done any aid climbing before, but years of frigging on sport routes served me well enough. Belayed beside the tree, I called to Scott to climb on up and was aware that the lower wall was now swarming with several parties. One pair, in particular, were really motoring and *simul* climbed the first four pitches – impressive. Scott methodically racked up for the next pitch, *The Split Pillar,* one of the real highlights of the climb. It is given a fairly low rating, 5.10b, but offers very sustained jamming or laybacking up an impeccable corner crack for 40m widening from thin hands through to wide fist.

My advice is take lots of cams with a double set being advisable. Scott had a hard time on the lead, neither of us were used to anything quite so long and sustained, but he managed to persevere and after some good old-fashioned thrutching up the final chimney he flopped onto the spacious ledge pumped but satisfied. I followed and amazed myself by really enjoying it. At least I was on the blunt end of the rope. By the time I joined Scott at the ledge there were a couple of parties at the base of the pillar and another climbing the left side of the split pillar – a somewhat more challenging 5.12a version complete with a 5.10 off-width-Friend 5 territory, hmm!

We took time to have a drink and another energy bar before I geared up for the next mega classic pitch, *The Sword.* This pitch is also truly amazing, it starts off very wide (Camalot 4) then quickly narrows to finger-tips width through a bulge which provides the technical crux. Above, an incredibly exposed step left led to a hidden crack on the otherwise blank face. Stretching out onto a foothold on the wall I reached blindly into the crack to gratefully grab a good hold. Quickly, committing myself, I swung onto the face and threw a sling over a hollow spike. The climbing above was pretty straight-forward on good holds, but I had to take care with a few rattling spikes. The crack faded after 5m, and again I had to step back right into the main corner line. The walls are pretty blank but the thin corner-crack provides perfect protection and succumbed with a few strenuous layback moves after which I could gratefully grab the belay chain over a small roof. This stance is hanging and I decided to link the next pitch, a 15m A0 bolt ladder. It was time to test those etriers again. Everything went very smoothly but it was time consuming and there was mutual relief when I reached the belay above.

By this time, there were two other parties right behind us and Scott wasted no time in seconding the long pitch. We were both now really psyched, and in particular, I was talking incoherent but enthusiastic gibberish. The next pitch is possibly the physical crux, a 5.11a offwidth/undercling crack, *Perry's Lieback*, that is, thankfully, bolted. There is an unusual rest near the top where you can lean backwards and brace your head against a large flake. Looking down at this point it is a sheer 250m to the valley floor.

By now we were on a fairly spacious ledge system and the sun had started to hit the face. Fortunately, the regular afternoon breeze had picked up so conditions were still ideal. I climbed a rather wandery 5.10a pitch that was mainly bolt protected then it was Scott's turn for the 10th and final pitch to *Bellygood Ledge,* a ledge system that runs across the face and provides an alternative to the notorious 5.1a *Roman Chimneys.* This last pitch provided more strenuous, exposed underclinging and laybacking and was a fitting end to what had been a fantastic climb. One of the parties had caught us up and we enthused about the route together at the top. They had climbed the original before and this time had done the much harder left side of the split pillar then higher up climbed a 5.12c variation with a couple of rests before French-freeing back into the original line at *Perry's Lieback.* These guys were no slouches! It is possible to free the whole climb at 5.13b, but I doubt it is more enjoyable than the original.

We kept the rope on for the 150m traverse along *Bellygood Ledge,* which is only a couple of feet wide at one point. In reality, it is little more than a walk, but there is a 330m drop, so a slip is not to be advised. We then stumbled back down the tourist trail and back to the car, the climb having taken eight hours. Not the fastest time but we were in no rush. It was a climb we wanted to savour and enjoy to the full. That night we treated ourselves to a (relatively) expensive meal and a few single malts to round off a perfect day and the highlight of my summer.

We woke up the next day to more perfect weather, although the forecast said it was going to get hot, up to 28°C, so an early start was required if we were going to get much done. I have never been an avid slab climber, but once in a while, have the urge to go out and purge the system. The Apron Slabs at Squamish seemed like a suitable destination – up to six or seven pitches long with some notable runouts between spaced bolts.

Routes such as *Dancing in the Light* 5.11b, *Unfinished Symphony* 5.11b and *White Lightning* 5.10c all have quite fearful reputations. There are numerous easier less scary classics too such as *Snake* 5.9 and *Diedre* 5.8, but expect to get up very early, or very late, if you want to avoid the queues. Being ambitious we thought we would see what one of the bolder routes was like – big mistake. I started up the first pitch and was about 25m up when, having clipped only one bolt, found myself sliding more than 11m back down again. Fortunately, I escaped with only some grazes to my ankle and hand – it could have been a lot worse. Scott declined when I offered him the lead and so we retreated with our tails firmly between our legs. Scott attempted a better protected 50m sport climb but it was equally thin, if not worse, and we eventually abseiled off having climbed little more than a rope-length between us. By now, the sun had moved around onto the face making friction climbing even more desperate. Today was not going to plan and proving a bit of a let down after the day before. We opted to go in search of some steep rock with holds and preferably in the shade. The Chek, which is halfway between Squamish and Whistler and only 25 minutes away fitted the bill. The short drive up was amazing with stunning views over to the glacier-ridden mountains of the Tantalus range. The rock at the Chek is also granite but much, much steeper than at the Chief and is home to some of the hardest sport climbs in Canada. We spent the late afternoon clipping bolts and although the routes were fun we both really wanted to be climbing somewhere else – the Chief.

We only had two days' climbing left, so the plan was to spend one day climbing some of the area's best cracks then do another long classic multi-pitch adventure on the Saturday to finish.

Top of the list of cracks for both of us was *Exasperator* 5.10c which is a stunning two-pitch finger crack and is a must-do for all E2+ leaders. It is just perfect. After this we thought we would try *Ghostdancing* a three pitch 5.11 face climb close to the base of the Grand Wall and a five-minute walk from *Exasperator.* I volunteered to lead the first pitch which at 5.11b was the hardest trad pitch either of us had tried so far this trip. I was pretty nervous but managed to solve the complexities of the initial overlap to become established on a nice footledge where I could suss out the rest of the pitch – a tricky rightward traverse across a steep slab with good footholds but no real handholds into yet another layback flake with a rather pokey section round a blankish bulge. It all went pretty well and I completed it in good style which was a real confidence booster. The next pitch was also rated 5.11b but was less steep and looked really thin. Also, rather ominously, there was a karabiner hanging off a bolt about halfway up, not a good sign, but at least it was Scott's lead.

It started off innocuously enough on really positive little flakes then the holds ran out just where it steepened above a slight recess and the bolt with krab beckoned. Scott had a brave attempt but just couldn't do it free and eventually decided he had had enough. My turn, I was feeling confident after the first pitch and gave it a real good go but it was desperate on tiny flakes and crystals for footholds. Needless to say I also failed miserably – these locals really know how to climb low angle face/steep slabs!

The sun had by this time come round onto the face and the temperature was really soaring so we just abseiled off. All wasn't lost, though, as we had spotted a very appealing rattley 5.10 finger crack called *Seasoned in the Sun* just down the path. It was only one pitch, but long, and pretty sustained with the hardest section at the top, another must-do area classic. It didn't disappoint.

After *Seasoned,* we were both feeling a bit tired and had a siesta for a couple of hours lazing around in the sun. I was still keen for a final challenging climb to round off the day but preferably one which had holds and was in the shade. We headed back off to Murrin Park where most of the cliffs are east or south-east facing and so get the sun in the morning and early afternoon but by late afternoon/ early evening are nice and cool. In order to maintain the day's theme of classic cracks, we headed over to Nightmare Rock which has a bunch of tough single-pitch climbs all rated 5.10-5.12 and all guaranteed to generate lactic acid overdoses. I led one of the easiest climbs there called *Perspective,* 5.11a, which was brilliant. It is about 30m long with strenuous hard climbing all the way interspersed with a couple of good bridging rests and perfect protection. Although not technically that hard it was a real pumper and felt E4 5c just for effort. I arrived at the belay with heavy arms but thoroughly psyched. The view from the top over to the Chief in the fading evening light was amazing and rounded off a perfect end to another great day's climbing.

Saturday morning, our last day's climbing, and *The Angel's Crest* was our final objective. This is one of the longest climbs on the Chief and is a 600m adventure that has five mild 5.10 pitches, a bunch of easier climbing, a little bit of scrambling, an exposed knife-edge arête and a 10m abseil off a gendarme. All in all, it feels a real Alpine experience. A quick stop at Tim Horton's for coffee and doughnuts then we drove the couple of miles to the trailhead. A steep 20-minute hike led up to the base of the climb. We kitted up then soloed the first pitch – scrambling with a short technical section over a bulge using a convenient tree root. The next pitch was the start of the proper technical climbing and more conventional techniques were employed. The third pitch is called *The Angel's Flake* and is one of the best pitches of the route – a beautiful diagonal 5.10 layback flake across a steep wall with the crux at the top (again). The efforts of the previous six days had started to take their toll and it felt a lot stiffer than it should have done, but really fun nonetheless. There then followed a couple of other 5.10-ish pitches and we caught sight of a couple of parties above us. Some people were also coming up behind us so it was turning out to be very Alpine-like. After a couple of short forest walks (I kid you not) interspersed with some more technical climbing we found ourselves at the start of the knife-edge arête. The climbing was no more than Hard Severe but the position spectacular and the exposure really wild. The ridge led to a little gendarme where a short abseil off followed by a short scramble led to the base of the final steep headwall. Three final steep pitches of sustained VS-E1 jamming led quickly to the top.

We were both pretty tired when we topped out, but elated, it was a fitting end to a superb week's climbing. The views from the summit of the Chief were incredible, down the Howe sound to the south and up north to the snow-capped Tantalus and Garibaldi mountains. It was also very busy with plenty of hikers enjoying the vistas. A quick stumble back down to the car in the late afternoon heat then it was time to hit the pub for a few final ales, another all-you-can eat barbeque, and to reflect on what had been a really excellent trip.

SIMON RICHARDSON REPORTS: Mount Gilbert (10,225ft) is an impressive granite peak that lies 90km south-east of Mount Waddington deep in Canada's Coast Mountains. Although it is the closest 10,000ft peak to Vancouver it is one of the most difficult mountains to access in the range and is rarely climbed. In early August, Chris Cartwright and I flew in by helicopter from Bluff Lake across the Homathko Icefield to the wide glacial bowl below Gilbert's west face. The West Pillar rose directly above our tents – it looked totally compelling – we just had to climb it.

Unfortunately, the weather had other ideas. It snowed for the next three days, dropping a couple of feet of snow. When it stopped we climbed the glacier shelf on the north-west face of Gilbert, and made the first ascent of a fine 8900ft rock peak via the East Ridge. It was bitterly cold and the rock on Gilbert showed little sign of clearing. The weather got bad again, but fortunately, this time it rained which cleared the rock of snow. Finally, after two more days waiting in the tent, the sun came out, so we packed our sacks with three days food and set off for the pillar.

Gilbert's 2500ft-high West Pillar is guarded by a large bergschrund system. Access is further complicated by a hanging serac and ice couloir that regularly spew rock and ice down the approach slopes. The whole approach would be unjustifiable if it were not for the Little Tower, a steep rocky crest that cuts into the left side of the serac and shields a narrow segment of the approach slopes from ice fall.

From a little way up the crest of the tower it is possible to cross the couloir to reach the West Pillar. The base of the pillar is undercut by a series of roofs, but these are breached on their right side by the Beak, a prominent prow with a corner running up its left side. The only weakness up the smooth central section of the pillar is the Great Flake, a hanging, left-facing flake system that leads through seemingly blank walls to the exit chimneys and summit snow slope.

We crossed the bergschrund at dawn, climbed the Little Tower and traversed across the couloir to reach the foot of the pillar. We expected the climbing to get very technical at this point, but the rock was superbly featured and gave a brilliant series of 5a and 5b pitches. All those days in the tent, snatching views of the face with the binoculars and working out the easiest way to go, had paid off.

The line slotted together perfectly and that evening we found ourselves racing towards the exit chimneys as a big storm approached. Fortunately, this fizzled out before it reached us, but we ran out of time and had a very uncomfortable bivvy in the chimneys. Next morning half-a-dozen more pitches took us to the top of a superb climb – perfect granite, all free and far easier than it had any right to be!

The Pennine Alps

COLWYN JONES REPORTS: SMC members Mark Litterick, Brian Shackleton, Colwyn Jones and Ann MacDonald assembled at a bustling Schipol Airport on Saturday, 20 April 2002, after early morning flights from Edinburgh and Glasgow. The connecting KLM flight to Geneva was on time, which is where they met the final member of the team, Colin Read from Keswick, arriving direct from Manchester. The following train journey, direct from the airport around Lake Geneva and up the Rhone valley, deposited them in Visp in time to catch an evening bus up the Saas Valley to Saas Grund. Proof that a co-ordinated transport policy can work.

After being repulsed by avalanche conditions the year before, Ann and Colwyn were planning a return to ski up the Weissmeis, but as the Hohsaas ski lifts had inconveniently closed for the season, everyone rose next morning to catch the first bus over to Saas Fee to access that all-important uplift. After the short walk through the car free village and last-minute shopping, the efficient lift system whisked them up through the crowds to the top of the Metro Alpin at a respectable 3454m. The cloud caused enough consternation at the bergschrund for a rope, but they soon skinned up the 573m via the Feejoch to bag the first 4000m peak of the trip, the Allalinhorn via the west-north-west ridge. Above the bergschrund the early cloud cleared and they all enjoyed fine views from the summit.

A splendid ski descent brought them to the short traverse of the Egginerjoch over to the Britanniahutte. This excellent, and busy, hut at 3030m was both the base and source of acclimatisation for the next two nights.

Sunday was taken up doing a training peak called the Flucthorn (3794m). This is a fine summit halfway up the Adlerpass on the same ridge as the Strahlhorn and they enjoyed another fine descent back down the Allalin Glacier to the junction with the Hohlaub Glacier before the snow got too soft. From there a short ascent back up to the hut ended a short and enjoyable day.

In the pre-dawn of the next morning, bathed in the eerie glow from LED headtorches, they followed quietly in the tracks of fellow guests back up the Allalin glacier. After dawn broke and halfway towards the pass, they displayed some independence from the crowds and branched off right between the Allalinhorn and the North Ridge of the target for the day, the Rimpfischorn (4199m). From the Allalinpass the approach was arduous contouring the entire length of the peak. Other teams abandoned their attempt that day, but perseverance paid off and the Rimpfischsattel, just below 4000m was finally reached.

Abandoning skis they romped up the well-protected west-south-west ridge to the foresummit and were soon exchanging places below the recently refurbished summit cross, posing for the obligatory photographs. Back at the skis the planned route down to Fluealp was abandoned in favour of the visually tempting direct descent of the Mellich Glacier by the side of the Vor Der Wand to Ottovan. Here, Brian assured them (although he later denied it!), they could call a taxi and get driven down to Tasch where they planned to spend the night.

The vision was realised and they enjoyed a splendid descent down untracked powder snow off the glacier into the Mellichbach Valley. Colwyn did his usual impersonation of a crevasse poodle when the group stopped for a comfort break, but moving with uncharacteristic speed promptly snapped back into his bindings. All too soon the snow ran out and they trudged cheerfully down the thawing valley to find that the village was closed. There was no phone to be found and no one to ask for directions. The village was literally closed for the winter. Walking down towards Tasch they discovered why. The road was blocked, not only by snow, but by some large and recent avalanches. However, by following a snowmobile track they made it to Tasch arriving at 8.45pm, where Mark negotiated a splendid chalet just in time for supper.

Next day started with a long lie and a late train up to Zermatt. The dependable Hotel Bahnhof had been booked and they squeezed into the typically crowded dormitories. Here, was another SMC member who had more palatial accommodation. John Bickerdike had just led a party along the High Level Route and had booked the luxury of a hotel room.

Next morning they were up early to catch the Klein Matterhorn lift up into the cloud. From the 3883m top station they had planned to attempt Castor but conditions dictated a more modest day and they skinned up the Briethorn (4184m) following a GPS bearing, achieving the summit just in front of the first guided party of the day. The cloud parted, but then closed in again and they skied back down to Furi where they, and everyone else, were forced to endure the attention seeking noise and chaos of a group of visiting French ski instructors. Abandoning the spectacle, they enjoyed a peaceful afternoon walk down to Zermatt.

The forecast was good for next morning and they caught the early train up to Gornergrat, with the workers, followed by the two vintage cable cars up to the Stockhorn. A short climb to the summit and a pleasant descent to the Stockhornpass preceded a traverse across the top of the Findel Glacier to pass between the Strahlchnubel and Adlerhorn. The steep ascent up the Adler Glacier to the Adlerpass confirmed the value of harschiesen, especially to those lacking this piece of gear. From the pass they ticked the Stralhorn (4190m) and skied down the splendid Allalin glacier and back to the Brittaniahutte to sunbathe for an hour before the snow started.

Low cloud and light snowfall on the final day dictated retreat from the hill so they skied down into what they thought would be a bustling ski area. However, as the resort had closed for the season the piste was deserted as they slowly skied back to Saas Fee for tea and cakes. A fine way to end a superb trip.

JOHN HIGHAM REPORTS: In the last two weeks of July and first week of August 2001, my son, Richard, my wife, Alison, and I joined the LSCC meet in Saas Grund. As we arrived a couple of days ahead of the main party and the sun was shining, Richard, Alison and I had an enjoyable training day climbing the Fletschhorn (NW Ridge PD).

As we finished and the rest of the party started arriving, including Jon Hutchison and Chris Gilmore (both SMC) the rain and snow fell and I began to have nightmares that this was going to be a repeat of 2000. That year's holiday had started with a week of some of the worst weather I had seen in the Alps and ruined long-laid plans. This time was not as bad although a planned ascent soon after of the Grand Cornier with Chris and Richard degenerated into a deep snow slog terminated on the conveniently nearer and lower peak the Bouquetins as exhaustion took its toll. The weather stabilised soon after and Richard, Alison and I accompanied by Chris and Eve Gilmore and probably a 100 other people made an ascent of the Weismeiss via the SW ridge (PD) on a bitterly cold, but crystal clear day.

High pressure had now settled over the Alps and I was keen to take as much advantage of it as possible. Richard and I started the campaign with a traverse of the Nordend and Dufourspitz via the North Flank (AD). Instead of being rock, the latter was still plastered with snow and ice from the recent storms and provided an exciting ascent at about Scottish IV. It also meant no crowds. Chris had been unable to accompany us because of a persistent knee problem but joined us when Richard and I decided to do the Northern Nadelgrat (AD).

Kate Ross and Mary Lothian of the LSCC made up a second team on the day. We traversed the Nadelgrat from the north starting at the Durrenhorn and gaining the ridge via the Durrenjoch Couloir, a long day followed with no technical problems, but considerable exposure and commitment. As the two weeks of the LSCC meet came to an end, lots of peaks had been done and people began to go home or move to a different area. Jon and Chris decided that it was time for some hot rocking and headed for Locarno where they reported excellent rock and plenty of sun. Richard had time for one more route before he had to return separately to the UK so we headed for the Weisshorn, a mountain I had wanted to do for a long time. I had tried it in the debacle of 2000, tempted during a short spell of good weather, but turned back in the face of deep snow. The conditions were much better this time although there was more snow on the East Ridge (AD) than normal and Richard and I had an uneventful and fast ascent, but with no views as the cloud rolled in at midday.

The end of the holiday was fast approaching but the weather was still just holding and we had time for one more route before returning home and decided to move across to Chamonix for this. Alison had had enough of the big mountains and went for a tour while I teamed up with Kate Ross to tackle the Jardin Ridge (D–) and continue to the Aiguille Verte over the Grand Rocheuse. A very early start ensured it was still dark when we reached the bergschrund and we stumbled around for quite a while looking for a way up the seemingly impassable wall of ice. We found the narrowest point and in the absence of any ice tools and with some dim memories of the Sixties returning, we soon cut our way up the ice and continued quickly up the gully above. A difficult chimney, loose and overhanging, led us onto the ridge proper which although narrow and intimidating was not too difficult and provided exciting positions on icy rock or corniced snow arêtes.

We made good time to the Verte but the weather had deteriorated through the day and as the wind picked up, we decided it was time to make our way down the Whymper Couloir. The descent was slow and frightening as the abseiling on one rope took forever and occasional massive rockfalls down the opposite side of the couloir showed us this was not the best place to be in this warm weather.

Unfortunately, the light ran out just above the seracs that run across the base of the couloir and we could not find a way through. As it stayed warm, a relatively comfortable night was spent on some rocks at the edge of the couloir. Some free abseils over the seracs the next morning saw us safely down to join the others and to head back home.

New Zealand

Ross Hewitt reports: Diana Ross and myself spent five weeks climbing in New Zealand during November and December 2002.

On arrival we headed straight into the mountains with a friend, Evan Cameron, who has been working as a Registrar in Dunedin Hospital. During this trip we climbed Mt. Beatrice and Nazomi in an attempt to get fit.

Poor weather in the mountains forced us onto the crags and we travelled around the South Island sampling quality rock routes at Castle Rock, Long beach, Wanaka, Paynes Ford, Quantum Field, Elephant Rocks, Doctor's Point, Mihiwaki and Duntroon.

All of these venues offer contrasting climbing in very different, but beautiful, settings from the white sandy beaches of Dunedin to the lakes and snowcapped mountains at Wanaka. The two places that stand out in my mind most for cragging and bouldering are the limestone at Quantum Field and Paynes Ford.

For sports climbing, Paynes Ford offers limestone climbing similar to our favourite Spanish winter venues complete with flowstones, tufas and pockets. If you like it steep then visit Thug's wall. Need I say more.

The end of the trip promised good weather in the mountains for a few days and we made a dash into the Plateau Hut via the Haast Ridge. A lot of fresh snow and time constraint to get back to Christchurch influenced our decision to give Mount Cook's Zubriggen Ridge a miss and go for the Linda Glacier Route. Climbing Cook in near perfect weather made a great end to the trip despite the slog in deep snow.

Spain

Jason Currie reports: In July and August 2002, with Adam Liversedge, I visited the Picos de Europa of northern Spain, basing ourselves in the tourist village of Potes.

We climbed a number of routes including Maraya (TD+) and the Regil route (TD-) on the south face of the Torre de los Horcados Rojos, Pilar de Nazaret (TD+) on the Torre de las Coteras Rojas, Las Placas (ED) on the Pena Olvidada and a traverse of the classic Madejuno-Tiro Llago ridge (AD).

The culmination of our trip was an ascent of the Rabada-Navarro (ED-) on the 500m west face of El Naranjo de Bulnes on August 7.

Visits were also made to the excellent sport-climbing venues of Valdehuesa, La Pedrosa-Valverdin and the impressive gorge of the Hoces de Vegacervera – all to the south of the Picos proper and within an hour's drive of Leon.

Throughout the trip the weather was largely very good in marked contrast to the reputation the area has for frequent frontal troughs. This coupled with a noticeable lack of other climbers made for a great experience that can be heartily recommended.

Indian Himalaya

THE first ascent of Suitilla West (6373m) in the Kumaon Himalaya was made by Graham Little and Jim Lowther.

After an abortive attempt on the 2000m north-west face (stopped by very poor snow conditions), they climbed the peak via the 1100m south face in 22 hours of continuous climbing (15hrs up and 7hrs down from a high camp at 5270m).

The face was climbed mostly on ice by a fairly central line with some objective danger from stonefall and avalanches. The route was christened *Moonlight Express* and was repeated a few days later by an Indian Navy team using extensive fixed ropes.

REVIEWS

The Evidence Of Things Not Seen – A Mountaineers Tale:– W. H. Murray
(Baton Wicks, 2002, hardback 325pp. 133 photos, ISBN1898573247). £20.

When the Journal editor offered me the opportunity of reviewing this book
I wondered whether it could turn out to be a bit of a poisoned chalice. After
all, the legendary W. H. Murray, Honorary President of the SMC at the time
of his death in 1996, was not only an inspirational figure to many but was as
distinguished a literary figure in the Scottish mountaineering realm as I was
ever likely to see. Additionally, I'm rather sceptical about book reviews with
their attempts to rationalise and categorise, efforts which often reveal more
about the reviewer than they do about the book. By what presumption, and I
ask the question of myself, do we sit in judgment of such a man? But, for me,
Murray has always had a cloak of mystery about him and, sooner or later, I
was going to have to read this book to try to understand the undercurrents that
influenced the author of those post-war classics *Mountaineering in Scotland*
and *Undiscovered Scotland.* If for no other reason, I would imagine that the
cognoscenti will already have done the same. So I offer you no definitive or
analytical approach but rather one of a sense of feeling which, I hope, is in
keeping with the theme of the book.

Basically, this is Bill Murray's autobiography with the apparently strange
title of *The Evidence of Things Not Seen.* This is, in fact, the title of chapter 22
in *Mountaineering in Scotland* (and is also included as an article in the *SMCJ*
23, 1946) but is not reproduced in this book, which seems odd given its crucial
and pivotal significance to Murray. But perhaps he intended his readers to do
a bit of homework for themselves. It concerns an incomparable night ascent
of the Buachaille in December 1939, with Douglas Laidlaw, a moonlit night
of utmost clarity. Murray describes the scene as…well, no, I cannot paraphrase
it. You'll have to read it, let it whisper its message, or shrug off the references
to Coleridge and Goethe as you decide.

W. H. would take his reader to the water and then leave it up to them whether
or not they drank but suffice to say that, for him, the hills that night were big
with the "truth made manifest". If trying to decipher his meaning sounds too
much like hard work and if, for you, reading a book should be pure
entertainment, then some of his writing may leave you struggling. But take
his advice – "therefore and above all persist" – because he was well aware of
the problems. Books, through all categories of literature, were a core part of
his life from his earliest years. By his own admission the writings of Plato
stretched his mind in his late teens but he persevered and they came to be as
"heavily bracing as hill winds…they enlarged all concepts of life and purpose".
Perhaps here was nourishing ground for an inbuilt tenaciousness, of a
resoluteness of purpose. Persist. On the Buachaille "something in that night
cried out to us, not low, nor faltering, but clear, true, urgent – that this was not
all".

Here, unseen, despite the brilliance of the moonlight, was Bill Murray's
evidence for his God. He is unequivocal, Providence was seen as a law of life

and, whatever fate held in store, there was no such thing as luck. Fighting in North Africa as an inexperienced subaltern in the Highland Light Infantry, Bill Murray first encountered the realities of battle in a suicidal mission over open ground, against massed German tanks at the Battle of the Cauldron in 1942. His battalion was decimated.

"One bomb landed just a yard to my right-hand side. It blew out a crater, but all stone and metal lifted close above my prone body. One golden rule in artillery attack is that no shell lands twice in the same spot ...therefore, get into a crater – the one safe place. I had tensed up my muscles to make the sideways move when I felt inwardly a sudden negative command: 'Stay put!' It came not from my own will or mind, which intended otherwise, yet while soundless, was so authoritative that I chose not to argue. I sank back in position. Just a few seconds later, another bomb came down exactly on that first crater."

Murray reflected on this episode for more than a year:

"My experience is that on rare occasions a human being may be open to direction from a power higher than his own. The direction is never over-riding of mind or will, but a simple impulse that one is free to ignore. I had chosen not to ignore. For want of another word, men often refer to such beneficent impulse as their guardian angel. Whatever the name given, I have no doubt of its reality."

William Hutchison Murray was just two years old when his father was killed in action at Gallipoli in the Dardanelles Campaign of 1915. Inevitably, a sense of deprivation came to him in his early teens and much had then to be learned alone, always the hard way, but he does not dwell upon these years. Perhaps here is an inkling as to the essence of the man. Mountains held no attraction for him until his attention was gripped by an overheard conversation about a traverse of An Teallach which inspired him to make a solo trip to the Cobbler and henceforth he was smitten. He joined the JMCS and, with Archie MacAlpine, who was to become his brother-in law, Bill Mackenzie, and Kenneth Dunn, formed an exceptional team which lifted Scottish mountaineering from the doldrums of the 1920s. It was a time when three of Scotland's finest glens – Affric, Cannich and Strathfarrar – had not been despoiled by dams and the West Highlands adulterated by a spreading coniferous monotony. Murray gives the background and captures the flavour of this bygone age with his customary flair. It fills one with envy for: "It was a golden age, and even felt like it at the time."

The section on pre-war climbing in Scotland, although brief, is highly informative, giving the background to those advances. The simple expedient of lengthening ropes from the 80 feet recommended by Raeburn for a party of three, and the use of waist belays, opened up alluring possibilities, allowing access onto the great walls, slabs and faces. Following the example of Colin Kirkus and others in England and Wales, who led long, unprotected run-outs on exposed faces, George Williams and Graham Macphee, both SMC members, climbed Route 1 on the Buachaille's Rannoch Wall. This demonstration of how nerve, control and balance could be more important than power-to-weight ratio and muscle size, cheered Murray who was tall and sparsely built. Unlike most of the SMC old-guard, who thoroughly disapproved of these unjustifiable new routes, J. H. B. Bell, then editor of the SMC Journal, took Murray and friends under his wing and it is clear that Bell, with his visionary approach to Scottish climbing, was highly influential, making the various new climbing groups known to each other.

Similarly, with winter climbing. Douglas Scott, realising the limitations imposed by long-shafted axes in confined spaces, had a new short axe made for him by a Glasgow blacksmith. When Murray and Bill Mackenzie saw this new tool they realised that slaters' hammers, with the side claw removed, would be just the right weight and length, and, using nailed boots, their various routes culminated in a first winter ascent of Garrick's Shelf on Crowberry Ridge in 1937. A couple of years more of intense climbing activity and then world war swallowed everyone up. "We knew only that in the last five years Scottish climbing had been re-founded."

The discomforts of winter mountaineering were to stand Bill Murray in good stead, enabling him to stand the strains of basic army training with relative ease. He was less comfortable with the dull and noisy life in barracks, but was eventually, commissioned in December 1940, and posted to the Highland Light Infantry. The chapters describing his war years, in two sections *Fortunes of War* and *Incarceration* are gripping, and full of sage observation, as relevant now as it was then. It is well documented that Murray sought escape from the sordid realities of prison camp, inspired by the sight of the first snows on the soaring Gran Sasso, the highest spire of the Abruzzi mountains, by writing about his own mountains. The only available material on which to write was toilet paper and so he set to work. But this was more than writing. It was a gateway to living in the mind as he sought to extract the detail of his memories from their pigeonholes, learning to concentrate by the very necessity of detachment, a trait that became ingrained.

Murray witnessed the depravities of a concentration camp called Moosburg in Bavaria, spending two months there before being moved to Czechoslovakia, where the Gestapo discovered his scribbled manuscript. Here, for the first time, were men with faces like corpses, who had the ability to send shivers down his spine. This was genuine evil and the justification for war. In the end they let him go but the manuscript was gone. It is a measure of his strength of purpose that he started again, even coming to the conclusion that the destruction of the original draft was a blessing in disguise for, believing that he would never climb mountains again, he wrote with an honesty about beauty and delight, effort and fun, of truth only.

About that time, Murray met a fellow prisoner, Herbert Buck, a man of real moral strength, who introduced him to the study and practice of mystical religion and meditation, which became an integral part of his life thereafter, and he describes this encounter as the most important and far-reaching personal experience of the war. That second manuscript was to become, of course, Murray's first book, *Mountaineering in Scotland*. There are accounts, too, of the exploits of fellow Scottish mountaineers, Alistair Cram and Tommy Wedderburn, who, like many others, risked all in their courageous escape attempts. "During this last year, I had not once thought of myself as imprisoned. I lived on mountains and had the freedom of them."

The next section of the book details Murray's post-war world. He took a decision, then, that would change the course of his life: to earn his living as a writer or to enter a monastery, or both. After a week's trial at a Benedictine Abbey, he rejected the monastic life, despite its attractions. A return to Scottish climbing and the highs and lows of the Alps are part of an attempt to shape his life. All this is followed by perhaps, the meat of the book, his accounts of his various Himalayan trips. Six chapters abridged from his 1950 Scottish Himalayan Expedition book are included. This was a trip to the Garhwal in northern India with Douglas Scott, Tom MacKinnon and Tom Weir and followed in the exploratory tradition of Tom Lonstaff, Eric Shipton and Bill Tilman. The Longstaff philosophy was one of always attempting to lose consciousness of self and the realisation that, should one do so, almost any part of the world is as good as another.

These were significant Himalayan trips – a 1951 Everest Reconnaissance Expedition and a 1953 trip to Api/Nampa in western Nepal with a clandestine entry into Tibet with John Tyson – and yet there occurred nothing to make a more lasting impression on his mind than the simple act of being given a small bunch of flowers by Matbir, a Dotial porter: "Again and again it recurs, accompanied by one or other of its witnessed opposites: Italian sentries at Tobruk staving in a prisoner's face with rifle butts ...from these I can turn to Matbir at Lampak and feel respect for man."

Throughout Murray's writings run the common threads of humanity and good sense. I can detect little of the so-called romanticism which is sometimes, often disparagingly, used to categorise his work. As he makes clear: "An author should not start writing in earnest until his feeling is aroused."

Murray can never be accused of writing without feeling. Some may call it romantic, I prefer to recognise it as honesty. After his return from the Himalaya, Bill Murray, turned his attention to full-time writing and enjoying the peace of Lochwood, his home by Loch Goil. He married Anne Clark whom he had met after a good day on the hills and became increasingly involved in conservation work, being a founder member, among many other bodies, of the John Muir Trust. He died before seeing his book published and he knew that it still needed much work. Anne, his wife, continued the editing and contributed all the poetry. Ken Wilson has contributed photo captions and various informative footnotes. There are several chapters and appendices towards the end of the book that may seem a bit out of place but it is a minor matter given the overall context.

I need not have worried, it has been a privilege to have reviewed this book for the Journal, for Bill Murray was an extraordinary man and one of a handful to have put his feelings on paper.

"The past was a good age to live in. I was lucky to view the world earlier when more was unspoiled, untouched. Looking back over a wide landscape, cloud shadows racing over the mountain, sun, wind. I know that I have known beauty."

Mike Jacob.

Escape From Lucania – An Epic Struggle For Survival:– David Roberts (Little Brown, ISBN 0 316724882).

What is the link between a Trans-Atlantic passenger liner and two of the world's greatest mountain photographers, and why should a well established writer like David Roberts want to write about it?

In 1897, His Royal Highness, Prince Luigi Amedo di Savoia, Duke of the Abruzzi, sailed across to North America and made the first ascent of Mount Saint Elias (18,008ft). Long thought to be the highest peak on that continent, it was subsequently overshadowed by McKinley (20,320ft) and Logan (19,550ft). From their summit, the Italians noted another major peak, which they named Lucania (17,147ft) after the ship on which they had sailed from Liverpool to New York.

Among the duke's companions on this and other notable expeditions was Vittorio Sella, whose magnificent photographs have inspired generations of mountain lovers. One such acolyte was the young Bradford Washburn. Graduating from Harvard in 1933, Washburn had developed an interest in aerial photography and a taste for climbing in the Far North, in a style described as "fast-and-light".

By 1937, remote Lucania remained the highest unclimbed peak on the continent, and with this objective Washburn put together a team of four, including fellow Harvard alumnus Bob Bates. With the help of bush pilot Bob Reeve, supplies were flown high onto a glacier, but plans went seriously awry when a change in the weather marooned the two climbers and their transport at the foot of the mountain. A few days later, Reeve managed to escape by the skin of his teeth in his empty plane, leaving the diminished party to climb their peak and walk 156 miles back to civilisation. Director of the Boston Museum of Science for 40 years, Washburn became a noted cartographer, photographer and leading authority on the mountains and glaciers of Alaska and the Yukon, while Bates, a teacher of English, went on to lead two American attempts on K2.

Apart from a few brief reports published at the time, the full details of this remarkable adventure have never been told. With the help of both protagonists, happily still hale and hearty in their Nineties, David Roberts sets the record straight with great enthusiasm. The author's own involvement in climbing in the Far North is extensive. *The Mountain of my Fear* (1968) remains a classic, describing his first ascent of the west face of Mt. Huntington (12,240ft) and he collaborated with Washburn on the superbly illustrated *Mount McKinley – The Conquest of Denali* (1991). In telling the story of Lucania, Roberts weaves in some of the climbing history of the main Alaska and Yukon peaks, along with a little biographical background of the personalities involved.

Over the years, British and English translation of European mountaineering literature has tended to focus on the Alps and the Himalayas and it is refreshing to be reminded that exciting things happened elsewhere in the world. Climbing and exploring the mountain ranges of the Far North of America presented its own unique problems and solutions. Developments in bush flying enabled climbers and their gear to be deposited on the glaciers at the foot of the mountains, doing away with very long and arduous approaches. Washburn also

Ross Hewitt climbing On Some Faraway Beach, Quantum Field, New Zealand. NZ 16 (F5+). Photo: Diana Ross.

Alastair Robertson on pitch 5 of Grand Wall, Squamish, Canada. Photo: (A. Robertson collection).

made use of reconnaissance flights to take aerial photographs which proved invaluable in the absence of accurate maps.

David Roberts's previous foray into mountaineering history, *True Summit: What Really Happened on the Legendary Ascent of Annapurna* (2000), was an unconvincing debunking of Maurice Herzog's seminal *Annapurna,* with more than a hint of sour grapes. In contrast, *Escape from Lucania* is a celebration of the people concerned and their achievements, and makes a much more uplifting read. The only hint of a cloud concerns bush pilot Bob Reeve. After one lucky escape he was clearly not prepared to risk his plane or his neck again, and made no attempt either to fly the other half of the team in, or bring Washburn and Bates back out.

Fortunately, neither climber seems to have expected anything different, and they went on to tackle the various difficulties that came their way with remarkable fortitude. Cutting gear down to an absolute minimum meant sharing just one sleeping bag, and inevitably supplies started to run out. Luckily, they kept hold of their revolver and a handful of ammunition and were able to bag a few squirrels and a rabbit for the pot. Swollen with summer meltwater, the rivers in the Far North become formidable barriers, but once again Lady Luck stayed on their side, enabling them to make the crucial crossing of the Donjek River.

Exciting right up to its nail-biting finish, the story of this adventure and the exploration of North America's highest mountains combined with a celebration of the long and remarkable lives of two of the continent's most active mountaineers makes for a great read.

David Broadhead.

The Classic Landforms of Skye:– D. Benn and C. Ballantyne, (The Geographic Association). £8.95.

As a mountaineer I have long been frustrated at being unable to obtain an account of the underlying geology of mountain areas which I could understand! Most geology books, even if they claimed to be written in a popular style, are to me like computer manuals – only accessible if you already understand what they are trying to teach you. 1 was very pleased therefore to come across the volume in the Geographical Society's series Classic Landforms (published in association with the British Geomorphological Research Group) of their book on the Misty Isle, which dispelled many of the clouds surrounding my knowledge of its staggering physical features.

This book has enthusiasm for its subject, an island which they say contains "some of the most spectacular scenery and varied geology in the British Isles". The Cuillin "form a mountain landscape unequalled anywhere in Britain" and "the buttresses and pinnacles of the Storr make an unforgettable impact."

This is not a general geology of Skye, instead it looks at specific landforms, among which are the most dramatic and gives a succinct and accessible account of the formation of each. In order to encourage the layman to get out and into this landscape a series of brief walks are attached to the end of each account of a specific landform. The Quirang and the Storr to the south are part of the most extensive landslide in Britain, which stretches 23km along the escarpment of

Ramtang in a sea of cloud from the North Col of Kanchenjunga with Makalu, Lhotse and Everest in the distance. Photo: Chris Comerie.

Louise Trave-Massuyes between the penitentes on the way to Camp 1, Aconcagua (6869m), Argentina. The Polish Glacier is visible in the upper left of the photograph. Photo: Rob Milne.

the Trotternish peninsula. After the retreat of the ice successive landslides, possibly triggered by earthquakes and the last some 6500 years ago, formed the present dramatic landscape. The Cuillin was formed by the retreat and re-advance of a glacier which stretched far beyond the present range, and resulted in the ice-polished slabs and smooth rocks of the Cuillin corries. But what of the shattered summits of the Cuillin? As the maximum height of the glacier was 800m, the summits remained proud of the ice, nunataks such as you can see presently on Iceland's glaciers. Repeated freezing and warming led to these shattering as we see them today.

As well as explaining things that had puzzled me, this book pointed out things I had never noticed before. The raised beaches at Braes, the huge moraine fields around Sligachan, the aolian (wind born) deposits at Storr causing a lush green meadow. It also dispelled some illusions. Like many, including those who reported that it was erupting in 1934, I thought Dun Caan on Raasay was an extinct volcano; apparently not. Despite that, this book shows that the geology of Skye is dramatic enough nevertheless. This is a book which will gladden the heart of all Skye folk with its praise for the island and delight all mountaineers with its explanation of the physical structure beneath the magic of Skye. My only reservation is that, even for such a well illustrated book, £8.95 is a tad pricey for 50-plus pages.

It can be obtained from The Geographic Association, 160 Solly Street, Sheffield S1 4BF.

Ian R. Mitchell.

Tigers of the Snow:– Jonathan Neale. (Little Brown, 338pp, £18.99, ISBN 0 316 85409 5).

Jonathan Neale is not a mountaineer. He has a Ph.D. in social history, spent part of his boyhood in India and speaks Nepali and a little Sherpa. Accordingly, his history of the progression of the (principally Sherpa) hill people of the Himalaya from 'coolies' to respected guide and entrepreneur status is not your average account of Himalayan epics. Nor does it make for comfortable reading – many reputations end up with a dent or two.

The author conducted interviews with surviving high-altitude Sherpas (including Ang Tensing who was on Everest in 1924 and Nanga Parbat in 1934) and with the relatives of dead Sherpas. This book gives the story of Himalayan 'conquest' from the point of view of the bearers of the White Man's burden; the men who, even in 1953, were expected to carry 65lb loads to Everest south col.

The main focus of the book is on the various German attempts on Nanga Parbat with their accompanying heavy loss of life. One of Neale's main themes is that Europeans in general and the Germans on Nanga Parbat in particular, did not understand two things – the psychology of their porters and high-altitude physiology. European attitudes to the indigenous people of the mountains were based on a mixture of paternalism and imperialism.

Those who went on expeditions as porters did so mainly for financial reasons. The pay was better than pulling a rickshaw in Darjeeling or carrying heavy loads over the passes to and from Tibet. A high-altitude porter allowed to keep his clothing and equipment at the end of an expedition could sell it for enough money to buy a house. Their attitude to danger was accordingly somewhat different to those of their prestige-driven employers. One telling statistic is that between 1953 and 1983, 116 men from Solu and Khumbu died working in the mountains. Little wonder that Sherpas were unhappy at using campsites or routes previously swept by avalanche or stonefall.

Neale's account of the gradual development of Sherpa self-confidence and their increasing role in the organisation and management of expeditions is interesting. A critical role was played by the post-war French and Swiss expeditions which included professional Alpine guides. They treated the high-altitude Sherpas as fellow professionals who might need to learn a technique or two but were perfectly acceptable tent companions. The influence of Raymond Lambert on Tensing was particularly strong.

This is a complex and thought-provoking book, if not particularly very well written. Don't bother if you are looking for tales of conquest and glory, but as a study of men on mountains it is highly recommended. At £18.99 most libraries could be persuaded to buy it if you tell them it's a sociological study.

R. T. Richardson.

The Fall:– Simon Mawer. (Little Brown, London, 2003, ISBN 0-316-72524-2. £12.99).
"Climb if you will but remember that courage and strength are naught without prudence, and that a momentary negligence may destroy the happiness of a lifetime. Do nothing in haste; look well to each step; and from the beginning think what may be the end."

These words of Whymper quoted as part of the funeral of Jamie Matthewson by Rob Dewar speak, as this novel does, about life as much as climbing. And the characters of this sensitive and complex book find the advice as difficult to follow on the mountains as in their lives.

The intricate plot weaves the lives of Rob and Jamie, Jamie's father (a famous climber) their mothers and lovers into a satisfying tale of climbing adventure and sexual intrigue.

The story opens with Rob, now an art dealer hearing about Jamie's death in a fall from Great Wall on Cloggy while climbing solo. An E4 at over 50; was it accident or suicide? Childhood friends and then climbing partners, they had become estranged but Rob heads for Wales to be with Jamie's wife and his mother. Through flashbacks both in their lives and in the lives of their partners of Guy, Jamie's father and of their mothers, the reasons for the loss of contact are explored.

Mawer handles the intricacies of the relationships with skill. None of the characters is wholly likeable, each in his or her own way is selfish and the reader finds none with which to identify easily. The women apart from Jamie's mother, Meg are the more sympathetic and seem to have more grip on their lives than the climbers. The latter are driven by forces almost outside their control. Life is fatalistic and self centred. Climbing as a death wish and "a substitute for feeling" is a resonant theme, though when Rob abandons the sport he seems no more sensitive.

There are many falls in the book, both metaphoric and real. The title, of course, invites one to think of the exit from Eden and perhaps there is a sense of a paradise lost in the wrong turns taken, the misery of the War, and the crippled relationships.

The climbing scenes are excellent and the evocation both of early days in Llanberis, Snowdon, and Gogarth, of Scottish ice climbs and the ascent of the Eiger ring true. What is absent is any exploration of the motivation of the protagonists. Sure, Jamie's father has been missing on Kanchengunga until, towards the end of the book, his body is found with consequences for the somewhat predictable denoument. But the characters seem to find little joy in the pursuit except perhaps during the exploration of a new sea cliff in Wales. Maybe that's where Mawer had his happiest experiences. The Eiger climb is well handled and dramatic, though I got the impression that the author was recycling others' accounts rather than drawing on personal experience. Another lack is any strong feeling of a climbing community. Jamie and Rob seem to be the only ones on the cliff or the mountain and there are few minor characters. Still, this is a work of fiction and there are no false steps in the climbing descriptions to distract from the story.

Mawer is already an accomplished novelist who explores serious themes.

So this is a good read and has a depth to it that much fiction set around mountaineering lacks, burying some big questions to lurk beneath the surface of this very readable novel.

Robin Shaw.

Scotland's Wild Land – what future?:– Edited by John Digney (Scottish Wild Land Group).

This slim publication celebrates the 20th anniversary of the founding of the Scottish Wild Land Group, whose aim is to raise public awareness of the threats posed to the wild character of Scotland's natural heritage. With brief essays, 10 contributors with diverse interests give their thoughts on some of the issues.

Martin Price, director of the Centre for Mountain Studies at Perth College, gives a highly personal view, based on his upbringing in London and his experiences in mountains around the world.

Nigel Hawkins, director of the John Muir Trust, explains how that organisation tries to apply the vision of John Muir, and its involvement in restoring damaged landscapes.

Alistair McIntosh, a Fellow of Edinburgh's Centre for Human Ecology, has something to say about the role of 'the fairies and all that', while Paul Johnson, head of Countryside Management with the National Trust for Scotland, outlines a more practical approach to the 75,000 hectares under his care. After setting out some objective indicators of wild land quality, he explains how the NTS, trying to learn from past mistakes, has developed the Unna Principles.

Nick Kempe, former president of the Mountaineering Council of Scotland, argues for the need to re-establish natural processes and Mark Wrightham, a National Strategy Officer with Scottish Natural Heritage, explains SNH policy.

With both feet firmly on the ground, *Angry Corrie* editor, Dave Hewitt, suggests leaving the guidebooks at home occasionally, and Alpine Club president, Alan Blackshaw, takes an international perspective on human rights and access freedoms.

An interview with John Love, SNH area officer for the Uists, Barra and St Kilda brings out some of the highlights of more than 30 years involvement in conservation, with some interesting comments on rock climbing on remote cliffs.

Finally, Alistair Cant, SWLG Steering Team Co-ordinator, examines progress on land reform in Scotland.

With all this packed into 34 pages of A4, along with a number of excellent colour photographs, this useful and interesting booklet stands out as one of the highlights of the International Year of The Mountain 2002.

Buy a copy by sending £5 (including p+p) to John Digney, SWLG, Creagmhor Lodge, Lochard Road, Aberfoyle, Stirling, FK8 3TD, or even better send £10 for the booklet plus membership of the Scottish Wild Land Group until December 2003. Highly recommended.

David Broadhead.

My Life – Eiger North Face, The Grandes Jorasses and Other Adventures:– Anderl Heckmair, Translated by Tim Carruthers, Foreword by Reinhold Messner, (Baton Wicks, hardback, 269pp. £17.99. ISBN 1-898-57355-7).

It was in the book *The White Spider* by Heinrich Harrer that I first became familiar with the name Anderl Heckmair. As one of the famous four that scaled the massive Eiger North Face in 1938, his name becoming thereafter immortalised in the annals of outstanding world mountaineering achievements, successes that go down in history as awe inspiring. Yet, although I acknowledged his role as the one person that led the way in the final hours of the first ascent through some desperate and dangerous ground to emerge alive on the summit, his presence seemed overshadowed by the powerful writing of the author.

It was not until we made the film documentary *Climbing for the Fatherland* on Channel Four and after having climbed the North Face of the Eiger for the film, that I realised just how fantastic Anderl's skills as a mountaineer, a technical climber on snow, rock and ice, his judgment and unbelievable route-finding skills really were. It was awe inspiring that he and his companions had such commitment and belief in their abilities, obviously built from years of prior training and experience. I knew he was coming for an interview for the documentary, which made me more nervous than the thought of climbing the route.

At the end of the Hinterstoiser traverse on his route on the North Face of the Eiger, I spoke with him by radio through Trudel his wife, who translated for us. He had arrived at Scheidegg as we had started climbing. I wasn't quite sure what to say and blurted an embarrassing: "That was an awesome and scary bit of route finding and climbing" or something to that effect, an awkward silence followed the translation, I felt a strong sense of calculation in his coming reply, yet a reserved silence as though he wished he was back in this magical place, where I now stood. "Get on with it young man, there are plenty of big holds up there!" came back. I knew what he had said before Trudel translated to English. His dry sense of humour was reassuring, I'm sure I'd heard someone else say that before! (like every time you're out with a Grand Old Master).

At Kleine Scheidegg, he sat straight, puffing on a small crème cigar, powerful looking and strong in presence, every wrinkle, of which there were few, on his face was wrought deep and hard, undoubtedly still a handsome and attractive man. Trudel again sat beside him translating, but I could swear he understood and could speak more than he cared to. He relived parts of his life that were fascinating for the privileged few at that table. Unbelievably, he was still guiding mountains at 87 and now sitting in front of us in his 90s, he appeared calmly excited and at home once more beneath the North Face.

His relationship with the famous German actress, Leni Riefenstahl, led him to meet with the Fuhrer, Adolf Hitler. A man who would eventually use them all as German propaganda 'supermen' in his quest to win the war. His membership of the 'SS' (Germany's Elite) has been a cross to bear for his whole life, in some ways surpassing and hiding his achievements. We tend to think less of those that were associated with some of the most horrific acts on humanity, yet his book, *My Life,* gives an insight into this side of his life and tells a story of a man who like all of us, couldn't quell his desire to climb more and more. *My Life* translated by Tim Carruthers goes down in my library along side *The Great Days* by Walter Bonatti and *Total Alpinism* by Rene Desmaison as inspirational and an essential read in appreciating the talent and achievements that shaped mountaineering world-wide. For me another chapter had closed, another ambition fulfilled. I had climbed one of my childhood dreams and met and spoke with the man who had led the way so confidently so many years ago. The route is still no push over and it will never get any less serious or scary, my hat is forever off.

Scott Muir.

Himalayan Vignettes:– Kekoo Naoroji. (The Himalayan Club, 2003, 234pp, ISBN 81-88204-23-4. £35. UK Distributors, Art Books International. Tel: 02079 538290.

This book arrived from India with a healthy thump and with goodness knows how many stamps attached.

It also came with a penned inscription on the flyleaf: "For Charlie Orr, Ed. Scottish Mountaineering," so I guess that means it's mine! But I'll tell you about it anyway.

This is essentially a large format photo book for the coffee table. It is the photographic record of the author's early explorations in the Garhwal and Sikkim areas in the 1950s.

The visual content is backed up by a narrative summary of the Garhwal trek and the author's diaries kept during the Sikkim expedition, as well as a number of maps.

These ground breaking treks were made in the days before such exploration became the mass participation 'pay your money and we'll take you' game it is today, when now, you are more likely to meet somebody from Milngavie than you are a local.

Anyway, enough of this drum beating. Being the Fifties, the majority of the photographs are black and white, although there are also some colour plates of the Sikkim trip which was the later of the two, being undertaken in 1958.

This is a book which I'm sure would be appreciated by any Himalayan aficionado, although the price might be a bit off-putting for some. You could always get a look at mine I suppose.

Charlie Orr.

Ben Nevis:– Simon Richardson. (Scottish Mountaineering Trust, 2002, ISBN 0-907521738, £19.95).

This guidebook is quite clearly a labour of love. Having climbed on the Ben over a period of 34 years, I thought I knew the place pretty well, but to leaf through the pages of Simon Richardson's book is to see the mountain in a new light. Every obscure nook and cranny is drawn, described and graded with loving precision, (a number of unclimbed lines are revealed in the process). The diagrams, drawn by Mark Hudson, deserve special mention for their clarity and differentiation between winter and summer conditions. Although Ben Nevis takes up the bulk of the guide, a variety of venues are included, from neighbours Aonach Mor and Aonach Beag to more distant winter climbing venues like Creag Meaghaidh and Ben Alder.

Although it's traditional for guidebook reviewers to find fault in route gradings or star ratings, the very nature of winter climbing ensures a degree of natural variability where grade, and to a lesser degree, quality, are at the whim of the weather. It is apparent that winter grades have been reviewed and a number of earlier anomalies resolved. I, therefore, have no real quibble. The rock grades also seem to have stabilised although a number of enigmatic 'Scottish VS' routes lurk throughout the guide, providing the more adventurous climber with extra value. Although I understand the logic of introducing a 'four star' rating, this will further exacerbate the queuing with all the associated hazards that currently plagues the premiere routes. In contrast, some star-less routes do provide excellent climbing and will repay those who stray from the beaten path.

The historical sections and first ascent lists will make good reading on storm-lashed days in the CIC Hut. The illustrations are a mixed bag, ranging from the inspirational to the uninteresting (including a classic 'bum shot'). The format of the Guidebook is a welcome departure from the small, ever more chunky, traditional style but needs a fairly generous pocket to slip into. Only serious field use will test the rather thin pages' resilience to Scottish weather.

In conclusion, this is the best guide ever to Ben Nevis and Central Highlands. At £20 it sounds expensive, but with 250 new routes since the last edition it's worth every penny. It should, global warming permitting, become the bible for international pilgrims and an inspiration to a new generation of local activists. I may even be tempted to brave the queues and falling bodies and return to the crucible of Scottish winter climbing.

Graham E. Little.

North East Outcrops:– Neil Morrison, (Scottish Mountaineering Trust, 2003, ISBN 0-907-52174-6. £19.95).

This is the latest in the new SMC Guidebook series and follows hot on the heels of Simon Richardson's widely-acclaimed Ben Nevis guide. Not having explored the territory covered by this guide I was impressed to learn that in the area covering Aberdeen, the Moray and Banff sea cliffs, Deeside, Clova and the Angus quarries and sea cliffs, that there are more than 100 separate major venues with minor outcrops on top of that.

The quality of the maps and diagrams and the 16 colour plates in this production is very high indeed, as I am sure is the detail and accuracy of the route descriptions it contains, compiled by a team of activists, all of whom could be considered specialists in their own given area. This is an excellent guide, both for those exploring the area for the first time and for the converted.

Everest – 50 Years On Top Of The World:– Mount Everest Foundation/George Band (Collins, 2003, 256pp, 300 colour/black and white plates, £20. ISBN 0-007-14748-1).

Published in association with the Royal Geographic Society, Alpine Club and the Everest Foundation, this is the official publication celebrating the 50th anniversary of the first ascent of Everest in 1953.

It puts the first successful ascent into context – detailing the adventures and deaths on the north face pre-World War II and the planning after the war that was nearly curtailed by a Swiss expedition in 1952.

Written by a member of the original Hunt team – George Band, who went on to climb the lower but much harder peak Kangchenjunga – the book contains details, photographs and material donated by team members and the RGS, much of which is previously unpublished.

The Villain – The Life of Don Whillans:– Jim Perrin, (Hutchison, January, 2004, hardback, 320pp, ISBN 0-0917-9438-2. £18.99).

This book hasn't even been published yet and nor has the Journal received a pre-publication copy for review. But hey – Don Whillans/Jim Perrin, I would be hard pushed to think up a more tantalising subject/author combination.

Anyone familiar with Perrin's writing will know that he will tell the proper story, cut through the layers of apocrypha and myth that build up around any iconic figure, and as importantly, tell it in a prose style that has placed him firmly at the forefront of mountaineering literature. You'll have to order yours; I'm just waiting for my review copy!

The Corbetts & Other Scottish Hills (Second Edition):– Rob Milne/Hamish Brown (Scottish Mountaineering Trust, 2002, hardback, 280pp and more than 200 colour plates. ISBN 0-907-52171-1. £18.95).

First published in 1990 as a companion volume to *The Munros.*

This new edition has been fully updated by both previous and new authors and is complemented throughout by new mapping and a large number of new photographs. The guidebook details routes up all 219 Corbetts and many other popular lower hills. Other hills include popular classics such as Criffel, Tinto, The Pentlands, The Eildons, Ochils, Ben Venue, Mount Blair, Bennachie, Stac Pollaidh and Suilven as well as a wide range of hills throughout the islands, from Lewis to Arran. An interactive PC CD-ROM to the Corbetts & Other Hills complements the book. Price £30.

Charlie Orr.

Also received

CICERONE continue apace with their guides and various manuals, all of which are
of their usual high standard and excellently produced in full glossy technicolour.
Among the titles received this year are:

Vanoise Ski Touring, by Paul Henderson.
Snowshoeing Mont Blanc and the Western Alps, by Hilary Sharp.
Alpine Ski Mountaineering, by Bill O'Connor.
The Isle Of Skye (A Walkers Guide), by Terry Marsh.
Via Ferratas of The Italian Dolomites, by John Smith and Graham Fletcher.

THE WEST HIGHLAND WAY

After overnighting at Achintee
I made speedy progress
taking long, powerful strides
along Glen Nevis
over the hill
and away from you.

From the top of the Devil's Staircase
I examined the long cleft of Glen Coe
all misty and wet, deep and mysterious
and for some reason thought of you.
The mobile didn't work.

Between Kingshouse and Inveroran
I heard my first geese of the year
this being late September
but couldn't see them.
Those lonely, poignant calls
reminded me of you again.

At Ba Bridge I heard a stag
roaring from high up on Clachlet.
The rut was coming on.
His hormones would be churning
his focus gathering.
I knew how he felt.

Looking through the trees
from the path south of Inverarnan
I saw Loch Lomond so beautiful
deep and reflective
so very dangerous to swim in
and thought: "How like her."

In Milngavie I had my picture taken
beside the sleek monolith
that marks the Way's end
a blond, granitic pillar
vertical, deep rooted, permanent
and wished I was home.

Hamish M. Brown.

OFFICE BEARERS 2002-2003

Honorary President: William. D. Brooker

Honorary Vice-President: Douglas Scott

President: Peter F. Macdonald

Vice-Presidents: Simon. M. Richardson, William S. McKerrow

Honorary Secretary: John R. R. Fowler, 4 Doune Terrace, Edinburgh, EH3 6DY. **Honorary Treasurer:** John A. Wood, Spout Close, Millbeck, Underskiddaw, Keswick, Cumbria CA12 4PS. **Honorary Editor:** Charles J. Orr, 28 Chesters View, Bonnyrigg, Midlothian EH19 3PU. **Convener of the Publications Sub-Committee:** Rob W. Milne, Four Winds, Westfield, near Bathgate, West Lothian, EH48 3DG. **Honorary Librarian:** Ian R. Angell, The Old Manse, 3 New Street, Largs, Ayrshire, KA30 9LL. **Honorary Custodian of Slides:** Graeme N. Hunter, Netheraird, Woodlands Road, Rosemount, Blairgowrie, Perthshire, PH10 6JX. **Convener of the Huts Sub-Committee:** William H. Duncan, Kirktoun, East End, Lochwinnoch, Renfrewshire, PA12 4ER. **Custodian of the CIC Hut:** Robin Clothier, 35 Broompark Drive, Newton Mearns, Glasgow G77 5DZ. **Custodian of Lagangarbh Hut:** Bernard M. Swan, 16 Knowes View, Faifley, Clydebank, Dunbartonshire, G81 5AT. **Custodian of the Ling Hut:** William Skidmore, 1 Kirkton Drive, Lochcarron, Wester Ross, IV54 8UD. **Custodian of the Raeburn Hut:** Gerry Peet, 6 Roman Way, Dunblane, Perthshire, FK15 9DQ. **Custodian of the Naismith Hut:** William S. McKerrow, Scotsburn House, Drummond Road, Inverness, IV2 4NA. **Committee:** John F. Ashbridge; Jonathon A. Baird; Bernard M. Swan; Rick Allen; Neil Marshall; Alastair P. Matthewson; Jamie R. Andrew; Heather Morning; Ronnie Robb.

SMC Internet Address – http://www.smc.org.uk SMC e-mail: smc@smc.org.uk

Journal Information

Editor:	Charles J. Orr, 28 Chesters View, Bonnyrigg, Midlothian EH19 3PU. (e-mail: charliejorr@hotmail.com).
New Routes Editor:	A. D. Nisbet, 20 Craigie Avenue, Boat of Garten, Inverness-shire PH24 3BL. (e-mail: anisbe@globalnet.co.uk).
Editor of Photographs:	Niall Ritchie, 18 Meadowlands Drive, Westhill, Skene, Aberdeen AB32 6EJ. (e-mail: niallritchie@aol.com).
Advertisements:	D. G. Pyper, 3 Keir Circle, Westhill, Skene, Aberdeen AB32 6RE. (e-mail: derek@pyper.fsbusiness.co.uk).
Distribution:	D. F. Lang, Hillfoot Hey, 580 Perth Road, Dundee DD2 1PZ.

INSTRUCTIONS TO CONTRIBUTORS

Articles for the Journal should be submitted before the end of January for consideration for the following issue. Lengthy contributions are preferably typed, double-spaced, on one side only, and with ample margins (minimum 30mm). Articles may be accepted on floppy disk, IBM compatible (contact Editor beforehand), or by e-mail. The Editor welcomes material from both members and non-members, with priority being given to articles of Scottish Mountaineering content. Photographs are also welcome, and should be good quality colour slides. All textual material should be sent to the Editor, address and e-mail as above. Photographic material should be sent direct to the Editor of Photographs, address as above.

Copyright.Textual matter appearing in the Miscellaneous section of the Journal, including New Climbs, is copyright of the publishers. Copyright of articles in the main section of the Journal is retained by individual authors.

SCOTTISH MOUNTAINEERING CLUB
SCOTTISH MOUNTAINEERING TRUST

HILLWALKERS' GUIDES

The Munros	£20
The Munros CD-ROM	£40
Munros GPS data disk – from SMC website	£10.48
The Corbetts and Other Scottish Hills CD-ROM	£30
The Cairngorms	£17.95
Central Highlands	£17.95
Islands of Scotland including Skye	£19.95
North-west Highlands	In preparation
Southern Highlands	£16.95
Southern Uplands	£16.95

SCRAMBLERS' GUIDE

Skye Scrambles	£14.50

CLIMBERS' GUIDES

Ben Nevis	£19.95
Glen Coe	£18.50
North-east Outcrops	£18.50
Scottish Winter Climbs	£17.95
Arran, Arrochar and Southern Highlands	£14.95
The Cairngorms Vol. 1	£11.95
The Cairngorms Vol. 2	£11.95
Highland Outcrops	£16.50
Lowland Outcrops	£14.95
Northern Highlands Vol. 1	£13.95
Northern Highlands Vol. 2	£13.95
Skye and the Hebrides (Two Vols)	£19.95

OTHER PUBLICATIONS

Munro's Tables	£15.95
A Chance in a Million – Avalanches in Scotland	£14.95
The Munroist's Companion	£16
Heading for the Scottish Hills	£6.95
Scottish Hill and Mountain Names	£9.95
Ben Nevis – Britain's Highest Mountain	£14.95
Ski Mountaineering in Scotland	£12.95

Visit our website for more details and to purchase on line:
www.smc.org.uk

Distributed by:
Cordee, 3a De Montfort Street, Leicester LE1 7HD
Tel: 0116 254 3579 Fax: 0116 247 1176
www.cordee.co.uk

*These publications are available from many bookshops and mountain
equipment suppliers*